KAY BOYLE
A Bibliography

KAY BOYLE

KAY BOYLE

A Bibliography

by M. Clark Chambers

Winchester Bibliographies
of 20th Century Writers

ST PAUL'S BIBLIOGRAPHIES   WINCHESTER

OAK KNOLL PRESS   NEW CASTLE   DELAWARE
2002

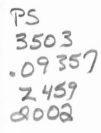

FIRST EDITION

Published by **Oak Knoll Press,**
310 Delaware Street, New Castle, Delaware, USA

Title: Kay Boyle: A Bibliography
Author: M. Clark Chambers
Editor: Mary Hallwachs
Typography: Spearhead Worldwide, Inc.
Publishing Director: J. Lewis von Hoelle

ISBN: 1-58456-063-0 (USA)

Library of Congress Cataloging-in-Publication Data

Chambers, M. Clark.
Kay Boyle : a bibliography / by M. Clark Chambers.– 1st ed.
p. cm.
Includes index.
ISBN 1-58456-063-0 (Oak Knoll Press : acid-free paper)
1. Boyle, Kay, 1902—Bibliography. I. Title.
Z8111.92 C47 2001
[PS3503.O9357]
016.813'52–dc21   2001050024

This work was printed in the United States of America on 60# archival,
acid-free paper meeting the requirements of the
American Standard for Permanence of Paper for
Printed Library Materials

Table of Contents

Capsule biography of Kay Boyle		vii
Introduction		xv
A.	Books and pamphlets by Kay Boyle	1
B.	Contributions and first appearances in books and pamphlets	129
C.	Contributions to periodicals	195
D.	Broadsides	233
E.	Translations by Kay Boyle	235
F.	Translations of the works of Kay Boyle	245
G.	Dust jacket blurbs by Kay Boyle	247
H.	Appearances of her work in anthologies	249
I.	Books about Kay Boyle and significant books which mention her work	265
J.	Articles in periodicals about Kay Boyle or reviews of her works	281
K.	Doctoral dissertations	335
L.	Audio and video recordings	337
Index		339

Capsule Biography of Kay Boyle

James Joyce, Gertrude Stein, Ernest Hemingway, Ezra Pound: all names very easily recognized and identified with Paris of the twenties and the expatriate generation. Kay Boyle, along with her friends Robert McAlmon, Nancy Cunard, Harry and Caresse Crosby, Eugene Jolas and Ernest Walsh, among others, were just as well known at the time in the literary circles of Paris.

Kay Boyle wrote fourteen novels, nine short story collections, three children's books, five collections of poetry and two collections of essays. She ghostwrote two books, co-edited two volumes, compiled and prefaced *The Autobiography of Emanuel Carnevali* and translated three books from French into English. She was a prolific contributor to literary quarterlies and commercial magazines from the middle twenties to the late eighties. She was awarded two Guggenheim Fellowships and was a member of the American Academy of Arts for her "extraordinary contribution to contemporary American literature over a lifetime of creative work." Yet despite all her achievements she is too often relegated to a minor role in the many chronicles of the so-called "Lost Generation." Kay Boyle is an American author who is long overdue to be rediscovered and finally given her rightful place in American letters.

Kay Boyle was born in St. Paul, Minnesota on February 19, 1902. Her father, Howard Peterson Boyle, who had attended the University of Pennsylvania law school, was a rather weak and ineffectual individual, without ambition or energy, and much under the control of his reactionary father, Jesse Peyton Boyle. Jesse Peyton Boyle had studied for the priesthood in England, but became a lawyer and was a co-founder of the West Publishing Company in St. Paul. He was a very strong personality who imposed a heavy patriarchal hand over the family and was its primary provider. Kay's maternal grandmother, Eva S. Evans, worked in the land-grant office in the Department of the Interior. Her aunt, Nina Evans Allender, was a political cartoonist and strongly supported the woman's suffrage campaign; her suffragist art is part of the collection in the Library of Congress. Her grandmother and aunt were "honorary co-chairmen" of the World Woman's Party founded in 1939 by Alice Paul. Kay's mother was a liberal political activist and took a lively interest in avant-garde artistic movements. She encouraged her daughters to be politically active and introduced them at an early age to the progressive writers and artists of the time. Most of the education that Kay and her older sister received was from their mother at home.

In 1916, after a family disaster, the family moved to Cincinnati. Here Kay studied architecture from 1917 to 1919 at the Ohio Mechanics Institute and took a secretarial course at night, one of her few short stints at formal education. She met and fell in love with Richard Brault, a French exchange student studying at the University of Cincinnati, and they planned to marry after his graduation.

Upon completing the secretarial course she took a job, and by the spring of 1922 had saved enough money to follow her sister Joan to New York. There with the help of her sister, who was an illustrator for *Vogue*, she got a job as a secretary to a fashion designer. Her wages enabled her to attend a creative writing course at Columbia University. She was soon able to get a job working for Lola Ridge, the New York editor *of Broom*, a literary quarterly published in Italy by Harold Bloom; this was Kay's introduction to the world of letters. Through her job with *Broom* she met writers such as William Carlos Williams, Marianne Moore, John Dos Passos, Glenway Westcott and others.

Richard Brault quickly followed Kay to New York, where they soon married. He took a job for a short time, but in May of 1923, with a loan of $250 form Marjorie Loeb, Harold Loeb's ex-wife, Kay and Richard set sail for France for a summer visit with Richard's parents. They expected to be gone for about three months; Kay was not to return to the states for eighteen years.

Kay and Richard soon tired of living with Richard's provincial parents, and with a loan from Richard's sister they set off for Paris, where Richard intended to look for work. During their short time in Paris Kay met for the first time Robert McAlmon, who was to become an important influence in her life.

Richard found work, not in Paris but in Le Havre, where they lived a poor existence in horrible conditions. During the fall and winter of 1923-24, Kay began corresponding with the Italian poet Emanuel Carnevali, whose autobiography she later compiled and edited. She also began her first novel, to be published in 1931 as *Plagued by the Nightingale*.

In May 1924, Kay and Richard moved to Harfleur, where they were to live for two years. Here she temporarily abandoned work on *Plagued by the Nightingale* to begin work on another novel, to be published in 1933 as *Gentlemen, I Address You Privately*.

In 1925 she was contacted by Ernest Walsh, who had read some of her poems in *Broom* and *Poetry Magazine*, asking her to contribute to a new literary quarterly that he was founding to be called *This Quarter*. During the winter of 1926 she was diagnosed with tuberculosis, and as her condition worsened with the harsh weather of Harfleur, with the help from Richard's parents and an advance of 1000 francs from Walsh for *Plagued by the Nightingale*, she left for the south of France for a four to six month stay in the sun.

Walsh and Ethel Morehead, the financial backer for *This Quarter*, helped Kay get situated. But Ethel Moorhead became increasingly jealous over the deepening involvement between Kay and Ernest and she moved to Monte Carlo. Consequently Kay and Ernest grew even closer. About this time it was determined that Kay did not have tuberculosis, but Ernest did suffer from the disease and his condition was deteriorating to the point that it became increasingly difficult for them to find a place to stay. Fortuitously, at this time, they met Archibald Craig and his cousin Gladys Palmer, the Dayang Muda of Sarawak. Gladys Palmer was the wife of the governor of Sarawak, a British Protectorate, and Dayang Muda was her title. As a result of their friendship with Gladys Palmer, she was able to get them a room at the back of a hotel in Annot, a small mountain village.

Relations between Ernest and Ethel continued to worsen and she frequently refused to continue to fund *This Quarter* or threatened to continue the quarterly on her own. However, Ernest's condition became critical and he died on October 26, 1926. Kay described her life with Ernest Walsh, the conflict with Ethel Morehead, and their life on the Riviera in her novel *The Year Before Last* (1932).

Soon after Ernest's death, Kay discovered she was pregnant with his child. For a while she continued to live with Ethel Morehead at her villa in Monte Carlo, and they worked together to edit and publish *This Quarter*. A baby girl, whom Kay named Sharon, was born, on March 11, 1927. Ethel lied to the American consulate, swearing that Kay and Ernest had been married at her family home in Scotland, so that Kay could receive a small pension as a veteran's widow.

Kay and Ethel labored at getting out a third issue of *This Quarter*, which was to be a memorial issue to Ernest Walsh. However, Ethel became increasingly difficult for Kay to live with, and finally, at the beseeching of her husband Richard, Kay moved to Stoke-on-Kent in England where Richard now had a good job. As a Catholic he had refuse to give her a divorce, and he continued to hope for a reconciliation.

Kay was to remain with Richard for a year, and during this time she finished *Plagued by the Nightingale* and returned to work on *Gentlemen, I Address You Privately*. She began a correspondence with Eugene Jolas, who was hoping to continue the work of Ernest Walsh with a new quarterly that he was founding, to be called *transition* [sic]. He asked her to send him stories and poems for inclusion.

But she longed to be in Paris, and when Archibald Craig, with whom she had remained in contact, wrote to her that his cousin, the Dayang Muda, wanted Kay to ghostwrite her memoirs, (to be published in 1929 as *Relations and Complications: Being the Recollections of H.H. the Dayang Muda of Sarawak)* she packed her belongings and in April of 1928 she left England with her daughter Sharon to move in with the Princess in Paris. Here her friendship with Robert McAlmon blossomed, and through him she met Hilaire Hiler, Man Ray, Kiki, Laura Riding, Robert Graves and others. Through Eugene Jolas she met James and Nora Joyce and Harry and Caresse Crosby, the publishers of Black Sun Press. The Crosby's Black Sun Press would later publish Kay's first book under her own name, *Short Stories*, a limited edition of 165 signed and numbered or lettered copies. It was also during this period that her works began to appear in many different small magazines, especially in *transition* as a result of her friendship with Eugene Jolas.

After concluding her work on the Dayang Muda's memoirs, Kay and Sharon moved into a commune led by Raymond Duncan, the brother of Isadora Duncan, probably a move impelled by expediency rather than ideology. Kay was assigned to work in one of the two gift shops owned by the commune on Rue du Fauboug St. Honoré and Boulevard St. Germain, where between customers she continued to write. But the commune members became increasingly demanding and possessive of Sharon, so, with the help of the Dayang Muda and Harry and Caresse Crosby she made her escape, and moved in with the Crosbys at their place in the country. Kay's novel *My Next Bride* (1934) describes her time in the commune and the events of her life during this period.

In 1929 she met Laurence Vail, and she and Sharon moved in with him in the village of St. Aulde, where he lived with his son Sinbad, the child of an earlier marriage
to Peggy Guggenheim. Kay and Laurence were married April 3, 1932, and by this
time their family had grown. Pegeen, Laurence's daughter by Peggy Guggenheim,
and Apple, a daughter born in December of 1929 to Kay and Laurence, had joined
them. A second daughter, Kathe, would be born in July 1934.

Kay's most productive literary decade began with the advent of the thirties. Seven
novels (one ghost written), three short story collections, a poetry collection, and her
first children's book were all published during the thirties, along with many short
stories, poems and essays in some of the best little and commercial magazines. In
1935 her short story "The White Horses of Vienna" won the O. Henry Memorial
Award prize. She also translated *Don Juan* by Joseph Delteil and *The Devil in the
Flesh* by Raymond Radiguet. She claims to have assisted her husband Laurence Vail
in the translation of *Bubu of Montparnasse* by Charles-Louis Philippe, but is not
given co-credit. She also translated René Crevel's *Babylone* for the Black Sun Press;
the first chapter, under the name "Mr. Knife, Miss Fork," was published as a limited
edition with illustrations by Max Ernst. The entire book was published by North
Point Press in 1985. Along with Vail and Nina Conarain Kay edited *365 Days,* a
collection of short stories to which she was the major contributor.

The thirties were also very nomadic years for the Vails as they moved to
Villefranche-sur-Mer and then to the Col-de-Villefranche near Nice, where they lived
from 1930 to 1933. Then in the summer of 1933 they moved first to Vienna and
then Kitzbühel, Austria, an experience out of which came her novel *Death of a Man*
(1936) and one of her best short stories, "The White Horses of Vienna." Here in
Austria they were first exposed to the encroaching threat of fascism and anti-semitism.

An uncle of Laurence's died and left him a considerable amount of money,
enabling he and Kay to move to Devon, England in the summer of 1936 so they
could be near Sinbad, who was at boarding school. In the summer of 1937 they
moved to Mégève in the Haute-Savoie, where they bought a chalet, which they
named "Les Cinq Enfants." In March of 1929 their third daughter, Clover, was
born. The family remained in Mégève until World War II forced them back to
America. Because of the inheritance Kay did not have to worry about selling her
work while they were in Mégève and she wrote two of her best works, *Monday Night,*
published in 1938, and *Three Short Novels,* published in 1940. She also won another
O. Henry Memorial Award prize for her 1940 short story "Defeat."

In August of 1939 Kay met Baron Joseph von Franckenstein, a refugee from Nazi
Austria. His mother was a countess and his father a Hapsburg. He was an expert
skier and mountain climber with a Ph.D. in classical languages from Innsbruck
University. He had been a tutor to the Vail children. When he reported to the French
to fight the Nazis, he was interred in a concentration camp where he remained until
the fall of France in 1940. Her novel, *Primer for Combat,* fictionalizes to some extent
their early relationship. With Kay's help Joseph was able to leave France, but his ship
was commandeered by the Dutch and only after another short interment in
Barbados did he finally make his way to the United States. When America declared

war on the Axis powers Joseph volunteered for service with the U.S. military. He was assigned to the ski troops in February 1943. During his training in Colorado, Kay's divorce from Laurence Vail was granted on February 19, 1943 and Kay and Joseph were married shortly thereafter. Joseph took part in the invasion of the Aleutians and afterwards was accepted by the OSS. He made seven parachute jumps into France, and later infiltrated into Austria, where he posed as a German NCO. He was captured and sentenced to death, but was liberated at the last moment by U. S. forces.

During the war years, Kay lived in and around New York City. Always desperate for money, she went on the lecture tour, talking about conditions in wartime Europe and about the French Resistance. She also taught creative writing at an adult night school, and wrote numerous book reviews. Her fiction writing was little more than thinly veiled propaganda, usually extolling the French Resistance movement. Her two novels *Avalanche* and *A Frenchman Must Die* were both serialized in *The Saturday Evening Post,* and her short stories appeared in publications such as *The Saturday Evening Post, Harper's Bazaar, Mademoiselle,* and *Women's Home Companion. Primer for Combat* was published in November 1942 and *Thirty Stories* in November 1946.

Kay now began also writing political essays for *The Nation, New Statesman and Nation,* and *The New Republic,* and her social and political conscience and interest began to mature. During the early years before Joseph was sent to the front Kay had given birth to two children by Joseph, Faith in December 1942 and Ian in November 1943.

In November 1946 Harold Ross hired Kay to be staff correspondent for *The New Yorker* in Europe and she was accredited by the War Department to travel to Germany and Austria. Her assignment was to write a minimum of six stories a year about occupied Germany. Joseph got a job as a civilian employee for the U.S. Army and was assigned to Offenbach, Germany. However, Kay refused to live in Germany and set up housekeeping with the children in Paris. Finally, in May 1948, she decided to move to Marburg, and then later to a U.S. military base in Frankfurt to be with Joseph and to unite the family. She traveled extensively during these years in Europe and apart from the promised stories for *The New Yorker,* she also wrote articles on postwar Europe for *The Nation.* Stories rejected by *The New Yorker* were sold to *The Saturday Evening Post, Harper's, The Nation* and *Tomorrow.* Among the stories written during her stay in Europe were some of her finest, and these were collected in *The Smoking Mountain, Stories Out of post war Germany,* published in 1951.

In 1951 began one of the most trying episodes in Kay Boyle's life. Joseph Franckenstein was brought before a Joseph McCarthy loyalty hearing and Kay found herself having to defend against the vaguest of charges. Those called to testify to Joseph's loyalty had to testify to Kay's as well. Janet Flanner gave eloquent testimony to the loyalty of both Kay and Joseph, but the other *New Yorker* staffers were not so helpful. While Kay did receive support from *The Ladies Home Journal* and *The Saturday Evening Post* and her editor Edward Aswell from McGraw-Hill, the attitude of *The New Yorker* was painful to her, and she instructed her agent to submit no more stories to that magazine.

Eventually the Consular Board cleared Joseph unanimously of all charges. Nevertheless, two of McCarthy's subcommittee staff members, Roy Cohn and G. David Schine were sent to look through the files of those employees brought before the loyalty hearings, and shortly thereafter Joseph and all others who had been tried were terminated from their positions. As a result of her loyalty being called into question, *The New Yorker* withdrew Kay's accreditation as a correspondent.

In 1953 Kay and Joseph returned from Germany to the United States and settled in Rowayton, Connecticut where Joseph taught at a girl's school. Kay found that she was essentially blacklisted and her agent could not find buyers for her stories. Thus, she was reduced to teaching and writing book reviews. In 1967 she taught a six-week course at the University of Delaware on the short story.

Kay, along with several other writers had, in 1929, signed a manifesto calling for the "Revolution of the Word," in which they declared that the writer should not be concerned "with the propaganda of sociological ideas," except to emancipate the creative elements from the present ideology." She now published a new manifesto, "A Declaration for 1955," in which she states that she believed that writers have a great moral responsibility to the world in which they live.

Kay and Joseph fought for Joseph's reinstatement until 1962 when he was finally rehired with apologies by the State Department. During the preceding years she had continued to write fiction and in 1955 Alfred A. Knopf published *The Seagull on the Step*, which unfortunately was not one of her better novels. She followed this, however, with a fine novel about post-war Germany, *Generation Without Farewell*, (Knopf, 1960) which was short-listed for The National Book Award. In 1959 she rewrote her children's story *The Youngest Camel* and it was published by Harper & Row as *The Youngest Camel Reconsidered and Rewritten*. In 1962 her second collection of poetry was published and she wrote a pamphlet for The American Jewish Committee entitled *Breaking the Silence; Why a Mother Tells Her Son About the Nazi Era*.

In 1962 Joseph was sent to Teheran as the cultural attaché. By the time Kay and their son Ian joined him there, Joseph was dying of cancer. He was operated on at the American military hospital at Landesstühl, Germany and then returned to Walter Reed Hospital in Washington, D.C. By now it was clear that his cancer was terminal and Kay began applying for employment. Her best offer came from San Francisco State University, where she was hired with full professor status. Joseph died in the hospital at the Presidio in San Francisco, and with his life insurance money Kay bought a house a few blocks from the corner of Haight and Ashbury. For the almost twenty years that she lived there her doors were always open to all minorities and disenfranchised groups of all sorts. She rented the second floor to students, always on a totally integrated basis, and made the main floor available to groups whose causes she supported.

Kay became increasingly active as an anti-Vietnam war protester, traveling to Cambodia in July 1966 with a pacifist group called "Americans Want to Know." In 1967 she was arrested and imprisoned twice for leading demonstrations and sit-ins at the Oakland Induction Center. During the 1968-1969 student strike at San Francisco

State she helped found the Faculty Action Committee. And was almost always at the front-of any protest or picket line, thus incurring the wrath of S. I. Hayakawa, the university president. In 1973 Kay founded a chapter of Amnesty International, the Nobel Peace Prize winning organization advocating rights for political prisoners around the world. This group met twice a week in her home. Also in the mid-seventies she was a member of the Committee for Intellectual and Artistic Freedom in Iran. When, in 1979, she was finally able to acquire her security file from the government under The Freedom of Information Act, it contained two thousand pages.

Her writings from this period reflect more and more her political and social involvement. In 1970 there first appeared a new collection of poetry entitled *Testament for My Students and Other Poems* and a book of essays, *The Long Walk at San Francisco State and Other Essays.* In 1972 she co-edited and wrote the introduction to a book of antiwar essays, *Enough of Dying! Voices for Peace,* Her last novel published in 1975, *The Underground Woman,* is a thinly veiled autobiography of these San Francisco years. It also fictionalizes another event which took place in 1970 while Kay was away for two semesters teaching a writing course at Hollins College in Virginia. Kay's youngest daughter Faith and her husband belonged to a cult headed by Mel Lyman. Kay's first contact with this cult had been in 1967, when on a one-semester leave of absence from San Francisco State to teach a course at the university of Massachusetts in Amherst, she had temporarily moved in with the cult in order to be with her daughter and her daughter's two children. Soon fed up with the cult members, Kay moved out. In the fall of 1970 when Kay was at Hollins the cult took over her Haight Ashbury home. It required intricate legal maneuvering by her attorney to free the house from the control of the Lyman commune members. After four years her son Ian left the commune, but her daughter Faith, with her husband and five children remained and Kay and her daughter were estranged almost up to the time of Kay's death.

In 1966 Doubleday published *Nothing Ever Breaks Except the Heart, and Other Stories* which included uncollected stories from the war years and some post war stories emphasizing some of her social themes. Two more children's books were published in 1966 and 1968. Doubleday also published, in 1968, *Being Geniuses Together,* in which Kay alternated chapters she had written with those of Robert McAlmon's book of the same title published in 1938. The book chronicles the lives and careers of the principals involved in expatriate Paris of the twenties. Kay's main reason for writing this book was to rekindle a new appreciation for McAlmon, whom she believed was an all too neglected writer of his era.

In 1988, North Point Press published a new collection of poetry, *This is Not a Letter and Other Poems,* and also in 1988, Sun and Moon Press brought out *Life Being the Best and Other Stories,* a compilation of early, uncollected stories. Kay never ceased to work up until her death. She rewrote *Gentlemen, I Address You Privately,* a book with which she had never been entirely satisfied, and it was published in 1991 by Capra Press. Kay Boyle died December 27, 1992.

In the twenties and thirties Kay Boyle was viewed by her contemporaries and her reviewers as one of the coming writers of her age. Unfortunately, most critics today would probably argue that she never fulfilled her promise. She is, however, a writer who needs reconsideration and reevaluation. In 1986 Sandra Whipple Spanier wrote an exceptionally good critical biography, *Kay Boyle; Artist and Activist*, which skill-fully integrates her life and her work. In 1994 Joan Mellen published an excellent comprehensive biography of Kay's life, *Kay Boyle; Author of Herself*. It seems that she may now get that long-overdue and deserved respect for a lengthy and prolific career.

Introduction

My original interest in Kay Boyle arose out of an interest in writers and publishers of Paris of the twenties and thirties. As a result of this interest I became an incidental collector of Kay Boyle's works. Burton Weiss, a book dealer from whom I had bought a great number of her books was a good friend of hers and was able to offer some exceedingly unique items and thus my interest in Kay Boyle expanded to the point that I became interested in any item that had to do with her or her work. Since there was no descriptive bibliography of her works, I began compiling exhaustive checklists that after years became this final effort. Of the A and B items almost all are in my personal collection plus a very large number of all the other categories. Hopefully this bibliography will prove helpful to other collectors and students of her works.

Conventions and Information. I am a book collector and not an academic. I have referred to a large number of bibliographies and have chosen the format and conventions from those bibliographies which I felt could impart the most information to scholars and collectors in the most straightforward manner. I have not used the ISCC-NBC Centroid Color Chart, but have simply tried to describe the colors of bindings, and dust jackets with general color descriptions. I have scoured academic and public libraries across the country for all editions and subsequent printings and dust jackets whenever possible. I have examined multiple copies whenever possible. I have made no effort to make a textual study for typographical errors or for textual variances between editions or printings.

A Items. This section is a chronological listing of books and pamphlets independently authored by Kay Boyle beginning with the true first edition whether English or American and then including all reprint editions both English and American. I have also noted uncorrected proof copies when found and examined.

B Items. This section is a chronological listing of the first apperances in book form of short stories, articles and poems. It also includes original contributions such as introductions, afterwords, autobiographical articles, appraisals or comments about artists' works in catalogs and the first appearances of unpublished letters or excerpts from letters. Also included is the transcript of her sworn deposition before a congressional committee regarding her alleged membership in the Communist party as published in the congressional record.

C Items. A chronological listing of Kay Boyle's contributions to magazines, newspapers and periodicals, whether a first appearance or a reprint, American or foreign. This includes short stories, poems, essays, book reviews and interviews. They are listed by title of publication, date of issue and page number. Volume and issue number are given when applicable and noted thus: 4.23 with the volume number before the period and the issue number after. Page numbers on which the piece occurs are in Parentheses.

D Items. A chronological listing of broadsides.

E Items. A chronological listing of books translated by Kay Boyle from French.

F Items. A chronological listing of foreign translations of her work.

G Items. A chronological listing of blurbs she contributed to the dust jackets of other peoples' work.

H Items. A chronological listing of appearances of short stories, poems and articles by Kay Boyle in anthologies regardless of whether or not it was a first appearance.

I Items. A chronological listing of books about Kay Boyle or that significantly mention Kay Boyle.

J Items. A chronological listing of articles and reviews about Kay Boyle or her works. See C Items for methodology of listings.

K Items. A chronological listing of doctoral dissertations written on Kay Boyle.

L Items. Audio and video recordings of Kay Boyle or other individuals reading from her works; also included are recorded interviews.

A

Books and Pamphlets by Kay Boyle

A1a   RELATIONS AND COMPLICATIONS   1929
                          (Ghostwritten by Kay Boyle)

First Edition:

RELATIONS & COMPLICATIONS | Being the Recollections of | H.H. THE
DAYANG MUDA OF SARAWAK | With a Foreword by the Rt. Hon. T. P.
O'Connor, p.c., m.p. | And 38 Illustrations from photographs | LONDON | JOHN
LANE THE BODLEY HEAD LIMITED

Collation: [i-iv], v, [vi], vii-xv, [xvi], xvii-xviii, [xix-xx], 1-249, [250], 251-253,
[254-260] pages; cream endpapers.   8 $\frac{1}{2}$" x 5 $\frac{5}{8}$". [A]^8 B-I^8 K-R^8 S^4

Contents: (i) half title page; (ii) blank; (iii) title page; (iv) copyright page; (v)
[dedication]: To | ARCHIE CRAIG and all young people, especially | JEAN |
ELIZABETH | ANNE | and ANTONI, | with my blessing;   (vi) blank; (vii-x)
foreword; (xi-xv) table of contents; (xvi) blank; (xvii-xviii) list of illustrations;
(xix) fly title; (xx) blank; (1-249) text; (250) blank; (251-253) index; (254) blank;
(255-260) book ads.

Plates: Plates of photographs, black and white printed on glossy machine finished
paper, facing the following pages: (iii), The Author; (24), My Father (from the pic-
ture by Frederick Sandys); (8), The Parchment Autograph Fan; (16), My Mother and
I; (24), George Meredith and My Mother; (28), The Author at Fifteen (from the pic-
ture by Frederick Sandys); (34), House Party at Frognal; (40), Sir Albert Seymour,
Bt., and Ellen Terry; (50), George Meredith waits for My Autograph Book; (54),
Kubelik tossing Hay at Kilby's Farm; (60), My Mother (from the picture by
Frederick Sandys); (68), My Husband, H.H. Tuan Muda of Sarawak; (74), My
Wedding Group; (84), The present Rajah; the late Tuan Bunsu; My Father-in-law;
My Husband, the Tuan Muda; (92), A Drawing of Jean by Sir Philip Burne-Jones;
(98), Mrs.—— as Burne-Jones saw Her on Her Honeymoon at Rottingdean; (102),
The Type of Man Burne-Jones couldn't Stand; (108), Sir James Brooke, First Rajah
of Sarawak; (114), A Sea Dayak Woman and Sea Dayaks; (124), A Sea Dayak Head
Feast and Kenyah Warfare; (128), Sir James Brooke's House in Sarawak (from an old
print); and The Race-course, Kuching, Sarawak; (136), My Father-in-law, the late
Rajah; (156), Ellen Terry and Our Children; (166), Dame Ellen Terry; (172), My
Daughter Jean; and My Son Antoni; (180), My Daughter Anne; and My Daughter
Betty; (188), Two Japanese Wrestlers that Burne-Jones saw at Olympia; and My
Husband, as Burne-Jones saw Him, off to Bathe; (206), Ernest Walsh, Editor of

"This Quarter;" (214), Portrait illustrating Burne-Jones' dislike for Fat Women; (226), Burne-Jones' terrible Dream, as described to My Husband; (232), Gertrude Stein with Archibald Craig, the Modern Poet; (236), Brancusi's Studio.

Copyright page: *First published in* 1929 | *Made and Printed in Great Britain by* | *Tonbridge Printers Peach Hall Works Tonbridge*

Binding: Black cloth covered boards printed in yellow. Top edge stained in yellow, and trimmed. Front and bottom edges rough trimmed. Front: RELATIONS AND | COMPLICATIONS | By H.H. THE DAYANG | MUDA OF SARAWAK Spine: RELATIONS | AND | COMPLICATIONS | BY | H.H. THE DAYANG | MUDA | OF SARAWAK | THE BODLEY HEAD

Dust jacket: Not seen

Note: Kay Boyle stated in a note written in the front of the compiler's copy of this book: "I did not contribute in any way to the final chapters of the book: pages 220 through 251. The Chapters I had written were typed up by Buffy Glasco in the Princess' apartment and I can only assume it was he and Archie [Craig] who finished the story of her life."

| A2a | SHORT STORIES | 1929 |

First Edition:

[red] SHORT STORIES | [black] BY | KAY BOYLE | THE BLACK SUN PRESS | [red] ÉDITIONS NARCISSE | [black] RUE CARDINALE | [red] PARIS | [black] MCMXXIX

Collation: [i-xii], 1-7, [8], 9-17, [18], 19-37, [38], 39-43, [44], 45-49, [50], 51-55, [56-64] pages. $9^1/_2$ " x $6^1/_4$ " [A-I]^4 [J]^2

Contents: (i-ii) blank and inserted under folding flap of front cover; (iii-iv) blank; (v) half title page; (vi) blank; (vii) title page; (viii) blank; (ix) [dedication]: [black] for | [red] Laurence Vail; (x) [publisher's note]: Acknowledgment is made to Transition | and to the London Calendar in which | certain of these stories have appeared.; (xi) contents; (xii) blank; (1-7) text; (8) blank; (9-17) text; (18) blank; (19-37) text; (38) blank; (39-43) text; (44) blank; (45-49) text; (50) blank; (51-55) text; (56) blank; (57) limitation statement; (58) Tous droits de reproduction et de traduction | réservés pour tous pays y compress la suède | la Norvège et la Russie. (59-62) blank; (63-64) blank and inserted under folding flap of back cover.

Limitation statement: This first edition of Short Stories | by Kay Boyle printed in Paris | March 1929 at the Black Sun Press | (Maître-Imprimeur Lescaret) for | Harry and Caresse Crosby is | limited to 15 copies on Japan | Paper signed by the author and | 150 numbered copies on Holland | Van Gelder Zonen to be sold at | the bookshop of Harry F. Marks | at 31 West 47 Street New York | [edition number (numbered copies are stamped) or letter (lettered copies are hand written)] | Il a été tiré en plus 20 exemplaires | sur Papier d'Arches pour la France

Copyright page: Blank

Binding: Beige wrappers printed in red and black with glassine dust jacket. Top edges unstained and trimmed. Front and bottom edge rough trimmed. Front: [red] SHORT STORIES | [black] BY | [black] KAY BOYLE | [black] THE BLACK SUN PRESS | [red] ÉDITIONS NARCISSE | [black] RUE CARDINALE | [red] PARIS | [black] MCMXXIX Spine: [red] S | H | O | R | T | S | T | O | R | I | E | S | [black] K | A | Y | B | O | Y | L | E Back: Black design in the middle of the back. The book comes in a gold gilt folder with a red ribbon tie at the front edge.

Publication: First published in March 1929 at the following prices: Holland Van Gelder copies at $10.00 and the Japanese vellum copies at $35.00.

Stories included with previous publication: "Theme" first appeared in *transition* 1, April 1927 "Bitte nehmen Sie die Blumen" first appeared in *transition* 9, December 1927. "Summer" first appeared in *London Calendar of Modern Letters* April 1927. "Portrait" first appeared in *transition* 3 June 1927. "Vacation Time" first appeared in *transition* 14 Fall 1928 "Uncle Anne," and "Spring Morning" appear for the first time.

A3a   WEDDING DAY AND OTHER STORIES   [1930]

First Edition:

WEDDING DAY | AND OTHER STORIES | KAY BOYLE | [five blue cranes moving from lower left to upper right in the center of the page.] | NEW YORK | JONATHAN CAPE & HARRISON SMITH |

Collation: [i-x], 1-35, [36], 37-53, [54], 55-65, [66], 67-89, [90], 91-101, [102], 103-107, [108-110], 111-122 pages; beige endpapers decorated with blue cranes. 7 3/4" x 5 1/8" [A-G]⁸ [H]⁶

Contents: (i) half title page; (ii) JONATHAN CAPE AND HARRISON SMITH, INCORPORATED, | 139 EAST 46th STREET, NEW YORK, N.Y. AND 91 WELLINGTON | STREET, WEST, TORONTO, CANADA; JONATHAN CAPE, LTD., | 30 BEDFORD SQUARE, LONDON, W.C. 1, ENGLAND; (iii) title page; (iv) copyright page; (v) [dedication]: for | Laurence Vail; (vi) blank; (vii) [publisher's note]: Acknowledgment is made to *Transition*, the *London | Calendar*, the *American Caravan*, and the | *Hound and Horn* | in which certain of these stories have appeared.; (viii) blank; (ix) table of contents; (x) blank; (1-35) text; (36) blank; (37-53) text; (54) blank; (55-65) text; (66) blank; (67-89) text; (90) blank; (91-101) text; (102) blank; (103-107) text; (108) blank; (109) LETTERS OF A LADY; (110) blank; (111-122) text.

Copyright page: COPYRIGHT, 1930, BY | JONATHAN CAPE AND | HAR-RISON SMITH INC. | ORIGINAL EDITION PUBLISHED IN 1929 BY THE | BLACK SUN PRESS, IN AN EDITION DE LUXE OF | ONE HUNDRED AND FIFTY COPIES | PUBLISHED BY JONATHAN | CAPE & HARRISON SMITH, 1930 | PRINTED IN THE UNITED STATES OF AMERICA | BY THE VAIL-BALLOU PRESS, BINGHAMTON, N.Y. | AND BOUND BY THE J.F. TAPLEY CO.

Binding: Light blue cloth spine stamped in gold. White paper covered boards with light blue crane design covering front and back. Top edge stained black and trimmed; bottom edge trimmed with rough trimmed fore edge. Spine: KAY | BOYLE | *Wedding* | *Day* | & | Other | Stories | [publisher's device]   Back: Blank.

Dust jacket: Gray paper printed in blue and gold. Front: [blue] WEDDING DAY | AND OTHER | STORIES | [six blue cranes flying from lower left to upper right] | KAY | BOYLE   Spine: [Gold] WEDDING | DAY AND | OTHER | STORIES | By | KAY | BOYLE | [publisher's device]   Back: Checklist of other titles by Cape and Smith with order blank. Front flap: A biographical note on Kay Boyle. [lower right] $2.00.   Back flap: Advertisement for *Brother and Sister* by Leonhard Frank and a plot outline.

Previous publication: "Episode in the Life of an Ancestor" first appeared in *Hound and Horn*, Fall 1930. "Bitte nehmen Sie die Blumen" first appeared in *transition* 9, December 1927. "Madame Tout Petit" first appeared in *The Second American Caravan*, New York: The Macaulay Company, 1928. "Theme" first appeared in *transition* 1, April 1927. "Summer" first appeared in *London Calendar* 4, April 1927. "Polar Bears and Others" first appeared in *transition* 6, September 1927 and also in *transition stories*, [sic] New York: Walter V. McKee, 1929. "Portrait" first appeared in *transition* 3, June 1927. "Vacation Time" first appeared in *transition* 14. "On the Run" first appeared in *transition* 16/17 June 1929. "Theme," "Bitte nehmen Sie die Blumen," "Summer," "Uncle Anne," "Portrait," "Vacation Time," and "Spring Morning" appeared in *Short Stories*. This is the first appearance of "Wedding Day" and "Letters of a Lady"

Publication: First published on November 3, 1930 at $2.00 according to a review copy.

A3b   WEDDING DAY AND OTHER STORIES   1932

First English Edition:

Wedding Day | *and Other Stories* | *Kay Boyle* | *author of* | *'Plagued by the Nightingale'* | [publishers device] | *London* | *Pharos Editions* | *1932*

Collation: [1-14], 15-26, [27-28], 29-36, [37-38], 39-47, [48-50], 51-56, [57-58], 59-65, [66-68], 69-77, [78-80], 81-87, [88-90], 91-98, [99-100], 101-104,

[105-106], 107-111, [112-114], 115-118, [119-120], 121-124, [125-126], 127-136 pages; cream endpapers. 8" x 5" [A]⁸ B-H⁸ I⁴

Contents: (1-2) blank; (3) half title page; (4) blank; (5) title page; (6) copyright page; (7) table of contents; (8) blank; (9) [publisher's note]: Acknowledgment is made to *Transition*, the | *London Calendar, the American Caravan* and the | *Hound and Horn* in which certain of these stories | have appeared.; (10) blank; (11) [dedication]: *for | Laurence Vail*; (12) blank; (13) [story title]: *Episode in the Life of an Ancestor*; (14) blank; (15-26) text; (27) [story title]: *Bitte Nehmen sie die Blumen*; (28) blank; (29-36) text; (37) [story title]: *Wedding Day*; (38) blank; (39-47) text; (48) blank; (49) [story title]: *Theme*; (50) blank; (51-56) text; (57) [story title]: *Madame Tout Petit*; 58) blank; (59-65) text; (66) blank; (67) [story title]: *Polar Bears and Others*; (68) blank; (69-77) text; (78) blank; (79) [story title]: *Summer*; (80) blank; (81-87) text; (88) blank; (89) [story title]: *Uncle Anne*; (90) blank; (91-98) text; (99) [story title]: *Portrait*; (100) blank; (101-104) text; (105) [story title]: *Vacation Time*; (106) blank; (107-111) text; (112) blank; (113) [story title]: *Spring Morning*; (114) blank; (115-118) text; (119) [story title]: *On the Run*; (120) blank; (121-124) text; (125) [story title]: *Letters of a Lady*; (126) blank; (127-136) text.

Copyright page: PRINTED IN GREAT BRITAIN IN THE CITY OF OXFORD | AT THE ALDEN PRESS | PAPER MADE BY JOHN DICKINSON & CO., LTD. | BOUND BY A. W. BAIN & CO., LTD.

Binding: Light blue cloth covered boards printed in yellow. Top edge unstained and all edges trimmed. Front: WEDDING DAY [small double zigzag decoration] KAY BOYLE | [zigzag decoration across bottom. Spine: W | E | D | D | I | N | G | D | A | Y [zigzag decoration] K | A | Y | B | O | Y | L | E | PHAROS   Back: Blank.

Dust jacket: Beige paper printed in blue. Front: WEDDING DAY | AND OTHER | STORIES | [six blue cranes flying from lower left of jacket to middle right] | KAY | BOYLE [a thick blue stripe from top to bottom along the left side of cover] Spine: [blue on beige] W | E | D | D | I | N | G | D | A | Y | by | K | A | Y | B | O | Y | L | E | PHAROS. Back: Blank.   Front flap: A short biographical note on Kay Boyle. [lower middle] *Six shillings net*.   Back flap: Blank.

Publication: Published in September 1932 at six shillings.

The story content and previous publication are the same as the American edition.

A3c   WEDDING DAY AND OTHER STORIES   [1972]

Library Edition:

WEDDING DAY | AND OTHER STORIES | KAY BOYLE | [five cranes ascending lower left to upper right] | *Short Story Index Reprint Series* | [publisher's device] BOOKS FOR LIBRARIES PRESS | FREEPORT, NEW YORK

Collation: [i-viii], 1-35, [36], 37-53, [54], 55-65, [66], 67-89, [90], 91-101, [102], 103-107, [108-110], 111-122, [123-124] pages; cream endpapers.   8" x   5" [A-C]^{16} [D]^{18}

Contents: (i) half title page; (ii) blank; (iii) title page; (iv) copyright page; (v) [dedication]: For | Laurence Vail; (vi) blank; (vii) table of contents; (viii) blank; (1-35) text; (36) blank; (37-53) text; (54) blank; (55-65) text; (66) blank; (67-89) text; (90) blank; (91-101) text; (102) blank; (103-107) text; (108) blank; (109) [story title]: LETTERS OF A LADY; (110) blank; (111-122) text; (123-124) blank.

Copyright page: First Published 1929 | Reprinted 1972 | [following enclosed in ruled rectangle] **Library of Congress Cataloging in Publication Data** | Boyle, Kay, 1903— | Wedding day and other stories. | (Short story index reprint series) | CONTENTS: Episode in the life of an ancestor.— | Bitte nehmen Sie die Blumen.— Wedding day, [etc.] | I. Title. | PZ3.B69796We7 [PS3503.09357] 813'.5'2 72-4420 | ISBN 0-8369-4171-3 | [outside of rectangle] PRINTED IN THE UNITED STATES OF AMERICA

Seen in two bindings with no priority established.

Binding one: Rose colored cloth covered boards stamped in gold.   All edges trimmed, top edge unstained.   Front: Blank.   Spine: [printed downward in gold] WEDDING DAY   Boyle | [printed horizontally and enclosed in small circle] B/L Back: Blank.

Binding two: Yellow cloth covered boards stamped in gold. Front : [blind imprint of publisher's device in lower right] Spine: [printed downward on brown rectangle] WEDDING DAY | [bell] | Boyle | design in brown] [a brown geometric design is to the top and the bottom of the brown rectangle on which the printing occurs] Back: Blank.

A4a   PLAGUED BY THE NIGHTINGALE   1931

First Edition:

PLAGUED | *BY THE* | *NIGHTINGALE* | * | KAY BOYLE | * | NEW YORK | *Jonathan Cape & Harrison Smith* | MCMXXXI [all enclosed in a double ruled box which is in turn enclosed in a larger triple ruled box]

Collation: [i-x], 1-334 pages; cream endpapers.   7 $^{7}/_{16}$" x 5 $^{1}/_{8}$".   [A-T]^{8} [U]^{4} [V]^{8}

Contents: (i-ii) blank; (iii) half title page; (iv) addresses for Jonathan Cape and Harrison Smith; (v) title page; (vi) copyright page; (vii) [dedication]: *For My Mother | and Her undying Flame;* (viii) blank; (ix) [quotation]: *Plagued by the nightingale | in the new leaves, | with its silence... | not its silence, but its | silences.* | MARIANNE MOORE (x) blank; (1-334) text.

Copyright page: COPYRIGHT, 1931, BY KAY BOYLE | FIRST PUBLISHED, 1931 | * | PRINTED IN THE UNITED STATES | OF AMERICA

Binding: Light green cloth covered boards stamped in gold. Top edge trimmed and stained black. Bottom edge trimmed and front edge rough trimmed. Front: [gold] *PLAGUED | BY THE | NIGHTINGALE |* * Spine: *PLAGUED | BY THE | NIGHTINGALE |* * | KAY | BOYLE | JONATHAN CAPE | HARRISON SMITH. Back: Blank.

Dust jacket: Beige paper printed in three shades of blue. Front: [dark blue] PLAGUED | [light blue] BY THE | [dark blue] NIGHTINGALE | [light blue horizontal rule] | [light blue] *KAY BOYLE* | [three vertical dots each in a different shade of blue] (all the preceding encircled in a beige vertical oval) | [beige script outside the oval] By the author of Wedding Day And Other Stories. Spine: [beige on blue] *KAY BOYLE* | [printed inside beige vertical oval] PLAGUED | BY THE | NIGHTIN- | GALE | [beige on blue outside of the oval] JONATHAN CAPE | HARRISON SMITH. Back: Advertisement for *The Story of Siegfried* by Angela Diller. Front flap: Short plot description and biographical note on Kay Boyle. $2.50 [lower right]. Back flap: Advertisement and description of *Epistle to Prometheus* by Babette Deutsch.

Publication: According to *Publisher's Weekly* the publication date was March 9, 1931 at $2.50.

A4b   PLAGUED BY THE NIGHTINGALE   1931

First Edition Second Printing:

PLAGUED | BY THE | NIGHTINGALE | * | KAY BOYLE | * | NEW YORK | *Jonathan Cape & Harrison Smith* | MCMXXXI. [all enclosed in a double ruled box which is in turn enclosed in a larger triple ruled box]

Collation: Second printing substitutes double quote for single after the word American 177.11.

Contents: Same as A4a.

Copyright page: COPYRIGHT, 1931, BY KAY BOYLE | FIRST PUBLISHED, 1931 | * | PRINTED IN THE UNITED STATES | OF AMERICA | *Second printing, April, 1931*

Binding: Same as A4a.

Dust jacket: The price does not appear on the front flap of the jacket. On the first printing jacket the price for *Epistle to Prometheus* is in the lower left corner of the back flap. It is omitted on the second printing jacket. In all other respects the first and second printing dust jackets are the same.

Publication: Reprinted in April 1931 at $2.50.

A4c   PLAGUED BY THE NIGHTINGALE   [1931]

First English Edition:

*PLAGUED | BY THE | NIGHTINGALE | * | KAY BOYLE | * | JONATHAN CAPE | LONDON AND TORONTO* [all enclosed in a double rectangular rule which is in turn enclosed in a larger triple rectangular rule]

Collation: [i-viii], 1-334 pages; cream endpapers.   7 $^1/_2$" x 5".   [A-T]^8 [U]^4 [V]^8

Contents: (i) half title page; (ii) addresses for Jonathan Cape and Harrison Smith in New York, Toronto and London; (iii) title page; (iv) copyright page; (v) [dedication]: *For My Mother | and Her undying Flame;* (vi) blank; (vii) [quotation]: *Plagued by the nightingale | in the new leaves, | with its silence... | not its silence, but its | silences. |* MARIANNE MOORE; (viii) blank; (1-334) text.

Copyright page: FIRST PUBLISHED, 1931 | * | PRINTED IN THE UNITED STATES | OF AMERICA | *Jonathan Cape, Ltd. | 30 Bedford Square, London, W. C. I, England | and 91 Wellington Street, West, Toronto, Canada | Jonathan Cape and Harrison Smith, Inc. | 139 E. 46th St., New York*

Binding: Light blue cloth covered boards stamped in gold. Top edge unstained and all edges trimmed. Front: Blank. Spine: PLAGUED | BY THE | NIGHTINGALE | [device] | KAY BOYLE | JONATHAN CAPE Back: [embossed publisher's device in the center of the rear panel]

Dust jacket: White paper printed in black and yellow.   Front: PLAGUED | BY THE | NIGHTINGALE [The preceding enclosed in a thick ruled black rectangle which is then also enclosed in a thick ruled yellow rectangle] KAY BOYLE [Repeat rectangle pattern] [The background is six rows of houses each row separated by a thin wavy black line, then a thick wavy yellow line and then a thick wavy black line] Spine: PLAGUED | BY THE | NIGHT- | INGALE [Enclosed in the same rectangle pattern as used on the front]   KAY BOYLE   [Repeat rectangle pattern] JONATHAN | CAPE [Repeat rectangle pattern]   [Front background design continues over to the spine]   Back: Blank.   Front flap: Story plot. *7s. 6d. net* [lower right corner]   Back flap: Blank.

Publication: First published in July 1931 at 7s6d.

A4d   PLAGUED BY THE NIGHTINGALE   [1951]

Second English Edition:

KAY BOYLE | [short double ruled line, thick over thin] | Plagued by the | Nightingale | LONDON | JOHN LEHMANN

Collation: [1-6], 7-190, [191-192] pages; cream endpapers.   7" x 4 $^5/_8$"   [A]^{16} B-F^{16}

Fig 1-A4c

Contents: (1) half title page; (2) blank; (3) title page; (4) copyright page; (5) [quotation]: *Plagued by the nightingale* | *in the new leaves,* | *with its silence...* | *not its silence, but its* | *silences.* | MARIANNE MOORE; (6) [dedication]: For | My Mother | and | her Undying Flame; (7-190) text; (191-192) blank.

Copyright page: FIRST PUBLISHED IN 1931 | FIRST PUBLISHED IN THE HOLIDAY LIBRARY IN 1951 | BY JOHN LEHMANN LTD | 25 GILBERT STREET LONDON W. 1 | MADE AND PRINTED IN GREAT BRITAIN BY | PURNELL AND SONS LTD | PAULTON (SOMERSET) AND LONDON

Binding: Blue cloth covered boards stamped in gold. Top edges unstained all edges trimmed. Front: Blank. Spine: [gold decoration tied into gold double rule] | [gold printed on maroon] *PLAGUED* | *BY THE* | *NIGHTINGALE* | KAY | BOYLE | [Gold double rule tied into gold decoration] | [gold on blue] *JOHN* | *LEHMANN* Back: Blank.

Dust jacket: White paper printed in black and blue. Front: light blue background. [black printing on white surrounded by black scroll design] *PLAGUED BY THE* | *NIGHTINGALE* | KAY BOYLE | [black printing on blue surrounded by similar scroll design all on white swatch] *THE* | *HOLIDAY* | *LIBRARY* Spine: [black scroll design at top of spine] | [black printing on blue, printed downward] *PLAGUED BY THE NIGHTINGALE* [design] KAY BOYLE | [black scroll design at bottom of spine] Back: List of modern reprints by Holiday Library. Front flap: Short reviews by *Manchester Guardian, The Observer,* and *John O'London Weekly.* 6 s. net [lower right]. Back flap: Blank.

Publication: First published in October 1951 at six shillings.

A4e   PLAGUED BY THE NIGHTINGALE   [1966]

Second American Edition:

Kay Boyle | PLAGUED BY | THE NIGHTINGALE | [three small designs arranged in a triangle] | SOUTHERN ILLINOIS UNIVERSITY PRESS | CARBONDALE AND EDWARDSVILLE

Collation: [i-vi], vii-x, [1-2], 3-203, [204-214] pages; gold endpapers.   8 $^1/_4$" x 4 $^7/_8$"   [A-G]^{16}

Contents: (i) CROSSCURRENTS/MODERN FICTION; (ii) CROSSCUR-RENTS/MODERN FICTION | HARRY T. MOORE, *General Editor* | MATTHEW J. BRUCCOLI, *Textual Editor* | PREFACE BY | HARRY T. MOORE | A NOTE ON THE TEXT BY | MATTHEW J. BRUCCOLI; (iii) title page; (iv) copyright page; (v) [dedication]: *For My Mother and Her undying Flame;* (vi) blank; (vii-x) preface by Harry T. Moore; (1) [quotation]: *Plagued by the nightingale* | *in the new leaves,* | *with its silence...* | *not its silence, but its* | *silences.* | MARIANNE

MOORE; (2) blank; (3-202) text; (203) A note on the text by Matthew Bruccoli; (204-214) blank.

Copyright page: COPYRIGHT © 1931,1959, by Kay Boyle | Preface by *Harry T. Moore* and A Note on the Text by *Matthew J.* | *Bruccoli*, COPYRIGHT © 1966, by SOUTHERN ILLINOIS UNI- | VERSITY PRESS | All rights reserved | Crosscurrents/Modern Fiction edition, March, 1966 | Library of Congress Card Catalog Number 65-19774 | Printed in the United States of America | *Designed Andor Braun*

Binding: Light reddish purple cloth covered boards stamped in gold. Top edge unstained and all edges trimmed. Front: Blank. Spine: [gold, printed downward] Kay Boyle [top line] Plagued by the Nightingale [bottom line] | Southern Illinois University Press   Back: Blank.

Dust jacket: Beige paper pictorial jacket printed in light purple, white and blue. Front: [white] Kay Boyle | [light purple] Plagued by the | [light purple] Nightingale | [light purple, white slashes] *CROSSCURRENTS/Modern Fiction/*Edited by HARRY T. MOORE   Spine: [printed downward] Kay Boyle [top line white] | Plagued by the Nightingale [bottom line light purple] | Southern Illinois University Press [light purple]   Back: blank.   Front flap: Short history of the novel with short plot outline and a review from *The Times Literary Supplement* and *The New Republic*. [upper right] $5.95.   Back flap: Short description of the Crosscurrents/Modern Fiction Series and titles published previously.

First published on March 21, 1966 at $5.95.

A4f   PLAGUED BY THE NIGHTINGALE   [1981]

First English Paperback Edition:

KAY BOYLE | [double ruled line thick over thin] | Plagued by the | Nightingale | *With a new Preface* | *by the author* | *Virago* | [apple with a bite taken out] | *London*

Collation: [i-ii], [1-6], 7-190 pages.   7 $^3/_4$" x 5"

Contents: (i) short biographical note on Kay Boyle; (ii) [quotation]: *Plagued by the nightingale* | *in the new leaves,* | *with its silence...* | *not its silence, but its* | *silences.* | MAR-IANNE MOORE; (1) title page; (2) copyright page; (3-6) preface; (7-190) text.

Copyright page: *For My Mother and* | *her undying Flame* | Published by VIRAGO Limited 1981 | Ely House, 37 Dover Street, | London W1X 4HS | First published 1930 | Copyright © Kay Boyle 1930, 1981 | Printed in Hong Kong by | Colorcraft Limited | This book is sold subject to the | condition that it shall not, by way of | trade or otherwise, be lent, re-sold, | hired out or otherwise circulated | without the publisher's prior consent, | in any form of binding or cover other | than that in which it is published and | without a similar condition including | this condition being imposed on the | subsequent purchaser. This book is | supplied subject to the Publishers | Association Standard Conditions of | Sale registered under the Restrictive | Trades Practices Act, 1956 | *British Library Cataloguing in Publication Data* | Boyle, Kay | Plagued by the nightingale | (Virago modern classic) | I.Title | 823'.9'1F PS3503.09357 | ISBN 0-86068-167-X

Binding: Stiff white pictorial wraps printed in green and white. Front: [light green] Virago Modern Classics | [white rule] | [white] Kay Boyle | [white rule] | [white] Plagued by the Nightingale [all the foregoing text printed on dark green background]   A picture of a standing woman, plant cutting in a vase, cello bow, scroll and red flower on stand with a cello leaning on a music stand. Spine: [continuation of white rule on the cover] | [apple with a bite taken out] | [continuation of white rule on the cover] | [printed downward in white] Plagued by the Nightingale Kay Boyle   0 86068 167 X   Back: Top three lines same as front cover. Notes and an excerpt from a review of the novel and cover credits. United Kingdom £2.50 Fiction 0 86068 167-X

Publication: First published in March 1981

A4g   PLAGUED BY THE NIGHTINGALE   [1990]

First American Paperback Edition:

KAY BOYLE | [double rule line thick over thin] | Plagued by the | Nightingale | *With a new Preface* | by the author | [Penguin Books publishing device] | PENGUIN BOOKS-VIRAGO PRESS

Collation: Same as A4f.

Contents: Same as A4f.

Copyright page: PENGUIN BOOKS | Published by the Penguin Group | Viking Penguin, a division of Penguin Books USA Inc., | 375 Hudson Street, New York, New York 10014, U.S.A. | Penguin Books Ltd, 27 Wrights Lane, | London W8 5TZ, England | Penguin Books Australia Ltd, Ringwood, | Victoria, Australia | Penguin Books Canada Ltd, 2801 John Street, | Markham, Ontario, Canada L3R 1B4 | Penguin Books (N.Z.) Ltd, 182-190 Wairau Road, | Auckland 10, New Zealand | Penguin Books Ltd, Registered Offices: | Harmondsworth, Middlesex, England | First published in Great Britain by | Jonathan Cape Limited 1931 | First published in the United States of America | by W.H. Smith 1931 | This edition published in Great Britain by | Virago Press Limited in 1981 | Published in Penguin Books 1990 | 1 3 5 7 9 10 8 6 4 2 | Copyright © Kay Boyle, 1931, 1981 | Copyright renewed Kay Boyle, 1959 | All rights reserved | LIBRARY OF CONGRESS CATALOGING IN PUBLICATION DATA | Boyle, Kay, 1902- | Plagued by the nightingale/Kay Boyle; with a new preface by the | author. | p. cm.— (Virago modern classics) | ISBN 0 14016.212 7 | I. Title. II. Series. | PS3503.O9357P5 1990 | 813'.52-dc20 90-7041 | Printed in the United States of America | Except in the United States of America, this | book is sold subject to the condition that it | shall not, by way of trade or otherwise, be lent, | re-sold, hired out, or otherwise circu-lated | without the publisher's prior consent in any form | of binding or cover other than that in which it | is published and without a similar condition | including this condition being imposed on the | subsequent purchaser.

Binding: Same as Virago edition other than small Penguin Books publishing device in the upper right hand corner of the front covers. This device also appears on the back cover along with a price of $7.95   Spine excludes the apple which is on the English edition and substitutes ISBN 014 [top line] 016.212 7 [bottom line] | [publisher's device] for 0 86068 167X

Publication: First published in October 1990

A5a   LANDSCAPE FOR WYN HENDERSON   [1931]

First Edition:

LANDSCAPE | FOR | WYN HENDERSON | BY KAY BOYLE | LONDON | 1931

Collation: [1-4], 5-7, [8] pages.   7" x 4$^1/_2$"

Contents: (1) cover and title page; (2) blank; (3) [limitation statement]: Seventy-five copies only of LANDSCAPE | FOR WYN HENDERSON have been privately | printed (and are not for sale) at | The Curwen Press, Plaistow. | This is number [ink number]; (4) blank; (5-8) text.

Copyright page: No copyright page.

Binding: Cream colored wraps. Two folded sheets sewn.

A6a   A STATEMENT   [1932]

First Edition:

A STATEMENT | by | KAY BOYLE | [two small decorations] | *Number 3* | *PAMPHLET SERIES ONE*

Collation: [1-12] pages.   9 $^1/_8$" x 5 $^7/_8$"   Three folded sheets sewn plus covers.

Contents: (1) blank; (2) drawing of head by Max Weber; (3) title page; (4) copyright page; (5-10) text; (11) blank; (12) [limitation statement]: *One hundred seventy five copies of this pamphlet* | *have been printed in handset Bernhard type,* | *on Utopian deckle-edged paper. One hun-* | *dred sixty five, numbered , and signed* | *by the author, are offered for sale.* | *Ten are hors-commerce.* | *This is* | [ink number] | [Kay Boyle's signature].

Copyright page: *Copyright 1932 The Modern Editions Press*

Binding: Yellow paper sewn wrappers printed in maroon. Top and bottom edges trimmed; front edge rough trimmed. Front: A STATEMENT | by KAY BOYLE | [yellow and maroon tulip design] | Pamphlet Three

Slipcase: Boxed in a pale green slipcase with a white paste on label on the front and printed in black. Front: [all the following in a black rectangular rule] Pamphlet Series One | 1. TWO POEMS by Dudley Fitts | *Decoration by Stuart Davis* | 2. TWO STO-RIES by John Kemmerer | *Decoration by Isami Doi* | 3. ONE POEM by Kay Boyle | *Decoration by Max Weber* | 4. THREE STORIES by K. T. Young | *Decoration by Stefan Hirsch* | 5. ONE POEM by Raymond Ellsworth Larsson | *Decoration by Jane Berlandino* | 6. ONE STORY by Albert Halper | *Decoration by Louis Lozowick* | THE MODERN EDITIONS PRESS | 725 Greenwich Street | New York City | $3.50

A7a   YEAR BEFORE LAST   [1932]

First Edition:

YEAR BEFORE LAST | BY | KAY BOYLE | LONDON | FABER AND FABER LIMITED | 24 RUSSELL SQUARE

Collation: [1-8], 9-67, [68-70], 71-230, [231-232], 233-320 pages; cream endpa-pers. 7 $^3/_8$" x 4 $^7/_8$"   [A]^8 B-I^8 K-U^8

Contents: (1) half title page; (2) blank; (3) title page; (4) copyright page; (5) [dedi-cation]: THIS BOOK | IS DEDICATED TO | EMANUEL CARNEVALI; (6) [dis-claimer]: AUTHOR'S NOTE | The characters in this novel are entirely fictitious and | have no reference whatsoever to real people, living | or dead.; (7) [divisional title]: PART I; (8) blank; (9-67) text; (68) blank; (69) [divisional title]: PART II; (70) blank; (71-230) text; (231) [divisional title]: PART III; (232) blank; (233-320) text.

Copyright page: FIRST PUBLISHED IN MCMXXXII | BY FABER AND FABER LIMITED | 24 RUSSELL SQUARE LONDON W.C.I | PRINTED IN GREAT BRITAIN | BY LATIMER TREND AND COMPANY PLYMOUTH | ALL RIGHTS RESERVED

Binding: Red cloth covered boards printed in black. Top edge unstained and all edges trimmed. Front: Blank Spine: YEAR | BEFORE | LAST | KAY | BOYLE | FABER | AND FABER Back: Blank

Dust jacket: Cream paper printed in greenish yellow, black and red.   Front: [black] by Kay Boyle | author of | 'Plagued by the Nightingale' | [red] YEAR | BEFORE | LAST | [black] 'Year Before Last' is the full | flower of that genius in fiction | which was first hailed in | 'Plagued by the Nightingale' | FABER AND FABER   Spine: [black] YEAR | BEFORE | LAST | [red] Kay | Boyle | [black] Faber | & Faber   Back: Other Fiction by Faber & Faber   Front flap: Story plot. 7s. 6d. net   [lower right]. Back flap: Note about current fiction and address of Faber & Faber.

Publication: First published in June 1932 at 7s6d.

A7b   YEAR BEFORE LAST   1932

First American Edition:

★ | *YEAR* | *BEFORE LAST* | ★ | KAY BOYLE | ★ | MCMXXXII | HARRRISON SMITH • NEW YORK   [All of the preceding enclosed in quadruple ruled rectangle]

Collation: [i-viii], [1-2], 3-71, [72-74], 75-265, [266-268], 269-373, [374-376] pages, cream endpapers. 7 $^5/_{16}$" x 5"   [A-X]^8

Contents: (i-ii) blank; (iii) half title page; (iv) [list]: BY KAY BOYLE [two titles]; (v) title page; (vi) copyright page; vii) [dedication]: ★ | *This book is for* | *Emanuel Carnevali* | ★   (viii) blank; (1) [divisional title and note]: PART ONE | Author's Note: None of the characters herein de- | picted have any connection with actual people, dead or | living.; (2) blank; (3-71) text; (72) blank; (73) [divisional title]: PART TWO; (74) blank; (75-265) text; (266) blank; (267) [divisional title]: PART THREE; (268) blank; (269-373) text; (374-376) blank.

Copyright page: COPYRIGHT, 1932, BY HARRISON SMITH, INC. | FIRST PUBLISHED, 1932 | ★ | PRINTED IN THE UNITED STATES | OF AMERICA

Binding: Red cloth stamped in gold. Top edge stained black and all edges trimmed. Front: ★ | *YEAR* | *BEFORE LAST* | ★   Spine: ★ | *YEAR* | *BEFORE* | *LAST* | ★ | KAY BOYLE | ★ | HARRISON SMITH   Back: Blank.

Dust jacket: Yellow paper printed in green and black. Front: Green, yellow, and black horizontal stripes with picture in the center. [yellow on green] KAY BOYLE | [yellow on black] AUTHOR OF "PLAGUED BY THE NIGHTINGALE" | yellow green and black picture of woman] | [yellow on black] YEAR BEFORE | LAST | [black on green drawn bow and arrow pointed up] Spine: [yellow on green] KAY BOYLE | [yellow on black] YEAR | [yellow on green] BEFORE | [yellow on green] LAST | [yellow on black] HARRISON | SMITH • INC   Back: Advertising for other books published by Harrison Smith   Front flap: Story plot. $2.50 [lower right]. Back flap: Description of Claire Spencer's *The Quick and the Dead.*

Fig 2-A7b

Publication: According to *Publisher's Weekly* it was published on June 16, 1932 at $2.50.

A7c   YEAR BEFORE LAST   1932

Crosby Continental Edition:

Year | Before Last | by | Kay Boyle | Harrison Smith and Robert Haas | NEW-YORK | Crosby Continental Editions | 2, Rue Cardinale | PARIS | 1932

Collation: [1-9], 10-19, [20], 21-26, [27], 28-35, [36], 37-43, [44], 45-49, [50], 51-56, [57], 58-63, [64], 65-68, [69], 70-76, [77], 78-81, [82], 83-90, [91], 92-100, [101], 102-107, [108], 109-114, [115], 116-122, [123], 124-130, [131], 132-138, [139], 140-146, [147], 148-157, [158], 159-165, [166], 167-172, [173], 174-179, [180], 181-186, [187], 188-192, [193], 194-198, [199], 200-207, [208], 209-214, [215], 216-221, [222], 223-228, [229], 230-235, [236], 237-243, [244], 245-252, [253], 254-262, [263], 264-268, [269], 270-276, [277], 278-282, [283], 284-288, [289], 290-300, [301], 302-307, [308], 309-313, [314], 315-317, [318-320] pages. $6\,^3/_8$" x $4\,^3/_4$" $[1]^8$ 2-20^8

Contents: (1-2) blank; (3) half title page; (4) blank; (5) title page; (6) blank; (7) [dedication]: THIS BOOK | IS DEDICATED TO | EMANUEL CARNEVALI; (8) [disclaimer]: AUTHOR'S NOTE | The characters in this novel are entirely fictitious | and have no reference whatsoever to real people, | living or dead.;   (9-317) text; (318) blank; (319) [note]: *Each volume of the C.C.E.* | *is published with continen-* | *tal rights acquired from the* | *author or his representative.* (320) PUBLISHED BY | THE BLACK SUN PRESS | 2, RUE CARDINALE [final E is inverted] | PARIS | [short rule] | PRINTED BY | F. PAILLART | PARIS——ABBEVILLE | [short rule] | SEPTEMBER 1932

Copyright page: Blank

Binding: Beige wraps printed in purple.   Front: Modern Masterpieces in English | Year | Before Last | by | Kay Boyle | [publishers device, curved e enclosed in a c both enclosed in another c] | Crosby Continental Editions | Paris   Spine: No 8 | Year | Before Last | [same publishers device as on front cover] | Kay Boyle | 16f; Back: *Not to be introduced* | *into the British Empire or U.S.A.* | *Sole distributors Hachette, Paris.*; Front flap: Advertisement for books which   have already appeared in Crosby Continental Editions;   Back flap: Advertisement for books next to appear.

Dust jacket: None

Publication: First published in September 1932 at 16 Francs.

A7d   YEAR BEFORE LAST   [1933]

Second American Edition:

★ | *YEAR* | *BEFORE LAST* | ★ | KAY BOYLE | ★ | [publisher's device: windmill] | NEW YORK | *GREENBERG : PUBLISHER*

Collation: Collation and size the same as the A7a.

Contents: Same as A7a.

Copyright page: Same as A7a.

Binding: Light rose cloth covered boards stamped in black. Front: ★ | *YEAR* | *BEFORE LAST* | ★   Spine: ★ | *YEAR* | *BEFORE* | *LAST* | ★ | KAY BOYLE | ★ | [publisher's device: windmill] | GREENBURG; Back: Blank.

Dust jacket: White paper printed in blue and red. Front: The same as A7a except the colors are red white and blue and there is no bow and arrow at the bottom. Spine: Same as A7a except done in red, white and blue and the Harrison Smith Inc. is deleted.   Back cover: Advertises new fiction titles published by Greenberg. Front flap: Same story description as A7a with Greenberg listed as publisher with address at the bottom of the flap. No price. Back flap: Order blank to receive announcements of forthcoming books by Greenberg.

A7e   YEAR BEFORE LAST   [1969]

Third American Edition:

Kay Boyle | YEAR BEFORE LAST | [Three small designs arranged in a triangle] | SOUTHERN ILLINOIS UNIVERSITY PRESS | CARBONDALE AND EDWARDSVILLE | FEFFER & SIMONS, INC. | LONDON AND AMSTERDAM

Collation: [i-vi], vii-viii, [ix-x], 1-41, [42], 43-157, [158], 159-224, [225-230] pages; gold endpapers.   8 $3/_{16}$" x 4 $7/_{8}$" [A-E]^{16} [F]^{8} [G-H]^{8}

Contents: (i) [publisher's device: pyramid, new moon and three dots enclosed in an oval]; (ii) CROSSCURRENTS/MODERN FICTION | HARRY T. MOORE, *General Editor* | MATTHEW J. BRUCCOLI, *Textual Editor* | PREFACE BY | HARRY T. MOORE | A NOTE ON THE TEXT BY | MATTHEW J. BRUCCOLI; (iii) title page; (iv) copyright page; (v) [dedication]: *This book is for* | *Emanuel Carnevali*; (vi) blank; (vii-viii) preface; (ix) fly title page; (x) blank; (1-220) text; (221-224) A note on the text; (225-230) blank.

Copyright page: Author's Note: None of the characters herein depicted have any | connection with actual people, dead or living. | Copyright 1932 Kay Boyle, © renewed 1959 | Preface by *Harry T. Moore* and A Note on the Text by *Matthew* | *J.*

Bruccoli, COPYRIGHT © 1969 by SOUTHERN ILLINOIS | UNIVERSITY PRESS | All rights reserved | Crosscurrents / Modern Fiction edition, November, 1969 | Printed in the United States of America | *Designed by Andor Braun* | Standard Book Number 8093-0390-6 | Library of Congress Catalog Number 74-76191

Binding: Light blue cloth covered boards printed in dark blue. Top edge unstained. All edges trimmed. Front: Blank. Spine: [printed downward] *Kay Boyle* [top line] YEAR BEFORE LAST [bottom line] | Southern Illinois [top line] University Press [bottom line]; Back: Blank.

Dust jacket: Cream paper printed in gray, light blue, black and white. Front: [white] *Kay Boyle* | [light blue] YEAR | BEFORE | LAST | [drawing of a woman with a man superimposed with arms crossed] | [black] Crosscurrents Modern Fiction Edited by Harry T. Moore; Spine: [printed downward] *Kay Boyle* [top line white] | YEAR BEFORE LAST [bottom line blue] | Southern Illinois [top line black] | University Press [bottom line black] Back: Blank. Front flap: Story description with excerpts from contemporary reviews. $6.95 [upper right]; Back flap: Description of Crosscurrents series with published titles.

First published on December 22, 1969 at $6.95.

A7f   YEAR BEFORE LAST   [1986]

First English Paperback:

YEAR BEFORE LAST | KAY BOYLE | [single line rule with design in center] | With a New Afterword by | DORIS GRUMBACH | Virago | [publisher's device – apple with bite taken out]

Collation: [i-ii], [1-8], 9-67, [68-70], 71-230, [231-232], 233-329, [330-334] pages.   7 $^3/_4$" x 5"

Contents: (i) biographical sketch of Kay Boyle; (ii) VIRAGO | MODERN | CLASSIC | NUMBER | 225 [enclosed in double rule with device breaking the rule at the bottom]; (1) title page; (2) copyright page; (3) [dedication]: THIS BOOK | IS DEDICATED TO | EMANUEL CARNEVALI; (4) blank; (5) author's disclaimer; (6) blank; (7) [divisional title]: PART I; (8) blank; (9-67) text; (68) blank; (69) [divisional title]: PART II; (70) blank; (71-230) text; (231) [divisional title]: PART III; (232) blank; (233-320) text; (321-329) afterword; (330) blank; (331) history and description of Virago Modern Classics; (332) advertisement and story plot for *My Next Bride*; (333) advertisement and story plot for *Plagued By the Nightingale*; (334) list of other American classics published by Virago.

Copyright page: Published by VIRAGO PRESS Limited 1986 | 41 William IV Street, London WC2N 4DB | First published in Great Britain by Faber & Faber Limited 1932 | Copyright Kay Boyle 1932 | Afterword Copyright © Doris

Grumbach 1986 | All rights reserved | *British Cataloguing in Publication Data* | Boyle, Kay | Year before last. ——(Virago modern | classics) | I. Title | 813'.52[F] PS3503.09357 | ISBN 0-86068-752-X | Printed in Great Britain by | Anchor Brendon, Tiptree, Essex

Binding: Stiff white pictorial wraps printed in lime green, dark green and white. Front: [lime green] Virago Modern Classics | [white rule] | [white] Kay Boyle | [white rule] | [white] Year Before Last | A picture of a woman playing solitaire. Spine: [continuation of white rule on cover] | [publisher's device-apple with bite taken out] | [continuation of white rule on cover] | [printed downward in white] Year Before Last Kay Boyle 0 86068 752 X   Back: Story plot and note about Kay Boyle. £3.95 net in UK only [lower left]

A7g   YEAR BEFORE LAST   [1986]

First American Paperback:

YEAR BEFORE LAST | KAY BOYLE | [single line rule with design in center] | With a New Afterword by | DORIS GRUMBACH | [publisher's device-penguin enclosed in oval] | Penguin Books——Virago Press

Collation: [i-ii], [1-8], 9-67, [68-70], 71-230, [231-232], 233-329,   [330-334] pages. $7^3/_4$" x 5"

Contents: (i) biographical sketch of Kay Boyle; (ii) blank; (1) title page;   (2) copyright page; (3) [dedication]: THIS BOOK | IS DEDICATED TO | EMANUEL CARNEVALI; (4) blank; (5) author's disclaimer; (6) blank; (7) [divisional title]: PART I; (8) blank; (9-67) text; (68) blank; (69) [divisional title]: PART II; (70) blank; (71-230) text; (231) [divisional title]: PART III; (232) blank; (233-320) text; (321-329) afterword; (330) blank; (331) history and description of Virago Modern Classics; (332) blank; (333) list of other Penguin/Virago Modern Classics in print; (334) blank.

Copyright page: PENGUIN BOOKS | Viking Penguin Inc., 40 West 23rd Street, | New York, New York 10010, U.S.A. | Penguin Books Ltd, Harmondsworth, | Middlesex, England | Penguin Books Australia Ltd, Ringwood, | Victoria, Australia | Penguin Books Canada Limited, 2801 John Street, | Markham, Ontario, Canada L3R 1B4 | Penguin Books (N.Z.) Ltd, 182-190 Wairau Road, | Auckland 10, New Zealand | First published in Great Britain by Faber & Faber Limited 1932 | This edition first published in Great Britain by | Virago Press Ltd 1986 | Published in Penguin Books 1986 | Copyright Kay Boyle, 1932 | Copyright renewed Kay Boyle, 1960 | Afterword copyright © Doris Grumbach, 1986 | All rights reserved | Printed in the United States of America by | R.R. Donnelley & Sons Company, Harrisonburg, Virginia | Set in Meridien | Except in the United States of America, | this book is sold subject to the condition | that it shall not, by way of trade or otherwise, | be lent, re-sold, hired out, or otherwise circulated | without the publisher's prior consent in any form of | binding or cover other than that in which it is | published and without a similar condition | including this condition being imposed | on the subsequent purchaser

Binding: Stiff white pictorial wraps printed in lime green yellow, dark green and white. Front: [lime green] Virago Modern Classics | [white rule] | [white] Kay Boyle | [white rule] | [white] Year Before Last | A picture of a woman playing solitaire, there is a publisher's device in the upper right hand corner, a white penguin enclosed in a white oval. Spine: [continuation of two white rules on cover] | [printed downward in white] Year Before Last   Kay Boyle ISBN 0 14 [top line] 016.146 5 [bottom line] | [same publisher's device as on the front is at the foot of the spine]. Back: Short description of the story and note about Kay Boyle. $6.95 [lower left].

Publication: First published in October 1986

A8a   THE FIRST LOVER AND OTHER STORIES   [1933]

First Edition:

THE | *FIRST LOVER* | *AND OTHER STORIES* | ★ | KAY BOYLE | [seven ★s arranged in a arch] | NEW YORK | HARRISON SMITH & ROBERT HAAS

Collation: [i-x], [1-2], 3-15, [16-18], 19-29, [30-32], 33-43, [44-46], 47-57, [58-60], 61-71, [72-74], 75-89, [90-92], 93-132, [133-134], 135-145, [146-148], 149-168, [169-170], 171-186, [187-188], 189-203, [204-206], 207-215, [216-218], 219-234, [235-236], 237-249, [250] pages; cream endpapers. $7 \frac{1}{2}$" x 5"   [A-O]^8 [P]^{10}

Contents: (i) half title page; (ii) blank; (iii) title page; (iv) copyright page; (v) [dedi- cation]: *This book is for Eugene Jolas who wrote* | *"Follow the voice that booms in the deepest* | *dream, deeper go, always deeper...."*; (vi) blank; (vii) [publisher's note]: Acknowledgment is hereby made to the following | magazines in which these stories first appeared: | "Scribners," "Harpers," "The Criterion," "The Adel- | phi," "The New Yorker," "Vanity Fair," "The Yale | Review," "Story," "Contempo," and "Comment." (viii) blank; (ix) table of contents; (x) contents continued; (1) [story title]: HIS IDEA OF A MOTHER; (2) blank; (3-15) text; (16) blank; (17) [story title]: KROY WEN; (18) blank; (19- 29) text; (30) blank; (31) [story title]: THE FIRST LOVER; (32) blank; (33-43) text; (44) blank; (45) [story title]: ONE OF OURS; (46) blank; (47-57) text; (58) blank; (59) [story title]: THREE LITTLE MEN | *I'm very brave generally, he went on in a* | *low voice: only to-day I happen to have* | *a headache* | THROUGH THE LOOKING GLASS; | (60) blank; (61-71) text; (72) blank; (73) [story title]: TO THE PURE; (74) blank; (75-89) text; (90) blank; (91) [story title]: THE MAN WHO DIED YOUNG; (92) blank; (93-132) text; (133) [story title]: BLACK BOY; (134) blank; (135-145) text; (144) blank; (146) [story title]: LYDIA AND THE RING DOVE; (148) blank; (149-168) text; (169)

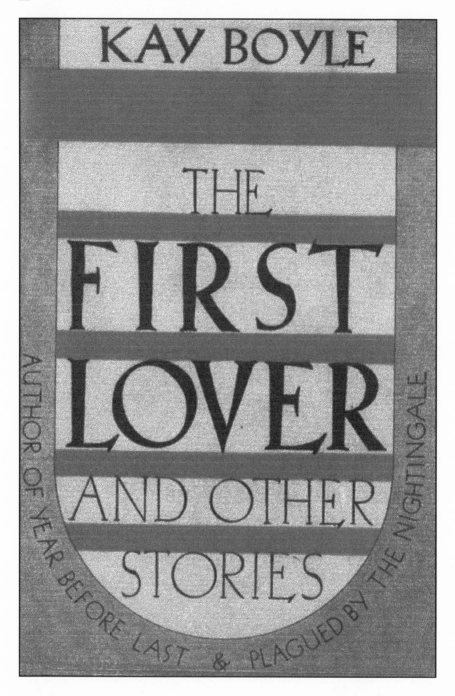

Fig 3-A8a

[story title]: FRIEND OF THE FAMILY; (170) blank; (171-186) text; (187) [story title]: REST CURE; (188) blank; (189-203) text; (204) blank; (205) [story title]: I CAN'T GET DRUNK; (206) blank; (207-215) text; (216) blank; (217) [story title]: THE MEETING OF THE STONES | . . . *for they sacrificed new-born babes at | the sowing-time, older children when the | grain had sprouted, and when it was fully | ripe they sacrificed old men. . . .*; (218) blank; (219-234) text; (235) [story title]: ART COLONY; (236) blank; (237-249) text; (250) blank.

Copyright page: *Copyright, 1933, by | Harrison Smith & Robert Haas, Inc. | Printed in the United States of America*

Binding: Dark blue cloth covered boards stamped in gold. Top edge stained yellow and trimmed. Bottom edge trimmed; front edge rough trimmed. Front: *THE | FIRST LOVER | AND OTHER STORIES | • | KAY BOYLE* Spine: [printed downward] *THE FIRST LOVER AND OTHER STORIES • KAY BOYLE* Back: Blank.

Dust jacket: Gray paper printed in dark blue, red, and dark gray. Front: KAY BOYLE | [wide red stripe across entire front] | THE | [narrower red stripe that does not extend to edges] | FIRST | [stripe identical to one just above] | LOVER | [repeat same stripe] | AND OTHER | [repeat stripe] | STORIES | [the following printed in a U shape encompassing the above text] AUTHOR OF YEAR BEFORE LAST & PLAGUED BY THE NIGHTINGALE. Spine: KAY | BOYLE | [continuation of wide red stripe on cover] | [printed downward] THE FIRST LOVER AND OTHER STORIES. Back: Advertisement for other titles by Smith & Haas. Front flap: Short biographical sketch of Kay Boyle. [lower right] $2.00. Back flap: Advertisement for William Faulkner's *A Green Bough*.

Publication: According to *Publisher's Weekly* it was first published on March 9, 1933 at $2.00.

Included stories and previous publication: "His Idea of a Mother" first appeared in *Scribner's* July 1931, "Kroy Wen" first appeared in *Front* December 1930, "The First Lover" first appeared in *Harper's Magazine* June 1931 and also appeared in *O. Henry Memorial Award Prize Stories of 1932*, Garden City: Doubleday, Doran & Company, 1932, "One of Ours" first appeared in *The New Yorker* October 17, 1931, "Three Little Men" first appeared in *Criterion* October 1932, "To the Pure" first appeared in *Scribner's* June 1932, "The Man Who Died Young" first appeared in *The Yale Review* June 1932, "Black Boy" first appeared in *The New Yorker* May 14, 1932, "Lydia and the Ring Dove" first appeared in *Vanity Fair* November 1932, "Friend of the Family" first appeared in *Harper's Magazine* September 1932, "Rest Cure" first appeared in *Story Magazine* April/May 1931 and also appeared in *The Best Short Stories 1931*, New York: Dodd, Mead and Company, [1931], "I Can't Get Drunk" first appeared in *Contempo* December 15, 1932, and "Art Colony" first appeared in *The New Yorker* December 10, 1932. This was apparently the first appearance of "The Meeting of the Stones" although acknowledgment is made in the front of the book to *Comment*. The compiler has been unable to find this magazine or confirm a Kay Boyle appearance.

A8b   THE FIRST LOVER AND OTHER STORIES   [1933]

First Edition Second Printing:

THE | *FIRST LOVER* | *AND OTHER STORIES* | ★ KAY BOYLE | [seven ★s arranged in a arch] | NEW YORK | HARRISON SMITH & ROBERT HAAS

Collation and contents: Same as A8a printing except the following line is added on copyright page: *Second Printing, April, 1933*

Binding: Same as A8a.

Dust jacket: Same as the A8a.

Publication: Printed in April 1933 at $2.00.

Note: All copies of the second printing examined were printed on lighter paper and were considerably thinner than the first printing.

A8c   THE FIRST LOVER AND OTHER STORIES   [1937]

First English Edition:

THE FIRST LOVER | and other stories | by | KAY BOYLE | FABER AND FABER | 24 Russell Square | London

Collation: [1-8], 9, [10], 11, [12-14], 15-30, [31-32], 33-46, [47-48], 49-62, [63-64], 65-77, [78-80], 81-93, [94-96], 97-114, [115-116], 117-164, [165-166], 167-179, [180-182], 183-206, [207-208], 209-226, [227-228], 229-246, [247-248], 249-259, [260-262], 263-282, [283-284], 285-299, [300-304] pages; cream endpapers.   7 $^3/_8$" x 4 $^3/_4$"   [A]^8 B-I^8 K-T^8

Contents: (1-2) blank; (3) half title page; (4) [list]: by the same author [7 titles]; (5) title page; (6) copyright page; (7) dedication same as American edition; (8) blank; (9) [pubisher's note]: Acknowledgment is hereby made to the fol- | lowing magazines in which these stories first | appeared: "*Scribners*," "*Harpers*," "*The Criterion*," "*The | Adelphi*," "*The New Yorker*," "*Vanity* Fair," "*The Yale | Review*," "*Story*," "*Contempo*," and "*Comment*." (10) blank; (11) contents; (12) blank; (13) [story title]: HIS IDEA OF A MOTHER; (14) blank; (15-30) text; (31) [story title]: KROY WEN; (32) blank; (33-46) text; (47) [story title]: THE FIRST LOVER; (48) blank; (49-62) text; (63) [story title]: ONE OF OURS; (64) blank; (65-77) text; (78) blank; (79) [story title]: THREE LITTLE MEN | *I'm very brave generally, he went on in a | low voice: only to-day I happen to have | a headache* | [story title]: THROUGH THE LOOKING GLASS; (80) blank; (81-93) text; (94) blank; (95) [story title]: TO THE PURE; (96) blank; (97-114) text; (115) [story title]: THE MAN WHO DIED YOUNG; (116) blank; (117-164) text; (165) [story title]: BLACK BOY; (166) blank; (167-179) text; (180) blank; (181) [story title]: LYDIA AND THE

RING DOVES; (182) blank; (183-206) text; (207) [story title]: A FRIEND OF THE FAMILY; (208) blank; (209-226) text; (227) [story title]: REST CURE; (228) blank; (229-246) text; (247) [story title]: I CAN'T GET DRUNK; (248) blank; (249-259) text; (260) blank; (261) [story title]: THE | MEETING OF THE STONES | . . . *for they sacrificed new-born babes at | the sowing-time, older children when the | grain had sprouted, and when it was fully | ripe they sacrificed old men. . . .*; (262) blank; (263-282) text; (283) [story title]: ART COLONY; (284) blank; (285-299) text; (300-304) blank.

Copyright page: *First published in October Mcmxxxvii | By Faber and Faber Limited | 24 Russell Square London W.C.1 | Printed in Great Britain by | Latimer Trend & Co Ltd Plymouth | All Rights Reserved*

Binding: Rose cloth covered boards stamped in gold and blue. Top edge unstained. All edges trimmed. Front: Blank. Spine: [gold] ★ | [enclosed in gold bordered dark blue rectangle with rose cloth showing through to form letters] THE | FIRST | LOVER | Kay | Boyle | [gold] ★ | [gold] FABER AND | FABER   Back: Blank.

Dust jacket: Pink paper printed in black and grayish green. Front: [black] Kay Boyle | [black surrounded by a grayish green square scroll design which is not closed] THE | FIRST | LOVER | [in black below the scroll] Faber and Faber Spine: [grayish green scroll at top of spine] | [black] THE | FIRST | LOVER | [grayish green] by | [black] Kay | Boyle | Faber and | Faber   Back: Advertisements for new fiction by Faber and Faber all printed in black.   Front flap: Reviews of *The White Horses of Vienna*.   7s. 6d. |net [lower right]   Back flap: Reviews of *Death of a Man* and *My Next Bride* and a notice from Faber and Faber.

Publication: First published in October 1937 at 7s6d.

The Included stories and first appearances are the same as the American edition.

A8d   THE FIRST LOVER AND OTHER STORIES   [1942]

Second English Edition:

THE FIRST LOVER | and other stories | by | KAY BOYLE | FABER AND FABER | 24 Russell Square | London

Collation: [1-8], 9, [10], 11, [12-14], 15-30, [31-32], 33-46, [47-48], 49-62, [63-64], 65-77, [78-80], 81-93, [94-96], 97-114, [115-116], 117-164, [165-166], 167-179, [180-182], 183-206, [207-208], 209-226, [227-228], 229-246, [247-248], 249-259, [260-262], 263-282, [283-284], 285-299, [300] pages; cream endpapers.   7" x 4 $^1/_2$"   [A]^8 B-S^8 T^6

Contents: (1-2) blank; (3) [half title page]: THE FABER LIBRARY—No. 54 [swelled rule] | THE FIRST LOVER; (4) [list]: by the same author | [seven titles];

(5) title page; (6) copyright page; (7) dedication same as American edition; (8) blank; (9) [publisher's note]: Acknowledgment is hereby made to the fol- | lowing magazines in which these stories first | appeared: *Scribners, Harpers, The Criterion, The | Adelphi, The New Yorker, Vanity Fair, The Yale | Review, Story, Contempo,* and *Comment.*; (10) blank; (11) table of contents; (12) blank; (13) [story title]: HIS IDEA OF A MOTHER; (14) blank; (15-30) text; (31) [story title]: KROY WEN; (32) blank; (33-46) text; (47) [story title]: THE FIRST LOVER; (48) blank; (49-62) text; (63) [story title]: ONE OF OURS; (64) blank; (65-77) text; (78) blank; (79) [story title]: THREE LITTLE MEN with quotation from *Through the Looking Glass*; (80) blank; (81-93) text; (94) blank; (95) [story title]: TO THE PURE; (96) blank; (97-114) text; (115) [story title]: THE MAN WHO DIED YOUNG; (116) blank; (117-164) text; (165) [story title]: BLACK BOY; (166) blank; (167-179) text; (180) blank; (181) [story title]: LYDIA AND THE RING DOVES; (182) blank; (183-206) text; (207) [story title]: FRIEND OF THE FAMILY; (208) blank; (209-226) text; (227) [story title]: REST CURE; (228) blank; (229-246) text; (247) [story title]: I CAN'T GET DRUNK; (248) blank; (249-259) text; (260) blank; (261) [story title]: THE MEETING OF THE STONES with quotation; (262) blank; (263-282) text; (283) [story title]: ART COLONY; (284) blank; (285-299) text; (300) blank.

Copyright page: *First published in October Mcmxxxvii | Reissued in this edition Mcmxlii | by Faber and Faber Limited | 24 Russell Square London W.C.1 | Printed in Great Britain by | Latimer Trend & Co Ltd Plymouth | All Rights Reserved*

Binding: Turquoise green cloth covered boards stamped in silver. Top edge unstained and all edges trimmed. Front: Blank. Spine: [design at top] | THE | FIRST | LOVER | [design] | KAY | BOYLE | FABER | AND FABER | [same design as at top inverted]. Back: Blank.

Dust jacket: Orange paper printed in blue. Front: THE | FIRST | LOVER | [the proceeding enclosed in a rectangle of small blue squares with an asterisk in the middle of each] | *by* | KAY | BOYLE | *The Faber Library.* Spine: The | First | Lover | ★ | KAY | BOYLE | [enclosed in same design as front and printed downward] THE FIRST LOVER [the following all horizontal] 54 | *The Faber | Library*   Back: List of books available from The Faber Library.   Front flap: Three short reviews of *The First Lover* from *Listener, Liverpool Daily Press* and *London Mercury.* THE *FABER LIBRARY | No. 54 |*   [lower right] 3s. 6d. | net   Back flap: Blank.

Publication: First published in May 1942 at 3s 6d.

A9a   GENTLEMEN, I ADDRESS YOU PRIVATELY   1933

First Edition:

Gentlemen, | I address you privately | BY KAY BOYLE | NEW YORK | *Harrison Smith and Robert Haas* | MCMXXXIII [all the preceding enclosed in a triple ruled box]

Fig 4-A9a

Collation: [1-10], 11-341, [342-344] pages; cream endpapers.   7 $\frac{1}{2}$" x 5 $\frac{1}{8}$"
[A-U]^8 [V]^4

Contents: (1) half title page; (2) blank; (3) title page; (4) copyright page; (5) [ded-
ication]: *Dedicated to* | Adelaide and Charles Walker | and their United States;   (6)
blank; (7) [quotation]: *"Gentlemen, I address you privately | and no woman is within
hearing."* | ERNEST WALSH;   (8) blank; (9) fly title; (10) blank; (11-341) text;
(342-344) blank.

Copyright page: COPYRIGHT, 1933, BY KAY BOYLE | FIRST PRINTING | * |
PRINTED IN THE UNITED STATES | OF AMERICA

Binding: Black cloth covered boards stamped in gold. Top edge stained yellow.
Top and bottom edge trimmed. Front edge rough trimmed.   Front: Gentlemen,
| I address you privately | BY KAY BOYLE   Spine: Gentlemen, | I address you |
privately | * | KAY BOYLE | HARRISON SMITH | & ROBERT HAAS   Back:
Blank.

Dust jacket: Cream paper pictorial jacket printed in beige, black and gold. Front:
[gold band at top] | [black rule] | [printed on black in gold] GENTLEMEN, | I
ADDRESS YOU | PRIVATELY | [black rule] | [picture of two men facing each
other enclosed in an oval, one on the right in military uniform on black background,
the other on the left in civilian clothes on a gold back ground with gold leaf
design top and bottom of oval with cover artist's name George Annand in black
between black rule and gold leaf design] | [black rule] | [printed   on black in
gold] *By* KAY BOYLE | [black rule] | [gold band across bottom] Spine: [continua-
tion of gold band from front] | [continuation of black rule from front] | [on
black band] GENTLE- | MEN, I | ADDRESS | YOU | PRIVATELY | [diamond] |
KAY | BOYLE | [continuation of black rule from front] | [picture of trees with
moon in the background all on a beige background] | [continuation of black rule
from the front] | [printed on black band in gold] HARRISON SMITH | &
ROBERT HAAS | [continuation of black rule from front] | [continuation of gold
band from the front]   Back: Advertisement for other books published by Smith and
Haas. Front flap: Story plot. $2.50 [lower right]. Back flap: Advertisement for
Southern Mail by Antoine de Saint-Exupéry.   NOTE: Two different jackets have
been noted. Presumed first state jacket lists four Kay Boyle books and does not
include *Gentlemen, I Address You Privately*.   Three books are listed by Maurice
Hindus and *The Great Offensive* is not listed. The assumed second state jacket lists
five Boyle books with *Gentlemen, I Address You Privately* listed first, but listed at
$2.00 instead of $2.50. Maurice Hindus' *The Great Offensive* is listed first among
his books.

Publication: First published on November 2, 1933 according to *Publisher's Weekly* at
$2.50.

A9b   GENTLEMEN, I ADDRESS YOU PRIVATELY   1933

First Edition Second Printing:

Gentlemen, | I address you privately | BY KAY BOYLE | NEW YORK | *Harrison Smith and Robert Haas* | MCMXXXIII [All the preceding enclosed in triple ruled box]

Collation: Same as A9a.

Contents: Same as A9a.

Copyright page: COPYRIGHT 1933, BY KAY BOYLE | *Second Printing November, 1933* | ★ | PRINTED IN THE UNITED STATES | OF AMERICA

Binding: Blue cloth covered boards stamped in gold. Top edge stained yellow and trimmed. Bottom edge trimmed and front edge rough trimmed. Front: Gentlemen, | I address you privately | BY KAY BOYLE   Spine: Gentlemen, | I address you | privately | ★ | KAY BOYLE | HARRISON SMITH | & ROBERT HAAS   Back: Blank.

Dust jacket: Same as A9a.

Publication: Published in November 1933 at $2.50.

A9c   GENTLEMEN, I ADDRESS YOU PRIVATELY   1934

First Edition Third Printing:

Gentlemen, | I address you privately | BY KAY BOYLE | NEW YORK | *Harrison Smith and Robert Haas* | MCMXXXIII [All the preceding enclosed in triple ruled box]

Collation: Same as A9a.

Contents: Same as A9a.

Copyright page: COPYRIGHT 1933, BY KAY BOYLE | *Third Printing January, 1934* | ★ | PRINTED IN THE UNITED STATES | OF AMERICA

Binding: Blue cloth covered boards stamped in gold. Top edge stained yellow and trimmed. Bottom edge trimmed and fore edge untrimmed. Front: Gentlemen, | I address you privately | BY KAY BOYLE   Spine: Gentlemen, | I address you | privately | ★ | KAY BOYLE | HARRISON SMITH | [gold decoration] ROBERT HAAS   Back: Blank.

Dust jacket: Same as A9a.

Publication: First published in January 1934 at $2.50.

A9d   GENTLEMEN, I ADDRESS YOU PRIVATELY   [1934]

First English Edition:

GENTLEMEN | I ADDRESS YOU PRIVATELY | BY | KAY BOYLE | LONDON | FABER AND FABER LIMITED | 24 RUSSELL SQUARE

Collation: [1-8], 9-311, [312] pages; cream endpapers.   7 $^5/_8$" x 4 $^7/_8$"   [A]^8 B-I^8 K-S^8, T^4 U^8

Contents: (1) blank; (2) blank; (3) [half title page and quotation]: GENTLEMEN | I ADDRESS YOU PRIVATELY | "Gentlemen, I address you privately, | and no woman is within hearing." | —-Ernest Walsh; (4) [list]: BY THE SAME AUTHOR [four titles]; | ★ | (5) title page; (6) copyright page; (7) [dedication]: DEDI-CATED TO | ADELAIDE & CHARLES WALKER | AND THEIR UNITED STATES; (8) blank; (9-311) text; (312) blank.

Copyright page: FIRST PUBLISHED IN MCMXXXIV | BY FABER AND FABER LIMITED | 24 RUSSELL SQUARE LONDON W.C.I | PRINTED IN GREAT BRITAIN BY | LATIMER TREND AND CO PLYMOUTH | ALL RIGHTS RESERVED

Binding: Light blue cloth covered boards stamped in gold. Top edge unstained with all edges trimmed. Front: Blank. Spine: *Gentlemen | I Address You | Privately |* [device] | *Kay Boyle | Faber and | Faber*   Back: Blank.

Dust jacket: White paper printed in two shades of green and black. Front: Pictorial jacket with four pictures; upper left corner a head of a man with left hand upraised; upper right corner three women's heads with one on right smoking a cigarette; lower left corner a standing women with both arms raised; and lower right corner a man running from right to left. [black at top] GENTLEMEN | I ADDRESS YOU PRIVATELY | gray green at bottom] BY KAY BOYLE Spine: [black in script] gen-tlemen, | I address | you | privately | [gray green in script] by Kay Boyle | [standing woman with both arms raised] | [printed in black and in script] Faber and Faber Back: Advertisements for other books published by Faber and Faber.   Front flap: Story plot. [lower right] 8s.6d. | net   Back flap: Review of *Year Before Last.*

First published in 1934 at 8s 6d.

A9e   GENTLEMEN, I ADDRESS YOU PRIVATELY   [1991]

Second American Edition:

Revised and rewritten

GENTLEMEN, | I ADDRESS YOU PRIVATELY | [series of double horizontal tear drops] | [thick rule] | [two trees showing roots below ground and two men] | [thick rule] | [repeat tear drop pattern] | KAY BOYLE | [publisher's device] | CAPRA PRESS | SANTA BARBARA

Collation: [1-6], 7-227, [228] pages; mustard colored endpapers, $8^1/_2$ " x $5^1/_2$ ".

Contents: (1) half title page; (2) blank; (3) title page; (4) copyright page; (5) [quotation]: *"Gentlemen,* I *address you privately* | *and no woman is within hearing."* | ERNEST WALSH; (6) blank; (7-227) text; (228) editor's note.

Copyright page: Copyright © 1991 by Kay Boyle | All rights reserved. | Printed in the United States of America | (Earlier version published in 1933 by | Harrison Smith and Robert Haas, New York.) | Cover design by Cyndi Burt. | Typesetting by Stanton, Minneapolis. | LIBRARY OF CONGRESS CATALOGING-IN-PUBLICATION DATA | Boyle, Kay, 1902- | Gentlemen, I address you privately / by Kay Boyle. | p. cm. | ISBN 0-88496-318-7 : $18.95 | I. Title. | PS3503.09357G43 1991 | 813' .52—dc20   90-19863 | CIP | CAPRA PRESS | Post Office Box 2068, Santa Barbara, CA 93120

Binding: Imitation dark green cloth spine stamped in gold with mustard yellow paper covered boards. Top edge unstained and all edges trimmed. Front: Blank. Spine: [printed downward] GENTLEMEN, [first line] I ADDRESS YOU [second line] PRIVATELY [third line] | [printed downward] KAY [top line] BOYLE [bottom line] | [horizontal] [publisher's device] CAPRA | PRESS Back: Blank.

Dust jacket: White paper printed in yellow, black and white. Front: [bottom half of yellow sun on black] | [white on black] GENTLEMEN I | ADDRESS YOU PRIVATELY | [horizontal tear drop pattern across page in black on yellow] | heavy black rule] | [picture of two trees showing roots below ground in black on yellow with white moon in back-ground with two men standing] | [heavy black rule] | [repeat tear drop pattern] | [top half of yellow sun on black with KAY BOYLE arched in black on the sun. Spine: [printed downward in white] GENTLEMEN, [top line] I ADDRESS YOU [second line] PRIVATELY [third line] | [continuation of tear drop pattern from front] | [continuation of heavy black rule from front] | [printed downward in black] KAY [top line] BOYLE [bottom line] | [continuation of heavy black rule from front] | [continuation of tear drop pattern from front] | [white publisher's device on black] | [horizontal in white] CAPRA | PRESS   Back: Dust jacket blurbs by Katherine Anne Porter, Janet Flanner and William Carlos Williams and Man Ray photograph of Kay Boyle. Front flap: Story plot. [upper right] $18.95   Back flap: Biographical sketch of Kay Boyle.

Publication: First published in March of 1991 at $18.95.

A10a   MY NEXT BRIDE   [1934]

First Edition:

Kay Boyle | MY NEXT | BRIDE | *"Knife will be my next bride"* | LAURENCE VAIL | HARCOURT, BRACE AND COMPANY | NEW YORK

Collation: [i-viii], [1-2], 3-93, [94-96], 97-239, [240-242], 243-327, [328] pages; cream endpapers.   7 $^{3}/_{8}$" x 5 $^{1}/_{8}$" [A-U]^{8}

Contents: (i) half title page; (ii) [list]: *Other books by Kay Boyle* [five titles]; (iii) title page; (iv) copyright page; (v) [dedication]: *for Caresse*; (vi) blank; (vii) contents; (viii) blank; (1) [divisional title]: *Part One* | SORREL; (2) [disclaimer]: *All the characters in this book* | *are imaginary*; (3-93) text;   (94) blank; (95) [divisional title]: *Part Two* | ANTONY; (96) blank; (97-239) text; (240) blank; (241) [divisional title and quotation]: *Part Three* | FONTANA | *"Bathe me in the vision of my youth, communi-* | *cate me forever. Do not let me go back with the* | *rest to fornicate and forget."* | (EMANUEL CARNELVALI); (242) blank; (243-327) text; (328) blank.

Copyright page: COPYRIGHT, 1934, BY | KAY BOYLE | *All rights reserved, including* | *the right to reproduce this book* | *or portions thereof in any form.* | *first edition* | *Typography by Robert Josephy* | PRINTED IN THE UNITED STATES OF AMERICA | BY QUINN & BODEN COMPANY, INC., RAHWAY, N.J.

Binding: Bound in light green cloth covered boards stamped in silver. Top edge stained dark green. Top and bottom edge trimmed; fore edge rough trimmed. Front: Blank. Spine: *Kay Boyle* | MY | NEXT | BRIDE | [design] |HARCOURT, BRACE | AND COMPANY   Back: Blank.

Dust jacket: Cream paper printed in beige, red and black.   Front: [thick red stripe] | MY | [thick red stripe] | NEXT | [thick red stripe] | BRIDE | [thick red stripe] | KAY BOYLE   Spine: [continuation of red stripe from front] | MY | NEXT | BRIDE | [continuation of red stripe from front] | KAY | BOYLE | [continuation of red stripe from front] | [continuation of red strip from front] | Harcourt, Brace | and Company   Back: Recent fiction by Harcourt, Brace and Company. Front flap: Story plot. $2.50 [upper right].   Back flap: Biographical information about Kay Boyle.

Publication: First published on November 1, 1934 according to *Publisher's Weekly* at $2.50.

A10b   My Next Bride   [1935]

First English Editon:

MY NEXT BRIDE | *by* | KAY BOYLE | *"Knife will be my next bride."* | —— Laurence Vail. | LONDON | FABER AND FABER LIMITED | 24 RUSSELL SQUARE

Fig 5-A10b

Collation: [i-iv], [1-6], 7-96, [97-98], 99-236, [237-238], 239-320 pages; cream endpapers. $7^1/_2$" x 5"   [A]^{10} B-I^8 K-U^8

Contents: (i) half title page; (ii) [list]: *by the same author* [five titles]; (iii) title page; (iv) copyright page; (1) [dedication]: FOR | CARESSE; (2) blank; (3) disclaimer; (4) blank; (5) [divisional title]: *Part One* | SORREL; (6) blank; (7-96) text; (97) [divisional title]: *Part Two* | ANTONY; (98) blank; (99-236) text; (237) [divisional title]: *Part Three* | FONTANA | [followed by quotation by Emanuel Carnevali]; (238) blank; (239-320) text.

Copyright page: FIRST PUBLISHED IN FEBRUARY MCMXXXV | BY FABER & FABER LIMITED | 24 RUSSELL SQUARE LONDON W.C.1 | PRINTED IN GREAT BRITAIN | BY BUTLER & TANNER LIMITED | FROME AND LONDON | ALL RIGHTS RESERVED

Binding: Dark blue cloth covered boards stamped in gold. Top edge unstained and all edges trimmed. Front: Blank.   Spine: MY | NEXT | BRIDE | [device] | Kay | Boyle | FABER | AND FABER   Back: Blank.

Dust jacket: Cream paper pictorial jacket printed in red, blues, browns and black. Front: [red on cream] My Next Bride, | [thick brown rule] | [picture of man and woman sitting by a stream] | [thick brown rule] | [red on cream] by Kay Boyle   Spine: [red on cream] MY NEXT | BRIDE | [blue on cream] KAY BOYLE | [continuation of thick brown rule from front of jacket] | [continuation of front picture with the following writing] [blue script slanting from top towards the bottom] Grand | [blue script slanting from bottom towards the top] Palais | [red slanting from the top towards the bottom] WALL | [red slanting from the bottom towards the top] STREET | [continuation of thick brown rule from the front] | [in blue on cream] FABER AND | FABER   Back: A list of the Faber and Faber Library.   Front flap: Story plot. [bottom right] 7s. 6d. | net   Black flap: Continuation from front flap and some press reviews of *Gentlemen, I Address You Privately.*

Publication: First published in February 1935 at 7s 6d.

A10c   MY NEXT BRIDE   [1986]

First English Paperback:

MY NEXT BRIDE | KAY BOYLE | [single rule separated in the middle by a decoration] | *"Knife will be my next bride"* | *-Laurence Vail* | With a New Afterword by | DORIS GRUMBACH | Virago | [apple with bite taken out]

Collation: [i-iv], [1-6], 7-96, [97-98], 99-236, [237-238], 239-330, [331-332] pages. $7^3/_4$" x 5"   [A]^{10} [B-T]^8 [U]^{14}

Contents: (i) biographical sketch about Kay Boyle; (ii) VIRAGO | MODERN | CLASSIC | NUMBER | 226 | [all enclosed in double rule box with decorative device separating double rule at the bottom of the box]; (iii) title page; (iv) copyright page; (1) [dedication]: For | CARESSE; (2) blank; (3) author's disclaimer; (4) blank; (5) [divisional title]: *Part One* | SORREL; (6) blank; (7-96) text; (97) [divisional title]: *Part Two* | ANTONY; (98) blank; (99-236) text; (237) [divisional title]: *Part Three* | FONTANA | quotation by Emanuel Carnevali; (238) blank; (239-320) text; (321-330) afterword; (331) blank; (332) short description about Virago Modern Classics.

Copyright page: Published by VIRAGO PRESS Limited 1986 | 41 William IV Street, London WC2N 4DB | First published by Harcourt, Brace & Company 1934 | First published in Great Britain by Faber & Faber Limited 1935 | Copyright Kay Boyle 1934 | Afterword Copyright © Doris Grumbach 1986 | All rights reserved | *British Cataloguing in Publication Data* | Boyle, Kay | My next bride.—(Virago modern | classics) | I. Title | 813'.52[F] PS3503.09357 | ISBN 0-86068-756-2 | Printed in Great Britain by | Anchor Brendon, Tiptree, Essex

Binding: Stiff white paper pictorial wrappers printed in lime green, dark green, browns and yellows. Top edge stained light yellow and all edges trimmed. Printed in yellow and white. Front: [lime green] Virago Modern Classics | [white rule] | [white] Kay Boyle | [white rule] | My Next Bride | [picture of a woman with crossed arms holding a bird cage with white bird]. Spine: [continuation of white rule on cover] | publisher's device, lime green apple with bite taken out] | [continuation of white rule on cover] | [printed downward in white] My Next Bride Kay Boyle 0 86068 756 2   Back: Story plot with short paragraph about Kay Boyle £3.95 [lower left]

A10d   MY NEXT BRIDE   [1986]

First American Paperback:

MY NEXT BRIDE | KAY BOYLE | [single rule divided by decorative device] | *"Knife will be my next bride"* | —*Laurence Vail* | With a New Afterword by | DORIS GRUMBACH | [Penguin's publishing device] | Penguin Books—-Virago Press

Collation: Same as A10c except signatures are signed. $7^3/_4$" x 5" $[A]^{10}$ B-T^8 U^{14}

Contents: Same as A10c except page ii is blank.

Copyright page: PENGUIN BOOKS | Viking Penguin Inc., 40 West 23rd Street, | New York, New York 10010, U.S.A. | Penguin Books Ltd, Harmondsworth, | Middlesex, England | Penguin Books Australia Ltd, Ringwood, | Victoria, Australia | Penguin Books Canada Limited, 2801 John Street, | Markham, Ontario, Canada L3R 1B4 | Penguin Books (N.Z.) Ltd, 182-190 Wairau Road, | Auckland 10, New Zealand | First published in the United States of America by | Harcourt, Brace & Company 1934 | This edition first published in Great Britain by | Virago Press Ltd

1986 | Published in Penguin Books 1986 | Copyright Kay Boyle, 1934 | Copyright renewed Kay Boyle, 1962 | Afterword copyright © Doris Grumbach, 1986 | All rights reserved | Printed in the United States of America by | R.R. Donnelley & Sons Company, Harrisonburg, Virginia | Set in Caslon No. 540 | Except in the United States of America, | this book is sold subject to the condition | that it shall not, by way of trade or otherwise, | be lent, re-sold, hired out, or otherwise circulated | without the publisher's prior consent in any form of | binding or cover other than that in which it is | published and without a similar condition | including this condition being imposed | on the subsequent purchaser

Binding: Same as A10c except top edge is unstained   Front: Same as A10c with exception of Penguin Books publishing device in upper right hand corner. Spine: [continuation of two white rules on cover] | [printed downward in white] My Next Bride Kay Boyle | ISBN 0 14 [top line] 016.147 3 [bottom line] | [Penguin Books publishing device in white]   Back: Same as English paperback except for Penguin Books publishing device in lower left corner. $6.95 [lower left]

Publication: First published in October 1986

A11a   THE WHITE HORSES OF VIENNA AND OTHER STORIES [1936]

First Edition:

The White Horses | *of Vienna* | AND OTHER STORIES | *Kay Boyle* | HARCOURT, BRACE AND COMPANY | NEW YORK

Collation: [i-x], [1-2], 3-27, [28-30], 31-55, [56-58], 59-74, [75-76], 77-104, [105-106], 107-121, [122-124], 125-144, [145-146], 147-154, [155-156], 157-182, [183-184], 185-193, [194-196], 197-209, [210-212], 213-217, [218-220], 221-251, [252-254], 255-265, [266-268], 269-295, [296-298], 299-305, [306-308], 309-317, [318-320], 321-345, [346-348], 349-355, [356-358] pages; cream endpapers. 7 $^3/_8$" x 5 $^1/_8$"   [A-W]^8

Contents: (i) half title page; (ii) [list]: *Books by Kay Boyle* [seven titles] ; (iii) title page; (iv) copyright page; (v) [dedication]: *This book is dedicated to Evelyn Scott;* (vi) blank; (vii) [publisher's note]: ACKNOWLEDGMENT is here made to the editors | of *Harper's Magazine, The New Yorker, The Ameri-* | *can Mercury, Brooklyn Daily Eagle, Harper's Bazaar,* | *Direction,* and *Story Magazine* for permission to re- | print stories first published in their pages; (viii) blank; (ix) table of contents; (x) blank; (1) [story title]: *The White Horses of Vienna;* (2) blank; (3-27) text; (28) blank; (29) [story title]: *Keep Your Pity;* (30) blank; (31-55) text; (56) blank; (57) [story title]: *Natives Don't Cry;* (58) blank; (59-74) text; (75) [story title]: *Life Being the Best;* (76) blank; (77-104) text; (105) [story title]: *White as Snow;* (106) blank; (107-121) text; (122) blank; (123) [story title]: *Count Lothar's Heart;* (124) blank; (125-144) text; (145) [story title]: *Career;* (146) blank; (147-154) text; (155) [story title]: *Major Alshuster;*

(156) blank; (157-182) text; (183) [story title]: *Astronomer's Wife;* (184) blank; (185-193) text; (194) blank; (195) [story title]: *Peter Foxe*; (196) blank; (197-209) text; (210) blank; (211) [story title]: *First Offense* (212) blank; (213-217) text; (218) blank; (219) [story title]: *Maiden, Maiden;* (220) blank; (221-251) text; (252) blank; (253) [story title]: *Convalescence*; (254) blank; (255-265) text; (266) blank; (267) [story title]: *Dear Mr. Walrus*; (268) blank; (269-295) text; (296) blank; (297) [story title]: *Rondo at Carraroe*; (298) blank; (299-305) text; (306) blank; (307) [story title]: *Security*; (308) blank; (309-317) text; (318) blank; (319) [story title]: *Your Body is a Jewel Box;* (320) blank; (321-345) text; (346) blank; (347) [story title]: *Winter in Italy*; (348) blank; (349-355) text; (356-358) blank.

Copyright page: COPYRIGHT, 1936, BY | KAY BOYLE | *All rights reserved, including | the right to reproduce this book | or portions thereof in any form.* | *first edition* | PRINTED IN THE UNITED STATES OF AMERICA | BY QUINN & BODEN COMPANY, INC., RAHWAY, N. J. | *Typography by Robert Josephy*

Binding: Light blue cloth covered boards stamped in silver. Top edge stained blue. Top and bottom edges trimmed and front edge rough trimmed. Front: Blank. Spine: KAY BOYLE | *The | White | Horses | of | Vienna* | [device] | *Harcourt, Brace | and Company*; Back: Blank. Note: Variant binding seen in dark blue; no priority established.

Dust jacket: White paper pictorial jacket printed in black, white, brown and blue. Front: [white letters shadowed with blue horizontal lines on light blue back ground] THE WHITE | HORSES | OF VIENNA | [black] *AND OTHER STORIES* | *by KAY BOYLE* | [picture of chalet with mountains in the background] Spine: [white letters on black background] THE | WHITE | HORSES | OF | VIENNA | *by | KAY | BOYLE* | [smaller repeat of picture on the front] | *HARCOURT, BRACE | AND COMPANY* Back: A selected list of fiction published by Harcourt Brace. Front flap: A short description of the book and the stories. Price $2.50 [upper right] Back flap: Story plot and description of Kay Boyle's novel *My Next Bride*.

Publication: First published on February 8, 1936 according to *Publisher's Weekly* at $2.50.

Stories included and previous publication: "The White Horses of Vienna" first appeared in *Harper's Magazine*, April 1935 and also appeared in *O. Henry Memorial Award Prize Stories of 1935*, Garden City: Doubleday, Doran & Company, 1935. "Keep Your Pity" first appeared in *The Brooklyn Daily Eagle* November 26, 1933. "Natives Don't Cry" first appeared in *The American Mercury*, March 1934. "Life Being the Best" first appeared in *Harper's Magazine*, November 1933. "White as Snow" first appeared in *The New Yorker*, August 5, 1933. "Count Lothar's Heart" first appeared in *Harper's Bazaar*, May 1935. "Career" first appeared in *Direction*, Autumn 1934. "Major Alshuster" first appeared in *Harper's Magazine*, December 1935. "Astronomer's Wife" first appeared in *London Mercury* December 1935. "Peter Foxe" first appeared in *Harper's Bazaar*, December 1933. "First Offense" first appeared in

The New Yorker, January 5, 1935. "Maiden, Maiden" first appeared in *Harper's Bazaar*, December 1934. "Convalescence" first appeared in *Story Magazine*, April 1933. "Rondo at Carraroe" first appeared in *The Spectator*, February 28, 1936. "Security" first appeared in *The New Yorker*, January 25, 1936. "Your Body Is a Jewel Box" first appeared in *New Writers*, February 1936. "Winter in Italy" first appeared in *The New Yorker*, November 23, 1935. "Dear Mr. Walrus" appears here for the first time.

A11b   THE WHITE HORSES OF VIENNA   [1937]

First English Edition:

BY KAY BOYLE | [double ruled line zigzagging and crossing in the center and forming three diamonds] | THE WHITE HORSES | OF VIENNA | FABER AND FABER LIMITED | 24 RUSSELL SQUARE | LONDON

Collation: [1-6], 7, [8], 9, [10], 11-147, [148], 149-213, [214], 215-247, [248], 249-295, [296], 297-340 pages; cream endpapers.   7 $^7/_{16}$" x 4$^3/_4$"   [A]^8 B-I^8 K-U^8 X^{10}

Contents: (1) half title page; (2) [list]: Other books by Kay Boyle [seven titles]; (3) title page; (4) copyright page; (5) [dedication]: This book is dedicated to | EVELYN SCOTT; (6) blank; (7) [publisher's note]: Acknowledgment is here made to the editors | of *Harper's Magazine, The New Yorker, The American* | *Mercury, Brooklyn Daily Eagle, Harper's Bazaar,* | *Direction,* and *Story Magazine* for permission to re- | print stories first published in their pages.; (8) blank; (9) table of contents; (10) blank; (11-147) text; (148) blank; (149-213) text; (214) blank; (215-247) text; (248) blank; (249-295) text; (296) blank; (297-340) text.

Copyright page: *First Published in January Mcmxxxvii | By Faber and Faber Limited | 24 Russell Square London W.C.1 | Printed in Great Britain | At The Bowering Press Plymouth | All Rights Reserved*

Binding: Black cloth covered boards stamped in silver. Top edge unstained and all edges trimmed. Front: Blank. Spine: THE WHITE | HORSES | OF VIENNA | Kay Boyle | Faber and | Faber   Back: Blank.

Dust jacket: White paper dust wrapper printed in red and black. Front: [in white on the red] The White Horses | of Vienna | Faber and Faber | Kay Boyle [jacket divided into three sections with wavy separation: black\red\black] Spine: [printed in white on the upper black] The White | Horses | of | Vienna | [in white on the red] by | Kay Boyle | [in red on the lower black] Faber and | Faber   Back: A list of Faber Library titles (34 books). Front flap: Story plot. 7s. 6d. | net [lower right]   Back flap: Faber's address for requesting their current list of available titles.

Publication: First published in January 1937 at 7s6d.

The included stories and previous publication are the same as the American edition.

A11c   THE WHITE HORSES OF VIENNA   [1937]

Second English Printing:

BY KAY BOYLE | [double ruled line zigzagging and crossing in the center] | THE WHITE HORSES | OF VIENNA | FABER AND FABER LIMITED | 24 RUSSELL SQUARE | LONDON

Collation: Same as A11b.

Contents: Same as A11b.

Copyright page: *First Published in January Mcmxxxvii* | *Second Impression February Mcmxxxvii* | *By Faber and Faber Limited* | *24 Russell Square London W.C.1* | *Printed in Great Britain* | *At The Bowering Press Plymouth* | *All Rights Reserved*

Binding: Same as A11b.

Dust jacket: Same as the first printing except that SECOND IMPRESSION is printed on front flap just before where the blurb about the book begins.

A11d   THE WHITE HORSES OF VIENNA   [1949]

First English Paperback:

THE WHITE HORSES | OF VIENNA | [rule] | KAY BOYLE | PENGUIN BOOKS | IN ASSOCIATION WITH | FABER AND FABER

Collation: [1-8], 9-27, [28], 29-47, [48], 49-60, [61], 62-83, [84], 85-95, [96], 97-111, [112], 113-117, [118], 119-138, [139], 140-146, [147], 148-157, [158], 159-161, [162], 163-186, [187], 188-195, [196], 197-217, [218], 219-222, [223], 224-229, [230], 231-249, [250], 251-256 pages.   7" x 4 $^1/_4$".   [1-8]^{16}

Contents: (1) PENGUIN BOOKS | 699 | THE WHITE HORSE OF VIENNA | BY KAY BOYLE | [publisher's device: penguin]; (2) blank; (3) title page; (4) copyright page; (5) [dedication]: ★ | *This book is dedicated* | *to* | EVELYN SCOTT | ★; (6) [publisher's note]: *Acknowledgment is here made to the editors of Harper's Magazine,* | *The New Yorker, The American Mercury, Brooklyn Daily Eagle,* | *Harper's Bazaar, Direction, and Story Magazine for permission to* | *reprint stories first published in their pages*; (7) table of contents; (8) blank; (9-256) text.

Copyright page: *First published in January* 1937 | *Published in Penguin Books* 1949 | MADE AND PRINTED IN GREAT BRITAIN | FOR PENGUIN BOOKS LTD, BY C. NICHOLLS & COMPANY LTD | LONDON   MANCHESTER READING

Binding: Stiff cream wrappers printed in orange and black. Front: [enclosed in white irregular oval] PENGUIN | BOOKS | [printed in black on white] THE |

WHITE HORSES | OF VIENNA | KAY BOYLE | [printed in black on orange] COMPLETE [publisher's device: penguin] UNABRIDGED | One shilling and sixpence   [printed in orange on the white band vertically along the spine edge bottom to top] FICTION [along the front edge top to bottom] FICTION Spine: [printed in black upward on the orange] KAY BOYLE [printed upward in black on the white] THE WHITE HORSES OF VIENNA | [publishers device] | [printed horizontally in black] 699   Back: Capsule biographical sketch of Kay Boyle with a photograph. Inside the front cover: A note about the book. Inside the back cover: A list of other books available from Penguin.

Publication: First published in February 1949 at one shilling and sixpence.

A12a   DEATH OF A MAN   [1936]

First Edition:

DEATH OF A MAN | by | KAY BOYLE | FABER AND FABER LTD | 24 Russell Square | London

Collation: [1-6], 7-372 pages; cream endpapers. $7^1/_4$" x 5"   [A]^8 B-I^8 K-U^8 X-Y^8 Z^{10}

Contents: (1) half title page; (2) [list]: *by the same author* [seven titles]; (3) title page; (4)   copyright page; (5) [dedication]: For | EUGENE JOLAS; (6) blank; (7-372) text.

Copyright page: FIRST PUBLISHED IN SEPTEMBER MCMXXXVI | BY FABER & FABER LIMITED | 24 RUSSELL SQUARE LONDON W.C.I | PRINTED IN GREAT BRITAIN | BY BUTLER & TANNER LIMITED | FROME AND LONDON | ALL RIGHTS RESERVED

Binding: Rust red cloth covered boards stamped in gold. Top edge unstained and all edges trimmed. Front: Blank. Spine: DEATH | OF A MAN | [device] | KAY BOYLE | FABER AND | FABER   Back: Blank.

Dust jacket: Yellow paper printed in purple. Front: [Yellow with large purple oval blot upon which is printed in yellow] KAY BOYLE | Death | of a | man | FABER AND | FABER   Spine: [printed in purple] DEATH | OF A | MAN | by | KAY | BOYLE | FABER & | FABER   Back: Advertisement and list for The Faber Library Front flap: Story plot. 7s.6d. net [lower right]   Back flap: Advertisement for Faber and Faber and mailing address.

Publication: First published in September 1936 at 7s 6d.

Note: An uncorrected proof copy was bound in yellow paper wrappers. $7^1/_8$" x 5" printed on the front in black: DEATH OF A MAN | by | KAY BOYLE | FABER AND FABER Spine: [printed downward] DEATH OF A MAN

A12b   DEATH OF A MAN   [1936]

First American Edition:

DEATH | OF | A MAN | *Kay Boyle* | HARCOURT, BRACE AND COMPANY | NEW YORK

Collation: [i-vi], [1-2], 3-321, [322] pages; cream endpapers. 8" x 5 $\frac{1}{4}$" [A-T]^8 [U]^4

Contents: (i) half title page; (ii) [list]: *Books by Kay Boyle* [eight titles] (iii) title page; (iv) copyright page; (v) [dedication]: *This book is dedicated to Eugene Jolas | because we sat in the summer of that year | in the wine-cellars and the Gasthauses of | that town.*; (vi) blank; (1) fly title; (2) blank; (3-321) text; (322) blank.

Copyright page: COPYRIGHT, 1936, BY | KAY BOYLE | *All rights reserved, including | the right to reproduce this book | or portions thereof in any form. | first edition | Typography by Robert Josephy* | PRINTED IN THE UNITED STATES OF AMERICA | BY QUINN & BODEN COMPANY, INC., | RAHWAY, N.J.

Binding: Gray cloth covered boards stamped in silver. Top edge stained orange. All edges trimmed. Front: Blank. Spine: KAY BOYLE | *Death | of a | Man* | [device] | *Harcourt, Brace | and Company*   Back: Blank.

Dust jacket: White paper pictorial jacket printed in orange, blue, black white and green. Front: [printed in black script on orange background] Death of a Man | by KAY BOYLE | [lower two thirds of jacket is a picture with a small village at the bottom with snow capped mountains rising up in the background]   Spine: [black script on orange background] Death | of a Man | KAY BOYLE | [picture on the front wraps around to the spine in a continuation.] Back: A description of *The White Horses of Vienna* with three reviews. [white printed in blue]   Front flap: Story plot. No price. Back flap: Description of *365 Days* edited by Kay Boyle, Laurence Vail, and Nina Conarain.

Publication: A slip in an advance review copy indicates publication was on October 8, 1936 at $2.50.

A12c   DEATH OF A MAN   [1989]

First Paperback Edition:

KAY BOYLE | [single rule] | DEATH OF A MAN | [single rule] | A NOVEL | With an Introduction by Burton Hatlen | and a Note from the Author | [publishers device] | [single rule] | A NEW DIRECTIONS BOOK

Collation: [i-iv], v-xii, [1-2], 3-324 pages.   8" x 5 $\frac{3}{8}$"

Contents: (i) A REVIVED | MODERN | CLASSIC | [single rule] | DEATH OF A MAN (ii) [list]: ALSO BY KAY BOYLE [nine titles]; (iii) title page; (iv) copyright page; (v-xii) introduction; (1) dedication same as in the first American edition; (2) blank; (3-321) text; (322-324) a note from the author.

Copyright page: Copyright © 1936, 1989 by Kay Boyle | Copyright © 1989 by Burton Hatlen | All rights reserved. Except for brief passages quoted in a newspaper, maga- | zine, radio, or television review, no part of this book may be reproduced in | any form or by any means, electronic or mechanical, including photocopy- | ing and recording, or by any information storage and retrieval system, with- | out permission in writing from the Publisher. | Manufactured in the United States of America | New Directions Books are   printed on acid-free paper. | First published clothbound by Harcourt Brace and Company in 1936; re- | issued as New Directions Paperback 670 in 1989 as part | of the Revived Modern Classics series | Published simultaneously in Canada by Penguin Books Canada Limited | Library of Congress Cataloging-in-Publication Data | Boyle, Kay, 1902- | Death of a man: a novel / by Kay Boyle : with an introduction by | Burton Hatlen and an afterword by the author. | p. cm.—(New Directions paperbook; 670) (Revised modern classics) | ISBN 0-8112-1089-8 (alk. paper) | 1. Title II. Series: Revived modern classic. | PS3503.O9357D4 1989 | 813'.52—dc 19   88-26799 | CIP | New Directions Books are published for James Laughlin | by New Directions Publishing Corporation, | 80 Eighth Avenue, New York 10011

Binding: Stiff white wraps printed in red, gray and black. Front: [a single black rule] | [red] A REVIVED MODERN CLASSIC [a red publisher device between revived and modern extending up and breaking the single rule] | [a double black rule, the bottom one being thicker] | [black] KAY BOYLE | [single black rule] | DEATH OF A MAN | [red] With an Introduction by Burton Hatlen | [red] and Note from the Author | [photograph of snow capped mountains]   Spine: [printed downward in black] KAY BOYLE [over and separated by a single rule] DEATH OF A MAN | [red publishers device] | [printed downward in black] NDP670   Back: Story plot with two reviews. $10.95 [lower left]

Publication: First published in April 1989 at $10.95.

A13a   YELLOW DUSK   [1937]
                    by Bettina Bedwell (ghost written by Kay Boyle)

First Edition:

[three rules, top one thicker than the other two] | YELLOW DUSK | *by* | BETTINA BEDWELL | [three rules] | *Publishers* | *Since 1812* | [publisher's device] | HURST & BLACKETT, LTD. | LONDON | [three rules, bottom one thicker than upper two]

Collation: [1-6], 7-304 pages; cream endpapers; [publisher's advertisements], [1-2], 3-55, [56].   7 $\frac{1}{8}$" x 4 $\frac{7}{8}$" [A]^8 B-I^8 K-T^8 [U]^{16} [X]^{12}

Contents: (1) half title page; (2) [list]: A SELECTED LIST OF HURST AND BLACKETT'S FICTION [23 titles]; (3) title page; (4) copyright page; (5) list of characters in the story; (6) disclaimer; (7-304) text [publisher advertisements] (1) Hurst and Blackett catalog of 1937 Spring books; (2) blank; (3-55) list of books available with descriptions; (56) blank.

Copyright page: Made and Printed in Great Britain | for Hurst & Blackett, Ltd., Pater- | noster House London, E. C. 4, at | The Gainsborough Press, St. Albans, | Fisher, Knight & Co., Ltd. | 1937

Binding: Rose pink cloth covered boards stamped in black. Top edge unstained and all edges trimmed. Front: Blank. Spine: *Yellow | Dusk | Bettina | Bedwell |* [publisher's device] | *Hurst & Blackett* Back: Blank.

Dust jacket: Not seen.

Publication: First published in September 1937 at 7s 6d. <u>Note</u>: According to The English Catalogue of Books volume 14, 1936-1941 Hurst and Blackett issued a Cheap Edition in January 1939 at 3s 6d. This edition was the same size and had the same number of pages. The compiler of this bibliography did not find or examine this edition.

A14a   MONDAY NIGHT   [1938]

First Edition:

[Script] Monday Night | KAY BOYLE | HARCOURT, BRACE AND COMPANY, NEW YORK

Collation: [i-viii], [1-2], 3-149, [150-152], 153-274, [275-280] pages; cream endpapers.   8" x 5 $^1/_4$"   [A-R]^8

Contents: (i) half title page; (ii) [list]: *Books by Kay Boyle* [nine titles]; (iii) title page; (iv) copyright page; (v) quotation]: ". . . those who speak it follow no political | leader and take no part in any persecution or | conquest; nor have they to do either with a | vocabulary of the rich or the poor or any | country or race; it being simply one way | of communication between the lost and the lost." | (*The Man Without a Nation*); (vi) blank; (vii) table of contents; (viii) blank; (1) [divisional title]: MONDAY NIGHT; (2) blank; (3-149) text; (150) blank; (151) [divisional title]: TUESDAY MORNING; (152) blank; (153-274) text; (275-280) blank.

Copyright page: COPYRIGHT, 1938, BY | KAY BOYLE | *All rights reserved, including | the right to reproduce this book | or portions thereof in any form. | first edition | Designed by Robert Josephy* | PRINTED IN THE UNITED STATES OF AMERICA | BY QUINN & BODEN COMPANY, INC., RAHWAY, N.J.

Binding: Dark blue cloth covered boards stamped in silver. Top edge unstained and all edges trimmed. Front: Blank. Spine: KAY BOYLE | *Monday* | *Night* | device | *Harcourt, Brace* | *and Company*   Back: Blank.

Dust jacket: White paper printed in shaded blues and white. Front: [all text on a slant] Monday | Night | [script] by | Kay Boyle Spine: [on a slant] Kay | Boyle | [printed downward] Monday Night | [on a slant] HARCOURT, BRACE | AND COMPANY Back: Advertisement with description and reviews of *The White Horses of Vienna* by Kay Boyle. Front flap: Story plot. $2.50 [upper right].   Back flap: Advertisement and short story description for *Death of a Man*. Review by Alfred Kazin.

First published on July 28, 1938 according to a review copy at $2.50.

A14b   MONDAY NIGHT   [1938]

First English Edition:

MONDAY NIGHT | by | KAY BOYLE | FABER AND FABER | 24 Russell Square | London

Collation: [1-10], 11-172, [173-174], 175-310, [311-312] pages; cream endpapers. 7 $^7/_{16}$" x 4 $^7/_8$"   [A]^8 B-I^8 K-T^8 U^4

Contents: (1-2) blank; (3) half title page; (4) [list]: *by the same author* [eight titles]; (5) title page; (6) copyright page; 7) [quotation]: ". . . those who speak it follow no political leader | and take no part in any persecution or conquest; | nor have they to do either with a vocabulary of | the rich or the poor or any country or race; it | being simply one way | of communication between | the lost and the lost." | (*The Man Without a Nation*); (8) blank; (9) [divisional title]: MONDAY NIGHT (10) blank; (11-172) text; (173) [divisional title]: TUESDAY MORNING; (174) blank; (175-310) text; (311-312) blank.

Copyright page: *First published in September Mcmxxxviii* | *by Faber and Faber Limited* | *24 Russell Square London W.C.1* | *Printed in Great Britain by* | *Latimer Trend & Co Ltd Plymouth* | *All Rights Reserved*

Binding: Light rose red cloth covered boards. Top edge unstained and all edges trimmed. Front : Blank. Spine: Small blue square surrounded by a single blue rule. Rose red cloth exposed in the square to read: MONDAY | NIGHT | * | Kay Boyle | [blue print, base of spine] FABER AND | FABER Back: Blank.

Dust jacket: Pink paper printed in pink, gray and maroon. Front: [a maroon rectangle surrounded by a series of small gray squares each with a star inside and printed in pink]. MONDAY | NIGHT | [gray print on pink] a novel by | Kay Boyle | [maroon print on pink] FABER AND FABER Spine: [maroon rectangle

Fig 6-A14b

surrounded by same gray squares as on front and printed vertical in pink] MONDAY NIGHT [top line] by Kay Boyle [bottom line] | Faber [top line] and Faber [bottom line]   Back: [gray print on pink] Advertisement for new fiction by Faber and Faber. Front flap: Story plot. 7s. 6d. | net [lower right]   Back flap: Short reviews of *The First Lover*, *The White Horses of Vienna*, *Death of a Man* and *My Next Bride* by Kay Boyle.

First published on September 29, 1938 at 7s 6d.

A14c   MONDAY NIGHT   [1947]

Second American Edition:

[script] Monday Night | KAY BOYLE | THE NEW CLASSICS

Collation: [i-x], [1-2], 3-149, [150-152], 153-274, [275-278] pages; cream end papers. 7" x 4 $^3/_4$"   [A-I]^{16}

Contents: (i-ii) blank; (iii) half title page; (iv) [list]: The New Classic Series [nineteen titles]; (v) title page; (vi) copyright page; (vii) [dedication]: *To J. Laughlin* | WHO, UNIQUE AMONG PUBLISHERS OF HIS | GENERATION, DEALS WITH IMPONDER- | ABLES: "WHAT THE ARTIST CALLS GOOD, | THE OBJECT OF ALL HIS PLAYFUL PAINS | HIS LIFE-AND-DEATH JESTING . . . THE | PARABLE OF THE RIGHT AND THE GOOD, | A REPRESENTA-TIVE OF ALL HUMAN STRIV- | ING AFTER PERFECTION" — | *in affectionate salute.*; (viii) blank; (ix) table of contents; (x) blank; (1) [divisional title]: MONDAY NIGHT; (2) blank; (3-149) text; (150) blank; (151) [divisional title]: TUESDAY MORNING; (152) blank; (153-274) text; (275-278) blank.

Copyright page: COPYRIGHT, 1938, BY | KAY BOYLE | *New Directions Books are published by James Laughlin* | NEW YORK OFFICE—-500 FIFTH AVENUE

Binding: Gray cloth covered boards stamped in dark blue. Top edge unstained and all edges trimmed.   Front: Blank. Spine: [printed downward] MONDAY NIGHT Back: Blank.

Dust jacket: White paper printed in mottled black, gray and blue. Front: [a black spiral expanding to occupy the upper three fourths of the jacket]. lustig (with small L), the jacket designer is in script in the upper right hand corner of the jacket. There is a large black bottle with a stylized skull and crossbones on the bottle in white. [white] monday night | [black] kay boyle   Spine: Same mottled design. [printed downward in black] MONDAY NIGHT KAY BOYLE | [printed horizontal and enclosed in square rule] NC 20   Back: Advertisements printed in black on white for the new classics series. Front flap: Story plot. $1.50 [lower right]   Back flap: Advertisement for three books in The Modern Readers Series also published by New Directions.

A14d   MONDAY NIGHT   1977

Third American Edition:

[script] Monday Night | KAY BOYLE | PAUL P. APPEL, PUBLISHER | MAMARONECK, NEW YORK | 1977

Collation: [i-x], [1-2], 3-149, [150-152], 153-274, [275-278] pages; white endpapers. 8$^1/_4$" x 5$^1/_2$" [A-I]^{16}

Contents: (i) half title page; (ii) facsimile of a letter to Kay Boyle from Dylan Thomas; (iii) title page; (iv) copyright page; (v) [list]: *Books by Kay Boyle* [nine titles]; (vi) blank; (vii) [quotation]: ". . . those who speak it follow no political | leader and take no part in any persecution or | conquest; nor have they to do either with a | vocabulary of the rich or the poor or any | country or race; it being simply one way of | communication between the lost and the lost." | (*The Man Without a Nation*); (viii) blank; (ix) table of contents; (x) blank; (1) [divisional title]: MONDAY NIGHT; (2) blank; (3-149) text; (150) blank; (151) [divisional title]: TUESDAY MORNING; (152) blank; (153-274) text; (275-278) blank.

Copyright page: Copyright © 1938 by Kay Boyle | All rights reserved, including the right to repro- | duce this book or portions thereof in any form. | Library of Congress Catalogue Card Number: 77-70179 | International Standard Book Number: 0-911858-35-0 | *Printed in the United States of America*

Binding: Dark blue cloth covered boards stamped in silver. Top edge unstained and all edges trimmed. Front: Blank. Spine: [single rule] | [heavy wavy rule] | [single rule] | KAY | BOYLE | [repeat above rule sequence] | printed downward] Monday Night | [printed horizontal] APPEL Back: Blank.

Dust jacket: White paper printed in dark blue and white. Front: Monday | Night | [large facsimile in white printed in dark blue of same letter on page ii from Dylan Thomas] | [script] by [block] Kay Boyle Spine: [printed downward] Monday Night [script] by [block] Kay Boyle | [printed horizontal] APPEL Back: Large photograph in blue tones of Kay Boyle. Front flap: Story plot. $10.00 [upper right].   Back flap: Advertisement for other books published by Paul P. Appel.

Publication: First published in December 1977.

A15a   A GLAD DAY   [1938]

First Edition:

[black] KAY BOYLE | [maroon] A GLAD DAY | [maroon publishers device] | [black] NEW DIRECTIONS | NORFOLK CONNECTICUT

Collation: [1-6], 7-85, [86-88] pages; cream endpapers. 8 $^1/_2$" x 6" [A]^4 [B-F]^8

Contents: (1) half title page; (2) blank; (3) title page; (4) copyright page; (5) table of contents; (6) blank; (7-85) text; (86) blank; (87) [limitation statement]: [small figure of a monk] | *Five Hundred Copies of "A Glad Day" were* | *printed in August, 1938 for New Directions* | *at The Rydal Press, Santa Fe, New Mexico;* (88) blank.

Copyright page: Copyright 1938 by New Directions | Some of the poems in this collection had their | first publication in "Transition," "Blues," | "The New Republic," "The American | Caravan," "Morada," "The Na- | tion," "This Quarter," & | "New Directions 1937." | *English Distributor* | *Gordon Fraser* | *Portugal Place* | *Cambridge* | *Printed in the United States of America*

Binding: Maroon cloth covered boards stamped in gold. Top edge unstained and all edges trimmed. Front: A GLAD DAY   Spine: [double wavy rule] | [printed downward] A GLAD DAY | [single wavy rule] | *by* KAY BOYLE | [single wavy rule] | NEW DIRECTIONS | [double wavy rule]   Back: Blank.

Dust jacket: Light yellow paper printed in red and blue. Front: [the following enclosed in a double red wavy ruled square] [blue] A GLAD | DAY [red] *poems by* | [blue] Kay Boyle   Spine: [printed downward in blue] A GLAD DAY *by* Kay Boyle [printed downward in red] NEW DIRECTIONS   Back: [red] Advertisements for new books from New Directions. Front flap: Short blurb on Kay Boyle's art and her poetry. $2.00 [bottom center]. Back flap: A continuation of the front flap.

First published October 18, 1938 at $2.00.

Included poems and their previous publication: "A Glad Day for Laurence Vail" first appeared in *transition* 21, March 1932, as "A Glad Day for L. V." "Landscape for Wyn Henderson" first appeared as an independent publication London: Curwen Press, 1931 and in *Readies for Bob Brown's Machine*, Cagnes-sur-Mer, Roving Eye Press, 1931. "A Complaint for Mary and Marcel" first appeared in *transition* 27, April/May 1938 as "A Complaint for M & M." "A Comeallye for Robert Carlton Brown" first appeared in *An Anthology of Younger Poets*, Philadelphia: The Centaur Press, 1932 and also in *Americans Abroad*, The Hague: Sevire Press, 1932. "A Waterfront for Allan Ross MacDougall" first appeared in *Direction* January/March 1935. "A Communication to Nancy Cunard" first appeared in *The New Republic*, June 9, 1937. "Angels for Djuna Barnes" first appeared in *Delta*, April 1938. "A Statement for El Greco and William Carlos Williams" first appeared in *Morada* 5, December 1930, as an independent publication, New York: Modern Editions Press, 1932 and in *An Anthology of the Younger Poets*, Philadelphia: The Centaur Press, 1932. "A Confession to Eugene Jolas" first appeared in *Blues*, July 1929. "A Christmas Carol for Emanuel Carnevali" first appeared in *The Second American Caravan*, New York: The Macaulay Company, 1928. "A Valentine for Harry Crosby" first appeared in *Blues*, Fall 1930. "A Letter to Francis Picabia" first appeared in *transition* 13, Summer 1928 as "Letter to Archibald Craig." "The Only Bird That Sang" first appeared in *transition* 19-20, June 1930. "Career" first appeared in *The Nation*, April 15, 1931. "Hunt" first appeared in *The Nation*,

March 4, 1931. "Dedicated to Guy Urquhart" first appeared in *transition* 18, November 1929. "To America" first appeared in *This Quarter*, April 1927. "For an American" first appeared in *This Quarter*, April 1927. "In Defense of Homosexuality" first appeared in *New Review*, April 1932. "Funeral in Hungary" first appeared in *New Directions In Prose and Poetry 1937*, Norfolk: New Directions, 1937. "And Winter" first appeared in *transition* 5, August 1927. "The United States" first appeared in *transition* 13, Summer 1928. "A Cloak for a Man Who Has No Heed for Winter" and "O This Is Not Spring" appear here for the first time.

A16a   THE YOUNGEST CAMEL   1939

First Edition:

THE YOUNGEST CAMEL | By Kay Boyle | [drawing of camel with wings in the clouds] | With illustrations by | FRITZ KREDEL | BOSTON | LITTLE, BROWN AND COMPANY | 1939

Collation: [i-viii], [1-2], 3-96 pages; cream endpapers. 8 $^1/_2$" x 6 $^1/_8$" [A-E]^8 [F]^4 [G]^8 Illustrations tipped in.

Contents: (i) half title page; (ii) blank; (iii) title page; (iv) copyright page; (v) [dedication]: *For Pegeen, Bobby, Apple-Joan, | Kathe, and Clover Vail*; (vi) blank; (vii) list of illustrations; (viii) blank; (1) [fly title]: *The Youngest Camel*; (2) blank; (3-96) text.

Illustrations: Illustrations done in yellow, gray and black facing the following pages: (iii) *"Now we have brought you to the pathway between | the winds."* (22) *The little camel said nothing at all, but simply followed in | her footsteps;* (28) *He lay there very meekly on one side;* (44) *And then they flew off, their legs floating on the air behind them;* (54) *"It's much wiser to be polite to everyone I meet, because one | never knows."* (68) *The little camel took another uncertain step towards the tent*

Copyright page: COPYRIGHT 1939, BY KAY BOYLE | ALL RIGHTS RESERVED, INCLUDING THE RIGHT | TO REPRODUCE THIS BOOK OR PORTIONS | THEREOF IN ANY FORM | FIRST EDITION | *Published August 1939* | [following enclosed in single ruled rectangle] THE ATLANTIC MONTHLY PRESS BOOKS | ARE PUBLISHED BY | LITTLE, BROWN AND COMPANY | IN ASSOCIATION WITH | THE ATLANTIC MONTHLY COMPANY | [following outside the rectangle] PRINTED IN THE UNITED STATES OF AMERICA

Binding: Beige cloth covered boards stamped in blue. Top edge unstained and all edges trimmed. Front: THE YOUNGEST | CAMEL | By Kay Boyle | [illustration of a baby camel] | Illustrated by Fritz Kredel Spine: [horizontal] BOYLE | [printed downward] THE YOUNGEST CAMEL | [horizontal] L. B. | & | CO. Back: Blank.

Dust jacket: Cream paper printed in rust and beige. Front: THE YOUNGEST | CAMEL | By Kay Boyle | [illustration of a baby camel] | Illustrated by Fritz Kredel Spine: [horizontal in rust] BOYLE | [printed downward in rust] THE YOUNGEST CAMEL | [a publisher's device] [horizontal in black] AN | ATLANTIC MONTHLY | PRESS BOOK | [in rust] L. B. | & | CO. Back: Advertisements for children's books published by Little, Brown & Company   Front flap: Story plot. $2.00 [upper right]. Back flap: Several reviews of *Mr. Popper's Penguins* by Richard and Florence Atwater.

First published on August 16,1939 at $2.00.

A16b   THE YOUNGEST CAMEL   1939

First Edition Second Printing:

THE YOUNGEST CAMEL | By Kay Boyle | [drawing of camel with wings in the clouds] | With illustrations by | FRITZ KREDEL | BOSTON | LITTLE, BROWN AND COMPANY | 1939

Collation: Same as A16a.

Contents: Same as A16a.

Copyright page: COPYRIGHT 1939, BY KAY BOYLE | ALL RIGHTS RESERVED, INCLUDING THE RIGHT | TO REPRODUCE THIS BOOK OR PORTIONS | THEREOF IN ANY FORM | *Published August 1939* | *Reprinted December 1939* | [following enclosed in single ruled rectangle] THE ATLANTIC MONTHLY PRESS BOOKS | ARE PUBLISHED BY | LITTLE, BROWN AND COMPANY | IN ASSOCIATION WITH | THE ATLANTIC MONTHLY COMPANY | [following outside the rectangle] PRINTED IN THE UNITED STATES OF AMERICA

Binding: Same as A16a.

Dust jacket: Same as A16a.

A16c   THE YOUNGEST CAMEL   1942

First Edition Third Printing:

THE YOUNGEST CAMEL | By Kay Boyle | [drawing of camel with wings in the clouds] | With illustrations by | FRITZ KREDEL | BOSTON | LITTLE, BROWN AND COMPANY | 1942

Collation: Same as A16a.

Contents: Same as A16a.

Copyright page: COPYRIGHT 1939, BY KAY BOYLE | ALL RIGHTS RESERVED, INCLUDING THE RIGHT | TO REPRODUCE THIS BOOK OR PORTIONS | THEREOF IN ANY FORM | *Published August 1939 | Reprinted December 1939 | Reprinted November 1942 |* [following enclosed in single ruled rectangle] THE ATLANTIC MONTHLY PRESS BOOKS | ARE PUBLISHED BY | LITTLE, BROWN AND COMPANY | IN ASSOCIATION WITH | THE ATLANTIC MONTHLY COMPANY | [following outside the rectangle] PRINTED IN THE UNITED STATES OF AMERICA

Binding: Same as A16a.

Dust jacket: Not seen.

A16d   THE YOUNGEST CAMEL   [1939]

First English Edition:

THE | YOUNGEST | CAMEL | by Kay Boyle | *illustrated by* | *Fritz Kredel* | [picture of camel with wings in the clouds] | Faber and Faber Limited | 24 Russell Square | London

Collation: [1-8], 9, [10], 11-107, [108-112] pages; cream endpapers. 8" x 5 $^{1}/_{8}$" [A]^8 B-G^8 Illustrations tipped in.

Contents: (1-2) blank; (3) half title page; (4) [list]: *by the same author* [five titles] ; (5) title page; (6) copyright page; (7) *For Pegeen, Bobby, Apple-Joan, | Kathe, and Clover Vail*; (8) blank; (9) list of illustrations; (10) blank; (11-107) text; (108-112) blank.

Illustrations: Illustrations done in yellow, gray and black facing the following pages: (5) *"Now we have brought you to the pathway | between the winds"* (12) *This was the first trip he had ever made across the | desert and he followed close behind his mother* (38) *He lay there very meekly on one side* (54) *And then they flew off, their legs floating on the | air behind them* (64) *"It's much wiser to be polite to everyone you meet, | because one never knows."* (80) *The little camel took another uncertain step | towards the tent.*

Copyright page: *First published in November Mcmxxxix | by Faber and Faber Limited | 24 Russell Square, London, W.C. 1 | Printed in Great Britain by | Western Printing Services Ltd., Bristol | All Rights Reserved*

Binding: Yellow cloth covered boards stamped in blue. Top edge unstained. All edges trimmed. Front: Picture of a baby camel. Spine: [stamped in blue out-lined in black] THE YOUNGEST CAMEL — KAY BOYLE   Back: Blank

Fig 7-A16d

Dust jacket: Beige paper printed in black, yellow and gray. Front: The | Youngest Camel | *by Kay Boyle* | [picture of baby camel facing two buzzards] | *Faber and Faber Limited* Spine: [printed vertical in black] The Youngest Camel —— Kay Boyle F & F   Back: List of other Faber & Faber books for children   Front flap: Story plot 3s 6p   [lower right] Back flap: Notice from Faber and Faber about lists for future publications.

First published in November 1939 at 3s 6d.

A17a   THE CRAZY HUNTER AND OTHER STORIES   [1940]

First Edition:

THE CRAZY HUNTER | and other stories | *by* | KAY BOYLE | FABER AND FABER LIMITED | 24 Russell Square | London

Collation: [1-6], 7, [8-10], 11-155, [156-158], 159-222, [223-224], 225-313, [314-320] pages; cream endpapers. 7 $^3/_8$" x 4 $^7/_8$" [A]^8 B-I^8 K-U^8

Contents: (1) half title page; (2) [list]: *by the same author* [eleven titles]; (3) title page; (4) copyright page; (5) To | KATHERINE ANN PORTER | in homage; (6) blank; (7) table of contents and acknowledgment for previous publication; (8) blank; (9) [divisional title]: *The Crazy Hunter* | [design]; (10) blank; (11-155) text (156) blank; (157) [divisional title]: *The Bridegroom's Body* | [design]; (158) blank; (159-222) text; (223) [divisional title]: *Big Fiddle* | [design]; (224) blank; (225-313) text; (314-320) blank.

Copyright page: *First published in March Mcmxl* | *by Faber and Faber Limited* | *24 Russell Square London W.C.* I | *Printed in Great Britain by* | *Latimer Trend & Co Ltd Plymouth* | *All Rights Reserved*

Binding: Light purple cloth covered boards stamped in yellow. Top edge unstained. All edges trimmed. Front: Blank.   Spine: THE | CRAZY | HUNTER | [decoration] | Kay | Boyle | Faber and | Faber Back: Blank.

Dust jacket: Cream paper printed in red, cream and blue.   Front: Blue background with red square edged in cream printed: THE | CRAZY | HUNTER | [on the blue] KAY | BOYLE Spine: [red square edged in cream] THE | CRAZY | HUNTER | [on the blue] KAY | BOYLE | FABER AND | FABER Back: [white printed in blue] A list of new fiction published by Faber and Faber Front flap: A short note about Kay Boyle and about the book. 8s. 3d. | net. [lower right]   Back flap: Excerpts from reviews of *Monday Night, The First Lover, The White Horses of Vienna, My Next Bride, Death of a Man* and *The Youngest Camel.*

First published in March of 1940 at 8s 3d.

The Included stories and their previous publication: "The Bridegroom's Body" first appeared in *The Southern Review*, Summer 1938. Part I of "Big Fiddle" first appeared in *The Phoenix*, Autumn 1938, Part II in *The Phoenix,* Spring 1939 and Part III in *The Phoenix*, Autumn 1939. "The Crazy Hunter" appears here for the first time.

A17b   THE CRAZY HUNTER: THREE SHORT NOVELS   [1940]

First American Edition:

The Crazy Hunter | THREE SHORT NOVELS | BY KAY BOYLE | HARCOURT, BRACE AND COMPANY, NEW YORK

Collation: [i-x], [1-2], 3-139, [140-142], 143-205, [206-208], 209-295, [296-302] pages; cream endpapers.   8" x 5 $^1/_4$" [A-S]^8 [T]^4

Contents: (i) blank; (ii) [list]: *Other books by Kay Boyle* [nine titles]; (iii) title page; (iv) copyright page; (v) [dedication]: DEDICATED IN HOMAGE TO | *Katherine Anne Porter;* (vi) blank; (vii) [publisher's note]: Acknowledgment is here made to the edi- | tors of *The Southern Review* and *The Phoe-* | *nix* for permission to reprint, respectively, | THE BRIDEGROOM'S BODY and BIG FIDDLE;   (viii) blank; (ix) table of contents; (x) blank; (1) [divisional title]: THE CRAZY HUNTER;   (2) blank; (3-139) text; (140) blank; (141) [divisional title]: THE BRIDEGROOM'S BODY; (142) blank; (143-205) text; (206) blank; (207) [divisional title]: BIG FIDDLE; (208) blank; (209-295) text; (296-302) blank.

Copyright page: COPYRIGHT, 1938,1940, BY | KAY BOYLE | *All rights reserved, including* | *the right to reproduce this book* | *or portions thereof in any form.* | *first edition* | *Designed by Robert Josephy* | PRINTED IN THE UNITED STATES OF AMERICA | BY QUINN & BODEN COMPANY, INC., RAHWAY, N. J.

Binding: Dark green cloth covered boards stamped in gold. Top edge stained green and all edges trimmed. Front: Blank. Spine: KAY BOYLE | *The* | *Crazy* | *Hunter* | [design] | *Harcourt, Brace* | *and Company*   Back: Blank.

Dust jacket: Cream paper printed in lime green, white and brown. Front: [the following printed in white on a large splash of brown] *The* | *Crazy Hunter* | *by* | *KAY BOYLE* | [the following printed on lime green in brown] *Three Short Novels*: | THE CRAZY HUNTER | THE BRIDEGROOM'S BODY | BIG FIDDLE   Spine: [all brown on lime green] KAY | BOYLE | ★ | THE | CRAZY | HUNTER | HARCOURT, | BRACE AND | COMPANY   Back: [brown on white] Appraising the work of Kay Boyle: three excerpts from reviews of her works. Front flap: Story plots of the stories in *The Crazy Hunter*. $2.50 [upper right]. Back Flap: Story plot for *Monday Night.*

First published on March 14, 1940 according to *Publisher's Weekly* at $2.50.

The Included stories and their previous publication are the same as in the first English edition.

A18a   PRIMER FOR COMBAT   1942

First Edition:

[black script] Primer for Combat | [small splash of blue with village and mountains] | [blue script] by | [black block] KAY BOYLE | [black] SIMON AND SCHUSTER • 1942

Collation: [i-viii], ix-xi, [xii], [1-2], 3-320, [321-324] pages; cream endpapers. 7 $^3/_4$" x 5 $^1/_2$" [A-U]^8

Contents: (i) publisher's device; (ii) blank; (iii) title page; (iv) copyright page; (v) [dedication]: For Ann and Roger Burlingame; (vi) blank; (vii) [publisher's note]: ACKNOWLEDGMENTS | The author and publishers of *Primer for Com-* | *bat* are grateful to the publishers of *Harper's* | *Bazaar, The New Yorker*, and *Mademoiselle* for | permission to reprint certain passages in this book. | Thanks are also due Greenberg Publisher, Inc., | for permission to quote from *Hell in the Foreign* | *Legion*, by Ernst F. Löhndorff; to D. Appleton- | Century Company Inc., for permission to quote | from *Lyautey*, by André Maurois; and to Double- | day, Doran and Company, Inc., for permission to | quote from *Revolt in the Desert*, by T.E. | Lawrence.; (viii) blank; (ix-xi) cast of characters; (xii) blank; (1) half title page; (2) blank; (3-320) text; (321) blank; (322) a note about the author; (323-324) blank.

Copyright page: ALL RIGHTS RESERVED | INCLUDING THE RIGHT OF REPRODUCTION | IN WHOLE OR IN PART IN ANY FORM | COPYRIGHT, 1942, BY KAY BOYLE | PUBLISHED BY SIMON AND SCHUSTER, INC. | ROCKEFELLER CENTER, 1230 SIXTH AVENUE, | NEW YORK, N.Y. | MANUFACTURED IN THE UNITED STATES OF AMERICA | BY THE AMERICAN BOOK-STRATFORD PRESS, INC., NEW YORK

Binding: Bound in blue cloth covered boards. Top edge stained blue with top and bottom edge trimmed. Front edge rough trimmed. Front: Blank. Spine: [beige paper paste on label printed in red and blue] Primer | for | Combat | [small village and mountains in blue] | KAY BOYLE | [stamped in red on the cloth] SIMON AND SCHUSTER Back: Blank.

Dust jacket: White paper printed in red, blue and white. Front: [script] Primer | for [church and tree with mountains in the back ground printed in white in this line] | [blue] Combat | [blue] KAY BOYLE Spine: [white] Primer | for | Combat | [blue block] KAY BOYLE | [white script] Simon and Schuster Back: White, with a paragraph printed in blue by Kay Boyle describing the plight of occupied countries and the necessity for citizens to buy war bonds to support the war effort. This is enclosed in a single red ruled rectangle. Front flap: Story plot. $2.50 [lower right]. Back flap: A continuation of the story plot from the front flap. Also a short biographical sketch about Kay Boyle.

Note: One publisher's presentation copy for Kay Boyle was bound in full dark brown leather stamped in gold with top edge gold gilt.

First published on October 27, 1942 according to *Publisher's Weekly* at $2.50.

A18b   PRIMER FOR COMBAT   1942

First Edition Second Printing:

[black script] Primer for Combat | [small splash of blue with village and mountains] | [blue script] by | [black block] KAY BOYLE | [black] SIMON AND SCHUSTER •1942

Collation and contents are the same as A18a.

Copyright page: ALL RIGHTS RESERVED | INCLUDING THE RIGHT OF REPRODUCTION | IN WHOLE OR IN PART IN ANY FORM | COPY-RIGHT, 1942, BY KAY BOYLE | PUBLISHED BY SIMON AND SCHUSTER, INC. | ROCKEFELLER CENTER, 1230 SIXTH AVENUE, | NEW YORK, N.Y. | SECOND PRINTING | MANUFACTURED IN THE UNITED STATES OF AMERICA | BY THE AMERICAN BOOK-STRATFORD PRESS, INC., NEW YORK

Binding: The same as A18a.

Dust jacket: The same as A18a with the following exception: There is a white band on the front of the jacket on which is printed in gray blue four short reviews of *Primer for Combat*. This band is between the word Combat and Kay Boyle's name. It extends around the spine with blurbs by Vicki Baum, Carson McCullers and Raoul de Roussy de Sales.

A18c   PRIMER FOR COMBAT   [1943]

First English Edition:

PRIMER FOR COMBAT | by | KAY BOYLE | FABER AND FABER | 24 Russell Square | London

Collation: [1-4], 5, [6], 7-240 pages; cream endpapers. $7 \, ^5/_{16}$" x $4 \, ^3/_4$" [A]^8 B-I^8 K-P^8

Contents: (1) half title page; (2) [list]: *by the same author* | ★ | [six titles]; (3) title page; (4) copyright page with dedication; (5) [publisher's note]: [publisher's note]: Acknowledgments | The author and publishers of *Primer for Combat* are grateful | to the publishers of *Harper's* | *Bazaar, The New Yorker,* and | *Mademoiselle* for permission to reprint certain passages in this | book. | Thanks are also due Greenberg Publisher, Inc., | for permission to quote from *Hell in the Foreign* | *Legion,* by Ernst F. Löhndorff; to D. Appleton- | Century Company inc., for permission to quote | from *Lyautey,* by André Maurois; and to Double- | day, Doran and Company, Inc., for permission to | quote from *Revolt in the Desert,* by T.E. | Lawrence; (6) blank; (7-8) cast of characters; (9-239) text; (240) note about the author.

Copyright page: FOR | ANNE AND ROGER BURLINGAME | *First published in Mcmxliii* | *by Faber and Faber Limited* | *24 Russell Square London W.C.1* | *Printed in Great Britain by* | *Western Printing Services Ltd. Bristol* | *All rights reserved* | *This book is produced in complete conformity* | *with the authorized economy standards*

Binding: Bright red cloth covered boards printed in gold. Top edge stained blue. Top and bottom edge trimmed. Front edge rough trimmed. Front: Blank. Spine: *Primer* | *for* | *Combat* | [single gold rule] | *Kay* | *Boyle* | Faber Back: Blank.

Dust jacket: Beige paper printed in dark blue and red. Front: [blue] Primer | for | Combat | a novel by | [red] KAY | BOYLE Spine: [blue] Primer | for | Combat | [single red rule] | [red] KAY | BOYLE | [blue] Faber | [red] and | [blue] Faber Back: A list of new fiction by Faber and Faber all printed in blue. Front flap: Story plot. 8s. 6d. | net. [lower right]. Back flap: A short description of *The White Horses of Vienna* by Kay Boyle with excerpts from reviews from the *Observer* and the *Sunday Times.*

Publication: First published in September 1943 at 8s 6d.

A18d   PRIMER FOR COMBAT   [1943]

Second English Printing:

PRIMER FOR COMBAT | by | KAY BOYLE | FABER AND FABER | 24 Russell Square | London

Collation and Contents: The same as A18c.

Copyright page: FOR | ANNE AND ROGER BURLINGAME | *First published in Mcmxliii* | *by Faber and Faber Limited* | *24 Russell Square London W.C.1* | *Second impression November Mcmxliii* | *Printed in Great Britain by* | *Western Printing Services Ltd. Bristol* | *All rights reserved* | *This book is produced in complete conformity* | *with the authorized economy standards*

Binding: The same as A18c.

Dust jacket: Same as A18c except that front and back flaps and the back of the jacket are a pale blue green. Also the advertisements on the back are in some cases different and also in a different order.

Publication: First printed in November 1943 at 8s 6d.

A19a   AVALANCHE   1944

First Edition:

[blue] *Avalanche* | [black] *a novel by KAY BOYLE* | [black] *1944* [blue] publishers device] [black] *Simon and Schuster, New York*

Collation: [i-vi], [1-2], 3-209, [210] pages; endpapers are a blue map printed in black. 8 $^1/_8$" x 5 $^1/_2$"   [A]^8 [B]^4 [C-N]^8

Contents: (i) publisher's device; (ii) blank; (iii) title page; (iv) copyright page; (v) [dedication]: TO | *Monsieur and Madame Rrose Sélavy*; (vi) [publisher's note]: A somewhat shorter version of | *Avalanche* | appeared serially in | *The Saturday Evening Post.*; (1) fly title; (2) blank; (3-209) text; (210) a note about Kay Boyle.

Copyright page: ALL RIGHTS RESERVED | INCLUDING THE RIGHT OF REPRODUCTION | IN WHOLE OR IN PART IN ANY FORM | COPY-RIGHT, 1944, BY KAY BOYLE | PUBLISHED BY SIMON AND SCHUSTER, INC. | ROCKEFELLER CENTER, 1230 SIXTH AVENUE, | NEW YORK 20, N.Y. | About the Appearance of Books in Wartime | A recent ruling by the War Production Board has cur- | tailed the use of paper by book publishers in 1944. | In line with this ruling and in order to conserve materials | and manpower, we are co-operating by: | 1. Using lighter-weight paper, which reduces the bulk of | our books substantially. | 2. Printing books with smaller margins and with more | words to each page. Result: fewer pages per book. | Slimmer and smaller books will save paper and plate | metal and labor. We are sure that readers will understand | the publishers' desire to co-operate as fully as possible | with the objectives of the War Production Board and our | government. | MANUFACTURED IN THE UNITED STATES OF AMERICA | BY VAIL-BALLOU PRESS, BINGHAMTON, N.Y.

Binding: Light blue cloth covered boards stamped in gold. Top edge stained blue. Top and bottom edges trimmed. Front edge rough trimmed. Front: Blank. Spine: *Avalanche* | BY | KAY | BOYLE | *Simon and* | *Schuster*   Back: Blank.

Dust jacket: White paper pictorial jacket printed in blue, blue green, brown, and white. Front: *Avalanche* | A NOVEL OF LOVE AND ESPIONAGE BY | *Kay Boyle* | A picture of a mountain climber's pick, rope and hat in the snow with snowcapped mountains in the background. The dust jacket designer's name, hoffman, with small h in white underneath the picture. Spine: AVALANCHE | *Kay Boyle* | *Simon and* |

Fig 8-A19a

Schuster   Back: An advertisement for other books published by Simon and Schuster printed in black and enclosed in a blue rule box. Front flap: Story plot. $2.50 [lower right]   Back flap: A continuation of the front flap and a short biographical note about Kay Boyle.

First published on January 10, 1944 according to *Publisher's Weekly* at $2.50.

A19b   AVALANCHE   1944

First Edition Second Printing:

[blue] *Avalanche* | [black] *a novel by KAY BOYLE* | [black] *1944* [blue] publishers device] [black] *Simon and Schuster, New York*

Contents: Same as A19a.

Collation: Same as A19a.

Copyright page: Same as A19a except the SECOND PRINTING appears between NEW YORK 20, N.Y. and the paragraph beginning: About the Appearance of Books

Binding: Same as A19a except in rust colored cloth instead of light blue.

Dust jacket: Same as A19a.

A19c   AVALANCHE   [1944]

First English Edition:

AVALANCHE | a novel by | KAY BOYLE | FABER AND FABER | 24 Russell Square | London

Collation: [1-4], 5-154, [155-156] pages; cream endpapers. 7 $^3/_8$" x 4 $^3/_4$". [A:A]^8 A:B-A:I^8 A:K^6

Contents: (1) half title page; (2) [dedication]: To | Monsieur et Madame Rose Sélavy; (3) title page; (4) copyright page; (5-153) text; (154) a note about the author; (155-156) blank.

Copyright page: *First published in Mcmxliv | by Faber and Faber Limited | 24 Russell Square London W.C. 1 | Printed in Great Britain by | Western Printing Services Limited Bristol | All rights reserved | This book is produced in complete conformity | with the authorized economy standards*

Binding: Light blue cloth covered boards stamped in gold. Top edge trimmed and unstained. Front and bottom edge untrimmed. Front: Blank. Spine: [printed downward] *AVALANCHE • KAY BOYLE | FABER* Back: Blank.

Dust jacket: Light pink paper printed in gray. Front: [at a slant from bottom to top] Avalanche | [a slash of pink starting in lower left hand corner and narrowing as it approaches the upper right hand corner with initials BLW in gray] | a novel | by | Kay Boyle Spine: [printed downward] *AVALANCHE • KAY BOYLE FABER* Back: [white printed in gray] A list of new fiction published by Faber and Faber. Front flap: A short note on the book   7s. 6d. | net [lower right]   Back flap: Blank.

Publication: First published in December 1944 at   5s.

A19d   AVALANCHE   [1944]

First English Edition Second Printing:

AVALANCHE | a novel by | KAY BOYLE | FABER AND FABER | 24 Russell Square | London

Collation: Same as A19c.

Contents: Same as A19c.

Copyright page: *First published in Mcmxliv | by Faber and Faber Limited | 24 Russell Square London W.C. 1 | Second impression January Mcmxlv | Printed in Great Britain by | Western Printing Services Limited Bristol | All rights reserved | This book is produced in complete conformity | with the authorized economy standards*

Binding: Same as A19c.

Dust jacket: Not seen.

Publication: First published in January 1945.

A19e   AVALANCHE   [1944]

First English Edition Third Printing:

AVALANCHE | a novel by | KAY BOYLE | FABER AND FABER | 24 Russell Square | London

Collation: Same as A19c.

Contents: Same as A19c.

Copyright page: *First published in Mcmxliv | by Faber and Faber Limited | 24 Russell Square London W.C. 1 | Second impression January Mcmxlv | Third impression June Mcmxlv | Printed in Great Britain by | Western Printing Services Limited Bristol | All rights reserved | This book is produced in complete conformity | with the authorized economy standards.*

Binding: Same as A19c.

Dust jacket: Not seen.

Publication: First published in June 1945.

A19f   AVALANCHE   [1944]

First English Edition Fourth Printing:

AVALANCHE | a novel by | KAY BOYLE | FABER AND FABER | 24 Russell Square | London

Collation: Same as A19c.

Contents: Same as A19c.

Copyright page: *First published in Mcmxliv | by Faber and Faber Limited | 24 Russell Square London W.C. 1 | Second impression January Mcmxlv | Third impression June Mcmxlv | Fourth impression May Mcmxlvi | Printed in Great Britain by | Western Printing Services Limited Bristol | All rights reserved | This book is produced in complete conformity | with the authorized economy standards*

Binding: Bound in blue cloth covered boards stamped in silver.

Dust jacket: White paper dust jacket printed in brown, gray, and blue. Front: [at an angle slanting upwards in blue] *AVALANCHE* | [in white] KAY BOYLE | [picture of a woman on the front with a small building in the background] Spine: [printed downward in blue] AVALANCHE [white] • [brown] KAY BOYLE [white] • [blue] *FABER* Back: Advertisements for other Faber fiction.

Publication: First published in May 1946.

Note: According to the English Catalogue of Books, volume 16   1948-1951, there was a cheap edition published at 5 shillings net in March of 1950. This book was not found or examined by the compiler.

A19g   AVALANCHE   1944

Book Club Edition:

Avalanche | a novel by KAY BOYLE | 1944 [publisher's device] *Simon and Schuster*, New York

Collation: [i-x], [1-2], 3-209, [210-214] pages; cream endpapers.   8" x 5 $^3/_8$" [A-G]^{16}

Contents: (i) publisher's device; (ii) blank; (iii) story plot; (iv) blank; (v) half title page; (vi)   blank; (vii) title page; (viii) copyright page; (ix) [dedication]:   TO | *Monsieur and Madame Rrose Sélavy*;   (x) blank; (1) fly title; (2) blank; (3-209) text; (210) blank; (211) a note about the author; (212-214) blank.

Copyright page: ALL RIGHTS RESERVED | INCLUDING THE RIGHT OF REPRODUCTION | IN WHOLE OR IN PART IN ANY FORM | COPY-RIGHT, 1944, BY KAY BOYLE | PUBLISHED BY SIMON AND SCHUSTER, INC. | ROCKEFELLER CENTER, 1230 SIXTH AVENUE, | NEW YORK 20, N.Y. | THIS BOOK HAS NOT BEEN CONDENSED. ITS BULK | IS LESS BECAUSE GOVERNMENT REGULATIONS | PROHIBIT USE OF HEAVIER PAPER. | MANUFACTURED IN THE UNITED STATES OF AMERICA

Binding: Teal blue cloth covered boards stamped in gold. Top edge stained orange and trimmed. Bottom edge trimmed and front edge rough trimmed. Front: Blank. Spine: [vertical on black rectangle] *Avalanche*———KAY BOYLE   Back: Blank.

Dust jacket: Front and spine same as first edition. Back has an advertisement for war bonds. Front flap: story plot with BOOK CLUB | EDITION in lower right hand corner in blue with no price on jacket. Back flap: Continuation of front flap with a note about the author.

A19h   AVALANCHE   1944

Armed Services Edition:

Avalanche | by KAY BOYLE | Editions for the Armed Services, Inc. | A NON-PROFIT ORGANIZATION ESTABLISHED | BY THE COUNCIL ON BOOKS IN WARTIME | NEW YORK [The title page is shared with the copyright page]

Collation: [1-5], 6-221, [222], 223-224 pages.   3 $^3/_4$" x 5 $^1/_2$"

Contents: (1) title page and copyright page; (2) *Manufactured in the United States of America*; (3) [dedication]: To | *Monsieur and Madame | Rrose Sélavy*;   (4) blank; (5-221) text; (222) blank; (223-224) a note about the author.

Copyright page: PUBLISHED BY ARRANGEMENT WITH | SIMON AND SCHUSTER, INC., NEW YORK | *All rights reserved, including | the right of*

reproduction in | *whole or in part in any form.* | *Copyright, 1944, by Kay Boyle*
[Copyright page shared with the title page.]

Binding: Bound in cream paper stapled wraps printed in blue, green and red. All
edges trimmed. Top edge unstained. Front: Left third in light blue with photograph
of the dust cover of the American first edition. I-241 in upper left hand corner.
Black circle in lower left hand corner with ARMED | SERVICES | EDITION
printed in white. Right two thirds in green printed thus: [white] *Avalanche* | [yellow]
A NOVEL OF LOVE AND ESPIONAGE BY | [white] *Kay Boyle* | [black] Overseas
edition for the Armed Forces. Distrib- | uted by the Special Services Division, A.S.F.,
| for the Army, and by the Bureau of Naval | Personnel for the Navy. U.S.
Government prop- | erty. Not for sale. Published by Editions for the | Armed
Services, Inc., a non-profit organization | established by the Council on Books in
Wartime. [half inch red band across the bottom printed in yellow] THIS IS THE
COMPLETE BOOK-NOT A DIGEST   Back: A short plot summary and
acknowledgment to Simon and Schuster. Inside front cover: A note on the Armed
Services Editions. Inside back cover: A list of other titles by the Armed Services
Editions.

A19i   AVALANCHE   [1944]

The Readers' League of America Edition:

Avalanche | *a novel by KAY BOYLE* | THE READERS' LEAGUE OF AMERICA |
NEW YORK, N.Y.

Collation: [i-vi], [1-2], 3-209, [210-218] pages; cream endpapers. 7 $^1/_4$" x 4 $^7/_8$"
[A-G]^{16}

Contents: (i-ii) blank; (iii) title page; (iv) copyright page; (v) [dedication]:
TO | Monsieur and Madame Rrose Sélavy; (vi) [publisher's note]: A somewhat
shorter version of | *Avalanche* | appeared serially in | *The Saturday Evening Post.*; (1)
half title page; (2) blank; (3-209) text; (210) a note about the author; (211-218)
blank.

Copyright page: ALL RIGHTS RESERVED | INCLUDING THE RIGHT OF
REPRODUCTION | IN WHOLE OR IN PART IN ANY FORM | COPY-
RIGHT, 1944, BY KAY BOYLE | About the Appearance of Books in Wartime | A
recent ruling by the War Production Board has cur- | tailed the use of paper by book
publishers in 1944. | In line with this ruling and in order to conserve materials | and
manpower, we are co-operating by: | 1. Using lighter-weight paper, which reduces
the bulk of | our books substantially. | 2. Printing books with smaller margins and
with more | words to each page. Result: fewer pages per book. | Slimmer and smaller
books will save paper and plate | metal and labor. We are sure that readers will under-
stand | the publishers' desire to co-operate as fully as possible | with the objectives of

the War Production Board and our | government. | MANUFACTURED IN THE UNITED STATES OF AMERICA

Binding: Bound in dark green vinyl covered boards printed in orange. Top edge unstained. All edges trimmed. Front: [ten orange wavy lines mid upper right] | AVALANCHE | [short rule] | KAY BOYLE | [repeat above pattern in mid lower left] Spine: [downward] AVALANCHE —— KAY BOYLE Back: Blank.

Dust jacket: Not seen. Probably not issued in dust jacket.

A20a   AMERICAN CITIZEN NATURALIZED   1944
                        IN LEADVILLE, COLORADO

First Edition:

AMERICAN | CITIZEN | NATURALIZED IN | LEADVILLE, COLORADO | A POEM BY | KAY BOYLE | [publisher's device] | SIMON AND SCHUSTER, NEW YORK | 1944

Collation: [i-ii], [1-5], 6-15, [16] pages.   8 $^3/_4$" x 6"

Contents: (i-ii) blank; (1) title page; (2) copyright page; (3) table of contents; (4) [dedication]: This poem is dedicated | to Carson McCullers. | Her husband, | like mine, | is serving overseas.; (5-15) text; (16) a note about the author.

Copyright page: ALL RIGHTS RESERVED | INCLUDING THE RIGHT OF REPRODUCTION | IN WHOLE OR IN PART IN ANY FORM | COPY-RIGHT, 1944, BY KAY BOYLE | PUBLISHED BY SIMON AND SCHUSTER, INC. | ROCKEFELLER CENTER, 1230 SIXTH AVENUE | NEW YORK 20, N.Y. | MANUFACTURED IN THE UNITED STATES OF AMERICA

Binding: Beige stapled wraps printed in red and black. Front: [ten very tight red rules edge to edge] | [black] AMERICAN | CITIZEN | [red] A POEM BY | [black] KAY BOYLE | [red publisher's device] | [black] SIMON AND SCHUSTER • NEW YORK • 1944 | [repeat above red rule sequence]   Back: Printed in red and black. A short description of the poem and a short note about the author. Front flap: FIFTY CENTS [lower right]   Back flap: Blank.

A21a   A FRENCHMAN MUST DIE   1946

First Edition:

KAY BOYLE | [a series of small linked diamonds forming a rule] | *A Frenchman* | *Must Die* | [a repeat of the above rule] | 1946 | SIMON AND SCHUSTER • NEW YORK

Fig 9-A21a

Collation: [i-x], 1-213, [214] pages; cream endpapers. 8" x 5 $^1/_2$" [A-G]^{16}

Contents: (i) publishers device; (ii) blank; (iii) title page; (iv) copyright page; (v) [dedication]: TO | *Allen Marple;* (vi) [publisher's note]: A somewhat shorter version of | *A Frenchman Must Die* | appeared serially in | *The Saturday Evening Post*; (vii-viii) an Introductory note on the French Milice; (ix) fly title; (x) blank; (1-213) text; (214) a note about the author.

Copyright page: ALL RIGHTS RESERVED | INCLUDING THE RIGHT OF REPRODUCTION | IN WHOLE OR IN PART IN ANY FORM | COPYRIGHT, 1946, BY KAY BOYLE | PUBLISHED BY SIMON AND SCHUSTER, INC. | ROCKEFELLER CENTER, 1230 SIXTH AVENUE, | NEW YORK 20, N. Y. | MANUFACTURED IN THE UNITED STATES OF AMERICA | BY VAIL-BALLOU PRESS, BINGHAMTON, N.Y.

Binding: Light blue cloth covered boards stamped in gold. Top edge unstained. Top and bottom edge trimmed. Front edge rough trimmed. Front: Blank. Spine: *A* | *Frenchman* | *Must Die* | BY | KAY | BOYLE | *Simon and* | *Schuster* Back: Blank.

Dust jacket: White paper pictorial jacket printed in yellow, rust brown, red white and blue. Front: A Frenchman | Must Die | [picture of a rifle, French flag stuck in the ground and a bombed building in the background.] | A story of Love and Intrigue by | KAY BOYLE [jacket is signed hoffman (the jacket designer) with small h] from bottom to top along the spine edge of the book. The silhouette of a curved knife is stenciled through the front of jacket allowing the binding to show through between the signature hoffman and the picture on the front of the jacket.] Spine: KAY | BOYLE | [printed downward] A Frenchman Must Die | [horizontal] SIMON AND | SCHUSTER Back: A selection of other books published by Simon and Schuster. Front flap: Story plot. $2.50 [lower right]. Back flap: A continuation of the story plot from the front flap and a short note about Kay Boyle.

Publication: First published on April 1, 1946 according to *Publisher's Weekly* at $2.50.

A21b   A FRENCHMAN MUST DIE   [1946]

First English Edition:

A FRENCHMAN | MUST DIE | by | KAY BOYLE | FABER AND FABER LTD | 24 Russell Square | London

Collation: [1-4], 5-194, [195-196] pages; cream endpapers. 7 $^3/_8$" x 4 $^3/_4$" [A]^8 B-I^8 K-MM^{10}

Contents: (1) half title page; (2) [dedication]: To | ALLEN MARPLE; (3) title page; (4) copyright page; (5-6) an introductory note on the French Milice; (7-194) text; (195-196) blank.

Copyright page: *First published in Mcmxlvi | by Faber and Faber Limited | 24 Russell Square London W.C.1 | Printed in Great Britain | at the Bowering Press Plymouth | All rights reserved*

Binding: Light blue cloth covered boards stamped in gold. Top edge unstained. All edges trimmed. Front: Blank. Spine: *A | French- | man | Must | Die |* [line device] | *Kay | Boyle | Faber*   Back: Blank.

Dust jacket: Cream paper printed in blue and red. Front: [blue] A | FRENCH- | MAN | MUST | DIE | *A Story of Love | and Intrigue by |* [red] KAY | BOYLE [A blue and a red strip from top to bottom on the flap edge of the jacket front] Spine: [printed horizontally in red] *Kay | Boyle |* [printed downward in blue] A Frenchman Must Die | [horizontal in red] *Faber*   Back: New fiction by Faber and Faber. Front flap: Story plot. 8s. 6d. | net [lower right]. Back flap: An excerpt from a review of Kay Boyle's *Avalanche* which appeared in the *Daily Telegraph*.

Publication: First published in November 1946 at 8s 6s.

A22a   THIRTY STORIES   [1946]

First Edition:

Thirty Stories | by | Kay Boyle | [publishers device] | SIMON AND SCHUSTER, NEW YORK

Collation: one extra leaf between free end paper and first paginated leaf [i-iv], v-vi, [vii-viii], ix-x, [1-2], 3-77, [78-80], 81-140, [141-142], 143-198, [199-200], 201-330, [331-332], 333-362, [363-372] pages; cream endpapers.   8" x 5 $^1/_2$" [A-L]^{16}

Contents: (i) publisher's device; (ii) blank; (iii) title page; (iv) copyright page and beginning of acknowledgments; (v-vi) continuation of acknowledgments; (vii) [dedication]: To Caresse Crosby | whose belief and fervor have never failed— | this book is dedicated in gratitude; (viii) blank; (ix-x) table of contents; (1) [divisional title]: Early Group | 1927-1934; (2) blank; (3-77) text; (78) blank; (79) [divisional title]: Austrian Group | 1933-1938; (80) blank; (81-140) text; (141) [divisional title]: English Group | 1935-1936; (142) blank; (143-198) text; (199) [divisional title]: French Group | 1939-1942; (200) blank; (201-330) text; (331) [divisional title]: American Group | 1942-1946; (332) blank; (333-362) text; (363) a note about Kay Boyle; (364-372) blank.

Copyright page: ALL RIGHTS RESERVED | INCLUDING THE RIGHT OF REPRODUCTION | IN WHOLE OR IN PART IN ANY FORM | COPYRIGHT, 1946, BY KAY BOYLE | PUBLISHED BY SIMON AND SCHUSTER, INC. | ROCKEFELLER CENTER, 1230 SIXTH AVENUE | NEW YORK 20, N. Y. | MANUFACTURED IN THE UNITED STATES OF AMERICA | BY THE HADDON CRAFTSMEN, INC., SCRANTON, PA. |

ACKNOWLEDGMENTS | [Then begins a list of acknowledgments which the extends to page v and vi.]

Binding: Cream cloth covered boards stamped in maroon and silver. Top edge stained maroon. Top and bottom edges trimmed and front edge rough trimmed. Front: Thirty Stories by Kay Boyle | [thick stamped silver rule] Spine: Thirty | Stories | by | Kay | Boyle | [thick stamped silver rule] | Simon and | Schuster Back: Blank.

Dust jacket: Cream paper printed with gray white marbling and rust red. Front: Thirty | Stories | by | Kay | Boyle | [single slash cutting through the lower part of the Y in Boyle] In the lower right hand corner of the jacket Woods is signed vertical top to bottom. Miriam Woods was the jacket designer. Spine: Thirty | Stories | by | Kay | Boyle | SIMON | and | SCHUSTER   Back: Photograph of Kay Boyle by George Platt Lynes. Also a short note about Kay Boyle. Front flap: A short note by Kay Boyle about the stories in the book. $3.50 [upper right].   Back flap: A continuation of the front flap.

Note: One publisher's presentation copy to Kay Boyle bound in light tan full leather. The top edge gold gilt. Top and bottom edges trimmed. Front: Blank   Spine: [gold] THIRTY | STORIES | KAY BOYLE | SIMON AND | SCHUSTER

Publication: First published on November 20, 1946 according to *Publisher's Weekly* at $3.50.

The included stories and their previous publication: "Ben" first appeared in *The New Yorker*, December 24, 1938. "How Birdie's Girl Was Won" first appeared in *Harper's Magazine*, March 1936. "The Herring Piece" first appeared in *The New Yorker*, April 10, 1977. "Major Engagement in Paris" first appeared in *The American Mercury*, August 1940. "Effigy of War" first appeared in *The New Yorker*, May 25, 1940. "Diplomat's Wife" first appeared in *Harper's Bazaar*, February 1940. "Men" first appeared in *Harper's Bazaar*, February 1941. "They Weren't Going to Die" first appeared in *The New Yorker*, October 12, 1940 and in *This Is My Best*, New York: The Dial Press, 1942. "Defeat" first appeared in *The New Yorker*, May 17, 1941 and also in *O. Henry Memorial Award Prize Stories of 1941*, Garden City: Doubleday, Doran & Company, 1941 and *American Harvest: Twenty Years of Creative Writing in the United States*, New York: L.B. Fisher, 1942. "Let There Be Honour" first appeared in *The Saturday Evening Post*, November 8, 1941 and also in *Saturday Evening Post Stories of 1941*, New York: Random House, 1942. "This They Took with Them" first appeared in *Harper's Bazaar*, October 1942 as "This They Carried with Them."   "Their Name Is Macaroni" first appeared in *The New Yorker*, January 3, 1942 and in *O. Henry Memorial Award Prize Stories of 1942*, Garden City: Doubleday, Doran & Company, 1942. "Hilaire and the Maréchal Pétard" first appeared in *Harper's Magazine*, August 1942 and in *Literature and Life in America*, Chicago: Scott Foreman, 1943. "The Canals of Mars" first appeared in *Harper's Bazaar*, February 1943 and in *O. Henry Memorial Award Prize Stories of 1943*,

Garden City: Doubleday, Doran & Company, 1943 and in *It's a Woman's World: A Collection of Stories from Harper's Bazaar*, New York: Whittlesey House/McGraw-Hill Book Company, 1944. "The Loneliest Man In the US Army" first appeared in *The Woman's Home Companion*, July 1943. "Winter Night" first appeared in *The New Yorker*, January 19, 1946 and in *O. Henry Memorial Award Prize Stories of 1946*, Garden City: Doubleday & Company, 1946. "Episode in the Life of an Ancestor" and "Wedding Day" were collected in *Wedding Day and Other Stories*. See A3a for previous publication. "Rest Cure," "Kroy Wen," "Black Boy" and "Friend of the Family" were collected in *First Lover and Other Stories*. See A8a for previous publication. "White As Snow," "Keep Your Pity," "Natives Don't Cry," "Maiden, Maiden," "The White Horses of Vienna," "Count Lothar's Heart," "Major Alshuster" and "Your Body Is a Jewel Box" were collected in *The White Horses of Vienna and Other Stories*. See A11a for previous publication.

| A22b | THIRTY STORIES | [1946] |

First Edition Second Printing:

Thirty Stories | by | Kay Boyle | [publishers device] | SIMON AND SCHUSTER, NEW YORK

Collation and contents: The same as A22a.

Copyright page: The same as A22a with the exception that SECOND PRINTING follows the line BY THE HADDON CRAFTSMEN, INC., SCRANTON, PA.

Binding: Coral cloth covered boards stamped in silver and blue. Top edge stained blue. Front, spine and the back are the same as A22a except printed in blue with same silver rule.

Dust jacket: The same as A22a except that back flap has a slanted dotted line across the lower left hand corner of the flap and the following is written in the resulting triangle: Thirty Stories | by Kay Boyle | Simon and Schuster

| A22c | THIRTY STORIES | [1948] |

First English Edition:

THIRTY STORIES | by | KAY BOYLE | FABER AND FABER LIMITED | 24 Russell Square | London

Collation: [1-6], 7-10, [11-12], 13-86, [87-88], 89-148, [149-150], 151-204, [205-206], 207-336, [337-338], 339-368 pages; cream endpapers.   7 $1/_4$" x 5"   [A]^{16} B^8 C-I^{16} K-M^{16}

Contents: (1) half title page; (2) [list]: *by the same author* | ★ | [eleven titles]; (3) title page; (4) copyright page; (5) [dedication]: To | CARESSE CROSBY | whose belief and fervour have never failed— | this book is dedicated in gratitude; (6) blank; (7-8) foreword; (9-10) table of contents; (11) [divisional title]: *Early Group* | *1927-1934*; (12) blank; (13-86) text; (87) [divisional title]: *Austrian Group* | *1933-1938*; (88) blank; (89-148) text; (149) [divisional title]: *English Group* | *1935-1936*; (149) blank; (151-204) text; (205) [divisional title]: *French Group* | *1939-1942*; (206) blank; (207-336) text; (337) [divisional title]: *American Group* | *1942-1946*; (338) blank; (339-368) text.

Copyright page: *First published mcmxlviii* | *by Faber and Faber Limited* | *24 Russell Square, London, W.C.1* | *Printed in Great Britain by* | *Purnell and Sons, Ltd.* | *Paulton, Somerset, and London* | *All rights reserved*

Binding: Tan cloth covered boards stamped in gold. Top edge unstained and all edges trimmed. Front: Blank. Spine: Thirty | Stories | Kay | Boyle | Faber Back: Blank.

Dust jacket: Light blue paper printed in black and red. Front: [black] THIRTY | STORIES | [red, enclosed in a ruled rectangle with thick vertical rules on both sides] KAY | BOYLE | [black outside the rectangle] THIRTY | STORIES Spine: [black] THIRTY | STORIES | by | KAY | BOYLE | [printed downward] THIRTY STORIES [top line black] BY KAY BOYLE [bottom line in red] | [horizontal in black] FABER & | FABER Back: Photograph of Kay Boyle with no credit. A short note about Kay Boyle. Front flap: A short note about the stories. 10s. 6d. | net [lower right]. Back flap: Reviews for *Avalanche*, *A Frenchman Must Die* and *1939* by Kay Boyle.

Publication: First published in June 1948 at 10s 6d.

The included stories and their previous publication are the same as the first American edition.

A22d   THIRTY STORIES   [1957]

First American Paperback:

Thirty Stories | BY | Kay Boyle | A NEW DIRECTIONS PAPERBOOK

Collation: Unpaginated leaf, [i-iv], v-vi, [vii-viii], ix-xvi, [1-2], 3-77, [78-80], 81-140, [141-142], 143-198, [199-200], 201-330, [331-332], 333-362, [363-366] pages.   7" X 4 $^1/_8$"

Contents: unpaginated leaf has a short note about Kay Boyle on the recto; (i) half title page; (ii) blank; (iii) title page; (iv) copyright page and beginning of acknowledgments; (v-vi) continuation of acknowledgments; (vii) [dedication]: To Caresse

Crosby | whose belief and fervor have never failed— | this book is dedicated in gratitude; (viii) blank; (ix-x) table of contents; (xi-xvi) introduction by David Daiches; (1) [divisional title]: Early Group | 1927-1934; (2) blank; (3-77) text; (78) blank; (79) [divisional title]: Austrian Group | 1933-1938; (80) blank; (81-140) text; (141) [divisional title]: English Group | 1935-1936; (142) blank; (143-198) text; (199) [divisional title]: French Group | 1939-1942; (200) blank; (201-330) text; (331) [divisional title]: American Group | 1942-1946; (332) blank; (333-362) text; (363-366) blank.

Copyright page: Copyright, 1946, by Kay Boyle | Copyright © 1957 by New Directions | First Published as New Directions | Paperbook No. 62, 1957 | Printed in the U.S.A. New Directions books | are published by James Laughlin. New York | Office: 333 Sixth Avenue. | ACKNOWLEDGMENTS | [beginning of acknowledgments]

Binding: White stiff wrappers printed in black and white. 7 $\frac{1}{8}$" x 4 $\frac{1}{8}$" Front: [white traced and shadowed in black] THIRTY [black shadowed in white] STORIES | [geometric montage of photographs of clouds] | [white traced and shadowed in black] by KAY [black shadowed in white] BOYLE | NEW DIRECTIONS [smaller photographic montage] PAPERBOOK $1.45 The name Mayen is printed vertical from bottom to top in the upper left hand corner. Apparently the cover designer or photographer. Spine: [printed downward] [white traced and shadowed in black] THIRTY [black shadowed in white] STORIES [black] BY [white traced and shadowed in black] KAY [black shadowed in white] BOYLE [black] ND PAPERBOOK | [horizontal] 62   Back: A short note on the stories and about Kay Boyle and an excerpt from a review from the San Francisco Chronicle. [bottom line] A NEW DIRECTIONS PAPERBOOK | 333 Sixth Avenue, New York 14

Publication: First published in 1957 at $1.45

A22e   THIRTY STORIES

First American Paperback Second Printing:

Thirty Stories | BY | Kay Boyle | A NEW DIRECTIONS PAPERBOOK

Collation: Same as A22d.

Contents: Same as A22d with following exceptions: The note on unpaginated leaf is altered slightly. Pages 363 and 364 now list other New Directions Paperbook titles available.

Copyright page: Copyright, 1946, by Kay Boyle | Copyright © 1957 by New Directions | First Published as New Directions | Paperbook No. 62, 1957 | Second Printing | Printed in the United States of America | New Directions books are published for James Laughlin by | New Directions Publishing | Corporation, 333 Sixth Avenue, | New York 10014

Binding: Front: Same as A22d except price is dropped. Spine: Same as A22d. Back: [top line added] FICTION   SECOND PRINTING | [same note as A22d] | [bottom line] A NEW DIRECTIONS PAPERBOOK NDP 62 $2.35

A22f   THIRTY STORIES

First American Paperback Third Printing:

Thirty Stories | BY | Kay Boyle | A NEW DIRECTIONS PAPERBOOK

Collation: Same as A22d.

Contents: Same as A22e.

Copyright page: Copyright 1946 by Kay Boyle | Copyright © 1957 by New Directions Publishing Corporation | Library of Congress Catalog Card No.: 57-8601 | All rights reserved. Except for brief passages quoted in a news- | paper, magazine, radio, or television review, no part of this book | may be reproduced in any form or by any means, electronic or | mechanical, including photocopying and recording, or by any | information storage and retrieval system, without permission in | writing from the Publisher. | Manufactured in the United States of America | First published as ND Paperbook 62 in 1957 | Published simultaneously in Canada | by McClellan & Stewart Limited | New Directions Books are published for James Laughlin | by New Directions Publishing Corporation, | 333 Sixth Avenue, New York 10114 | THIRD PRINTING | ACKNOWLEDGMENTS | [begin acknowledgments]

Binding: Same as A22d with the following exceptions: Front: Price is dropped. Spine: The same. Back: FICTION   THIRD PRINTING is added at the top. Bottom line now reads: A NEW DIRECTIONS PAPERBOOK NDP 62 $2.75.

A22g   THIRTY STORIES

First American Paperback Fourth Printing:

Thirty Stories | BY | Kay Boyle | A NEW DIRECTIONS PAPERBOOK

Collation: Same as A22d.

Contents: Same as A22e.

Copyright page: Same as A22f except FOURTH PRINTING is substituted for Third Printing and (ISBN: 0-8112-0013-2) is inserted between line three and four.

Binding: Same as A22f except top line on the back now reads: FICTION/ISBN 0-8112-0013-2   FOURTH PRINTING. The price on the examined copy had been obliterated. Book is enlarged to 7 $^7/_8$" x 5 $^1/_8$"

A23a   1939   [1948]

First American Edition:

[A large ruled square the bottom of which is broken by the title] *1939* | *a novel by KAY BOYLE* | [publisher's device enclosed in small square] *Simon and Schuster, New York*

Collation: [i-vi], [1-2], 3-152, [153-154] pages; cream endpapers.   8" x 5 $^3/_8$" [A-E]^{16}

Contents: (i) publisher's device; (ii) blank; (iii) title page; (iv) copyright page; (v) [dedication]: FOR | *Bessie Breuer* | AND | *Henry Varnum Poor;* (vi) disclaimer; (1) fly title; (2) blank; (3-152) text; (153) a note about Kay Boyle; (154) blank.

Copyright page: ALL RIGHTS RESERVED | INCLUDING THE RIGHT OF REPRODUCTION | IN WHOLE OR IN PART IN ANY FORM | COPYRIGHT, 1948, BY KAY BOYLE | PUBLISHED BY SIMON AND SCHUSTER, INC. | ROCKEFELLER CENTER, 1230 SIXTH AVENUE, | NEW YORK 20, N.Y. | MANUFACTURED IN THE UNITED STATES OF AMERICA | BY THE H. WOLFF BOOK   MFG. CO., INC., NEW YORK

Binding: Rust orange cloth covered boards printed in black.   Top edge stained black and all edges trimmed.   Front: [A facsimile of Kay Boyle's signature in the middle]. Spine: *Kay* | *Boyle* | *1939* [this breaks the bottom line of a small square] | *Simon* | *and* | *Schuster*   Back: Blank.

Dust jacket: Cream paper printed in brown, blue, white and black.   Front: The jacket is divided with the left side being done in brown tones and the right side in browns and light blue.   There is a chalet with mountains in the background.   S. Fisher is printed in white at the right under the mountains. [light blue] a novel | [black] 19 [white] 39 | [brown] by | [white] Kay [black] Boyle Spine: [white] 1 | 9 | [black] 3 | 9 | [mountains and man walking with ski poles] | [white] Kay | Boyle | *Simon and* | *Schuster*   Back: Excerpts from five reviews of *Thirty Stories*.   Front flap: Story plot. *Jacket design by Sam Fisher.* | $2.50 [lower right].   Back flap: A continuation of the front flap and a short note about Kay Boyle.

Publication: First published on February 16, 1948 according to *The Kirkus Review* at $2.50.

A23b   1939   [1948]

First Edition Second Printing:

[A large ruled square the bottom of which is broken by the title] *1939* | *a novel by KAY BOYLE* | [publisher's device enclosed in small square] *Simon and Schuster, New York*

Collation: Same as A23a.

Contents: Same as A23a.

Copyright page: Same as A23a except that *Second Printing* is inserted between NEW YORK 20, N.Y. and MANUFACTURED IN THE UNITED STATES OF AMERICA

Binding: Same as A23a.

Dust jacket: Same as A23a.

A23c   1939   [1948]

First English Edition:

[enclosed in double rule box, thin rule out thick rule in, which is flanked on two sides with decorations] 1939 | [outside of the box] *a novel by* | KAY BOYLE | FABER AND FABER | 24, Russell Square | London

Collation: [1-8], 9-154, [155-156] pages; cream endpapers. 7 $^5/_{16}$" x 4 $^7/_8$"   [A]^{16} B-D^{16} E ^{16} with back pastedown included in this gathering.

Contents: (1-2) blank; (3) half title page; (4) [list]: *other books by the same author* [three titles]; (5) title page; (6) copyright page; (7) [dedication]: For | BESSIE BREUER | and | HENRY VARNUM POOR; (8) disclaimer; (9-154) text; (155-156) Blank.

Copyright page: *First published in mcmxlviii by* | *Faber and Faber Limited* | *24 Russell Square London W.C. 1* | *Printed in Great Britain by* | *Purnell and Sons Limited* | *Paulton (Somerset) and London* | *All rights reserved*

Binding: Light blue cloth covered boards stamped in gold. Top edge unstained and all edges trimmed. Front: Blank. Spine: [four rules increasing in length top to bottom] | 1939 | [four rules inverse of above] | *a* | *novel* | *by* | Kay | Boyle | *Faber* | *&* | *Faber*   Back: Blank.

Dust jacket: Cream paper printed in pale green, black and red. Front: [Thick red rule] | [seven large black dots] | [shorter thick red rule] | [black] 1939 | [repeat shorter red rule] | [repeat seven black dots] | [repeat longer red rule] | [black] *A novel by* | [red] KAY | BOYLE | [black] *Faber*   Spine: [red pyramid with top cropped] |

[black] 1939 | [same pyramid inverted] | [black] *a novel* | [black] *by* | [red] KAY | BOYLE | FABER | & | FABER Back: Short biographical sketch about Kay Boyle with photograph of her framed in red. Front flap: Story plot. 7s. 6d. | net   [lower right]. Back flap: Advertisements and a review of *Avalanche, A Frenchman Must Die* and *Thirty Stories* by Kay Boyle

Publication: First published in July 1948 at 7s 6d.

A24a   HIS HUMAN MAJESTY   [1949]

First Edition:

HIS HUMAN MAJESTY | By KAY BOYLE | [sketch of mountains] | WHITTLESEY HOUSE | *McGraw-Hill Book Company, Inc* • *New York* • *London* • *Toronto*

Collation: [i-viii], [1-2], 3-131, [132-134], 135-295, [296] pages; cream endpapers, 8" x 5 $^1/_2$"   [A-S]^8

Contents: (i) half title page; (ii) [list]: Books by Kay Boyle [nineteen titles]; (iii) title page; (iv) copyright page; (v) [dedication]: *This book is dedicated to* | EDWARD ASWELL | *whose devotion and understanding* | *gave the men who live in it their life*; (vi) disclaimer; (vii) a quotation from William Blake; (viii) blank; (1) [divisional title]: PART ONE | ENEMY DETAIL; (2) blank; (3-131) text; (132) blank; (133) [divisional title]: PART TWO | THE MAIN DRAG; (134) blank; (135-295) text; (296) blank.

Copyright page: HIS HUMAN MAJESTY | *Copyright, 1949, by Kay Boyle. All rights in this book are reserved.* | *It may not be used for dramatic, motion-, or talking-picture purposes* | *without written authorization from the holder of these rights. Nor* | *may the book or parts thereof be reproduced in any manner whatsoever* | *without permission in writing, except in the case of brief quotations* | *embodied in critical articles and reviews. For information, address* | *Whittlesey House, 330 West 42nd Street, New York 18, New York.* | PUBLISHED BY WHITTLESEY HOUSE | A division of the McGraw-Hill Book Company, Inc., | PRINTED IN THE UNITED STATES OF AMERICA

Binding: Dark green cloth covered boards stamped in gold. Top edge unstained and all edges trimmed. Front: Blank. Spine: HIS HUMAN | MAJESTY | [sketch of mountain in outline] | BY KAY BOYLE | WHITTLESEY | HOUSE Back: Blank.

Dust jacket: white paper pictorial jacket printed in black, blue, brown, green and yellow. Front: Scenic mountain landscape. [white] A Novel by KAY BOYLE | [black] HIS HUMAN | MAJESTY [signed in lower right hand corner]: Adolf Dehn [the designer of the jacket]   Spine: [continuation of the mountain landscape]. [white] KAY BOYLE | [black] HIS | HUMAN | MAJESTY | [white] Whittlesey | House Back: [further continuation of the mountain landscape].   Front flap: Story plot. $3.00 [upper right]. Back flap: A continuation of the front flap with a photograph of Kay Boyle.

Publication: According to advance review slip it was published April 11, 1949 at $3.00.

Note: A publisher's presentation copy was bound for Kay Boyle in green cloth with green leather spine and corners, stamped in gold. Spine: [design] HIS | HUMAN | MAJESTY | [design] | BOYLE | [design] marble endpapers. Top edge in gilt.

A24b   HIS HUMAN MAJESTY   [1950]

First English Edition:

HIS HUMAN MAJESTY | by | KAY BOYLE | FABER AND FABER | 24 Russell Square | London

Collation: [1-12], 13-144, [145-146], 147-312 pages; cream endpapers. 7 $^1/_2$" x 5" [A]^8 B-I^8 K-T^8 U^4

Contents: (1-2) blank; (3) half title page; (4) [list]: *by the same author* [eighteen titles]; (5) title page; (6) copyright page; (7) [dedication]: *This book is dedicated to* | EDWARD ASHWELL | *whose devotion and understanding* | *gave the men who live in it their life*; (8) disclaimer; (9) a quotation from William Blake; (10) blank; (11) [divisional title]: *Part One* | ENEMY DETAIL; (12) blank; (13-144) text; (145) [divisional title]: *Part Two* | THE MAIN DRAG; (146) blank; (147-313) text. NOTE: Aswell is misspelled in the dedication. He was senior editor at Whittlesey House.

Copyright page: *First published in mcml* | *by Faber and Faber Limited* | *24 Russell Square London W.C. 1* | *Printed in Great Britain by* | *Latimer Trend & Co Ltd Plymouth* | *All rights reserved*

Binding: Bound in orange cloth covered boards stamped in gold. Top edge unstained. All edges trimmed. Front: Blank. Spine: His | Human | Majesty | [design] | Kay | Boyle | Faber & | Faber Back: Blank.

Dust jacket: White paper printed in red, gray and light blue. Front: [red] HIS | HUMAN | MAJESTY | *A Novel by* | KAY | BOYLE [There is a large snowcapped mountain in the background] Spine: [gray] His | Human | Majesty | [red] *a novel by* | KAY | BOYLE | Faber | and | Faber [a continuation of mountain] Back: A list of new fiction published by Faber and Faber. Front flap: Story plot. 12s. 6d. | net [lower left]. Back flap: Reviews of *A Frenchman Must Die, Thirty Stories, 1939* and *Avalanche* by Kay Boyle.

Publication: First published in May 1950 at 12s 6d.

A25a   THE SMOKING MOUNTAIN :   [1951]
                       STORIES OF POST WAR GERMANY

First Edition:

The Smoking Mountain | STORIES OF POSTWAR GERMANY | BY KAY
BOYLE | McGraw-Hill Book Company, Inc. | NEW YORK • LONDON •
TORONTO

Collation: [i-xii], 1-77, [78], 79-117, [118], 119-127, [128], 129-167, [168], 169-
205, [206], 207-225, [226], 227-243, [244], 245-273, [274-276] pages; cream
endpapers.   8" x 5½"   [A]⁸ [B-I]¹⁶ [J]⁸

Contents: (i) half title page; (ii) [list]: Books by Kay Boyle [twenty titles]; (iii) title
page; (iv) copyright page; (v) [dedication]: TO HAROLD ROSS | WHO WANTED
FICTION OUT OF GERMANY; (vi) blank; (vii) acknowledgments; (viii) blank;
(ix) table of contents; (x) blank; (xi) quotation from Theodor Plievier; (xii) blank; (1-
77) introduction; (78) blank; (79-117) text; (118) blank; (119-127) text; (128)
blank; (129-167) text; (168) blank; (169-205) text; (206) blank; (207-225) text;
(226) blank; (227-243) text; (244) blank; (245-273) text; (274-276) blank.

Copyright page: THE SMOKING MOUNTAIN | Copyright, 1950,1951, by
Kay Boyle. All rights in this book are reserved. | It may not be used for dramatic,
motion-, or talking-picture purposes | without written authorization from the holder
of these rights. Nor may the | book or parts thereof be reproduced in any manner
whatsoever without | permission in writing, except in the case of brief quotations
embodied in | critical articles and reviews. For information, address the McGraw-Hill
| Book Company, Inc., Trade Department, 330 West 42nd Street, New York | 18,
New York. | "Begin Again," "Fife's House," "Summer Evening," "The Criminal," and
| "Adam's Death," copyright, 1949, by *The New Yorker Magazine, Inc.* | *Published by
the McGraw-Hill Book Company, Inc.* | *Printed in the United States of America*

Binding: Dark gray cloth covered boards printed in light gray. Top edge unstained.
All edges trimmed. Front: Blank. Spine: KAY BOYLE | [printed downward in
script] The Smoking Mountain | [horizontal] McGRAW-HILL   Back: Blank.

Dust jacket: White paper printed in blue and white. KAY BOYLE | The | Smoking
| Mountain | [black mountain tops in the background] Spine: [printed downward]
KAY BOYLE The Smoking Mountain | [horizontal] McGRAW-HILL Back: [white
printed in black] A note about Kay Boyle with a photograph. Front flap: A note
about the stories. $3.50 [upper right]. Back flap: A continuation of the front flap.

Note: Special publisher's presentation copy for Kay Boyle was bound in blue cloth
with blue leather spine and corners. Printed in gold with gold gilt top edge. Spine:
THE | SMOKING | MOUNTAIN | BOYLE

Publication: First published on April 23, 1951 according to *Publisher's Weekly* at
$3.50.

The included stories and their previous publication: "Begin Again" first appeared in *The New Yorker*, May 7, 1949. "Fife's House" first appeared in *The New Yorker*, October 15, 1949. "Summer Evening" first appeared in *The New Yorker*, June 25, 1949 and in *Prize Stories of 1950 the O. Henry Awards*, Garden City: Doubleday & Company, 1950. "Frankfurt in Our Blood" first appeared in *The Nation*, October 15, 1949. "Cabaret" first appeared in *Tomorrow*, April 1951. "Home" first appeared in *Harper's Magazine*, January 1951. "The Lovers of Gain" first appeared in *The Nation*, June 24, 1950. "The Lost" first appeared in *Tomorrow*, March 1951. "The Criminal" first appeared in *The New Yorker*, March 5, 1949. "Adam's Death" first appeared in *The New Yorker*, September 10, 1949. "Aufwiedersehn Abend" first appeared in *Harper's Magazine*, April 1951.

A25b   THE SMOKING MOUNTAIN :   [1951]
                 STORIES OF POST WAR GERMANY

First Edition Second Printing:

The Smoking Mountain | STORIES OF POSTWAR GERMANY | BY KAY BOYLE | McGraw-Hill Book Company, Inc. | NEW YORK LONDON TORONTO

Collation: Same as A25a.

Contents: Same as A25a.

Copyright page: Same as A25a except that SECOND IMPRESSION is stated.

Binding: Brown cloth covered boards printed in white. The rest the same as A25a.

Dust jacket: Same as A25a.

A25c   THE SMOKING MOUNTAIN :   [1952]
                 STORIES OF POST WAR GERMANY

First English Edition:

THE | SMOKING MOUNTAIN | [short double ruled line closing at ends] | *Stories of Post-War Germany* | *by* | KAY BOYLE | FABER AND FABER LIMITED | 24 Russell Square | London

Collation: [1-8], 9, [10], 11, [12], 13, [14], 15-232 pages; cream endpapers. 7 $7/_8$" x 5" [A]^8 B-I^8 K-O^8 P^4

Contents: (1-2) blank; (3) half title page; (4) [list]: *by the same author* [nineteen titles]; (5) title page; (6) copyright page; (7) [dedication]: *To* | HAROLD ROSS |

who wanted fiction out of Germany;   (8) blank; (9) acknowledgments; (10) blank; (11) table of contents; (12) blank; (13) a quotation from Theodor Plievier; (14) blank; (15-77) introduction; (78-232) text.

Copyright page: *First published in mcmlii | by Faber and Faber Limited | 24 Russell Square London W,C.1 | Printed in Great Britain by | Latimer Trend & Co Ltd Plymouth | All rights reserved*

Binding: Burgundy cloth covered boards printed in black. Top edge unstained and all edges trimmed. Front: Blank. Spine: The | Smoking | Mountain | KAY | BOYLE | FABER   Back: Blank.

Dust jacket: Rust colored paper printed in reddish orange and black. Front: THE | SMOKING | MOUNTAIN | BY | KAY BOYLE   Spine: KAY | BOYLE | The | Smoking | Mount- | ain | [red orange dot] | Stories | of | Post-War | Germany | [repeat dot] | FABER   Back: New fiction published by Faber and Faber. Front flap: Story plot. 15s | net [lower right].   Back flap: Advertisements with reviews of *His Human Majesty, Avalanche* and *Thirty Stories* by Kay Boyle.

Publication: First published in April 1952 at 15s.

The included stories and their previous publication are the same as the first American edition.

A25d   THE SMOKING MOUNTAIN :   1963
                         STORIES OF POST WAR GERMANY

Second American Edition:

[device] | [nine small flags] | [double rule: thick-thin] | [row of fifteen small circles] | THE Smoking | MOUNTAIN | *Stories of | Germany during the Occupation* | BY | KAY BOYLE | *With a Foreword by* WILLIAM L. SHIRER | [publisher's device] | *New York* : *Alfred • A • Knopf* | 1963

Collation: One unpaginated leaf, [i-viii], ix-xix, [xx-xxii], [1-2], 3-260, [261-264] pages; cream endpapers. 8 $^3/_8$" x 5 $^5/_8$" [A-I]^{16}

Contents: [list on the verso of unpaginated leaf] BOOKS BY | *Kay Boyle* [twenty-five titles]; (i) half title page; (ii) blank; (iii) title page; (iv) copyright page; (v) [dedication]: TO | *Harold Ross* | WHO WANTED FICTION | OUT OF GERMANY; (vi) blank; (vii) quotation by Theodor Plievier; (viii) blank; (ix-xx) foreword; (xxi) table of contents; (xxii) blank; (1) [device] | THE Smoking | MOUNTAIN; (2) blank; (3-76) introduction; (77-261) text; (262) a note on the type; (263) A note about Kay Boyle; (264) blank.

Copyright page: [A list of acknowledgments] | L.C. catalog card number: 63-9120 | [double rule: thick-thin] | THIS IS A BORZOI BOOK | PUBLISHED BY

ALFRED A. KNOPF, INC. | [repeat rule: thin-thick] | Copyright 1949, 1950 by The New Yorker Maga- | zine, Inc.; copyright 1950,1951 by Kay Boyle. | Foreword copyright © 1963 by William L. Shirer. | All rights reserved. No part of this book may be | reproduced in any form without permission in | writing from the publisher, except by a reviewer, | who may quote brief passages in a review to be | printed in a magazine or newspaper. Manufactured | in the United States of America, and distributed | by Random House, Inc. Published simultaneously | in Toronto, Canada, by Random House of Can- | ada, Limited. | FIRST BORZOI EDITION | This collection of stories was first published by | McGraw-Hill Book Company, Inc., in 1951.

Binding: Rust orange cloth spine with blue paper covered boards stamped in black and gold. Top edge stained rust. Top and bottom edge trimmed. Front edge rough trimmed. Front: gold loop design with K B in the loops. Spine: [black design] | [gold] THE | Smoking | Mountain | [gold rule] | *KAY* | *BOYLE* | [black design] | [black] *Knopf* Back: Blind impression of Borzoi device.

Dust jacket: Cream paper printed in black, orange and white. Front: [black] *KAY BOYLE* | [white] *the Smoking* | *Mountain* | [black] *Stories of* | *Germany* | *during* | *the* | *Occupation* | [white] *with a foreword by William L. Shirer* [A black German eagle with yellow beak and talons in lower right quarter of front panel] Spine: [printed downward] *KAY BOYLE* [top line printed in black] *the Smoking Mountain* [bottom line printed in white] | [borzoi device] | [horizontal white] *ALFRED A.* | *KNOPF* Back: White printed in black and orange. An advertisement for *Generation Without Farewell* with excerpts from four reviews. Front flap: A short note about *The Smoking Mountain*. $4.95 | S.M. | A.A.K. [upper right]. Jacket design by Muriel Nasser. Back flap: Continuation of front flap,

Publication: First published in March 18, 1963 at $4.95.

A25e   THE SMOKING MOUNTAIN: [1968]
                     STORIES OUT OF POST WAR GERMANY

Second American Edition Second Printing:

[device] | [nine small flags] | [double rule: thick-thin] | [row of fifteen small circles] | THE Smoking | MOUNTAIN | *Stories of* | *Germany during the Occupation* | BY | KAY BOYLE | *With a Foreword by* WILLIAM L. SHIRER | [publisher's device] | *New York* : *Alfred • A • Knopf* | 1968

Collation: Same as A25d.

Contents: Same as A25d except on the verso of the unpaginated leaf the following books are added: *Nothing Ever Breaks Except the Heart* (1966), *Pinky, the Cat Who Liked to Sleep* (1965), *Being Geniuses Together, 1920-1930* (1968) and *Autobiography of Emanuel Carnevali* (Edited by Kay Boyle 1967).

Copyright page: Same as A25d with following exception: Text after All rights reserved now becomes: All rights reserved under International and Pan- | American Copyright Conventions. Published in the | United States by Alfred A. Knopf, Inc., New York, | and in Canada by Random House of Canada | Limited, Toronto. Distributed by Random House, | Inc., New York. | This collection of stories was first published by | McGraw-Hill Book Company, Inc., in 1951. | BORZOI EDITION PUBLISHED MARCH 18, 1963 | SECOND PRINTING, JULY 1968

Binding: Everything the same as A25d except bound totally in teal green cloth covered boards.

Dust jacket: Same as A25d with following exceptions: Back flap now states that Miss Boyle makes her home in San Francisco and the blurbs on the back of the jacket about *Generation Without Farewell* are replaced with blurbs about *The Smoking Mountain.*

Publication: Published in July 1968 at $4.95.

A26a   THE SEAGULL ON THE STEP   1955

First Edition:

Kay Boyle | the | Seagull | on | the | Step | NEW YORK | ALFRED A KNOPF |1955 [There is a publisher's device on line with Alfred A Knopf and 1955]

Collation: [i-viii], [1-2], 3-247, [248] pages; cream endpapers. 8 $^1/_8$" x 5 $^1/_2$" [A-H]^{16}

Contents: (i) blank; (ii) [list]: *Books by Kay Boyle* [twenty-one titles]; (iii) half title page; (iv) blank; (v) title page; (vi) copyright page; (vii) [dedication]: THIS BOOK IS DEDICATED IN LOVE TO | those young people who are the flesh and spirit | of the new France (and who have, in consequence, | no time or need to read these pages), among | them my children who are there.; (viii) blank; (1) fly title; (2) blank; (3-247) text; (248) a note on the type.

Copyright page: THIS IS A BORZOI BOOK, PUBLISHED BY ALFRED A. KNOPF, INC. | L.C. catalog card number: *55-5604* | © Kay Boyle, *1955* | Copyright *1955* by KAY BOYLE. All | rights reserved. No part of this | book may be reproduced in any | form without permission in | writing from the publisher, | except by a reviewer who may | quote brief passages in a review to | be printed in a magazine or | newspaper. Published | simultaneously in Canada by | McClelland & Stewart Limited. | Manufactured in the United | States of America. | FIRST EDITION

Binding: Yellow cloth covered boards stamped in green and red. Top stained light blue and top and bottom edges trimmed. Front edge rough trimmed. Front: A yellow K and B outlined in green with alternating slanting green and red lines under the K and B. Spine: [a single slanting red line] | [green] *Kay Boyle* | [another series of green and red rules at different slants across the spine] | [red] the | Sea- | -gull | on

| the | Step | [more alternating blue and red lines] | [green] ALFRED A | KNOPF | [single slanting red line]   Back: A red Borzoi publisher's device.

Dust jacket: White paper printed in gold, maroon, blue and white. Front: An alternating maroon and gold design from top to bottom of the jacket with one blue segment. Printed in white and gold. [white] THE | SEAGULL | ON THE | STEP | [gold] A NOVEL BY | [white] KAY BOYLE There is a white stylized gull in the blue segment. Spine: The spine has the same alternating pattern as the front. [white] THE | SEA | GULL | [maroon] ON THE | [white] STEP | KAY | BOYLE | [blue segment with stylized white gull] | [Borzoi device in gold] | ALFRED | A | KNOPF Back: KAY BOYLE across top. A photograph of Kay Boyle by Louise Dahl-Wolfe. Front flap: Story plot. $3.50 [upper right]. [blue] JACKET DESIGN: Harry Ford. Back flap: A continuation of the front flap.

Publication: First published on May 9, 1955 according to *Publisher's Weekly* at $3.50.

A26b   THE SEAGULL ON THE STEP

First Edition Second Printing:

Kay Boyle | the | Seagull | on | the | Step | NEW YORK | ALFRED A KNOPF |1955 [There is a publisher's device on line with Alfred A Knopf and 1955]

Collation: Same as A26a.

Contents: Same as A26a.

Copyright page: THIS IS A BORZOI BOOK, PUBLISHED BY ALFRED A. KNOPF, INC. | L.C. catalog card number: *55-5604* | © Kay Boyle, *1955* | Copyright *1955* by KAY BOYLE. All | rights reserved. No part of this | book may be reproduced in any | form without permission in | writing from the publisher, | except by a reviewer who may | quote brief passages in a review to | be printed in a magazine or | newspaper. Published | simultaneously in Canada by | McClelland & Stewart Limited. | Manufactured in the United | States of America. | PUBLISHED MAY 9, 1955 | SECOND PRINTING, MAY 1955

Binding: Same as A26a except top edge is not stained.

Dust jacket: Same as A26a.

A26c   THE SEAGULL ON THE STEP   [1955]

First English Edition:

The Seagull on the Step | KAY BOYLE | FABER AND FABER | 24 Russell Square | London

Collation: [1-8], 9-277, [278-280] pages; cream endpapers, 7 $^3/_8$" x 4 $^7/_8$"   [A]^8
B-I^8 K-R^8 S^4

Contents: (1-2) blank; (3) half title page; (4) blank; (5) title page; (6) copyright page; (7) [dedication]: This book is dedicated in love to those young | people who are the flesh and spirit of the new | France (and who have, in consequence, no | time or need to read these pages), among | them my children who are there.; (8) blank; (9-277) text; (278-280) blank.

Copyright page: *First published in mcmlv | by Faber and Faber Limited | 24 Russell Square London W.C.1 | Printed in Great Britain by | Latimer Trend & Co Ltd Plymouth | All rights reserved*

Binding: Light blue cloth covered boards stamped in white.   Top edge unstained. All edges trimmed.   Front: Blank. Spine: *The | Seagull | on the | Step* | [design] | *Kay | Boyle* | Faber   Back: Blank.

Dust jacket: Cream paper printed in gold, maroon, blue and white.   Front and spine: Identical to American edition except that FABER between Kay Boyle and the blue segment replaces the Alfred A. Knopf at the bottom of the spine.   Back: Advertisement for new fiction published by Faber and Faber. Front flap: Story plot. 15s net [lower right].   Back flap: Advertisement and reviews for two novels by William Golding.

Publication: First published on December 2, 1955 at 15s.

A27a   THREE SHORT NOVELS   [1958]

First American Edition:

[script] Three Short Novels | *by* KAY BOYLE | BEACON PRESS *Beacon Hill* Boston

Collation: [i-viii], [1-2], 3-139, [140-142], 143-205, [206-210], 211-262, [263-264] pages.   8" x 5 $^3/_8$"

Contents: (i) blank; (ii) note about Kay Boyle; (iii) title page; (iv) copyright page; (v) [dedication]: To James Stern, no matter how many oceans | or hedgerows stand between; (vi) blank; (vii) table of contents; (viii) blank; (1) [story title]: THE CRAZY HUNTER; (2) blank; (3-139) text; (140) blank; (141) [story title]: THE BRIDEGROOMS BODY; (142) blank; (143-205) text; (206) blank; (207) [story title]: DECISION; (208) blank; (209) [publisher's note]: This novel was first published by the | *Saturday Evening Post* in 1948, under the | title *Passport to Doom.*; (210) blank; (211-262) text; (263-264) blank.

Copyright page: Copyright 1938, 1940, by Kay Boyle; Copyright 1948 by the | Curtis Publishing Company. | *The Crazy Hunter* and *The Bridegroom's Body* were pre- | viously published in a collection called *The Crazy Hunter* by | Harcourt, Brace and Company. | The present collection is first published as a Beacon Paper- | back in 1958. | Manufactured in the United States of America.

Binding: Stiff white wrappers printed in red and black. Top edge unstained. All edges trimmed. Front: Beacon BP 55 $1.60 | kay boyle | The Crazy Hunter | The Bridegroom's Body | Decision | THREE SHORT NOVELS; There are three connected triangles, red, black and yellow top to bottom on the front. Spine: [black] BP | 55 | [downward in red] KAY BOYLE [downward] in black] THREE SHORT NOVELS | [horizontal in black] BEACON | PRESS Back: Statement by Kay Boyle and excerpts from four reviews.

Note: Issued with a yellow wrap around-band printed front and back thus: "THE CRAZY HUNTER *is* | *the story closest to perfection that* | *I have ever read.*" | [A facsimile of Katherine Anne Porter's signature.]

The included stories and their previous publication: "The Crazy Hunter" and "The Bridegroom's Body" were collected in *The Crazy Hunter and Other Stories.* See A17a for previous publication. "Decision" first appeared as "Passport to Doom" in *The Saturday Evening Post*, May 15, 1948.

A27b   THREE SHORT NOVELS   [1982]

Second American Edition:

[script] Three Short Novels | *by* KAY BOYLE | Introduction by Margaret Atwood | [Penguin publishing device] | PENGUIN BOOKS

Collation: [i-vi], vii-x, [1-2], 3-139, [140-142], 143-205, [206-210], 211-262 pages. 7 $^3/_4$" x 5"

Contents: (i) a note on Kay Boyle; (ii) [list]: Books by Kay Boyle [thirty-two titles]; (iii) title page; (iv) copyright page; (v) table of contents; (vi) blank; (vii-x) Introduction; (1) [story title]: THE CRAZY HUNTER; (2) blank; (3-139) text; (140) blank; (141) [story title]: THE BRIDEGROOM'S BODY; (142) blank; (143-205) text; (206) blank; (207) [story title]: DECISION; (208) blank; (209) [publisher's note]: This novel was first published by the | *Saturday Evening Post* in 1948, under the | title *Passport to Doom.* (210) blank; (211-262) text.

Copyright page: *To James Stern, no matter how many oceans* | *or hedgerows stand between* | Penguin Books Ltd, Harmondsworth, | Middlesex, England | Penguin Books, 625 Madison Avenue, | New York, New York 10022, U.S.A. | Penguin Books Australia Ltd, Ringwood, | Victoria, Australia | Penguin Books Canada Limited, 2801 John Street, | Markham, Ontario, Canada L3R 1B4 | Penguin Books (N.Z.) Ltd, 182-190 Wairau Road, | Auckland 10, New Zealand | This collection first published in the United States of America by | the Beacon Press 1958 |

Published in Penguin Books 1982 | Copyright 1938, 1940, by Kay Boyle | Copyright 1948 by the Curtis Publishing Company | Introduction copyright © Margaret Atwood, 1982 | All rights reserved | LIBRARY OF CONGRESS CATALOGING IN PUBLICATION DATA | Boyle, Kay, 1903- | Three short novels. | Reprint. Originally published: Boston: Beacon Press, 1958. | Contents: The crazy hunter—The bridegroom's body—Decision. | I. Title. | PS3503.O9357T54 1982 813'.52 81-21034 | ISBN 0 14 00.6109 6 AACR2 | Printed in the United States of America by | Offset Paperback Mfrs., Inc., Dallas, Pennsylvania | Set in Janson | " The Crazy Hunter" and "The Bridegroom's Body" were previously | published in a collection called *The Crazy Hunter* by Harcourt, Brace | and Company. "Decision" was first published in the *Saturday Evening* | *Post* under the title "Passport to Doom." | Except in the United States of America, this book is sold subject to | the condition that it shall not, by way of trade or otherwise, be lent, | re-sold, hired out, or otherwise circulated without the publisher's prior | consent in any form of binding or cover other than that in which it is | published and without a similar condition including this condition | being imposed on the subsequent purchaser

Binding: Stiff white wraps printed in purple and silver. [large silver 3 with KAY BOYLE IN BLACK printed over and over on the three] | SHORT NOVELS | [rule | THE CRAZY HUNTER • DECISION | • THE BRIDEGROOM'S BODY • | [rule] BY KAY BOYLE | [rule] | INTRODUCTION BY MARGARET ATWOOD | [rule] | "MISS BOYLE IS ONE OF THE BEST SHORT-STORY | WRITER'S IN AMERICA." | —*The New York Times*   Penguin trademark in upper right corner. Spine: [printed downward in black] KAY BOYLE [printed downward in white] THREE SHORT NOVELS [printed downward in black] ISBN 0 14 [over] 00.6109 6 | [publisher's device: Penguin]   Back: Story plots $5.95 [lower left] Printed vertically from bottom to top in white along spine: *Cover design by Neil Stuart.*

A27c   THREE SHORT NOVELS   1991

New Directions:

KAY BOYLE | [rule] | THREE SHORT NOVELS | The Crazy Hunter | The Bridegroom's Body | Decision | Introduction by Doris Grumbach | [publisher's device] | A NEW DIRECTIONS BOOK

Collation: [i-vi], vii-x, [1-2], 3-139, [140-142], 143-205, [206-210], 211-262 pages.   8" x 5 $^1/_4$"

Contents: (i) A REVIVED | MODERN | CLASSIC | [rule] | THREE SHORT NOVELS;   (ii) [list]: ALSO BY KAY BOYLE | [ten tiles]; (iii) title page; (iv) copyright page; (v) table of contents; (vi) blank; (vii-x) introduction;   (1) [story title]: THE CRAZY HUNTER; (2) blank; (3-139) text; (140) blank; (141) [story title]: THE BRIDEGROOM'S BODY; (142) blank; (143-205) text; (206) blank; (207) [story title]: DECISION; (208) blank; (209) [publisher's note]: This novel was first published by the | *Saturday Evening Post* in 1948, under the | title *Passport to Doom*.; (210) blank; (211-262) text.

Copyright page: *To James Stern, no matter how many oceans or hedgerows stand between* | Copyright 1938,1940 by Kay Boyle | Copyright 1948 by the Curtis Publishing Company | Introduction copyright © 1991 by Doris Grumbach | All rights reserved. Except for brief passages quoted in a newspaper, maga- | zine, radio, or television review, no part of this book may be reproduced in | any form or by any means, electronic or mechanical, including photocopying | and recording, or by any information storage and retrieval system, without | permission in writing from the Publisher. | This collection first published by Beacon Press in 1958; Reissued by Penguin | Books in 1982; reissued as a New Directions Paperbook 703 in 1991 as part of | the Revived Modern Classics series. | Manufactured in the United States of America | New Directions Books are printed on acid-free paper. | Published simultaneously in Canada by Penguin Books Canada, Limited | "The Crazy Hunter" and "The Bridegroom's Body" were previ- | ously pub- | lished in a collection called *The Crazy Hunter* by Harcourt, Brace and Com- | pany. "Decision" was first published in the *Saturday Evening Post* under the | title "Passport to Doom." | Library of Congress Cataloging-in-Publication Data | Boyle, Kay, 1902— | [Novels. Selections] | Three short novels / Kay Boyle ; intro- | duction by Doris Grumbach. | p. cm.—(New Directions paperback ; 703) (A Revived modern | classic) | "This collection first published by Beacon Press in 1958"—T.p. | verso. | Contents: The crazy hunter—The bridegroom's body — Decision. | ISBN 0-8112-1149-5 | I. Title. II. Series. | PS3503.09357A6 1991 | 813'.52—dc20 90-47955 | CIP | New Directions Books are published for James Laughlin | by New Directions Publishing Corporation, | 80 Eighth Avenue, New York 10011

Binding: Stiff white wrappers printed in black and red. Front: [black rule inter- | rupted by red publisher's device] | [red] A REVIVED [extension of publisher's device from above] MODERN CLASSIC | [thin black rule] | [thick black rule] | [black] KAY BOYLE | [thin black rule] | [black] THREE SHORT NOVELS | [black] The Crazy Hunter • The Bridegroom's Body • Decision | [red] Introduction by Doris Grumbach | [photograph of the painting The English Blood-Horse "Fidget" by Henry Barnard Chalon]. Spine: [black printed downward] KAY BOYLE [top line] | [thin rule] | THREE SHORT NOVELS [bottom line] | [red publisher's device] | [black printed downward] NDP703 Back: Story plots. Review from *The New York Times Book Review*. Cover painting credit. [price] $10.95 Canada: $15.95 [lower right]

Publication: First published in January 1991 at $10.95.

A28a   THE YOUNGEST CAMEL   [1959]
                   RECONSIDERED AND REWRITTEN

First Edition:

[double spread title page] The YOUNGEST | CAMEL | Reconsidered and
Rewritten | by KAY BOYLE | *Pictures by Ronni Solbert* | HARPER & BROTHERS
| *Publishers* NEW YORK [an illustration of a camel amidst some foliage on both
sides of the double spread page]

Collation: [1-6], 7, [8-9], 10-12, [13-14], 15-18, [19], 20-24, [25], 26-27, [28-29],
30-31, [32], 33-38, [39], 40, [41], 42-43, [44-46], 47-52, [53], 54-55, [56],
57-65, [66], 67-71, [72-73], 74, [75-76], 77-88, [89], 90-94, [95-96] pages; cream
endpapers. 9" x 6 ¹/₂" [A-F]⁸

Contents: (1) half title page; (2-3) title page; (4) copyright page; (5) [dedication]:
For | *Sindbad, Pegeen, Bobby, Apple,* | *Kathe, Clover, Faith,* and *Ian* | and *their chil-
dren;* (6) blank; (7) text; (8-9) text with illustrations on bottom half of the pages;
(10-12) text; (13) illustration; (14) blank; (15-18) text; (19) illustration; (20-24)
text; (25) half text, half illustration; (26-27) text; (28) half text, half illustration; (29)
illustration; (30-31) text; (32) blank; (33-38) text; (39) illustration; (40) text; (41)
illustration; (42-44) text; (45) half text, half illustration; (46) blank; (47-49) text;
(50-51) half text, half illustration; (52) text; (53) half text, half illustration; (54-55)
text; (56) blank; (57-58) text; (59) half text, half illustration; (60-63) text; (64) half
text, half illustration; (65) text; (66) half text, half illustration; (67-71) text; (72-73)
half text, half illustration; (74) text; (75) half text, half illustration; (76) blank;
(77-83) text; (84-85) half text, half illustration; (86-88) text; (89) illustration;
(90-94) text; (95) half text, half illustration; (96) blank.

Copyright page: THE YOUNGEST CAMEL | *Copyright © 1939, 1959 by Kay
Boyle* | *Printed in the United States of America* | *All rights in this book are reserved.* | *No
part of the book may be used or reproduced* | *in any manner whatsoever without written
per-* | *mission except in the case of brief quotations* | *embodied in critical articles and
reviews. For* | *information address Harper & Brothers,* | *49 East 33rd Street, New York
16, N.Y.* | *Library of Congress catalog card number: 58-5286*

Binding: Beige cloth covered boards printed in brown. Top edge unstained and all
edges trimmed. Front: Outline of a sun or a moon. An adult camel laden with goods
being led by an Arab with a small camel following. Spine: [printed downward]
BOYLE THE YOUNGEST CAMEL HARPER Back: Blank.

Dust jacket: White paper pictorial jacket printed in orange and white. Front: THE
YOUNGEST | CAMEL | by KAY BOYLE | pictures by Ronni Solbert. There is an
illustration of a white camel in a sultan's conveyance towed by two camels front and
back with a small camel alongside. Spine: [printed downward] BOYLE THE
YOUNGEST CAMEL HARPER Back: A photograph of Kay Boyle by Pach
Brothers, New York and a short note about Kay Boyle. No. 5633 [lower left]. Front

flap: Story plot. $2.75 [upper right] 70 up | No. 8999A [lower left]. Back flap: A continuation of the front flap and a short note about the artist Ronni Solbert. No. 9000A [lower left].

Note: A Harpercrest library binding was also examined with the following differences: the binding was orange cloth printed in black and white with the same design on the front and the same printing on the spine. The back states that "This is the Harpercrest Library Binding" with the binding specifications all enclosed in a black ruled rectangle. The endpapers are cream with a repeating Harpercrest interlocking design. The dust jacket is the same except that there is a Harpercrest label around the lower portion of the spine with instructions to see the back cover of the book for the Harpercrest binding specifications.

Publication: First published on August 5, 1959 according to *Publisher's Weekly* at $2.75.

A28b   THE YOUNGEST CAMEL   [1963]
                         RECONSIDERED AND REWRITTEN

First Edition Second Printing:

[double spread title page] THE YOUNGEST | CAMEL | Reconsidered and Rewritten | by KAY BOYLE | *Pictures by Ronni Solbert* | HARPER & ROW, PUBLISHERS | *New York, Evanston, and London*

Collation: Same as A28a except end papers are dark blue heavy paper.

Contents: Same as A28a.

Copyright page: THE YOUNGEST CAMEL | *Copyright © 1939, 1959 by Kay Boyle | Printed in the United States of America | All rights in this book are reserved. | No part of the book may be used or reproduced | in any manner whatsoever without written per- | mission except in the case of brief quotations | embodied in critical articles and reviews. For | information address Harper & Row, Publishers, | Incorporated, | 49 East 33rd Street, New York, N.Y.* 10016 | *Library of Congress catalog card number:* 58-5286

Binding: Bound in orange pictorial cloth identical to the dust jacket of the first issue with Harper Row on the spine instead of Harper.   Spine: [printed downward in white] BOYLE THE YOUNGEST CAMEL HARPER [top row] & ROW [bottom row]   Back: [a small box in the lower right corner in which was printed in black] This is the | HARPER [design] CREST | LIBRARY BINDING

Dust jacket: The dust jacket was identical to A28a except HARPER | & ROW instead of just HARPER at the base of the spine. There is a small gold paste-on band on which is printed HARPER [design] CREST. Back: Omits No. 5633. Front flap: States HARPER & ROW instead of HARPER & BROTHERS | *Publishers.* Omits

70 up | No. 8999A   [lower right] $2.92. Upper right hand corner is clipped. Back flap: HARPER AND ROW | *Publishers* instead of HARPER & BROTHERS. Omits No. 9000A.

A28c   THE YOUNGEST CAMEL   1960
                    RECONSIDERED AND REWRITTEN

First English Edition:

Publication: Book not located or examined but published June 10, 1960 by Faber & Faber at 12s 6d according to The English Catalogue of Books, volume XIX, 1960-1962.

A29a   GENERATION WITHOUT FAREWELL   1960

First Edition:

Generation | Without Farewell | by Kay Boyle | [publishers device] *1960 | Alfred A. Knopf / New York*

Collation: [i-xii], [1-2], 3-300, [301-308] pages; cream endpapers. 7 $^7/_8$" x 5" [A-J]^{16}

Contents: (i-iii) blank; (iv) [list]: BOOKS *by Kay Boyle* [twenty-two titles]; (v) half title page; (vi) a quotation from Wolfgang Borchert (vii) title page; (viii) copyright page; (ix) [dedication]: *For Siegfried*; (x) blank; (xi-xii) list of principal characters; (1) [fly title]: Generation | Without Farewell | [single rule]; (2) blank; (3-301) text; (302) blank; (303) a note about Kay Boyle; (304) a note on the type; (305-308) blank.

Copyright page: [publisher's device] | L.C. Catalog card number: 59-11822 | © Kay Boyle, 1959 | [single rule] | THIS IS A BORZOI BOOK, | PUBLISHED BY ALFRED A. KNOPF, INC. | [single rule] | Copyright 1959 by Kay Boyle. | All rights reserved. No part of this book may be re- | produced in any form without permission in writing from | the publisher, except by a reviewer who may quote brief | passages in a review to be printed in a magazine or news- | paper. Manufactured in the United States of America. | Published simultaneously in Canada by McClelland & | Stewart Ltd. | FIRST EDITION | The title, epigraph, and other quotations used in this | book are from *The Man Outside* by Wolfgang Borchert, | translated by David Porter, published by New Directions | and reprinted with their permission. All rights reserved.

Binding: Bound with green cloth spine and red paper covered boards printed in black and red. Top edge stained black. All edges trimmed. Front: [black loop design with the initials K and B in the loops.] Spine: [red design] | [black] *Genera-* |

tion | *Without* | *Farewell* | [black rule] | *Kay* | *Boyle* | [red design] | [red] *Knopf* Back: [blind stamp of the Borzoi device]

Dust jacket: White paper printed in gold, cream, blue, green, and red. Front: From top to bottom there is a series of multi-colored slats like a venetian blind broken at the bottom with the last slat dangling. [white on red slats] GENERATION | WITHOUT | FAREWELL | [red printed on cream in script] A Novel by | Kay Boyle | [bottom right hand corner in blue] Salter   Spine: [red] Gener- | ation | Without | Farewell | [Short gold bar] | [blue script] Kay Boyle | [red and white Borzoi device] | [blue script] Alfred A. | Knopf   Back: Photograph of Kay Boyle in blue sepia by Louise Dahl-Wolfe.   Front flap: Story plot. $3.95 [upper right].   *Typography, binding, and jacket designs by* George Salter.   Back flap: A biographical note about Kay Boyle.

Publication: First published on January 18, 1960 according to *Publisher's Weekly* at $3.95.

A29b   GENERATION WITHOUT FAREWELL   1960

First Edition Second Printing:

Generation | *Without Farewell* | *by Kay Boyle* | [publisher's device] *1960* | *Alfred A. Knopf* | *New York*

Collation: Same as A29a.

Contents: Same as A29a.

Copyright page: PUBLISHED JANUARY 18, 1960 | SECOND PRINTING, JANUARY 1960 substituted for FIRST EDITION; otherwise the same as A29a.

Binding: Same as A29a.

Dust jacket: Same as A29a.

Publication: Printed in January 1960.

A29c   GENERATION WITHOUT FAREWELL   1960

First Edition Third Printing:

Generation | *Without Farewell* | *by Kay Boyle* | [publisher's device] *1960* | *Alfred A. Knopf* | *New York*

Collation: Same as A29a.

Contents: Same as A29a.

Copyright page: PUBLISHED JANUARY 18, 1960 | SECOND PRINTING, JANUARY 1960 | THIRD PRINTING, FEBRUARY 1960 substituted for FIRST EDITION; otherwise the same as the first printing.

Binding: Same as A29a.

Dust jacket: Same as A29a except that seven excerpts from reviews for *Generation Without Farewell* replace the photograph.

Publication: Printed in February 1960 at $3.95.

A29d   GENERATION WITHOUT FAREWELL   [1960]

First English Edition:

Generation | Without Farewell | by Kay Boyle | Faber and Faber | 24 Russell Square London

Collation: [i-viii], [1-2], 3-300, [301-304] pages; cream endpapers.   7 $\frac{1}{4}$" x 4 $\frac{7}{8}$" [A]⁶ B-I⁸ K-T⁸ U⁶

Contents: (i) blank; (ii) [list]: *by the same author* [nineteen titles]; (iii) half title page; (iv) a quotation by Wolfgang Borchert; (v) title page; (vi) copyright page; (vii) [dedication]: For Siegfried; (viii) blank; (1-2) list of characters; (3-301) text; (302-304) blank.

Copyright page: *First published in England in mcmlx | by Faber and Faber Limited | 24 Russell Square London W.C.1 | Printed in Great Britain | by D. R. Hillman & Sons Ltd., Frome | All rights reserved |* The title, epigraph, and other quotations used in this | book are from *The Man Outside* by Wolfgang Borchert, | translated by David Porter, published by Hutchinson & | Co. and reprinted with their permission. All rights reserved. | Copyright Kay Boyle, 1959

Binding: Bound in reddish orange cloth covered boards stamped in yellow. Top edge unstained. All edges trimmed. Front: Blank. Spine: [printed downward] GENERATION WITHOUT FAREWELL [top line] by Kay Boyle [bottom line] | [horizontal] Faber Back: Blank.

Dust jacket: White paper with same design and colorization as the American edition. Front: Same as American edition except the name Salter is not present at the bottom. Spine: [black] Gener- | ation | Without | Farewell | [red bar] | by | KAY | BOYLE | [blue bar] | [red] Faber | [yellow bar]   Back: Story plot and advertisement for *The Youngest Camel* by Kay Boyle.   Front flap: Story plot. 18s | net [lower right] *Jacket design by George Salter.* Back flap: Reviews for *The Seagull on the Step* by Kay Boyle.

Publication: First published on July 8, 1960 at 18s.

A30a COLLECTED POEMS 1962

First Edition:

COLLECTED | POEMS | KAY BOYLE | [design] | [single rule] | [borzoi device] | *New York • Alfred • A • Knopf* | 1962

Collation: [i-xii], [1-2], 3-25, [26-28], 29-37, [38-40], 41-95, [96-98], 99-105, [106-116] pages; cream endpapers. 8 $^3/_8$" x 5 $^1/_4$" [A-D]^{16}

Contents: (i) blank; (ii) [list]: BOOKS BY *Kay Boyle* [twenty-three titles]; (iii) half title page; (iv) blank; (v) title page; (vi) copyright page; (vii) [dedication]: FOR | *William Carlos Williams* | WHO, AS MAN AND POET, | ILLUMINATES THE WAY; (viii) blank; (ix) [publisher's note]: ACKNOWLEDGMENTS | The Poems in Part II: 1926-1943 of this volume appeared | in the collection *A Glad Day*, published by New Directions | in 1938. *American Citizen* was originally published by | Simon and Schuster, Inc., in 1944. Grateful acknowledg- | ment is made to the above pub- lishers to reprint these | poems in this book, and to the editors of the following | pub- lications, where some of the poems from Part I: 1954- | 1961 first appeared: *Ladies' Home Journal, The Nation,* | *Poetry, Saturday Review,* and *The Outsider.*; (x) blank; (xi-xii) table of contents; (1) [divisional title]: *PART • I* | 1954-1961; (2) blank; (3-25) Text; (26) blank; (27) [divisional title]: Poems for a Painter; (28) blank; (29-37) text; (38) blank; (39) [divisional title]: *PART • II* | 1926-1943; (40) blank; (41-95) text; (96) blank; (97) [divisional title]: AN EXCERPT FROM THE POEM | *American Citizen* | *Dedicated to* Carson McCullers; (98) blank; (99-106) text; (107) blank; (108) a note about the author; (109) blank; (110) a note on the type; (111-116) blank.

Copyright page: *L.C. catalog card number: 62-14759* | [rule] | THIS IS A BORZOI BOOK, | PUBLISHED BY ALFRED A. KNOPF, INC. | [rule] | Copyright 1938, 1944, 1954, © 1956, 1959, 1960, 1961, | 1962 by Kay Boyle; © 1957 by The Curtis Publishing | Company. All rights reserved. No part of this book may be | reproduced in any form without permission in writing from | the publisher, except by a reviewer, who may quote brief | passages in a review to be printed in a magazine or news- | paper. Manufactured in the United States of America, and | distributed by Random House, Inc. Published simultane- | ously in Toronto, Canada, by Random House of Canada, | Limited. | FIRST EDITION

Binding: Bound in pinkish red cloth covered boards and stamped in dark red. Top edge stained blue. Top and bottom edges trimmed. Front edge untrimmed. Front: [a dark red stamp allowing the initials KB show through in the red cloth. Spine: [printed downward in dark red] KAY BOYLE [design] COLLECTED POEMS [horizontal design in dark red] | [horizontal] *Knopf* Back: Stamped Borzoi device in lower right corner.

Dust jacket: Cream paper printed in cream, rust and black. Front: [cream] Collected | Poems | [black] Kay Boyle | [white] Alfred A. Knopf [black]

PUBLISHER | [black] NEW YORK.   [black Borzoi device on line with PUBLISHER and NEW YORK]   Spine: [printed downward in black] KAY BOYLE [design] [printed downward in cream] COLLECTED POEMS | [black Borzoi device] | [horizontal in cream] *Knopf*   Back: A 1961 poem: "Print from a Lucite Block" printed in black on cream. Front flap: Discussion of Kay Boyle's poetry. $4.00 [upper right].   *Typography, binding and jacket design by* Vincent Torre. Back flap: A short note about Kay Boyle.

Publication: First published on August 13, 1962 at $4.00.

The included poems and their previous publication: "Dreams Dreamed" first appeared in *The Saturday Review*, April 4, 1959. "October 1954" first appeared in *The Nation*, October 30, 1954. "Spring" first appeared in *The Ladies Home Companion*, March 1957. "A Poem of Gratitude" first appeared in *Poetry Magazine*, March 1959. "Two Poems for a Poet" first appeared in *Poetry Magazine*, February 1961. "Two Twilights for William Carlos Williams" first appeared in *Poetry Magazine*, March 1960. "A Dialogue of Birds for Howard Nemerov" first appeared in *Poetry Magazine*, March 1960. "The New Emigration" first appeared in *The Nation*, September 22, 1956. "Rendezvous" first appeared in *Poetry Magazine*, January 1962. "A Poem for a Painter Who Drinks Wine" first appeared in *The Nation*, January 14, 1961. "Print from a Lucite Block" first appeared in *Outsider*, Fall 1960. "Seascape for an Engraver" first appeared in *Poetry Magazine*, January, 1962. "Carnival 1927" first appeared in *This Quarter*, April 1927. "A Glad Day for Laurence Vail," "A Landscape for Wyn Henderson," "A Complaint for Mary and Marcel," "A Comeallye for Robert Brown," "A Communication to Nancy Cunard," "A Statement for El Greco and William Carlos Williams," "A Christmas Carol for Emanuel Carnevali," "The Only Bird That Sang," "Hunt," "O This Is Not Spring," "Dedicated to Guy Urquhart," "To America," "For an American," "Funeral in Hungary," and "And Winter" were all collected in *A Glad Day*. See A15a for previous publication. "American Citizen" was originally published by Simon and Schuster, 1944. "A Night Letter," "A Winter Fable," "The Artist Speaks—The Woman Answers," "The Painter Speaks—The Woman Answers," and "The Evening Grass" appear here for the first time.

A31a   BREAKING THE SILENCE   [1962]

First Edition:

Breaking the Silence | Why A Mother Tells Her Son | About the Nazi Era | by Kay Boyle | INSTITUTE OF HUMAN RELATIONS PRESS | The American Jewish Committee | 165 East 56 Street, New York 22, N.Y.

Collation: [1-2], 3-39, [40] pages.   Stapled wrappers.   9" x 6"

Contents: Inside the front cover: a note on the Institute of Human Relations Press. (1) title page; (2) copyright page; (3-4) foreword by John Slawson; (5-38) text;

(39) bibliography of references; (40) [price]: *Single Copy*, 35¢ | *Quantity prices on request*

Copyright page: [A short note about Kay Boyle] | *Copyright © 1962 by Kay Boyle* | *All Rights Reserved* | *Printed in the United States of America* | *First Edition*

Binding: White stapled wrappers printed in two-toned green, black and white. All edges trimmed. Front: [black] *Breaking the Silence* | [white] Why A Mother Tells Her Son | About the Nazi Era | [black] by Kay Boyle | [white] INSTITUTE OF HUMAN RELATIONS PRESS | PAMPHLET SERIES [white shield]. There is a photo in lower left hand corner of Nazi youths giving the Nazi salute. Back: [all in black] INSTITUTE OF HUMAN RELATIONS PRESS | The American Jewish Committee | 165 East 56 Street, New York 22, N.Y. | September 1962 [DESIGN] 150

Publication: First published in September 1962.

A31b   BREAKING THE SILENCE   [1963]

First Edition Second Printing:

Breaking the Silence | Why A Mother Tells Her Son | About the Nazi Era | by Kay Boyle | INSTITUTE OF HUMAN RELATIONS PRESS | The American Jewish Committee | 165 East 56 Street, New York 22, N.Y.

Collation: Contents, and copyright page the same as A31a.

Binding: The same as A31a except that on the back cover in the lower left corner the following appears: Second Printing, January 1963 instead of September 1962

A32a   NOTHING EVER BREAKS EXCEPT THE HEART   1966

First Edition:

KAY BOYLE | [single rule] | *Nothing Ever Breaks* | *Except the Heart* | [design] | 1966 | *Doubleday & Company, Inc., Garden City, New York*

Collation: [1-11], 12-25, [26], 27-49, [50], 51-81, [82], 83-98, [99-101], 102-129, [130], 131-197, [198], 199-218, [219-221], 222-338, [339], 340-345, [346], 347-357, [358-360] pages; red endpapers. 8 $^3/_{16}$" x 5 $^1/_2$"   1-7^{12} [8-15] ^{12}

Contents: (1) half title page; (2) [list]: *Books by Kay Boyle* [twenty-six titles]; (3) title page; (4) copyright page; (5) [dedication]: For Ann Watkins Burlingame | with my devotion; (6) blank; (7) table of contents; (8) blank; (9) [divisional title]: PEACE | [rule] | [design]; (10) blank; (11-98) text; (99) [divisional title]: WAR YEARS |

[rule] | [design]; (100) blank; (101-218) text; (219) [divisional title]: MILITARY OCCUPATION | [rule] | [design]; (220) blank; (221-357) text; (358-360) blank.

Copyright page: *All of the characters in this book | are fictitious, and any resemblance | to actual persons, living or dead, | is purely coincidental.* | From *The New Yorker:* "Nothing Ever Breaks Except the Heart," "Army of | Occupation," and "Evening at Home" Copyright © 1941,1947, 1948, re- | spectively, by The New Yorker Magazine, Inc. | From *Tomorrow:* "French Harvest" Copyright 1948 by Garrett Publications, | Inc. | LIBRARY OF CONGRESS CATALOG CARD NUMBER 66-15667 | COPYRIGHT © 1939, 1942, 1943, 1945, 1950, 1953, 1955, | 1963, 1964,1965, 1966 BY KAY BOYLE | ALL RIGHTS RESERVED | PRINTED IN THE UNITED STATES OF AMERICA | FIRST EDITION

Binding: Bound in black cloth covered boards stamped in gold. Top edge unstained. Top and bottom edge trimmed. Front edge rough trimmed. Front: The initials KB blind stamped. Spine: KAY | BOYLE | *Nothing | Ever | Breaks | Except | the Heart* | DOUBLEDAY   Back: Blank.

Dust jacket: White paper jacket printed in black, maroon, red, and green. Front: [black script] Nothing | ever | breaks | [maroon script] except | the | [red script] heart | [green script] Kay Boyle   Spine: Printed downward. [black] Nothing ever breaks [maroon] except the [red] heart [green] Kay Boyle [horizontal in black] Doubleday   Back: Photograph of Kay Boyle by Phiz Mozesson. Front flap: A note about the stories. $4.95 in upper right corner with the corner clipped. Back flap: A continuation of the front flap with a short note about Kay Boyle.

Publication: First published on June 24, 1966 at $4.95.

The included stories and their previous publication: "Seven Say You Can Hear Corn Grow" first appeared in *The Saturday Evening Post*, April 9, 1966 as "Wild Horses." "You Don't Have to Be a Member of the Congregation" first appeared in *Liberation*, April 1966. "The Ballet of Central Park" first appeared in *The Saturday Evening Post*, November 28, 1964. "One Sunny Morning" first appeared in *The Saturday Evening Post*, July 3, 1965. "Should Be Considered Extremely Dangerous" first appeared in *Story Magazine*, January/February 1963. "Evening at Home" first appeared in *The New Yorker*, October 9, 1948. "Anschluss" first appeared in *Harper's Magazine*, April 1939 and also in *O. Henry Memorial Award Prize Stories of 1939*, Garden City: Doubleday, Doran & Company, 1939 and in *The Best Short Stories 1940*, Boston: Houghton, Mifflin Company, 1940. "Nothing Ever Breaks Except the Heart" first appeared in *The New Yorker*, October 4, 1941 and also in *The Best American Short Stories 1942*, Boston: Houghton Mifflin Company, 1942 and in *Fifty Best American Short Stories: 1915-1965*, Boston: Houghton Mifflin Company, 1965. "Luck for the Road" first appeared in *The Woman's Home Companion*, January 1944 and also in *A Diamond of Years*, Garden City: Doubleday and Company, 1961. "The Little Distance" first appeared in *The Saturday Evening Post*, March 6, 1943. "Frenchman's Ship" first appeared in *The Saturday Evening Post*, November 21, 1942 and also in

The Best American Short Stories 1943, Boston: Houghton Mifflin Company, 1943 and in *The Saturday Evening Post Stories: 1942-1945*, New York: Random House, 1946. "Hotel Behind the Lines" first appeared in *The Nation*, January 9 and 16, 1945. "The Kill" first appeared in *Harper's Magazine*, August 1955. "A Disgrace to the Family" first appeared in *The Saturday Evening Post*, September 23, 1950 and also in *Saturday Evening Post Stories 1950*, New York: Random House, 1951. "The Soldier Ran Away" first appeared in *The Saturday Evening Post*, February 28, 1953 and also in *Saturday Evening Post Stories 1953*, New York: Random House, 1954. "French Harvest" first appeared in *Tomorrow*, May 1948. "Army of Occupation" first appeared in *The New Yorker*, June 7, 1947. "A Puzzled Race" first appeared in *The Nation*, June 4, 1955. "Fire in the Vineyards" first appeared in *The Saturday Evening Post*, July 2, 1966. "A Christmas Carol for Harold Ross" appears here for the first time.

A33a   PINKY, THE CAT WHO LIKED TO SLEEP   [1966]

First Edition:

Pinky, the Cat | Who Liked to Sleep | [design] | *by* Kay Boyle | *illustrated by* Lilian Obligado | The Crowell-Collier Press, *New York* | Collier-Macmillan Ltd., *London*

Collation: [1-4], 5-6, [7], 8, [9-10], 11-12, [13], 14-15, [16-17], 18-20, [21], 22, [23], 24, [25], 26-28, [29-32] pages; white endpapers. 8 $^1/_2$" x 6" [A-B] ^{8}

Contents: (1) half title page; (2) illustration; (3) title page; (4) copyright page; (5) text with illustration; (6) text; (7) text with illustration; (8) text; (9-11) text with illustrations; (12) text; (13) text with illustration; (14) text; (15-18) text with illustrations; (19-20) text; (21) illustration; (22) text; (23) text with illustration; (24) text; (25) text with illustration; (26) text; (27-32) text with illustration.

Copyright Page: *Copyright © 1966 by Kay Boyle | Copyright © 1966 by The Macmillan Company | All rights reserved. No part of this book may be reproduced or | utilized in any form or by any means, electronic or mechanical, including | photocopying, recording or by any information storage and retrieval | system, without permission in writing from the Publisher. | Library of Congress Catalog Card Number: 66-15375 | The Macmillan Company, New York | Collier-Macmillan Canada Ltd., Toronto, Ontario | Printed in the United States of America | First Printing*

Binding: Bound in yellow pictorial cloth covered boards printed in black, white, blue and green.   Front: Pinky, the Cat | who liked to sleep | by KAY BOYLE | Illustrated by LILIAN OBLIGADO | [illustration of a cat sleeping with its head on a broken flower pot with a toad looking out of the broken side of the pot and with a grasshopper in the lower right corner.] | A BEGINNING READER   Spine: [printed downward] Kay Boyle Pinky, the Cat Who Liked to Sleep | Crowell-Collier Press   Back: [sketch of a dog and a dragonfly]   Note: Library edition has the following text on the back panel.   CROWELL-COLLIER PRESS | LIBRARY EDITION | 71179

Dust jacket: White paper jacket printed identically to the covers without the text on the back panel. Front flap: Story plot. Back flap: A short note about Kay Boyle and one about Lilian Obligado.

Publication: First published in October 1966 at $2.95.   Library Edition: $3.24

A33b   PINKY, THE CAT WHO LIKED TO SLEEP   [1968]

First Edition Second Printing:

Pinky, the Cat | Who Liked to Sleep | [design] | *by* Kay Boyle | *illustrated by* Lilian Obligado | Crowell-Collier Press, *New York* | Collier-Macmillan Ltd., *London*

Collation: Same as A33a.

Contents: Same as A33a.

Copyright Page: Copyright © 1966 by Kay Boyle | Copyright © 1966 by The Macmillan Company | All rights reserved. No part of this book may be | reproduced or transmitted in any form or by any means, | electronic or mechanical, including photocopying, recording | or by any information storage and retrieval system, without | permission in writing from the Publisher. | Library of Congress Catalog Card Number: 66-15375 | The Macmillan Company, New York | Collier-Macmillan Canada Ltd., Toronto, Ontario | Printed in the United States of America | Second Printing 1968

Binding: Same as A33a except that A BEGINNING READER is dropped on the front cover.

Dust jacket: Same as A33a except that A BEGINNING READER is dropped on the front cover.

A33c   PINKY, THE CAT WHO LIKED TO SLEEP   [1970]

First Edition Third Printing:

Pinky, the Cat | Who Liked to Sleep | [design] | *by* Kay Boyle | *illustrated by* Lilian Obligado | Crowell-Collier Press | Collier-Macmillan Limited., *London*

Collation: Same as A33a.

Contents: Same as A33a.

Copyright Page: Copyright © 1966 by Kay Boyle | Copyright © 1966 by The Macmillan Company | All rights reserved. No part of this book may be | reproduced or transmitted in any form or by any means, | electronic or mechanical, including photocopying, recording | or by any information storage or retrieval system, without | permission in writing from the Publisher. | Library of Congress Catalog Card Number: 66-15375 | The Macmillan Company | 866 Third Avenue, New York, New York 10022 | Collier-Macmillan Canada Ltd., Toronto, Ontario | Printed in the United States of America | Third Printing 1970

Binding: Bound in yellow pictorial cloth covered boards printed in black, white, blue and green.   Front: [all of the following on yellow square background] Pinky, the Cat | who liked to sleep | by KAY BOYLE | [illustration on the yellow square of a cat sleeping with its head on a broken flower pot with a toad looking out of the broken side of the pot and with a grasshopper in the lower right corner.]   Spine: Kay Boyle   PINKY, THE CAT WHO·LIKED TO SLEEP Crowell Collier Press Back: [black sketch of a dragonfly] | 71177   Note: Also seen in alternate binding thus: Bound in green cloth covered boards printed in black, white, yellow and gray with no number on the back.

Dust jacket: Not seen.

Publication: First printed on April 3, 1970.

A33d   PINKY, THE CAT WHO LIKED TO SLEEP   [1967]

First English Edition:

Publication: No copy located or examined, but published in February 1967 at 15s by Collier-Macmillan Limited according to *British Books in Print 1969*. Title is listed as *Pinky, the Cat Who Loved to Sleep*. Also there was a note in the *London Times Literary Supplement* on November 30, 1967 about this book using the correct title.

A34a   PINKY IN PERSIA   [1968]

First Edition:

PINKY in PERSIA | [a drawing of a cat and a frog under an umbrella surrounded in a decorative frame] | *by* KAY BOYLE | *Illustrated by Lilian Obligado* | *Crowell-Collier Press, New York*

Collation: [1-32] pages; orange endpapers. 8 $^1/_2$" x 6" [A-B]^8

Contents: (1) title page; (2) copyright page; (3) half title page; (4) illustration; (5-7) illustration and text; (8) illustration; (9-10) illustration and text; (11-12) illustrations; (13-15) illustrations and text; (16) text; (17-18) illustrations; (19) illustration and text: (20) text; (21) illustration and text; (22) illustration; (23) text; (24) Illustration and text; (25) illustration; (26) illustration and text; (27) text; (28) illustration and text; (29) illustration; (30) illustration and text; (31) illustration; (32) illustration and text.

Copyright page: Copyright © 1968 by Kay Boyle | Copyright © 1968 by The Macmillan Company | All rights reserved. No part of this book may be | reproduced or transmitted in any form or by any means, | electronic or mechanical, including photocopying, recording | or by any information storage and retrieval system, without | permission in writing from the Publisher. | Library of Congress Catalog Card Number: 68-18472 | The Macmillan Company, New York | Collier-Macmillan Canada Ltd., Toronto, Ontario | Printed in the United States of America | FIRST PRINTING

Binding: Bound in white imitation cloth covered boards. Printed in orange, pink, yellow, and black. Front: [orange] PINKY in PERSIA | [A gray cat sitting on a pink Persian rug, yellow background with a pink border; all framed in a black decorative design.] | *by* KAY BOYLE | *Illustrated by Lilian Obligado* | [The preceding two lines bracketed by a floral design on each side.] Spine: [printed downward] [black] BOYLE [orange] PINKY in PERSIA | [black] *Crowell-Collier Press*   Back: A repeat of the picture on the front with the number 71182 in the lower right corner.

Dust jacket: White paper printed in orange, pink, yellow, and black. Front: Identical to the front of the binding. Spine: Same as the binding. Back: Same as binding. Front flap: Story plot. $3.50 [upper right]. Back flap: Continuation of front flap, with a note on Kay Boyle and Lilian Obligado.

Publication: Published the week of October 8, 1968 according to *Publisher's Weekly* at $3.50.

A35a   BEING GENIUSES TOGETHER   1968

First Edition:

[double spread title page] [Left Page] *Robert McAlmon* | *Revised and with supplementary chapters by* | *Kay Boyle* [right page] *Being* | *Geniuses* | *Together* | *1920-1930* | *Doubleday & Company, Inc., Garden City, New York* | 1968

Collation: [i-xi], xii, [xiii], xiv, [xv-xvi], [1], 2-10, [11], 12-26, [27], 28-42, [43], 44-53, [54-55], 56-70, [71], 72-80, [81], 82-90, [91], 92-97, [98-99], 100-112, [113], 114-120, [121], 122-132, [133], 134-143, [144-145], 146-153, [154-155], 156-174, [175], 176-189, [190-191], 192-215, [216-217], 218-231, [232-233], 234-245, [246-247], 248-262, [263], 264-272, [273], 274-288, [289], 290-304, [305], 306-317, [318-319], 320-340, [341], 342-348, [349], 350-373, [374-375], 376-392 pages; olive green endpapers. 9 $^1/_8$" x 6" 1-8^{12} [9-17]^{12}

Contents: (i) blank; (ii) [list]: *Books by Kay Boyle*; (iii) half title page; (iv-v) double spread title page; (vi) acknowledgments and copyright page; (vii) [dedication]: *To my five daughters | and the memory of Pegeen*; (viii) blank; (ix) acknowledgments; (x) photo credits; (xi) list of illustrations; (xii) list of illustration continued; (xiii-xiv) a note on Robert McAlmon; (xv) an excerpt from a poem by Robert McAlmon; (xvi) blank; (1-53) text; (54) blank; (55-97) text; (98) blank; (99-143) text; (144) blank; (145-153) text; (154) blank; (155-189) text; (190) blank; (191-215) text; (216) blank; (217-231) text; (232) blank; (233-245) text; (246) blank; (247-317) text; (318) blank; (319-373) text; (374) blank; (375-392) index.

Copyright page: [List of Acknowledgments of previous publication.] | LIBRARY OF CONGRESS CATALOG CARD NUMBER 68-11759 | COPYRIGHT © 1968 BY KAY BOYLE | ALL RIGHTS RESERVED | FIRST EDITION IN THE UNITED STATES OF AMERICA

Illustrations: Black and white glossy photographs. 1 through 27 between pages 128 and 129. 29 through 53 between pages 248 and 249.

Binding: Spine is beige cloth, the front and the back in brown cloth covered boards stamped in rust brown and gold. Top edge unstained and all edges trimmed. Front: [blind stamp] *R • McA | K • B* Spine: [rust] *Robert | McAlmon |* [*rust square printed in gold*] *BEING | GENIUSES | TOGETHER |* [outside the square in rust] *Kay | Boyle* | [gold] *Doubleday*. Back: Blank.

Dust jacket: White paper printed in black, yellowish brown and rust with four photos on the front. Front: [rust] BEING | GENIUSES | TOGETHER | A moving and entertaining diptych *Kay Boyle—* | that reveals what Paris | meant to the lost generation *Robert McAlmon* | [grouping of four framed photographs] Spine: [black] *Kay | Boyle— | Robert | McAlmon* | [printed downward in rust] BEING GENIUSES [top line] TOGETHER [bottom line] | [horizontal in black] Doubleday. Back: [printed in black on white] Excerpts from reviews by Harry T. Moore and Padraic Colum. Front flap: Story plot. $6.95 [upper right]. Back flap: A note on Kay Boyle. Jacket typography by Patricia Saville Voehl. Jacket design by Alex Gotfryd.

Note: A book was originally published under this title by Robert McAlmon in 1938. Kay Boyle revised it and wrote alternating chapters and republished it in 1968.

Publication: First published on June 7, 1968 according to *Publisher's Weekly* at $6.95.

A35b   BEING GENIUSES TOGETHER   [1970]

First English Edition:

Robert McAlmon | Being Geniuses | Together | 1920-1930 | *Revised and with supplementary chapters by* | Kay Boyle | [publishers device] | *Michael Joseph | London*

Collation: [i-ix], x, [xi], xii, [xiii-xiv], [1], 2-9, [10-11], 12-24, [25], 26-38, [39], 40-48, [49], 50-62, [63], 64-71, [72-73], 74-81, [82-83], 84-88, [89], 90-101, [102-103], 104-109, [110-111], 112-120, [121], 122-129, [130-131], 132-138, [139], 140-156, [157], 158-169, [170-171], 172-193, [194-195], 196-207, [208-209], 210-219, [220-221], 222-234, [235], 236-242, [243], 244-256, [257], 258-270, [271], 272-282, [283], 284-301, [302-303], 304-309, [310-311], 312-332, [333-335], 336-350, [351-354] pages; white endpapers.   8 $^7/_{16}$" x 5 $^3/_8$" [1]^{16} 2-11^{16} 12^8

Contents: (i) half title page; (ii) [list]: *Also by Kay Boyle* [twenty-eight titles]; (iii) title page; (iv) acknowledgment of previous publication and copyright page; (v) [dedication]: *To my five daughters | and the memory of Pegeen*; (vi) blank; (vii) acknowledgments; (viii) photo credits; (ix-x) list of illustrations; (xi-xii) a note on Robert McAlmon; (xiii) excerpt from poem by Robert McAlmon; (xiv) blank; (1-9) text; (10) blank; (11-71) text; (72) blank; (73-81) text; (82) blank; (83-101) text; (102) blank; (103-109) text; (110) blank; (111-129) text; (130) blank; (131-169) text; (170) blank; (171-193) text;   (194) blank; (195-207) text; (208) blank; (209-219) text; (220) blank; (221-301) text; 302) blank; (303-309) text; (310) blank; (311-332) text; (333) index title page; (334) blank; (335-350) index text; (351-354) blank.

Copyright page: [list of acknowledgments of previous publication.] | First Published in Great Britain 1970 by | Michael Joseph Limited, 52 Bedford Square, London, W.C.1. | Copyright © 1968 by Kay Boyle | Printed in Great Britain by Ebenezer Baylis and Sons Limited | The Trinity Press, Worcester, and London. Bound by James Burn Limited | Royal Mills, Esher, Surrey | 7181 0724 1 | *All Rights Reserved. No part of this publication may be reproduced, | stored in a retrieval system, or transmitted, in any form or by any | means, electronic, mechanical, photocopying, recording, or otherwise, | without the prior permission of the Copyright owner.*

Illustrations: Black and white photographs on glossy paper. Photos 1 through 27 between pages 114 and 115. Photos 28 through 53 between pages 242 and 243.

Binding: Brown cloth covered boards stamped in gold. Top edge unstained. All edges trimmed. Front: Blank. Spine: *Being | Geniuses | Together | 1920-1930* | [design] | ROBERT | McALMON | KAY | BOYLE | [publisher's device] | MICHAEL | JOSEPH Back: Blank.

Dust jacket: White paper jacket printed in rust and black with a grouping of four photographs. Front: [black] Being Geniuses | Together | [rust] 1920-1930 [the preceding three lines boxed in by four rust corner designs] | [group of four sepia photographs] | [black] Robert McAlmon | Revised and with supplementary chapters by | Kay Boyle [the preceding boxed in by identical four rust colored corner designs] Spine: [printed downward in black] Being Geniuses Together 1920-1930 [top line] Robert McAlmon & Kay Boyle [bottom line in rust] | [horizontal in black] MICHAEL | JOSEPH   Back: A list of non fiction books for 1970 printed in black and rust. Front flap: Note about the book. 60s. net | £ 3.00 Jacket design by TURNER/SMITH   Back flap: Short note on Kay Boyle with photograph.

Note: See note for first American edition.

Publication: Published in April 1970 at £3.

A35c   BEING GENIUSES TOGETHER   1984

First American Paperback:

Robert McAlmon | Being Geniuses | Together | 1920-1930 | *Revised with supplementary chapters | and an afterword by* | Kay Boyle | 1984 | *North Point Press | San Francisco*

Collation: One blank leaf. [i-xi], xii, [xiii-xiv], [1], 2-9, [10-11], 12-24, [25], 26-38, [39], 40-48, [49], 50-62, [63], 64-71, [72-73], 74-81, [82-83], 84-88, [89], 90-101, [102-103], 104-109, [110-111], 112-120, [121], 122-129, [130-131], 132-138, [139], 140-156, [157], 158-169, [170-171], 172-193, [194-195], 196-207, [208-209], 210-219, [220-221], 222-234, [235], 236-242, [243], 244-256, [257], 258-270, [271], 272-282, [283], 284-301, [302-303], 304-309, [310-311], 312-332, [333], 334-343, [344-347], 348-362, [363-368] pages. 8 $^1/_4$" x 5 $^3/_{16}$" [A-L]^{16}

Contents: blank leaf; (i) small arrow enclosed in small square in upper right hand corner of the page; (ii) photograph of Robert McAlmon by Bernice Abbott; (iii) title page; (iv) copyright page; (vi) [dedication]: *To my five daughters | and the memory of Pegeen*; (vi) blank; (vii) acknowledgments by Kay Boyle; (viii) blank; (ix) photo credits; (x) blank; (xi-xii) a note on Robert McAlmon; (xiii) excerpt form a poem by Robert McAlmon; (xiv) blank; (1-9) text; (10) blank; (11-71) text; (72) blank; (73-81) text; (82) blank; (83-101) text; (102) blank; (103-109) text; (110) blank; (111-129) text; (130) blank; (131-169) text; (170) blank; (171-193) text; (194) blank; (195-207) text; (208) blank; (209-219) text; (220) blank; (221-301) text; (302) blank; (303-309) text; (310) blank; (311-343) text; (344) blank; (345) index title page; (346) blank; (347-362) index text; (363-368) blank.

Copyright page: Copyright © 1968 by Kay Boyle | Afterword copyright © 1984 by Kay Boyle | Printed in the United States of America | Library of Congress Catalogue Card Number: 83-063128 | ISBN: 0-86547-149-5

Illustrations: Black and white photographs on glossy paper numbered 1 through 47 between pages 208 and 209.

Binding: Stiff white paper wraps in dust jacket. Wrappers printed in silver gray with all edges trimmed. Front: BEING GENIUSES | TOGETHER 1920-1930 | Robert McAlmon | Revised with supplementary chapters and an afterword by | Kay Boyle   Spine: Being | Geniuses | Together | 1920- 1930 | ROBERT | McALMON | KAY | BOYLE | [Small arrow enclosed in small square].   Back: Blank.

Dust jacket: White paper photographic jacket printed in green, black & white. Front: Top third of cover is green printed in white. BEING GENIUSES | TOGETHER 1920-1930 | Robert McAlmon | Revised with supplementary chapters and an afterword by | Kay Boyle | [Lower two-thirds of the cover is a photograph of the cafe Le Dome which wraps around entire jacket from front to back] Spine: Being | Geniuses | Together | 1920-1930 | ROBERT | McALMON | KAY | BOYLE. Back: [paragraph from a review in the New York Times Book Review] | NORTH POINT • PRESS SAN FRANCISCO. [lower two-thirds is a continuation of the front photograph] Front flap: History and synopsis of the book. $13.50 [upper right]. Back flap: Short biographical notes about Robert McAlmon and Kay Boyle.

Publication: First published in April 1984 at $13.50.

Note: There is also a advance page proof issued in light blue stiff paper wraps.

A35d   BEING GENIUSES TOGETHER   1984

First American Paperback Second Printing:

Robert McAlmon | Being Geniuses | Together | 1920-1930 | *Revised with supplementary chapters | and an afterword by* | Kay Boyle | *1984 | North Point Press | San Francisco*

Collation: Same as A35c.

Contents: Same as A35c.

Copyright page: Same as A35c except SECOND PRINTING is just below ISBN number.

Illustrations: Same as A35c.

Binding: Same as A35c.

Dust jacket: Same as A35c.

A35e   BEING GENIUSES TOGETHER   [1984]

First English Paperback Edition:

[The following enclosed in a ruled square with the top of the square intersected with the head of a fox] BEING | GENIUSES | TOGETHER | 1920-1930 | Robert McAlmon | [outside the square] *Revised, with supplementary chapters | and New Afterword by Kay Boyle* | THE HOGARTH PRESS | LONDON

Collation: [i-viii], [1], 2-9, [10-11], 12-24, [25], 26-38, [39], 40-48, [49], 50-62, [63], 64-71, [72-73], 74-81, [82-83], 84-88, [89], 90-101, [102-103], 104-109, [110-111], 112-120, [121], 122-129, [130-131], 132-138, [139], 140-156, [157], 158-169, [170-171], 172-193, [194-195], 196-207, [208-209], 210-219, [220-221], 222-234, [235], 236-242, [243], 244-256, [257], 258-270, [271], 272-282, [283], 284-301, [302-303], 304-309, [310-311], 312-332, [333], 334-343, [344-347], 348- 362 pages. 7 $^3/_4$" x 5"

Contents: (i) a note about Robert McAlmon and Kay Boyle; (ii) blank; (iii) title page; (iv) copyright page; (v) acknowledgements by Kay Boyle; (vi) photo credits; (vii-viii) a note on Robert McAlmon; (1-9) text; (10) blank; (11-71) text; (72) blank; (73-81) text; (82) blank; (83-101) text; (102) blank; (103-109) text; (110) blank; (111-129) text; (130) blank; (131-169) text; (170) blank; (171-193) text; (194) blank; (195-207) text; (208) blank; (209-219) text; (220) blank; (221-301) text; (302) blank; (303-309) text; (310) blank; (311-343) text; (344) acknowledgements for material included in the book; (345-362) index.

Copyright page: To my five daughters | and the memory of Pegeen | Published in 1984 by | The Hogarth Press | 49 William IV Street, London WC2N 4DF | First published in Great Britain by Michael Joseph 1970 | Hogarth edition offset from North Point Press 1984 edition | Copyright © Kay Boyle 1968 | Afterword copyright © Kay Boyle 1984 | All rights reserved. | No part of this publication may be reproduced, stored in a | retrieval system, or transmitted in any form, or by any means, electronic, | mechanical, photocopying, recording or otherwise, without the prior | permission of the publisher. | British Library Cataloguing in Publication Data | McAlmon, Robert | Being geniuses together. — Rev. ed | I. McAlmon, Robert — Biography | I. Title II. Boyle, Kay | 818'.5203 PS3525.A1143Z5 | ISBN 0 7012 0563 6 | This book has been published with sub-sidy from | the Arts Council of Great Britain | Printed in Great Britain by | Cox & Wyman Ltd | Reading, Berkshire

Illustrations: Black and white photographs on glossy paper numbered 1 through 24 between pages 56 and 57 and 25 through 47 between pages 296 and 297.

Binding: Stiff white paper pictorial wraps printed in purple, black and blue. Top edge unstained and all edges trimmed. Front: [stylized head of a fox] | [black and white photograph of Robert McAlmon] | Being Geniuses Together | [rule] 1920 [short rule] 1930 [rule] | ROBERT McALMON & KAY BOYLE | [black and white photograph of Kay Boyle] [the preceding on a blue decorative background] Spine: [stylized head of a fox] | [printed downward in white on purple] Being Geniuses Together [top line] ROBERT McALMON & KAY BOYLE [bottom line] Back: Notes about the book. Robert McAlmon and Kay Boyle printed in white on purple.

Published in 1984 at £4.95.

A36a   TESTAMENT FOR MY STUDENTS AND OTHER POEMS   1970

First Edition:

[Double spread title page] KAY BOYLE | Testament for my students | and other poems | 1970 | DOUBLEDAY & COMPANY, INC. | GARDEN CITY, NEW YORK

Collation: [1-8], 9-10, [11-12], 13-90, [91-96] pages; blue endpapers. 8 $^1/_8$" x 5 $^1/_2$" 1-2^{12} [3-4]^{12}

Contents: (1) blank; (2) [list]: *Books by Kay Boyle* [thirty titles]; (3) half title page; (4-5) double spread title page; (6) copyright page; (7) [dedication]: THIS BOOK IS DEDICATED TO SONIA SANCHEZ; (8) blank; (9-10) table of contents; (11) fly title; (12) blank; (13-90) text; (91-96) blank

Copyright page: [Acknowledgment of prior publication] | Library of Congress Catalog Card Number 76-100494 | Copyright © 1938, 1956, 1959, 1962, | 1965, 1967, 1968, 1970, by Kay Boyle | All Rights Reserved | Printed in the United States of America | First Edition

Binding: Blue cloth covered boards stamped in gold. Top edge unstained and all edges trimmed. Front: Facsimile of Kay Boyle's signature in gold. Spine: [printed downward] KAY BOYLE Testament for my students DOUBLEDAY. Back: Blank.

Dust jacket: White paper printed in gold, blue and black. Front: [gold] KAY BOYLE | [thick blue rule] | [black] TESTAMENT | FOR MY | STUDENTS | [thick blue rule] | [gold] AND OTHER POEMS Spine: [printed downward in gold] KAY BOYLE [printed downward in black] TESTAMENT FOR MY STUDENTS *Doubleday* Back: Photograph by Robert Wax of a protest march at San Francisco State College in 1968 including Kay Boyle with a protest sign. Front flap: A short note about the poems. $4.95 [upper right]. Back flap: A short note about Kay Boyle. Jacket by Peter Rauch.

Publication: First published on March 20, 1970 according to *Publisher's Weekly* at $4.95.

The included poems and their previous publication: "Testament for My Students" first appeared in *Southern Review*, Winter 1970. "A Poem in One Sentence" first appeared in *Twigs* IV 1968. "For James Schevill, on the Occasion of His Arrest" first appeared in *Poem* 3 & 4, November 1968. "For Marianne Moore's Birthday, November 15, 1967" first appeared in *Twigs* IV, 1968. "The Lost Dogs of Phnom Penh" first appeared in *Lace Curtain* 1, Winter 1969/1970. "A Poem of Love" first appeared in *Love (Incorporating Hate)*, 1966. "Dedicated to *Terre des Hommes*" first appeared in *The Catholic Worker*, December 1966. "A Poem about Black Power" first appeared in *Liberation*, January 1967. "Thunderstorm in South Dakota" first appeared in *Southern Review*, October 1967. "A Short Poem in Color" first appeared in *Southern Review*, Summer 1965. "A Poem about the Jews" first appeared in *The Harvard Advocate*, Fall 1966. "A Poem for Arthur" first appeared in *Southern Review*, Summer 1965. "A Square Dance for a Square" first appeared in *Southern Review*, Summer 1965. "World Tour, for My Daughter, Sharon" first appeared in *Seven* 4, Spring 1939. "A Communication to Nancy Cunard," "A Glad Day for Laurence Vail," "A Comeallye for Robert Carlton Brown," "A Valentine for Harry Crosby," "Dedicated to Robert McAlmon" (as "Dedicated to Guy Urquhart"), "The Only Bird That Sang," "A Letter to Francis Picabia" and "In Defense of Homosexuality" all were collected in *A Glad Day*. See A15a for previous publication. "A Winter Fable," "A Poem of Gratitude, for Caresse Crosby" and "The New Emigration" were collected in *Collected Poems*. See A30a for previous publication. "For James Baldwin" and "The Jews among the Nations" appear here for the first time.

A36b   TESTAMENT FOR MY STUDENTS AND OTHER POEMS   1970

First Paperback Edition:

Published simultaneously with hardcover edition

[Double spread title page] KAY BOYLE | Testament for my students | and other poems | 1970 | DOUBLEDAY & COMPANY, INC. | GARDEN CITY, NEW YORK

Collation: Same as A36a.

Contents: Same as A36a.

Copyright page: [Acknowledgement of prior publication] | *Testament for my students and other poems* | was published simultaneously in a hardcover edition | by Doubleday and Company, Inc. Copyright © 1938, 1956, 1959, 1962, | 1965, 1967, 1968, 1970 by Kay Boyle | All Rights Reserved | Printed in the United States of America

Binding: White wrappers printed in blue gold and black. Top edge unstained and all edges trimmed. Front: [black] $1.95 | [gold] KAY BOYLE | [thick blue rule] | [black] TESTAMENT | FOR MY | STUDENTS | [thick blue rule] | [gold] AND OTHER POEMS Spine: [printed downward in gold] KAY BOYLE [printed downward in black] TESTAMENT FOR MY STUDENTS *Doubleday* Back: A note about the poems and a short note about Kay Boyle. Cover by Peter Rauch.

Publication: First published on March 20, 1970 according to *Publisher's Weekly* .

A37a   THE LONG WALK AT SAN FRANCISCO   [1971]
                    STATE AND OTHER ESSAYS

First Edition:

The | Long | Walk | at | San | Francisco | State [with] *and* | *other essays* [on the same
line as State] | by KAY BOYLE | GROVE PRESS, INC., NEW YORK

Collation: [i-viii], [1-2], 3-78, [79-90], 91-96, [97], 98-122, [123-124], 125-137,
[138-140], 141-150, [151-152] pages; white endpapers. 7" x 4 $^3/_8$" [A-E]^{16}

Contents: (i) half title page; (ii) [list]: BOOKS BY KAY BOYLE [twenty-seven
titles]; (iii) title page; (iv) copyright page; (v) [dedication]: *for* Ira Morris; (vi)
blank; (vii) table of contents; (viii) blank; (1) [divisional title]: The | Long |
Walk | at | San | Francisco | State; (2) blank; (3-78) text; (79-90) photographs;
(91-96) text; (97) [divisional title]: Notes | on | Jury | Selection | in the | Huey P.
Newton | Trial; (98-122) text; (123) [divisional title]: No | One | Can | Be | All |
Things | to | All | People; (124) blank; (125-137) text; (138) blank; (139) [divisional
title]: Seeing | the | Sights | in | San Francisco; (140) blank; (141-150) text;
(151-152) blank.

Copyright page*: Copyright* © *1967,1968,1970 by Kay Boyle | ALL RIGHTS
RESERVED | First Evergreen Black Cat Edition, 1970 | First Printing | Library of
Congress Catalog Number:* | *70-126593* | *Portions of* The Long Walk at San Francisco
State *originally* | *appeared in* Evergreen Review, *No.76, March 1970.* Notes on | Jury
Selection in the Huey P. Newton Trial *originally ap-* | *peared in* The Progressive,
October 1968; No One Can Be All | Things to All People *originally appeared in*
Evergreen Re- | view, *No. 81, August 1970;* and Seeing the Sights in San Fran- | cisco
originally appeared in The Progressive, *December 1967.* | *No part of this book may be
reproduced, for any reason, by* | *any means, including any method of photographic
repro-* | *duction, without the permission of the publisher.* | *Designed by Ruth Smerechniak
| Manufactured in the United States of America*

Binding: Bound in red cloth covered boards stamped in black. Top edge unstained
and all edges trimmed. Front: Blank. Spine: [printed downward in black] THE
LONG WALK AT SAN FRANCISCO STATE KAY BOYLE [horizontal] GROVE
| PRESS Back: Blank.

Dust jacket: White paper pictorial jacket printed in red, black and white. Front:
Photograph toned in black and red of several riot police with clubs. [white] THE
LONG WALK AT | SAN FRANCISCO STATE | [red] BY KAY BOYLE
Spine: [printed downward in black] THE LONG WALK AT SAN FRANCISCO
STATE [printed downward in red] KAY BOYLE | [horizontal in black] GP-656 |
GROVE | PRESS Back: Photograph of Kay Boyle with caricature of S.I. Hayakawa
and a short note about her. Front flap: Short quote by Kay Boyle and a note on the
book and the times about which it is written. $5.00 [upper right]. Back flap: A
continuation of the front flap.

Publication: Published January 29, 1971 According to *Publisher's Weekly* and a laid in review slip at $5.00.

The included essays and their previous publication: Portions of "The Long Walk at San Francisco State" first appeared in *Evergreen Review*, March 1970. "Notes on Jury Selection in the Huey P. Newton Trial" first appeared in *The Progressive*, October 1968. "No One Can Be All Things to All People" first appeared in *Evergreen Review*, August 1970. "Seeing the Sights of San Francisco" first appeared in *The Progressive*, December 1967.

A37b   THE LONG WALK AT SAN FRANCISCO   [1971]
                STATE AND OTHER ESSAYS

First Paperback Edition:

The | Long | Walk | at | San | Francisco | State | [with] *and* | *other essays* [on the same line as State] | by KAY BOYLE | GROVE PRESS, INC., NEW YORK

Collation: [i-viii], [1-2], 3-78, [79-90], 91-96, [97], 98-122, [123-124], 125-137, [138-140], 141-150, [151-152] pages; 7" x 4 $^1/_8$"

Contents: Same as A37a with exception of page i which has short biographical note about Kay Boyle rather than half title.

Copyright page: Same as A37a.

Binding: Wrappers with same design on cover as hardcover dust Jacket. [upper right corner in white] B-263 [publisher's device] $1.25 | [at the bottom in white] THE LONG WALK AT | SAN FRANCISCO STATE | [red] BY KAY BOYLE   Spine: [printed downward in black] THE LONG WALK AT SAN FRANCISCO [printed downward in red] KAY BOYLE | [horizontal in black] [publisher's device] | B-263 | GROVE | PRESS   Back: Short excerpt from essays and short biographical sketch of Kay Boyle.

A38a   THE UNDERGROUND WOMAN   1975

First Edition:

THE | UNDERGROUND | WOMAN | Kay Boyle | Doubleday & Company, Inc. | Garden City, New York | 1975

Collation: [1-9], 10-18, [19], 20-33, [34], 35-44, [45], 46-54, [55], 56-64, [65], 66-76, [77], 78-90. [91], 92-101, [102], 103-114, [115], 116-126, [127], 128-143, [144], 145-153, [154], 155-161, [162], 163-171, [172], 173-187, [188], 189-200,

[201], 202-213, [214], 215-227, [228], 229-239, [240], 241-255, [256], 257-264 pages; white endpapers. 8 $^3/_{16}$" x 5 $^3/_8$" 1-6^{12} [7-11] ^{12}

Contents: (1) half title page; (2) [list]: BOOKS BY KAY BOYLE| [thirty-two titles]; (3) title page; (4) copyright page; (5) [dedication]: This book is for | Bessie Breuer, | great writer and beloved friend.; (6) blank; (7) fly title; (8) blank; (9-264) text.

Copyright page: "A portion of this novel first appeared as excerpts | in *Icarbs* and a portion appeared under the title | "Nolo Contendere" in *Antaeus*, Copyright © 1974 | by Antaeus. | Library of Congress Cataloging in Publication Data | Boyle, Kay, 1903— | The underground woman. | I. Title. | PZ3.B69796Un   813'.5'2 | ISBN 0-385-07047-0 | Library of Congress Catalog Card Number 72-186008 | Copyright © 1973, 1975 by Kay Boyle | All Rights Reserved | Printed in the United States of America | First Edition

Binding: Bound with black cloth spine and gray paper covered boards stamped in silver. Top edge unstained and all edges trimmed. Front: Blank. Spine: Kay | Boyle | [printed downward] THE UNDERGROUND WOMAN | [horizontal] Doubleday Back: Blank.

Dust jacket: White paper printed in black. Front: Photograph of a rock cliff front. Kay | Boyle | the | Underground | Woman | a novel by the author of | Nothing Ever Breaks | Except the Heart   Spine: [printed downward in black] the [top line] Kay Underground [second line] Boyle Woman [bottom line] | [Printed horizontally] Doubleday   Back: Photograph of Kay Boyle by Thomas Victor. A short biographical note about Kay Boyle. Front flap: Story plot. $7.95 [upper right].   Back flap: Continuation of front flap.

Publication: First published on January 10, 1975 according to *Publisher's Weekly* at $7.95.

A39a   FIFTY STORIES   1980

First Edition:

[series of contiguous tiny triangles, tips up, forming a line] | *Fifty Stories* | KAY BOYLE | [same series of triangles, tips down forming a line] | 1980 | DOUBLEDAY & COMPANY, INC. | GARDEN CITY, NEW YORK

Collation: [1-7], 8, [9], 10-14, [15-17], 18-116, [117-119], 120-129, [130], 131-165, [166], 167-178, [179-181], 182-197, [198], 199-236, [237-239], 240-287, [288], 289-304, [305], 306-365, [366], 367-375, [376-379], 380-431, [432], 433-546, [547], 548-574, [575-577], 578-586, [587], 588-606, [607], 608-648 pages; white endpapers 8 $^1/_8$" x 5 $^3/_8$"   1-14^{12} [15-28] ^{12}

Contents: (1) half title page, (2) [list]: BOOKS BY KAY BOYLE [thirty-one titles]; (3) title page; (4) copyright page and acknowledgment of previous publication; (5) continuation of the acknowledgments; (6) blank; (7-8) contents; (9-14) introduction by David Daiches; (15) [divisional title]: [line as on title page, tips up] | *Early Group* | 1927-1934 | [repeat line tips down]; (16) blank; (17-116) text; (117) [divisional title]: [line as on title page, tips up] | *Austrian Group* | 1933-1938 | [repeat line, tips down]; (118) blank; (119-178) text; (179) [divisional title]: [line as on title page, tips up] | *English Group* | 1935-1936 | [repeat line tips down]; (180) blank; (181-236) text; (237) [divisional title]: [line as on title page, tips up] | *French Group* | 1939-1966 | [repeat line, tips down]; (238) blank; (239-375) text; (376) blank; (377) [divisional title]: [line as on title page, tips up] | *Military* | *Occupation Group* | 1945-1950 | [repeat line, tips down]; (378) blank; (379-574) text; (575) [divisional title]: [line as on title page, tips up] | *American Group* | 1942-1966 | [repeat line, tips down]; (576) blank; (577-648) text.

Copyright page: Library of Congress Catalog Number 78-22151 | ISBN: 0-385-14996-4 | COPYRIGHT © 1945, 1950, 1955, 1964, 1966, 1980 BY KAY BOYLE | ALL RIGHTS RESERVED | PRINTED IN THE UNITED STATES OF AMERICA | FIRST EDITION | ACKNOWLEDGMENTS | [acknowledgment of previous publication follows]

Binding: Blue cloth spine stamped in gold. Beige paper covered boards. Top edge unstained and front and bottom edges trimmed. Front edge rough trimmed. Front: Blank. Spine: [small contiguous triangles, tips up forming a line] | *Fifty* | *Stories* | KAY | BOYLE | [repeat line, tips down] | DOUBLEDAY Back: Blank.

Dust jacket: White paper printed in beige, brown, black and blue. Front: [brown] *fifty* | *Stories* | [black] *THE SELECTED STORIES* | *BY* | Kay | Boyle Spine: [printed downward in blue] KAY BOYLE [printed downward in brown] *·fifty Stories* | [printed horizontally in black] DOUBLEDAY Back: Photograph of Kay Boyle by Bob Doty. A short biographical note about Kay Boyle. Front flap: Short quote from the introduction by Bob Daiches. A note about Kay Boyle. $15.95. [upper right] Back flap: Continuation of the front flap. Jacket design by George Bacso.

Publication: First published on September 26, 1980 according to advance review slip at $15.95.

Note: Also examined an uncorrected proof copy in lime green wraps. 10 $^3/_4$" x 5 $^1/_2$"

The included Stories and their previous publication: "Security," "Dear Mr. Walrus" and "Rondo at Carraroe" were all collected in *The White Horses of Vienna and Other Stories*. See A11a for previous publication. "Episode in the Life of an Ancestor," "Wedding Day," "Rest Cure," "Ben," "Kroy Wen," "Black Boy," "Friend of the Family," "White as Snow," "Keep Your Pity," "Natives Don't Cry," "Maiden, Maiden," "The White Horses of Vienna," "Count Lothar's Heart," "Major

Alshuster," "How Birdie's Girl Was Won," "The Herring Piece," "Your Body Is a Jewel Box," "Major Engagement in Paris," "Effigy of War," "Diplomat's Wife," "Men," "They Weren't Going to Die," "Defeat," "Let There Be Honour," "This They Took with Them," "Their Name Is Macaroni," "The Canals of Mars," "The Loneliest Man in the U. S. Army" and "Winter Night" were all collected in *Thirty Stories*. See A22a for previous publication. "Summer Evening," "The Criminal," "Fife's House," "The Lovers of Gain," "Cabaret," "The Lost," "Adam's Death" and "Aufwiedersehen Abend" were all collected in *The Smoking Mountain*. See A25a for previous publication. "French Harvest," "Fire in the Vineyard," "Hotel Behind the Lines," "Army of Occupation," "The Kill," "A Disgrace to the Family," "A Puzzled Race," "Evening at Home," "The Ballet of Central Park" and "Seven Say You Can Hear Corn Grow" were all collected in *Nothing Ever Breaks Except the Heart*. See A32a for previous publication.

A39b   FIFTY STORIES

First Edition Second Printing:

[series of contiguous tiny triangles, tips up, forming a line] | Fifty Stories | KAY BOYLE | [same series of triangles, tips down forming a line] | DOUBLEDAY & COMPANY, INC. | GARDEN CITY, NEW YORK"

Collation: Same as A39a.

Contents: Same as A39a.

Copyright page: Same as A39a except that FIRST EDITION is omitted.

Binding: Same as A39a.

Dust jacket: Same as A39a.

A39c   FIFTY STORIES   [1981]

First Paperback Edition:

[small contiguous triangles, tips up, forming a line] | *Fifty Stories* | KAY BOYLE | [repeat of above line with triangle tips pointing down] | [publisher's device: small penguin enclosed in oval] | PENGUIN BOOKS

Collation: [1-7], 8, [9], 10-14, [15-17], 18-116, [117-119], 120-129, [130], 131-165, [166], 167-178, [179-181], 182-197, [198], 199-236, [237-239], 240-287, [288], 289-304, [305], 306-365, [366], 367-375 [376-379], 380-431, [432], 433-546, [547], 548-574, [575-577], 578-586, [587], 588-606, [607], 608-648, [649-656] pages. 7 $^3/_4$" x 5"

Contents: (1) a short note on Kay Boyle; (2) [list]: BOOKS BY KAY BOYLE [thirty-one titles]; (3) title page; (4) copyright page and acknowledgment of previous publication; (5-6) continuation of the acknowledgments; (7-8) table of contents; (9-14) introduction by David Daiches; (15) [divisional title]: [line as on title page, tips up] | *Early Group* | 1927-1934 | [repeat line tips down]; (16) blank; (17-116) text; (117) [divisional title]: [line as on title page, tips up] | *Austrian Group* | 1933-1938 | [repeat line, tips down]; (118) blank; (119-178) Text; (179) [divisional title]: [line as on title page, tips up] | *English Group* | 1935-1936 | [repeat line tips down]; (180) blank; (181-236) text; (237) [divisional title]: [line as on title page, tips up] | *French Group* | 1939-1966 | [repeat line, tips down]; (238) blank; (239-375) text; (376) blank; (377) [divisional title]: [line as on title page, tips up] | *Military* | *Occupation Group* | 1945-1950 | [repeat line, tips down]; (378) blank; (379-574) text; (575) [divisional title]: [line as on title page, tips up] | *American Group* | 1942- 1966 | [repeat line, tips down]; (576) blank; (577-648) text. (649) a note on books available from Penguin Books, both American and Canadian enclosed in a double ruled box, one thick rule and one thin, with the Penguin publisher's device at the top; (650-656) blank.

Copyright page: Penguin Books Ltd, Harmondsworth, | Middlesex, England | Penguin Books, 625 Madison Avenue, | New York, New York 10022, U.S.A. | Penguin Books Australia Ltd, Ringwood, | Victoria, Australia | Penguin Books Canada Limited, 2801 John Street, | Markham, Ontario, Canada L3R 1B4 | Penguin Books (N.Z.) Ltd. 182-190 Wairau Road, | Auckland 10, New Zealand | First published in the United States of America by | Doubleday & Company, Inc., 1980 | Published in Penguin Books by arrangement with | Doubleday & Company, Inc., 1981 | Copyright 1945, 1950, by Kay Boyle | Copyright © Kay Boyle, 1955, 1964, 1966, 1980 | All rights reserved | LIBRARY OF CONGRESS CATALOGING IN PUB-LICATION DATA | Boyle, Kay, 1903— | Fifty stories. | Originally published: Garden City, N.Y.: Doubleday, 1980. | I. Title. | [PS3503.09357F5 1981] | 813'.52 81-7361 | ISBN 0 14 00.5922 9 AACR2 | Printed in the United States of America by | Offset Paperbacks Mfrs., Inc., Dallas, Pennsylvania | Set in Caledonia | [single rule] | ACKNOWLEDGMENTS | [follows at the bottom of page 4, all of page 5, and the top of page 6 a long list of acknowledgments of previous publication] | [continue middle of page 6] Except in the United States of America, | this book is sold subject to the condition | that it shall not, by way of trade or otherwise, | be lent, re-sold, hired out, or otherwise circulated | without the publisher's prior consent in any form of | binding or cover other than that in which it is | published and without a similar condition | including this condition being imposed | on the subsequent purchaser

Binding: White wrappers printed in silver and black and blue. Front: Dark blue. [a large silver 50 covering the top two thirds with KAY BOYLE in black written inside the outline of the 50. | [single silver rule] | STORIES | [single silver rule] | BY KAY BOYLE | [single silver rule] | STORIES FROM 1927 THROUGH 1966, | CHOSEN BY THE AUTHOR | "A MOVING AND MEMORABLE COLLEC-TION" | —*The New York Times Book Review* [a small publisher's device, a penguin, inside an orange oval lower right].   Spine: Spine is orange. [printed downward in black] Kay Boyle [printed downward in white] Fifty Stories [printed downward in black] ISBN 0 14 [top line] 00.5922 9 [bottom line] | [publisher's device]   Back: Dark blue printed in white. Quotes from two reviews and a short note on the stories. Cover design by Neil Stuart. Price in lower left hand corner: U.K. £ 2.95. Australia $8.95. Canada $7.95. U.S.A. $7.95.

A39d   FIFTY STORIES   [1992]

Second Paperback Edition:

KAY BOYLE | [rule] | FIFTY STORIES | Introduction by Louise Erdrich | [publisher's device] | A NEW DIRECTIONS BOOK

Collation: No examined copies had pages 1-8.   [9-17], 18-116, [117-119], 120-129, [130], 131-165, [166], 167-178, [179-181], 182-197, [198], 199-236, [237-239], 240-287, [288], 289-304, [305], 306-365, [366], 367-375, [376-379], 380-431, [432], 433-546, [547], 548-574, [575-577], 578-586, [587], 588-606, [607], 608-648 pages.   8" x 5 $^1/_8$"

Contents: pagination begins on page 9.   (9) title page;   (10) copyright page;   (11) table of contents;   (12-14) introduction by Louise Erdrich;   (15) [divisional title]: [small contiguous triangles, tips up, forming a line] | *Early Group* | 1927-1934 | [repeat line tips down]; (16) blank; (17-116) text; (117) [divisional title]: [line as on first divisional title page, tips up] | *Austrian Group* | 1933-1938 | [repeat line, tips down]; (118) blank; (119-178) Text; (179) [divisional title]: [line as on first divisional title page, tips up] | *English Group* | 1935-1936 | [repeat line tips down]; (180) blank; (181-236) text; (237) [divisional title]: [line as on first divisional title page, tips up] | *French Group* | 1939-1966 | [repeat line, tips down]; (238) blank; (239-375) text; (376) blank; (377) [line as on first divisional title page, tips up] | *Military | Occupation Group* | 1945-1950 | [repeat line, tips down]; (378) blank; (379-574) text; (575) [divisional title]: [line as on first divisional title page, tips up] | *American Group* | 1942- 1966 | [repeat line, tips down]; (576) blank; (577-648) text.

Copyright page: Copyright © 1945, 1950, 1955, 1964, 1966, 1980 by Kay Boyle | Introduction copyright © 1992 by Louise Erdrich | All rights reserved. Except for brief passages quoted in a newspaper, magazine, | radio, or television review, no part of this book may be reproduced in any form or by | any means, electronic or mechanical, including photocopying and recording, or by | any information storage and retrieval system, without permission in writing from | the Publisher. | This collection was first published by Doubleday & Company, Inc. in 1980 and is | reissued as New Directions Paperbook 741 in 1992 as part of the Revived Modern | Classics series. (*Fifty Stories* incorporates an earlier collection, *Thirty Stories*, first | published by Simon & Schuster in 1946 and reissued as New Directions Paperbook | 62 in 1957.) | Acknowledgments for the first publication of the stories included in this volume are | given on page 648. | Manufactured in the United States of America | New Directions Books are printed on acid-free paper. | Published simultaneously in Canada by Penguin Books Canada, Limited | **Library of Congress Catalogine** [sic] **-in-Publishing Data** | Boyle, Kay, 1902— | [Short stories. Selections] | Fifty stories / Kay Boyle. | p.cm.— (A Revived modern classic) (New Directions | paperbook ; 741) ISBN 0-8112-1206-8 : $19.95 | I. Title. II. Title: 50 stories. III. Series. | [PS3503.09357A6 1992] | 813' .52—dc20 91-40229 | CIP | New Directions Books are published for James Laughlin | by New Directions Publishing Corporation, | 80 Eighth Avenue, New York 10011

Binding: White wrappers printed in black and blue. Front: [black rule broken by blue publisher's device] | [blue] A REVIVED [same publisher's device extends down] MODERN CLASSIC | [black] KAY BOYLE | [black rule] | FIFTY STORIES | [blue] INTRODUCTION BY LOUISE ERDRICH | [geometric montage of photographs of clouds] Spine: [printed downward in black] KAY BOYLE [top line] | [rule] | FIFTY STORIES [bottom line] | [horizontal blue publisher's device] | [printed in black horizontally] NDP741 Back: Paragraph about Kay Boyle and *Fifty Stories*. Price in lower left corner. USA $15.95 | CAN $19.99

Publication: First published on June 30, 1992 at $15.95.

Also examined: An uncorrected proof copy. 8 $^{1}/_{2}$" x 11"

A40a WORDS THAT MUST SOMEHOW BE SAID 1985

First Edition:

[The following printed in a long rectangular box with dividers separating the years from the line of text] 1927 SELECTED ESSAYS OF KAY BOYLE 1984 | Words that | Must Somehow | Be Said | Edited and with an Introduction by Elizabeth S. Bell | *North Point Press San Francisco 1985*

Collation: one blank leaf, [i-viii], ix-xiv, [1-2], 3-23, [24-26], 27-89, [90-92], 93-151, [152-154], 155-262, [263-272] pages; light brown endpapers, 7 $^{7}/_{8}$" x 4 $^{7}/_{8}$" [A-I]^{16}

Contents: blank unpaginated leaf; (i) [small square with enclosed arrow pointing up]; (ii) blank; (iii) title page; (iv) copyright page; (v) [dedication]: To E.R. Hagemann | E.B.; (vi) blank; (vii-viii) table of contents; (ix-xiv) introduction by Elizabeth Bell; (1) [divisional title]: [enclosed in ruled box] I. ON THE BEGIN-NINGS | *"Look into Memory's Dreamy,* | *Evasive Eyes"* (2) blank; (3-23) text; (24) blank; (25) [divisional title]: [enclosed in ruled box] II. ON WRITERS AND WRITING | *"Interpreters of This Deep Concern"* (26) blank; (27-89) text; (90) blank; (91) [divisional title]: [enclosed in ruled box] III. ON THE BODY POLITIC | *"Shout Aloud Our Disputed Tongue"* (92) blank; (93-151) text; (152) blank; (153)

[divisional title]: [enclosed in ruled box] IV. ON THE HUMAN CONDITION | *"A Quite Humble Pageant"* (154) blank; (155-262) text; (263-264) blank; (265) design by David Bullen | Typeset in Mergenthaler Caslon Old Face #2 | by Wilsted & Taylor | Printed by Maple-Vail | on acid-free paper; (266-272) blank.

Copyright page: Copyright © 1985 by Kay Boyle | Introduction copyright © 1985 by Elizabeth S. Bell | Printed in the United States of America | Library of Congress Catalogue Card Number: 84-62301 | ISBN: 0-86547-187-8 | The editor and author extend their thanks to the | original publishers of these essays.

Binding: Beige cloth stamped in gold. Top edge unstained and all edges trimmed. Front: Blank. Spine: [printed downward] WORDS THAT MUST SOMEHOW BE SAID [top line] KAY BOYLE [bottom line] | [publisher's device] Back: Blank.

Dust jacket: White paper printed in beige, blue and white. Front: [white letters highlighted in blue on a blue background] WORDS THAT | MUST SOME- | HOW BE SAID | Selected Essays of | KAY BOYLE | 1927-1984 | [blue on beige background] Edited and with an Introduction | by Elizabeth S. Bell | [All preceding text enclosed in a white ruled rectangle broken by a beige swatch] Spine: [blue lettering high-lighted in beige printed downward] WORDS THAT MUST SOMEHOW BE SAID [top line] KAY BOYLE [bottom line] | [publisher's device] Back: Photograph of Kay Boyle by Terrence McCarthy and a short biographical note. Front flap: A note on Kay Boyle's political activism and about the essays.] $16.50. [upper right] Back flap: A note on Elizabeth Bell. A list of other books of essays published by North Point Press. Jacket design by David Bullen.

Publication: First published on June 15, 1985 at $15.50.

The included essays and their previous publication: "The Family" first appeared in *Contemporary Authors Autobiography Series*, Detroit: Gale Research Company, 1984. "In the American Grain" first appeared in *transition* 1, April 1927. "Mr. Crane and His Grandmother" first appeared in *transition* 10, January 1928. "Preface to *The Autobiography* of *Emanuel Carnevali*," New York: Horizon Press, 1967. "Elizabeth Bowen" first appeared in *The New Republic*, September 21, 1942. "Katherine Mansfield: A Reconsideration" first appeared in *The New Republic*, October 20, 1937. "Tattered Banners" first appeared in *The New Republic*, March 9, 1938. "A Declaration for 1955" first appeared in *The Nation*, January 29, 1955. "A Man in the Wilderness" first appeared in *The Nation*, May 29, 1967. "Farewell to New York" first appeared in *The Nation*, March 8, 1947. "Excerpt from *The Long Walk at San Francisco State*" first appeared in *Evergreen Review*, March 1970. "The Teaching of Writing" first appeared in the *NEA Journal*, March 1964. "Farewell to Europe" first appeared in *The Nation*, December 12, 1953. "No Time to Listen" first appeared in *The Nation*, November 16, 1957. "A Day on Alcatraz with the Indians" first appeared in *The New Republic*, January 17, 1970. "The Crime of Attica" first appeared in *The New Republic*, March 15, 1975. "Report from Lockup" first appeared in *Four Visions of America*, Santa Barbara: Capra Press, 1977. "Battle of the Sequins" first appeared in *The Nation*, December 23, 1944. "The Jew Is a Myth" first appeared in *The Nation*, October 13, 1945. "Frankfurt in Our Blood" first appeared in *The Nation*, October 15, 1949 and in *The Smoking Mountain*, New York: McGraw-Hill Book Company, 1951. "Lucky Eyes and a High Heart" first appeared in *The New Republic*, October 28, 1978. "Sisters of the Princess" first appeared in *The Nation*, March 6, 1976. "Seeing the Sights of San Francisco" first appeared in *The Progressive*, December 1967. "The Triumph of Principals" first appeared in *Liberation*, June 1960 and also in *Seeds of Liberation*, New York: George Braziller, 1964, and in *Enough of Dying*, New York: Liveright, 1972. The "Preface from *The Smoking Mountain*" first appeared in *The Smoking Mountain*, New York: McGraw-Hill, 1951.

Proof copy: In green wraps 8 $^1/_4$" x 5 $^1/_4$". Title page is different and the dedication is missing. Front cover: UNCORRECTED PAGE PROOF | [enclosed in a ruled box] WORDS THAT | SOMEHOW MUST BE SAID | Selected Essays of | KAY BOYLE | 1927-1984 | Edited and with an Introduction by Elizabeth S. Bell | NORTH POINT PRESS | [The following three lines preceded by publisher's device] 850 Talbot Avenue | Berkeley, CA 94706 | (415) 527-6200 | [underlined] publication data: | 288 Pages, 5 x 8 | CLOTH, 0-86547-187-8, $16.50 | [underlined] DATE OF PUBLICATION: | JUNE 15, 1985 | FOR FURTHER INFORMATION PLEASE CONTACT : LISA ROSS/PUBLICITY/ (415) 527-6260. Spine: [vertical] WORDS THAT MUST [over] SOMEHOW BE SAID KAY BOYLE NORTH POINT

A40b   WORDS THAT MUST SOMEHOW BE SAID   [1985]

First English Edition:

Words That | Must Somehow | Be Said | Selected Essays 1927-1984 | KAY BOYLE | Edited and with an Introduction by Elizabeth S. Bell | *Chatto & Windus* | [rule] | *The Hogarth Press* | London

Collation: [i-viii], ix-xiv, [1-2], 3-23, [24-26], 27-89, [90-92], 93-151, [152-154], 155-262 pages; cream end papers. 7 $^3/_4$" x 5" [A-H]^{16} [I]^{10} [J]^{16}

Contents: (i) Words That Must Somehow Be Said | [publisher's device]; (ii) [list]: *Among the author's other works* | [five titles]; (iii) title page; (iv) copyright page; (v) [dedication]: To E. R. Hagemann | E.B. (vi) blank; (vii-viii) table of contents; ix-xiv) introduction; (I) [divisional title]: enclosed in a ruled box] 1. ON THE BEGINNINGS | *"Look into Memory's Dreamy, | Evasive Eyes"* (2) blank; (3-23) text; (24) blank; (25) [divisional title]: [enclosed in a ruled box] II. ON WRITERS AND WRITING | *"Interpreters of This Deep Concern"* (26) blank; (27-89) text; (90) blank; (91) [divisional title]: [enclosed in a ruled box] III. ON THE BODY POLITIC | *"Shout Aloud Our Disputed Tongue"* (92) blank; (93-151) text; (152)

blank; (153) [divisional title]: [enclosed in a ruled box] IV. ON THE HUMAN CONDITION | *"A Quite Humble Pageant"* (154) blank; (155-262) text.

Copyright page: Published in 1985 by | Chatto & Windus • The Hogarth Press | 40 William IV Street, London WC2N 4DF | All rights reserved. No part of this publication may be | reproduced, stored in a retrieval system, or transmitted in | any form, or by any means, electronic, mechanical, photocopying | recording or otherwise, without the prior permission of the | publisher. | ISBN 0-7011-2967-0 | Copyright © 1985 Kay Boyle | Introduction copyright © 1985 Elizabeth S. Bell | The editor and author extend their thanks to the | original publishers of these essays. | Printed in Great Britain by | Redwood Burn Limited, Trowbridge, Wiltshire

Binding: Black cloth covered boards stamped in gold. Top edge unstained. All edges trimmed. Front: Blank. Spine: [printed downward] KAY BOYLE | *Words That Must* [top line] *Somehow Be Said* [bottom line] | [horizontal] CHATTO | [rule] | HOGARTH Back: Blank.

Dust jacket: White paper printed in black white and red. Front: [Man Ray photograph of Kay Boyle] [white] KAY BOYLE | [lower right hand corner print on a slant in red] Words That | Must Somehow | Be Said [lower left hand corner printed in white horizontal] EDITED BY | ELIZABETH BELL Spine: [printed downward in white] KAY BOYLE | [printed downward in red] *Words That Must* [top line] *Somehow Be Said* [bottom line] | [white publisher's device] Back: A short blurb printed in white on the essays and a short plug for *Being Geniuses Together 1920-1930.*   Front flap: Note about the book.   £10.95 net | in UK only [lower right]   Back flap: Short biography of Kay Boyle.

Publication: First published in August 1985 at £10.95.

A40c   WORDS THAT MUST SOMEHOW BE SAID   [1985]

First Paperback Edition:

[The following printed in a long rectangular box with dividers separating the years from the line of text] 1927 SELECTED ESSAYS OF KAY BOYLE 1984 | Words that | Must Somehow | Be Said | Edited and with an Introduction by Elizabeth S. Bell | *North Point Press San Francisco 1985*

Collation: Same as A40a. 7 $^7/_8$" x 5". [A-I]^{16}

Contents: Same as A40a.

Copyright page: Copyright © 1985 by Kay Boyle | Introduction copyright © 1985 by Elizabeth S. Bell | Printed in the United States of America | Library of Congress Catalogue Card Number: 84-62301 | ISBN: 0-86547-188-6 | The editor and author extend their thanks to the | original publishers of these essays, in particular to Gale

| Research (Detroit, Michigan) for "The Family" (p.3), | excerpted from *Contemporary Authors Autobiography* | *series*, vol. I, 1984. | North Point Press | 850 Talbot Avenue | Berkeley, California | 94706

Binding: White wraps printed in gray, black and red. Front: [red] KAY BOYLE | [black] enclosed in a black ruled box with the dates separated by a black horizontal rule] 1927 SELECTED ESSAYS 1984 | [red] *Words That Must* | *Somehow Be Said* [Man Ray photograph of Kay Boyle] | Edited and with an Introduction | by Elizabeth S. Bell Spine: [printed downward in red] *Words That Must Somehow Be Said* [black] KAY BOYLE | [Publisher's device]   Back: Reviews of the book. Cover photograph by © Man Ray, 1930 $8.95 [upper right] Cover design: David Bullen

The Included essays and their previous publication are the same as the American edition.

A41a   THIS IS NOT A LETTER   [1985]

First Limited Edition:

THIS IS NOT A LETTER | AND OTHER POEMS | BY | [device] KAY BOYLE [device] | [publisher's logo] | Sun & Moon Press | Los Angeles

Collation: [1-6], 7-66, [67-72] pages; green endpapers. 7 $^3/_4$" x 5 $^1/_4$" [A-C]^8 [D]^4 [E]^{16}

Contents: (1) half title page; (2) blank; (3) title page; (4) copyright page; (5) table of contents; (6) [dedication]: *for Grace Paley*; (7-66) text; (67-68) blank; (69) limitation statement; (70-72) blank. Note: There is an errata slip tacked onto the front free end paper.

Limitation statement: Of an edition of 26 copies signed by the author | this is letter_____ [hand written letter and signature.

Copyright page: Copyright © Kay Boyle, 1985 | Some of the poems in this collection appeared previously in | *The Malahat Review* (Canada), *Pearl* (Sweden), *Rolling Stock*, | *Willow Springs Magazine*, and *Wind*. | Cover: Page I from the Japanese volume *Iseshu* | Design: Katie Messborn | Publication of this book was made possible, in part, by a | grant from the National Endowment for the Arts and contributions | to the Contemporary Arts Educational Project, Inc. | [rule] | Library of Congress Cataloging-in-Publication Data | Boyle, Kay, 1902- | This is not a letter and other poems. | I. Title. | PS3503.09357T538 1985   811' .52   85-20778 | ISBN 0-940650-61-4 | ISBN 0-940650-62-2 (signed) | [rule] | FIRST EDITION | 10 9 8 7 6 5 4 3 2 1 | Sun & Moon Press | 6363 Wilshire Blvd. Suite 115 | Los Angeles, California 90048

Binding: Orange cloth covered boards printed in black. Front: [horizontal across the top] [device] THIS IS NOT A LETTER [printed down the right edge of the cover]

AND OTHER POEMS by KAY BOYLE [device] Spine: [printed downward] Kay Boyle This Is Not a Letter   Sun & Moon Press   Back : Blank.

Dust jacket: White paper printed in black and several other colors.   Front: Multicolored pattern on front with script printed in black.   [across the top in black] [device] THIS IS NOT A LETTER [printed down the right edge of the jacket] AND OTHER POEMS by KAY BOYLE [device]   Spine: [printed downward] Kay Boyle This Is Not a Letter Sun & Moon Press   Back: Reviews with address of Sun and Moon Press. $30.00 [lower left]

Publication: First published on October 21,1985 at $30.00.

The included poems and their previous publication: Excerpt from "A Poem for Samuel Beckett" part 3. "Reincarnation" first appeared in *Rolling Stock*, Number 5, 1983. "Poets" first appeared in *Pacific Sun Literary Quarterly*, May 27, 1976. "On Taking Up Residence in Virginia" first appeared in *Hart,* ca. 1970-1971. "On the Death of My Student, the Poet Serafin" first appeared in *Wind* 11, Spring 1974. "Branded for Slaughter" first appeared in *Anteus* 3, Spring 1971. "A Poem for Vida Hadjebi Tabrizi" first appeared in a Committee for Artistic and Intellectual Freedom news letter, March 1977. "This Is Not a Letter" first appeared in *Twigs* 7, 1971. "What Parents Do Not Know Yet" first appeared in *Pearl* 9, Spring 1982. "A Poem for the Students of Greece" first appeared in *New York Quarterly* 17, 1975. "A Poem for the Teesto Diné of Arizona" first appeared in *The Mahlahat Review*, 1983. "Advice to the Old (Including Myself)," "The Stones of a Seventeenth Century Village," "A Poem for February First 1975," "After the Earth Quaked," and "Poem for a Painter Bent on Suicide" all appear here for the first time.

Note: A Special copy bound for the author has been examined identical to the first edition except that it was bound in green leather printed in gold and with marbled endpapers. printed in gold thus: Front: "This Is Not A Letter | and Other Poems" | [inkwell with feather pen] | Kay Boyle | LOS ANGELES TIMES BOOK PRIZE 1986 Spine: [vertical] "This Is Not A Letter" SUN & MOON PRESS"

A41b   THIS IS NOT A LETTER   [1985]

First Trade Edition:

THIS IS NOT A LETTER | AND OTHER POEMS | BY | [device] KAY BOYLE [device] | [publisher's device] | Sun & Moon Press | Los Angeles

Collation: [1-6], 7-66, [67-72] pages; green endpapers. $7\ ^3/_4$" x 5 $^1/_4$".   [A-C] ^{8} [D] ^{4} [E] ^{8}

Contents: (1) half title page; (2) blank; (3) title page; (4) copyright page; (5) table of contents; (6) [dedication]: *for Grace Paley* ; (7-66) text; (67-72) blank. Note: There is an errata sheet tacked onto the front free end paper.

Copyright page: Copyright © Kay Boyle, 1985 | Some of the poems in this collection appeared previously in | *The Malahat Review* (Canada), *Pearl* (Sweden), *Rolling Stock,* | *Willow Springs Magazine,* and *Wind.* | Cover: Page I from the Japanese volume *Iseshu* | Design: Katie Messborn | Publication of this book was made possible, in part, by a | grant from the National Endowment for the Arts and contributions | to the Contemporary Arts Educational Project, Inc. | [rule] Library of Congress Cataloging-in-Publication Data | Boyle, Kay, 1902- | This is not a letter and other poems. | I. Title. | PS3503.09357T538 1985 811'.52 85-20778 | ISBN 0-940650-61-4 | ISBN 0-940650-62-2 (signed) | [rule] | FIRST EDITION | 10 9 8 7 6 5 4 3 21 | Sun & Moon Press | 6363 Wilshire Blvd. Suite 115 | Los Angeles, California 90048

Binding: Orange cloth covered boards printed in black. Front: [horizontal across the top] [device] THIS IS NOT A LETTER [printed down the right edge of the cover] AND OTHER POEMS by KAY BOYLE [device] Spine: [printed downward] Kay Boyle This Is Not a Letter Sun & Moon Press Back : Blank.

Dust jacket: White paper printed in black and several other colors. Front: Multicolored pattern on front with script printed in black. [across the top in black] [device] THIS IS NOT A LETTER [printed down the right edge off the jacket] AND OTHER POEMS by KAY BOYLE [device] Spine: [printed downward] Kay Boyle This Is Not a Letter Sun & Moon Press Back: Reviews with address of Sun and Moon Press. $9.95 [lower left] Front flap: Note about Kay Boyle and the book. Back flap: List of other books published by Sun and Moon Press and The New American Fiction Series.

Publication: First published on October 21, 1985 at $9.95.

A42a   LIFE BEING THE BEST & OTHER STORIES   [1988]

First Edition:

[rule] | A REVIVED MODERN CLASSIC | [rule] | KAY BOYLE | [rule] | LIFE BEING THE BEST | & OTHER STORIES | EDITED WITH AN INTRODUCTION | BY SANDRA WHIPPLE SPANIER | [publisher's device] | [rule] | A NEW DIRECTIONS BOOK

Collation: [i-vi], vii-xviii, [1-2], 3-41, [42], 43-51, [52], 53-61, [62], 63-91, [92], 93-117, [118], 119-129, [130], 131-140, [141-142] pages; cream endpapers. 8" x 5 ³/₈". [A-E] ¹⁶

Contents: (i) half title page; (ii) [list]: ALSO BY KAY BOYLE [seven titles]; (iii) title page; (iv) copyright page; (v) table of contents; (vi) blank; (vii-xviii) introduction; (1) LIFE BEING THE BEST | & OTHER STORIES; (2) blank; (3-41) text; (42) blank; (43-51) text; (52) blank; (53-61) text; (62) blank; (63-91) text; (92) blank; (93-117) text; (118); (119-129) text; (130) blank; (131-140) text; (141-142) blank.

Copyright page: Copyright © 1930, 1931, 1932, 1933, 1935,1936, 1988, by Kay Boyle | Introduction copyright © 1988 by Sandra Whipple Spanier | All rights reserved. Except for brief passages quoted in a newspaper, | magazine, radio, or television review, no part of this book may be repro- | duced in any form or by any means, electronic or mechanical, including | photocopying and recording, or by any information storage and retrieval | system, without permission in writing from the Publisher. | The contents of this selection of stories are taken from the earlier collec- | tions *Wedding Day and Other Stories* (1930), *The First Lover and Other Stories* | (1933), and *The White Horses of Vienna and Other Stories* (1936). Some of | the stories first appeared in the following magazines to which grateful ac- | knowledgment is made: *Contempo, Harper's Magazine, London Mercury, The* | *New Yorker, Scribner's Magazine,* and *Spectator.* | Manufactured in the United States of America | First published clothbound and as New Directions Paperbook 654 in | 1988 | Published simultaneously in Canada by Penguin Books Canada Limited | **Library of Congress Cataloging-in-Publication Data** | Boyle, Kay, 1902- | Life being the best and other stories / by Kay Boyle ; edited with an | introduction by Sandra Whipple Spanier. | (A New Directions Book) | ISBN 0-8112-1052-9 | ISBN 0-8112-1053-7 (pbk.) | I. Spanier, Sandra Whipple, 1951-   II. Title | PS3503. 09357L5 1988 87-32059 | 813'.52-dc 19   CIP | New Directions Books are published for James Laughlin | by New Directions Publishing Corporation | 80 Eighth Avenue, New York 10011

Binding: Rust orange cloth covered boards stamped in gold.   Front: Blank. Spine: [printed downward] KAY BOYLE [top line] | rule] | LIFE BEING THE BEST & OTHER STORIES [bottom line] | [horizontal publisher's device] [printed downward] NEW DIRECTIONS

Dust jacket: White paper pictorial jacket printed in red and black. Front: [black rule broken by red publisher's device] | [red] A REVIVED [same publisher's device extending down] MODERN CLASSIC | [black] KAY BOYLE | [black rule] | [black] LIFE BEING THE BEST | [black] & OTHER STORIES | [red] | Edited with an introduction | [red] by Sandra Whipple Spanier | [color photograph of a painting by Marcel Duchamp: The Chess Game] Spine: [printed downward in black] KAY BOYLE [top line] | [rule] | LIFE BEING THE BEST & OTHER STORIES [bottom line] | [red publisher's device] | [printed downward in black] NEW DIRECTIONS Back: Same as the top of the front. List of other Revived Modern Classics. Bottom line: NEW DIRECTIONS 80 EIGHTH AVENUE NEW YORK 10011   Front flap: short biographical sketch about Kay Boyle. $18.95 [upper right]. Bottom: Credits for front cover. Back flap: 1930 photograph of Kay Boyle and continuation of front flap text.

Publication: First published in April 1988 at $18.95.

Included stories and previous publication: "Letters of a Lady" was collected in *Wedding Day and Other Stories*. See A3a for previous publication. "I Can't Get Drunk," "Art Colony," "The Meeting of the Stones," "The First Lover," "To the Pure" and "His Idea of a Mother" were all collected in *The First Lover and Other Stories*. See A8a for previous publication. "Life Being the Best," "Astronomer's Wife," "Winter in Italy," "Peter Foxe," "Convalescence" and "Career" were all collected in *The White Horses of Vienna and Other Stories*. See A11a for previous publication.

A42b   LIFE BEING THE BEST & OTHER STORIES   [1988]

First Paperback Edition:

[rule] | A REVIVED MODERN CLASSIC | [rule] | KAY BOYLE | [rule] | LIFE BEING THE BEST | & OTHER STORIES | EDITED WITH AN INTRODUCTION | BY SANDRA WHIPPLE SPANIER | [publisher's device] | [rule] | A NEW DIRECTIONS BOOK

Collation: [i-vi], vii-xviii, [1-2], 3-41, [42], 43-51, [52], 53-61, [62], 63-91, [92], 93-117, [118], 119-129, [130], 131-140, [141-142] pages. 8" x 5 $^1/_4$". [A-E] ^{16}

Contents: (i) half title page; (ii) [list]: ALSO BY KAY BOYLE [seven titles]; (iii) title page; (iv) copyright page; (v) table of contents; (vi) blank; (vii-xviii) introduction; (1) LIFE BEING THE BEST | & OTHER STORIES; (2) blank; (3-41) text; (42) blank; (43-51) text; (52) blank; (53-61) text; (62) blank; (63-91) text; (92) blank; (93-117) text; (118) blank; (119-129) text; (130) blank; (131-140) text; (141-142) list with blurbs of other titles by the Revived Modern Classics.

Copyright page: Same as hardcover edition.

Binding: white pictorial wraps printed in red and black. Front: [black rule broken by red publisher's device] | [red] A REVIVED [same publisher's device extending down] MODERN CLASSIC | [black] KAY BOYLE | [black rule] | [black] LIFE BEING THE BEST | [black] & OTHER STORIES | [red] | Edited with an introduction | [red] by Sandra Whipple Spanier | [black and white photograph of a painting by Marcel Duchamp: The Chess Game]   Spine: [printed downward in black] KAY BOYLE [top line] | [rule] | LIFE BEING THE BEST & OTHER STORIES [bottom line] | [red publisher's device] | [printed downward in black] NDP654   Back: A blurb about Kay Boyle, her work, and the included stories with a photograph of her; also a blurb by Margaret Atwood. $8.95 [lower right]

Publication: First published in April 1988 simultaneously with the hardcover at $8.95.

A43a   COLLECTED POEMS OF KAY BOYLE   [1991]

First Edition:

[Large rectangular design] | COLLECTED POEMS OF | KAY BOYLE | [repeat rectangular design inverted] | COPPER CANYON PRESS / PORT TOWNSEND

Collation: [i-ii], [1-10], 11-172, [173-174] pages; cream endpapers. 9" x 6" [A-B] [16] [C] [8] [D-F] [16]

Contents: (i) half title page; (ii) blank; (1) title page; (2) copyright page; (3) publisher's note; (4) blank; (5-7) table of contents; (8) blank; (9) [dedication]: TO SHAWN WONG; (10) blank; (11-172) text; (173-174) blank.

Copyright page: Copyright 1938, 1944, 1954, © 1956, 1959, 1960, 1961, 1962, 1970, 1985, and 1991 | by Kay Boyle. All rights reserved. | ISBN I-55659-038-5 (Cloth) | ISBN I-55659-039-3 (Paper) | Library of Congress Catalog Card Number 90-85089 | The publication of this book was supported by a grant from the National Endowment | for the Arts. | Copper Canyon Press is in residence with Centrum at Fort Worden State Park. | Copper Canyon Press | Post Office Box 271 | Port Townsend, Washington 98368

Binding: Black cloth spine stamped in pink with yellow paper covered boards embossed in pink. Top edge unstained and all edges trimmed. Front: [short rule] | K B | [square design]   Spine: [printed downward] COLLECTED POEMS OF KAY BOYLE | COPPER [top line] CANYON [bottom line]   Back: Blank.

Dust jacket: White paper printed in yellow, coral, pink and black Front: [design in yellow and orange in upper left quadrant with black and white photograph of Kay Boyle in upper right quadrant] | [black rule] | [black printing on pink band] COLLECTED POEMS OF | KAY BOYLE | [black rule] | [solid black left lower quadrant with right lower quadrant of similar design of upper left quadrant] Spine: [printed downward in pink on black] COLLECTED POEMS OF KAY BOYLE | COPPER [top line] CANYON [bottom line]   Back: Entire back done in yellow and coral design Front flap: Short biographical sketch of Kay Boyle. $19.00 [upper right]   Back flap: Reviews with cover photo credit.

Published July 1, 1991 at $19.00.

Included poems and previous publication: "In Defense of Homosexuality," "Career," "Hunt," "To America," "For an American," "And Winter," "A Letter to Francis Picabia," "O This Is Not Spring," "A Christmas Carol for Emanuel Carnevali," "A Confession to Eugene Jolas," "Dedicated to Robert McAlmon, " The United States," "The Only Bird That Sang," "A Valentine for Harry Crosby," "A Cloak for a Man Who Has No Heed for Winter," "A Glad Day for Laurence Vail," "A Comeallye for Robert Carlton Brown," "A Landscape for Wyn Henderson," "A Statement for El Greco and William Carlos Williams," "A Waterfront for Allan Ross MacDougall," "Funeral in Hungary," "A Complaint for

Mary and Marcel," "A Communication to Nancy Cunard" and "Angels for Djuna Barnes" were all collected in *A Glad Day*. See A15a for previous publication. "Carnival 1927," "American Citizen," "October 1954," "Spring," "The New Emigration," "Dreams Dreamed," "A Poem of Gratitude," "Two Twilights for William Carlos Williams," "A Dialogue of Birds for Howard Nemerov," "A Night Letter," "Rendezvous," "A Winter Fable," "Poem for a Painter Who Drinks Wine," "Print from a Lucite Block," "Seascape for an Engraver," "The Artist Speaks—The Woman Answers," "The Painter Speaks—The Woman Answers," "The Evening Grass" and "Two Poems for a Poet" were all collected in *Collected Poems*. See A30a for previous publication. "A Square Dance for a Square," "Thunderstorms in South Dakota," "A Short Poem in Color," "A Poem about the Jews," "A Poem for Author," "The Lost Dogs of Phnom Penh," "A Poem of Love," "Dedicated to *Terre des Hommes*," "A Poem about Black Power," "A Poem in One Sentence," "For James Schevill," "For Marianne Moore's Birthday," "Testament for My Students," "For James Baldwin" and "The Jews Among the Nations" were all collected in *Testament for My Students and Other Poems*. See A36a for previous publication. "World Tour," "Poets," "On Taking up Residence in Virginia," "On the Death of My Student, the Poet Serafin," "Branded for Slaughter," "This Is Not a Letter," "What Parents Do Not Yet Know," "A Poems for the Students of Greece," "A Poem for the Teesto Diné of Arizona" "Advice to the Old," "The Stones of a Seventeenth Century Village," "To a Woman Watching the Tearing Down of a Hurricane Shed," and "Poem for a Painter Bent on Suicide" were all collected in *This Is Not a Letter and Other Poems*. See A41a for previous publication. Part III of "A Poem for Samuel Beckett" first appeared in *Rolling Stock* 5, 1983. "A Poem for Vida Hadjebi Tabrizi" first appeared in a *Committee for Artistic and Intellectual Freedom in Iran*, March 1977 and as a small letter size Broadside. "A Poem for February First 1975" was first published as a Broadside, San Francisco: The Quercus Press, 1975. "After the Earth Quaked" was first published as a Broadside and included as one of ten broadsides in an issue by Copper Canyon Press, 1983. "To a Proud Old Woman Watching the Tearing Down of a Hurricane Shed," "December 1989," "A Lesson in Anatomy," "A Poem on Getting Up Early in the Morning," Weather," "Ode to a Maintenance Man and His Family," and "The Crows" all appear here for the first time. "A Letter to Archibald Craig" first appears here in this form. However, it is very similar to a poem of the same name which first appeared in *transition* in the Summer of 1928. The name was change to "A Letter for Francis Picabia" and was collected in *A Glad Day*, *Testament for My Students and Other Poems* and also appears on page 24 of this item.

A43b   COLLECTED POEMS OF KAY BOYLE   [1991]

First Paperback Edition:

[Large rectangular design] | COLLECTED POEMS OF | KAY BOYLE | [repeat rectangular design inverted] | COPPER CANYON PRESS / PORT TOWNSEND

Collation: [i-ii], [1-10], 11-172, [173-174] pages.   9" x 6"   [A-B] ^{16} [C] ^{8} [D-F] ^{16}

Contents: (i) half title page; (ii) blank; (1) title page; (2) copyright page; (3) publisher's note; (4) blank; (5-7) table of contents; (8) blank; (9) [dedication]: TO SHAWN WONG; (10) blank; (11-172) text; (173-174) blank.

Copyright page: Copyright 1938, 1944,1954, © 1956,1959, 1960, 1961, 1962, 1970, 1985, and 1991 | by Kay Boyle. All rights reserved. | ISBN 1-55659-038-5 (Cloth) | ISBN 1-55659-039-3 (Paper) | Library of Congress Catalog Card Number 90-85089 | The publication of this book was supported by a grant from the National Endowment | for the Arts. | Copper Canyon Press is in residence with Centrum at Fort Worden State Park. | Copper Canyon Press | Post Office Box 271 | Port Townsend, Washington 98368

Binding: Stiff white paper wraps. Front: Printed identically to the hardcover dust wrapper. Back: Short biographical sketch and note about *The Collected Poems of Kay Boyle* with excerpts from reviews.

Publication: Published simultaneously with hardback edition at $10.00.

A44a   THE CRAZY HUNTER   [1993]

First Separate Edition:

Kay | Boyle | The Crazy | Hunter | A NEW DIRECTIONS BOOK | [black rectangle with Bibelot written in white

Collation: [i-iv], [1-2], 3-139, [140] pages. 7" x 4 $^3/_4$"

Contents: (i) half title page; (ii) list of other New Directions publications; (iii) title page; (iv) copyright page; (1) fly title; (2) blank; (3-139) text; (140) blank.

Copyright page: Copyright © 1940 by Kay Boyle | All rights reserved. Except for brief passages quoted in a | newspaper, magazine, radio, or television review, no part of this | book may be reproduced in any form or by any means, | electronic or mechanical, including photocopying and | recording, or by any information storage and retrieval system, | without permission in writing from the Publisher. | *The Crazy Hunter* is also available in the New Direction Revived | Modern Classic edition of Kay Boyle's *Three Short Novels: The Crazy | Hunter, The Bridegroom's Body, and Decision.* | Manufactured in the United States of America. | New Directions Books are printed on acid-free paper. | First published as a New Directions Bibelot in 1993. | Published simultaneously in Canada by Penguin Books of Canada | Limited. | Library of Congress Cataloging-in-Publication Data | Boyle, Kay, 1902-92 | The crazy hunter / Kay Boyle | p. cm. | ISBN 0-8112-1233-5 (alk. paper) | 1. Family-England-Fiction. 2. Horses-Fiction. I. Title | PS3503.09357C73

1993 | 813' .54—dc20 | 93-8246 | CIP | New Directions Books are published for James Laughlin | by New Directions Publishing Corporation, | 80 Eighth Avenue, New York 10011

Binding: White paper wraps printed in black, white and orange.   Top edge unstained and all edges trimmed.   Front: [white on black] ND [white on orange] Bibelots | [photograph of Kay Boyle] | [white on black The Crazy | Hunter | [torn orange corner] | [white on black] Kay | Boyle   Spine: [white on black printed downward] Kay Boyle   The Crazy Hunter [repeat torn orange corner] | [white on black printed horizontally] ND   Back: Story plot with reviews and cover credits. Price USA $6.00 | CAN $6.99 in lower left corner.

Published September 28, 1993 at $6.00.

Note: Also examined: An 8 $^1/_2$" x 11" uncorrected proof copy in spiral bound wraps.

B

Contributions and First Appearances in
Books and Pamphlets

B1   ANTHOLOGY OF MAGAZINE VERSE FOR 1923   1923
     AND YEARBOOK OF AMERICAN POETRY

a. First Limited Edition:

Anthology of Magazine Verse | for 1923 | and | Yearbook of American Poetry | Edited by | WILLIAM STANLEY BRAITHWAITE | [Ink drawing of boy with laurel wreath sitting under a tree, a bird and deer with scroll lettered thus: ANTHOLOGY | of | MAGAZINE | VERSE | WILLIAM STANLEY | BRAITHWAITE] | BOSTON | B.J. BRIMMER COMPANY | 1923

[i-viii], ix, [x], xi-xix, [xx], [1-2], 3-376 pages, part 1; [1-4], 5-165, [166-168], 169-188 pages, part 2; cream endpapers. $9^1/_2$" x $6^1/_2$" Published November 26, 1923 at $7.50. Issued in dark brown paper covered boards with lighter brown cloth spine and corners. Top and bottom edge trimmed with top edge gilt. Front edge rough trimmed. Front cover has small rectangular paste on. [following enclosed in ruled rectangle printed in black] BRAITHWAITE'S ANTHOLOGY | OF MAGAZINE VERSE | FOR 1923 | YEAR-BOOK OF AMERICAN POETRY [following enclosed in smaller rectangle] WILLIAM STANLEY BRAITHWAITE [both previous rectangles then enclosed in a larger rectangle] Spine has small square paste on printed in black: [double rule] | Anthology *of* | Magazine | Verse | 1923 | [short rule] BRAITHWAITE | [double rule]   Issued without dust jacket.

Limitation Statement: *This Special Edition of the | ANTHOLOGY OF MAGAZINE VERSE FOR 1923 | AND YEARBOOK OF AMERICAN POETRY | consists of 245 signed and numbered | copies, of which this is | Number.....*[ink number] | [signed in ink: William Stanley Braithwaite]

Contains: "Monody to the Sound of Zithers" (47) which originally appeared in *Poetry, A Magazine of Verse*   December 1922   (125)

b. First Trade Edition:

Anthology of Magazine Verse | for 1923 | and | Yearbook of American Poetry | Edited by | WILLIAM STANLEY BRAITHWAITE | [Ink drawing of boy with laurel wreath sitting under a tree, a bird and deer with scroll lettered thus: ANTHOLOGY | of | MAGAZINE | VERSE | WILLIAM STANLEY | BRAITH-WAITE] | BOSTON | B.J. BRIMMER COMPANY | 1923 [i-viii], ix, [x], xi-xix, [xx], [1-2], 3-376 pages, part 1; [1-4], 5-165, [166-168], 169-188 pages, part 2; cream endpapers. 8$^1/_4$" x 5$^1/_2$" Published November 26, 1923 at $3.00. Issued in dark brown paper covered boards with lighter brown cloth spine. Top and bottom edge trimmed with top edge stained brown.   Front edge rough trimmed. Front cover has small rectangular paste on. [following enclosed in ruled rectangle printed in black] BRAITHWAITE'S ANTHOLOGY | OF MAGAZINE VERSE | FOR 1923 | YEARBOOK OF AMERICAN POETRY   [following enclosed in smaller rectangle] WILLIAM STANLEY BRAITHWAITE [both previous rectangles then enclosed in a larger rectangle]   Spine has small square paste on printed in black: [double rule] | Anthology *of* | Magazine | Verse | 1923 | [short rule] BRAITHWAITE | [double rule]   Issued in cream paper dust jacket printed in black.

B2   THE SECOND AMERICAN CARAVAN   1928

a. First Limited Edition:

[enclosed in double rule thick-thin, the thin rule is red] THE SECOND | AMERICAN | CARAVAN | [red rule] | A YEARBOOK | OF AMERICAN | LITERATURE | EDITED BY | ALFRED KREYMBORG | LEWIS MUMFORD | PAUL ROSENFELD | [red design] | [red rule] | NEW YORK | THE MACAULAY COMPANY | MCMXXVIII

[i-vi], vii-ix, [x], xi-xii, 1-872 pages; cream endpapers. 9$^3/_{16}$" x 6$^1/_4$"   Published September 24,1928 at $15.00. Issued in full black leather stamped in gold. Top edge gilt. Top and bottom edges trimmed. Front edge rough trimmed. Front: Blank. Spine: [stamped in gold] THE SECOND | AMERICAN | CARAVAN | EDITED BY | ALFRED KREYMBORG | LEWIS MUMFORD | PAUL ROSENFELD | [rule] | MACAULAY   First deluxe limited edition 250 copies signed by the editors.

Limitation statement on page ii: THIS EDITION OF "THE SECOND AMERICAN | CARAVAN" CONSISTS OF TWO HUNDRED FIFTY | SPECIALLY BOUND COPIES, OF WHICH | THIS IS NUMBER   [Signed by all three editors]

Contains "A Christmas Carol for Emanuel Carnevali" and "Madame Tout Petit." "Madam Tout Petit" (307-311) was collected in *Wedding Day and Other Stories*. "A Christmas Carol for Emanuel Carnevali" on (302-306) was collected in *A Glad Day*, *Collected Poems* and *Collected Poems of Kay Boyle*

b. First Trade Edition:

[enclosed in double rule] THE SECOND | AMERICAN | CARAVAN | [rule] | A YEARBOOK | OF AMERICAN | LITERATURE | EDITED BY | ALFRED KREYMBORG | LEWIS MUMFORD | PAUL ROSENFELD | [design] | [rule] | NEW YORK | THE MACAULAY COMPANY | MCMXXVIII [i-vi], vii-ix, [x], xi-xii, 1-872 pages; cream end papers. $9^3/_{16}$" x $6^1/_4$" Published September 24,1928 at $5.00. Issued in beige cloth covered boards stamped. Top edge unstained. Top and bottom edges trimmed. Front edge untrimmed. Front: [gray rectangle enclosed in a double rule thick-thin printed in gold] THE SECOND | AMERICAN | CARAVAN Spine: [gray rectangle enclosed in double rule thick-thin printed in gold] THE SECOND | AMERICAN | CARAVAN | EDITED BY | ALFRED KREYMBORG | LEWIS MUMFORD | PAUL ROSENFELD | [rule] | MACAULAY Issued in beige paper dust jacket printed in red and black.

B3   TRANSITION STORIES   1929

a. First Limited Edition:

transition stories | Twenty-three stories from "transition" | selected and edited by | Eugene Jolas | and | Robert Sage | [red publisher's device] | New York | Walter V. McKee | 1929

tipped in page for limitation statement. [i-vi], vii, [viii], ix-xii, [1-2], 3-16, [17-18], 19-25, [26-28], 29-30, [31-32], 33-38, [39-40], 41-47, [48-50], 51-63, [64-66], 67-77, [78-80], 81-95, [96-98], 99-136, [137-138], 139-147, [148-150], 151-160, [161-162], 163-176, [177], 178-191, [192-194], 195-211, [212-214], 215-226, [227-228], 229-239, [240-242], 243-248, [249-250], 251-267, [268-270], 271-289, [290-292], 293-307, [308-310], 311-333, [334-336], 337-346, [347], 348-349, [350], 351-354, [355-356] pages; cream endpapers. $9^1/_2$" x $6^1/_4$" Published in the Spring of 1929 at $10.00. Issued in decorative paper covered boards with lime green cloth spine. Top edge stained and trimmed. Front and bottom edge rough trimmed. Spine: [printed in black] t | r | a | n | s | i | t | i | o | n | s | t | o | r | i | e | s | [triangle pointing down] | mckee   Issued in plain black paper covered cardboard slipcase.

Limitation statement: One hundred copies of the first edition | of *transition stories* have been printed on | large paper, specially bound and numbered. | This copy is | No._____

Contains : "Polar Bears and Others" (17-25) which originally appeared in *transition* Number 6 September 1927 and was collected in *Wedding Day and Other Stories*.

b. First Trade Edition:

transition stories | Twenty-three stories from "transition" | selected and edited by | Eugene Jolas | and | Robert Sage | [publisher's device] | New York | Walter V. McKee | 1929

[i-vi], vii, [viii], ix-xii, [1-2], 3-16, [17-18], 19-25, [26-28], 29-30, [31-32], 33-38, [39-40], 41-47, [48-50], 51-63, [64-66], 67-77, [78-80], 81-95, [96-98], 99-136, [137-138], 139-147, [148-150], 151-160, [161-162], 163-176, [177], 178-191, [192-194], 195-211, [212-214], 215-226, [227-228], 229-239, [240-242], 243-248, [249-250], 251-267, [268-270], 271-289, [290-292], 293-307, [308-310],

311-333, [334-336], 337-346, [347], 348-349, [350], 351-354, [355-356] pages; cream endpapers. 7 $^3/_8$" x 5 $^1/_8$" Published in the spring of 1929 at $2.50. Issued in decorative paper covered boards with cloth covered spine. Front and back designed by Albert Schiller. Top edge stained brownish red and trimmed. Front and bottom edge rough trimmed. Black cloth spine printed in red: t | r | a | n | s | i | t | i | o | n | s | t | o | r | i | e | s | [triangle pointing down] | mckee Issued in cream paper dust wrapper printed in orange and black.

B4   DON JUAN   [1931]

DON JUAN | BY JOSEPH DELTEIL | *Translated from the French by* KAY BOYLE | *Illustrated by* CHARLES SANDFORD | [design] | NEW YORK | JONATHAN CAPE & HARRISON SMITH

[i-xii], xiii-xvii, [xviii-xx], [1-3], 4-28, [29-30], 31-36, [37-39], 40-42, [43-44], 45-63, [64-67], 68-84, [85-86], 87-88, [89-91], 92-102, [103-104], 105-110, [111-112], 113-115, [116 -119], 120-122, [123-124], 125-146, [147-149], 150-166, [167-168], 169-174, [175-176], 177, [178-181], 182-206 pages; cream endpapers. 7 $^3/_8$" x 4 $^7/_8$" Published April 6, 1931 at $2.50. Issued in glossy dark blue cloth covered boards stamped in gold. Top edge stained black with all edges trimmed. Front: DON JUAN | JOSEPH DELTEIL | [design]   Spine: [design] | [rule] | DON | JUAN | [dot enclosed in a small circle] | DELTEIL | [rule] | [design] | [publisher's device]   Cream paper dust jacket printed in black and light blue. ALSO: Seen in dark matte blue cloth covered boards stamped in gold; the same as the above except that the publisher's device at the bottom of the spine is replaced with BLACKFRIAR | PRESS No priority established.

Contains: A translator's foreword by Kay Boyle (xiii-xvii).

B5   THE BEST SHORT STORIES 1931   1931

THE | BEST SHORT STORIES | OF 1931 | AND THE | YEARBOOK OF THE AMERICAN | SHORT STORY | EDITED BY | EDWARD J. O'BRIEN | [publisher's device] | DODD, MEAD AND COMPANY | NEW YORK [three spaced colons] 1931

[i-viii], ix, [x], xi-xxvii, [xxviii], [1-2], 3-15, [16-18], 19-36, [37-38], 39-46, [47-48], 49-68, [69-70], 71-76, [77-78], 79-83, [84-86], 87-106, [107-108], 109-133, [134-136], 137-146, [147-148], 149-161, [162-164], 165-192, [193-194], 195-199, [200-202], 203-213, [214-216], 217-242, [243-244], 245-268, [269-270], 271-315, [316] pages; cream endpapers. 7$^3/_4$" x 5$^1/_2$" Published October 9, 1931 at $2.50. Issued in dark blue cloth covered boards printed in gold. Top edge stained red. Top and bottom edges trimmed. Front edge rough trimmed. Front: THE |

BEST SHORT STORIES | OF 1931 | And the | Yearbook of the American | Short Story | Edited by | Edward J. O'Brien Spine: THE | BEST | SHORT | STORIES | OF | 1931 | [rule] | O'Brien | DODD, MEAD | & COMPANY Issued in a yellow paper dust jacket printed in gold, green and black.

Contains: "Rest Cure" (47-54) which originally appeared in *Story Magazine* April-May 1931 and was collected in *The First Lover and Other Stories*, *Thirty Stories* and *Fifty Stories*.

B6 READIES FOR BOB BROWN'S MACHINE 1931

READIES | for | Bob Brown's Machine | by | A. Lincoln Gillespie Jr. John A. Farrell | Alfred Kreymborg John Banting | Axton Clark Kay Boyle | B.C. Hagglund K.T. Young | Carlton Brown Laurence Vail | Charles Beadle Lloyd Stern | Clare L. Brackett Manuel Komroff | Charles Henri Ford Nancy Cunard | Daphne Carr Norman Mac Leod | Donal MacKenzie Paul Bowles | Eugene Jolas Peter Neagoè | Ezra Pound Richard Johns | Filippo Tommaso Marinetti Robert Mc Almon | George Kent Rose Brown | Gertrude Stein Rue Menken | Herman Spector Samuel Putnam | Hilaire Hiler Sydney Hunt | Hiler, *pere* Theodore Pratt | J. Jones Walter Lowenfels | James T. Farrell Wambly Bald | Jay du Von William Carlos Williams | Roving Eye Press | Cagnes-sur-Mer (A.-M.) | 1931

[i-vi], [1-4], 5-208 pages. $8^1/_2$" x $5^1/_4$". Published in late December of 1931 at $2.00. 300 copies. Issued in stiff green paper wraps printed in black with top edge unstained and all edges trimmed. Front: READIES | for | BOB BROWN'S | Machine Spine: [printed upward] 1931 | [double rule] | READIES | [double rule] | For [first line] BOB BROWN'S [second line] Machine [third line]

Contains: "Change of Life" and "Landscape for Wyn Henderson." "Change of Life" (37-38), uncollected. "Landscape for Wyn Henderson" (39-41) was collected in *A Glad Day*, *Collected Poems* and *Collected Poems of Kay Boyle*.

B7 O. HENRY MEMORIAL AWARD PRIZE STORIES OF 1932 1932

O. HENRY | MEMORIAL AWARD | *Prize Stories of 1932* | SELECTED AND EDITED BY | BLANCHE COLTON WILLIAMS | *Author of* "A HANDBOOK ON STORY WRITING" | "OUR SHORT STORY WRITERS," *Etc.* | *Head*, *Department of English*, | *Hunter College of the* | *City of New York* | [red publisher's device] | DOUBLEDAY, DORAN & COMPANY, INC. | GARDEN CITY, NEW YORK | 1932

[i-viii], ix, [x], xi-xxvii, [xxviii], [1-2], 3-15. [16-18], 19-36, [37-38], 39-46, [47-48], 49-68, [69-70], 71-76, [77-78], 79-83, [84-86], 87-106, [107-108], 109-133, [134-136], 137-146, [147-148], 149-161, [162-164], 165-192, [193-194], 195-199,

[200-202], 203-213, [214-216], 217-242, [243-244], 245-268, [269-270], 271-315, [316] pages; cream endpapers. $7^3/_4$" x $5^3/_8$". Published October 26, 1932 at $2.50. Issued in black cloth covered boards with top edge unstained and all edges trimmed. Stamped in gold. Front: Blank. Spine: [gold square with black showing through] O. HENRY | MEMORIAL | AWARD | [another gold square as above] | PRIZE | STORIES | OF 1932 | [another gold square as above] EDITED BY | BLANCHE | COLTON | WILLIAMS | [gold on black] DOUBLEDAY | DORAN There is a series of slanting gold rules above, between and below the three gold squares. Back: Blank. Issued in a cream paper dust jacket striped in gold and printed in cream and black.

Contains: "The First Lover" (71-76) which originally appeared in *Harper's Magazine* in June 1931. It was collected in *The First Lover and Other Stories* and *Life Being the Best and Other Stories*. With short biographical note (70)

B8   AN ANTHOLOGY OF THE YOUNGER POETS   1932

a. First Limited Edition:

An Anthology *of the* Younger Poets | [double rule thick thin] | Edited by Oliver Wells | [single rule] | With a Preface by Archibald MacLeish | [publisher's device, centaur] | PHILADELPHIA – THE CENTAUR PRESS | 1932

[i-iv], v-xiv, 1-184, [185-186] pages; gray endpapers. $9^1/_4$" x $6^1/_4$". Published December 1932.   Issued in red paper covered boards with heavy beige cloth spine. Top and bottom edge trimmed. Front edge rough trimmed. Spine: [on beige paste on paper label] [double rule, thick thin] | An | Anthology | *of the* | Younger | Poets | [short rule] | Edited | *by* | Oliver | Wells | [double rule, thin thick] Issued in a tissue paper dust jacket.

Contains: "A Comeallye for Robert Carleton Brown"   (85-90) and "A Statement" (91-95) "A Comeallye for Robert Carleton Brown" appearing for the first time and was later collected in *A Glad Day, Collected Poems,* and *Collected Poems of Kay Boyle*. "A Statement" appeared by itself in a pamphlet published by Modern Editions Press, New York, 1932 and was collected in *A Glad Day, Collected Poems* and *Collected Poems of Kay Boyle*

Limitation Statement: THIS EDITION IS LIMITED TO | 500 COPIES OF WHICH THIS IS | NUMBER [ink number]

b. First Trade Edition:

An Anthology *of the* Younger Poets | [double rule thick thin] | Edited by Oliver Wells | [single rule] | With a Preface by Archibald MacLeish | [publisher's device, centaur] | PHILADELPHIA – THE CENTAUR PRESS | 1932

[i-iv], v-xiv, 1-184, [185-186] pages; gray endpapers. $9^1/_4$" x $6^1/_4$". Published December 1932 at $3.00.   Issued in red paper covered boards with heavy beige

cloth spine. Top and bottom edge trimmed. Front edge rough trimmed. Spine: [on beige paste on paper label] [double rule, thick thin] | An | Anthology | *of the* | Younger | Poets | [short rule] | Edited | *by* | Oliver | Wells | [double rule, thin thick] Issued in a tissue paper dust jacket.

B9   AMERICANS ABROAD   1932

AMERICANS | ABROAD | An Anthology | edited by | PETER NEAGOE | WITH AUTOGRAPHED PHOTOGRAPHS AND | BIOGRAPHIC SKETCHES OF THE AUTHORS | 1932 | THE SERVIRE PRESS • THE HAGUE (HOLLAND)

[i-iv], v-xi, [xii], [1-2], 3-6, [7-8], 9-18, [19-20], 21-26, [27-29], 30-36, [37-38], 39-41, [42-43], 44-49, [50-51], 52-62, [63-64], 65-72, [73-74], 75-82, [83-84], 85-88, [89-91], 92-101, [102-103], 104-107, [108-109], 110-111, [112-113], 114-121, [122-123], 124, [125-126], 127, [128-129], 130-134, [135-136], 137-138, [139-140], 141, [142-143], 144-148, [149-150] 151-156, [157-158], 159-160, [161-162], 163-166, [167-168], 169-174, [175-176], 177-182, [183-184], 185-201, [202-203], 204-205, [206-207], 208-215, [216-217], 218-221, [222-223], 224-231, [232-233], 234, [235-236], 237-249, [250-251], 252-262, [263-264], 265-269, [270-271], 272-278, [279-280], 281-295, [296-297], 298-314, [315-316], 317-321, [322-323], 324-325, [326], 327, [328-329], 330-333, [334-335], 336-356, [357-360], 361-374, [375-376], 377-378, [379-380], 381-402, [403-404], 405-417, [418-419], 420-423, [424-425], 426-427, [428-429], 430-457, [458-459], 460-461, [462], 463-467, [468-469], 470-475, [476], pages; brown endpapers. 9 $^1/_8$" x 6" Published December 1, 1932 at $2.50. Top edge stained red and all edges trimmed. Issued in beige cloth covered boards stamped in blue Front: AMERICANS | ABROAD   Spine: AMERICANS | ABROAD | edited by | Peter Neagoe | [publisher's device]   Issued in white paper dust jacket printed in red and blue. Note: Not seen but also apparently issued in white paper covered boards printed in red and blue and in yellow paper covered boards printed in brown on the front cover with gray cloth covered back stamped in brown, top edges stained gray.

Contains: An autobiographical statement and bibliography by Kay Boyle and "A Comeallye for Robert Carlton Brown" (37-41)

B10   AUTHORS TODAY AND YESTERDAY   1933

AUTHORS | TODAY and YESTERDAY | A Companion Volume to | LIVING AUTHORS | Edited By | STANLEY J. KUNITZ | HOWARD HAYCRAFT WILBUR C. HADDEN | Managing Editor   Editorial Assistant | ILLUSTRATED WITH 320 PHOTOGRAPHS | AND DRAWINGS | [publisher's device] | NEW YORK | THE H. W. WILSON COMPANY | NINETEEN HUNDRED THIRTY-THREE [i-iv], v-vii, [viii], [1], 2-717, [718-721], 722-726, [727-728] pages; cream endpapers. 10" x 6 $^5/_8$" Published in December 1933 at $5.00. Issued in green cloth covered boards stamped in gold. Top edge unstained and all edges trimmed. Front: Blank. Spine: [double rule-thick/thin] | AUTHORS | TODAY AND | YESTERDAY | [doubled rule] | KUNITZ | [double rule-thin/thick] | [double rule-thick\thin | THE | H.W. WILSON | COMPANY | [double rule-thin\thick] Dust jacket not seen and maybe not issued.

Contains: Autobiographical sketch.   (85-87)

B11   O. HENRY MEMORIAL AWARD PRIZE STORIES OF 1935   1935

O. HENRY | MEMORIAL AWARD | *Prize Stories of 1935* | SELECTED AND EDITED BY | HARRY HANSEN | *Literary Editor* | *of the New York World-Telegram* | [publisher's device] | DOUBLEDAY, DORAN & COMPANY, INC. | GARDEN CITY, NEW YORK | 1935

[i-iv], v, [vi], vii-xviii, [1-2], 3-20, [21-22], 23-53, [54-56], 57-59, [60-62], 63-67, [68-70], 71-84, [85-86], 87-100, [101-102], 103-121, [122-124], 125-138, [139-140], 141-149, [150-152], 153-167, [168-170], 171-186, [187-188], 189-202, [203-204], 205-208, [209-210], 211-216, [217-218], 219-226, [227-228], 229-234, [235-236], 237-256, [257-258], 259-263, [264-266], 267-273, [274-276], 277-284, [285-286] pages; cream endpapers. 7 $^1/_2$" x 5 $^1/_8$". Published November 8, 1935 at $2.50. Issued in black cloth covered boards stamped in gold. Top edge stained green and trimmed. Bottom edge trimmed and front edge rough trimmed. Front: Blank. Spine: [gold square with black showing through] O. HENRY | MEMORIAL | AWARD | [another gold square as above] | PRIZE | STORIES | OF 1935 | [another gold square as above] SELECTED AND | EDITED BY | HARRY | HANSEN | [gold on black] DOUBLEDAY | DORAN There is a series of slanting gold rules above, between and below the three gold squares. Back: Blank. Issued in a cream paper dust jacket and printed in green, pale yellow, gold and black.

Contains: "The White Horses of Vienna." (3-20) Originally published in *Harper's Magazine* in April 1935. Later collected in *The White Horses of Vienna and Other Stories*, *Thirty Stories* and *Fifty Stories*. Short biographical note (2)

B12   365 DAYS   [1936]

a. First Edition:

365 DAYS | *Edited by* |KAY BOYLE | LAURENCE VAIL | NINA CONARAIN | [publisher's device] | JONATHAN CAPE | THIRTY BEDFORD SQUARE | LONDON

[1-6], 7-12, [13-14], 15-47, [48-50], 51-81, [82-84], 85-118, [119-120], 121-154, [155-156], 157-189, [190-192], 193-225, [226-228], 229-262, [263-264], 265-298, [299-300], 301-335, [336-338], 339-374, [375-376], 377-412, [413-414], 415-449, [450] pages; cream endpapers. 7 $7/_8$" x 5 $3/_8$" Published in September 1936 at 8s 6d. Issued in tan cloth covered boards lettered in blue. Top edge stained blue. Top and fore edge trimmed and bottom edge rough trimmed. Front: 365 | DAYS Spine: 365 | DAYS | *Edited by* | KAY BOYLE | LAURENCE VAIL | NINA CONARAIN | [publisher's device] Issued in a white paper dust jacket printed in black and red.

Contains: Ninety six short pieces under her own name and apparently several others under pseudonyms.

b. First American Edition:

365 DAYS | *Edited by* | KAY BOYLE | LAURENCE VAIL | NINA CONARAIN | [design] HARCOURT, BRACE AND COMPANY | NEW YORK

[i-vi], vii, [viii], ix, [x], xi-xiii, [xiv], xv. [xvi], [1-2], 3-33, [34-36], 37-65, [66-68], 69-99, [100-102], 103-133, [134-136], 137-167, [168-170], 171-201, [202-204], 205-236, [237-238], 239-270, [271-272], 273-305, [306-308], 309-342, [343-344], 345-377, [378-380], 381-411, [412], 413-414, [415-416] pages; cream end-papers. 8 $7/_{16}$" x 5$3/_4$". Published November 14, 1936 at $3.00. Issued in gray cloth covered boards stamped in silver. Top edge stained grape. Top and bottom edge trimmed. Front edge rough trimmed. Spine: 365 | DAYS | *edited by* | KAY BOYLE | LAURENCE VAIL | NINA CONARAIN | design] | HARCOURT, BRACE | AND COMPANY Issued in a cream paper dust jacket printed in green and purple.

Contains: Ninety-six short pieces under her own name and apparently several others under pseudonyms.

Note: In a copy owned by the compiler Kay Boyle has written the following: August 1980—- "As it was not an easy matter to procure stories of the required length, or, rather of the restricted length, for this odd collection, I was obliged to write a number of stories under various noms de plume in order to complete the volume. And as all this took place forty-seven years ago, I am somewhat uncertain as to my claims to authorship of some of the stories herewith listed. To the best of my belief I am: Graham Boswell, Morris Cohen, Susan S. Grant, Donald Holloway, Mary Knaggs, Kamarov, Jane Martin, Florence Park, Kerker Quinn, Angus Rudge, Imre Suryani (?) In addition to these names, I may also be (or have been) Malachi Whitaker, but I am in some doubt about this. It is also just possible that I was Ambrose Caddy. It is also more than possible that Laurence Vail was Imre Suryani. It is also quite likely that I was Wallace H. Short for a brief moment, and that Laurence Vail was Hiram White. I Think I was Larry Boyle, but am far from sure."

"If I have in the above statement claimed the work of others as Laurence Vail's or mine, I hereby offer my apologies."

B13   NEW DIRECTIONS IN PROSE AND POETRY 1937   [1937]

NEW DIRECTIONS | IN PROSE & POETRY | 1937 | [publisher's device] | NEW
DIRECTIONS | NORFOLK — CONN

328 unpaginated pages; white endpapers. 9" x 6". Published December 29, 1937
at $2.50. Issued in white paper covered boards printed black, blue, gray and white.
Top edge unstained and all edges trimmed. Front: [white] • NEW • DIREC-
TIONS • | [gray] 37 | | [black] MIL- [gray] COC- | [black] LER • [gray] TEAU |
[black] • STEIN • [gray] WIL- | [black] MUNSEN [gray] LIAMS | • SAROYAN |
[gray] • CUM- | [black] O'REILLY • | [gray] MINGS • | • SCHWARTZ • [gray] •
BOYLE • [black] HAMPDEN [gray] FITZGERALD | [black] • NIEDECKER • |
[gray] WHEELWRIGHT | [black] YOUNG and [gray] • O'DONNELL • | [black]
• OTHERS • | AND OTHERS • [white] PROSE POETRY   Spine: [printed in
black] N | E | W | • | D | I | R | E | C | TI | O | N | S | [white] '37   Issued in a
white paper dust jacket printed identically to the boards.

Contains: "Funeral in Hungary"   (79-80)   which was collected in *A Glad Day*,
Collected Poems and *Collected Poems of Kay Boyle*.

B14   JUST WHAT THE DOCTOR ORDERED   1938

Fun in Bed——*Series Four* | R Just What the | Doctor Ordered | *edited by* FRANK
SCULLY | *and an* | ALL-STAR CAST | *including* | ROBERT BENCHLEY, WOL-
COTT GIBBS, FRED ALLEN, | OGDEN NASH, DONALD OGDEN
STEWART, MARK | HELLINGER, KAY BOYLE, CEDRIC BELFRAGE, | HEY-
WOOD BROUN, WILLIAM SAROYAN, | JACK BENNY, STEWART
EDWARD WHITE, | ERNEST HEMINGWAY, GEORGE E. SO- | KOLSKY,
WILLIAM SHAKESPEARE | AND MANY, MANY MORE | *SIMON AND
SCHUSTER, INC.* | New York 1938

[i-vi], vii-x, [1], 2-15, [16], 17-42, [43], 44-102, [103], 104-122, [123], 124-152,
[153], 154-172, [173], 174-188, [189-190] pages with cream endpapers. 10" x
$6^3/_4$"   Published September 15, 1938 at $2.00. Top edge unstained and all edges
trimmed. Issued in orange cloth covered boards printed in dark blue. Front:
[script] "Just What the Doctor Ordered" | FUN IN BED | [picture of a butler
offering a bed pan to bedridden patient in a covered serving dish. Drawing by O.
Soglow.] Spine: [printed downward] FUN IN BED SERIES 4 [top line] FRANK
| [bottom line] SCULLY [horizontal] SIMON AND | SCHUSTER   Issued in a
yellow paper dust jacket printed in dark blue and red. Comes with a pencil in a special holder attached to the back cover.

Contains: "I Am Ready to Drop Dead" (127) which originally appeared in *The
New Yorker* July 6, 1935.

B15   NEW DIRECTIONS IN PROSE AND POETRY 1939   [1939]

NEW DIRECTIONS | IN PROSE & POETRY | 1939 | [publisher's device] | NEW
DIRECTIONS • NORFOLK • CONN.

[i-vi], vii-xi, [xii], xiii-xxii, [xxiii-xxiv], [1-2], 3-159, [160-162], 163-189, [190], 191-
231, [232], 233-336, [337], 338-390, [391-426] pages, cream endpapers. 9" x 6"
Published November 1, 1939 at $3.00 Issued in blue paper covered boards printed
in red and white. Front: [red enclosed in thick red oval with thin red oval inside the
thick] NEW | DIRECTIONS | 1939 | [white outside the oval] *Prose Poetry Design*
| EDITED BY JAMES LAUGHLIN IV   Spine: [white printed downward] NEW
DIRECTIONS 1939 Back boards are white instead of blue. Issued in white paper
dust jacket printed in red and blue of the exact same design as the boards.

Contains: "World Tour" (63-65) "World Tour" originally appeared in *Seven* #4,
Tauton, England, (2-3) in the Spring of 1939. It was later collected in *Testament
for My Students and Other Poems* and *Collected Poems of Kay Boyle*.. In *Seven* and in
New Directions the poem was dedicated to Nancy Cunard. In *Testament for My
Students and Other Poems* and *Collected Poems of Kay Boyle* it was dedicated to her
daughter Sharon.

B16   O. HENRY MEMORIAL AWARD PRIZE STORIES OF 1939   1939

O. HENRY | MEMORIAL AWARD | *Prize Stories of 1939* | SELECTED AND
EDITED BY | HARRY HANSEN | *Literary Editor* | *of the New York World-Telegram*
| [publisher's device] | DOUBLEDAY, DORAN & COMPANY, INC. | NEW
YORK | 1939

[i-iv], v, [vi], vii-xv, [xvi], [1-2], 3-29, [30-32], 33-48, [49-50], 51-62, [63-64], 65-
76, [77-78], 79-102, [103-104], 105-118, [119-120], 121-130, [131-132], 133-
144, [145-146], 147-160, [161-162], 163-177, [178-180], 181-204, [205-206],
207-224, [225-226], 227-234, [235-236], 237-254, [255-256], 257-275, [276-
278], 279-288 pages; cream endpapers. $7^1/_2$" x $5^1/_8$". Published November 17,
1939 at $2.50. Issued in black cloth covered boards stamped in gold. Top edge
stained yellow and trimmed. Bottom edge and fore edge rough trimmed. Front:
Blank. Spine: [gold square with black showing through] O. HENRY | MEMO-
RIAL | AWARD | [another gold square as above] | PRIZE | STORIES | OF 1939 |
[another gold square as above] EDITED BY | HARRY | HANSEN | [gold on black]
DOUBLEDAY | DORAN There is a series of slanting gold rules above, between
and below the three gold squares. Back: Blank. Issued in a white paper dust jacket
printed in black, blue, yellow and gold.

Contains: "Anschluss" (79-102). "Anschluss" originally appeared in *Harper's
Magazine* in April 1939. It was later collected in *Nothing Ever Breaks Except the
Heart and Other Stories*. Short biographical note (78)

B17   WE MODERNS   [1939]

a. Spiral Binding Issue:

[At the top in an irregularly shaped white box] WE MODERNS | GOTHAM
BOOK MART | 1920-1940 | [Reproduction of Carl Van Vechten's photograph of
painting by Ruth Bower] | [within white rectangle at bottom] The Life of the Party
at FINNEGAN'S WAKE in our Garden | on Publication Day | Painting by Ruth
Bower Photograph by Carl Van Vechten

Cover-title, 3-88, [89-90] pages. $7^3/_4$" x $5^1/_2$" Published December 17, 1939 for
$1.00. Issued in stiff white paper wrappers printed in black with spiral loose-leaf
binding. Printed on coated paper. Note: This item issued as catalog No. 42 of the
Gotham Book Mart to celebrate their 20th anniversary.

Contains: "Peter Neagoe" a tribute to Peter Neagoe (51).

b. Stapled Wrappers Issue:

[At the top in an irregularly shaped white box] WE MODERNS | GOTHAM
BOOK MART | 1920-1940 | [Reproduction of Carl Van Vechten's photograph of
painting by Ruth Bower] | [within white rectangle at bottom] The Life of the Party
at FINNEGAN'S WAKE in our Garden | on Publication Day | Painting by Ruth
Bower Photograph by Carl Van Vechten

Cover-title, 3-88, [89-90] pages. 8" x $5^1/_2$" Published December 17, 1939 and distributed free. Stapled wrappers printed in black on uncoated paper. Note: This
item issued as catalog No. 42 of the Gotham Book Mart to celebrate their 20th
anniversary.

B18   O. HENRY MEMORIAL AWARD PRIZE STORIES OF 1940   1940

O. HENRY | MEMORIAL AWARD | *Prize Stories of 1940* | SELECTED AND
EDITED BY | HARRY HANSEN | *literary Editor | of the New York World-Telegram*
| [publisher's device] | DOUBLEDAY, DORAN & COMPANY, INC. | NEW
YORK | 1940

[i-iv], v, [vi], vii-xvii, [xviii], [1-2], 3-21, [21-24], 25-41, [42-44], 45-56, [57-58],
59-69, [70-72], 73-83, [84-86], 87-94, [95-96], 97-116, [117-118], 119-143, [144-
146], 147-166, [167-168], 169-177, [178-180], 181-205, [206-208], 209-235,
[236-238], 239-248, [249-250], 251-254, [255-256], 257-268, [269-270], 271-
286, [287-288], 289-305, [306-308], 309-317, [318] pages; cream endpapers. $7^1/_2$"
x $5^1/_8$". Published November 15, 1940 at $2.50. Issued in black cloth covered
boards stamped in gold. Top edge trimmed and unstained. Bottom and fore edge
rough trimmed. Front: Blank. Spine: [gold square with black showing through] O.
HENRY | MEMORIAL | AWARD | [another gold square as above] | PRIZE |

STORIES | OF 1940 | [another gold square as above] EDITED BY | HARRY | HANSEN | [gold on black] DOUBLEDAY | DORAN There is a series of slanting gold rules above, between and below the three gold squares. Back: Blank. Issued in a white paper dust jacket printed in black and rose.

Contains: "Poor Monsieur Panalitus" (59-69) originally appeared in *The New Yorker* January 20, 1940. (19-22) Uncollected. Short biographical note (58)

B19   O. HENRY MEMORIAL AWARD PRIZE STORIES OF 1941   1941

O. HENRY MEMORIAL AWARD | *PRIZE STORIES* | OF | *1941* | [decorative rule] | SELECTED AND EDITED BY | HERSCHEL BRICKELL | [repeat decorative rule] | [publisher's device] | DOUBLEDAY, DORAN AND COMPANY, INC. | GARDEN CITY *1941* NEW YORK

[i-iv], v-xix, [xx], [1-2], 3-14, [15-16], 17-27, [28-30], 31-46, [47-48], 49-57, [58-60], 61-67, [68-70], 71-89, [90-92], 93-102, [103-104], 105-110, [111-112], 113-136, [137-138], 139-152, [153-154], 155-169, [170-172], 173-194, [195-196], 197-209, [210-212], 213-219, [220-222], 223-231, [232-234], 235-243, [244-246], 247-269, [270-272], 273-286, [287-288], 289-304, [305-306], 307-319, [320-322], 323-330, [331-332] pages; cream endpapers. 7 $^7/_8$" x 5 $^1/_2$" Published November 7, 1941 at $2.50. Issued in red cloth covered boards stamped in gold. Top edge stained gray and trimmed. Bottom and fore edge rough trimmed. Front: Blank. Spine: O. HENRY | MEMORIAL | AWARD | PRIZE | STORIES | OF | 1941 | [decorative rule] | EDITED BY | HERSCHEL | BRICKELL | [publisher's device] | DOUBLEDAY DORAN   Back: Blank. Issued in a white paper dust jacket printed in black, red and gold.

Contains: "Defeat" (3-13) which originally appeared in *The New Yorker* May 17, 1941. (18-22) Collected in *Thirty Stories* and *Fifty Stories*. Short biographical note (2)

B20   VERTICAL   [1941]

a: Limited Edition of 100:

[red] V | E | R | T | I | C | A | L [along side and to the left a swirling design by Alexander Calder] | A YEARBOOK FOR ROMANTIC- | MYSTIC ASCEN-SIONS. Edited | by Eugene Jolas. Published by The | Gotham Bookmart Press • New York

[i-iv], [1-4], 5-8, [9-10], 11-14, [15-16], 17-71, [72-74], 75-102, [103-108] with two leaves with drawings not accounted for in the pagination], 109, [110], 111-153,

[154-156], 157-186, [187-188], 189-201, [202-204] pages; cream endpapers. 9$^1/_4$" x 5$^7/_8$". Published November 30, 1941 at $4.50. 100 copies signed by Eugene Jolas on special rag paper. Top edge stained red and trimmed. Bottom edge trimmed. Fore edge rough trimmed. Bound in black cloth covered boards with a cover design by Alexander Calder stamped in gold. Spine: [printed in red on beige paste on] V | E | R | T | I | C | A | L Issued with a tissue paper jacket printed in red on the front underside: V | E | R | T | I | C | A | L

Limitation statement: OF THIS EDITION, SET IN ELECTRA TYPES | AND PRINTED ON SPECIAL RAG PAPER | ONE HUNDRED COPIES HAVE BEEN PRINTED | AT THE WALPOLE PRINTING OFFICE | MOUNT VERNON, NEW YORK [ink signature—Eugene Jolas]

Contains: "Two Fragments from an Aviation Epic." (20-29)   First appearance. Uncollected.

b: Limited Edition of 400:

[red] V| E | R | T | I | C | A | L [along side and to the left a swirling design by Alexander Calder] | A YEARBOOK FOR ROMANTIC- | MYSTIC ASCEN-SIONS. Edited | by Eugene Jolas. Published by The | Gotham Bookmart Press • New York

[i-iv], [1-4], 5-8, [9-10], 11-14, [15-16], 17-71, [72-74], 75-102, [103-108] with two leaves with drawings not accounted for in the pagination],109, [110], 111-153, [154-156], 157-186, [187-188], 189-201, [202-204] pages; cream endpapers.   9" x 6". Published November 30, 1941 at $2.75.   Top edge stained red and all edges trimmed. Bound in black cloth covered spine and white paper covered boards printed in black with a cover design by Alexander Calder. Spine: [printed in red on beige paste on paper] V | E | R | T | I | C | A | L   Issued with a tissue paper jacket printed in red on the front underside: V | E | R | T | I | C | A | L

Limitation statement: OF THIS EDITION, SET IN ELECTRA TYPES | AND PRINTED ON SPECIAL ANTIQUE PAPER | FOUR HUNDRED COPIES HAVE BEEN PRINTED | AT THE WALPOLE PRINTING OFFICE | MOUNT VERNON, NEW YORK

B21   SELECTED WRITING   [1942]

SELECTED | WRITING | *edited by – – REGINALD MOORE* | *poetry selected by TAMBIMUTTU* | [part of a rectangle with the top line beginning at the middle of the page going to the right and down the page about 3 inches and then returning to the left side of the page] | NICHOLSON & WATSON | NUMBER ONE, CRAVEN HOUSE, KINGSWAY, LONDON, W. C. 1 [to the left of these last two lines and on level with both is a publishers device: a circle enclosing an N & W [i-iv], v-vii, [viii-xii], 13-158, [159-160] pages.   7 $^{1}/_{4}$" x 4 $^{3}/_{4}$"   Published in May 1942 at 3s. 6d.. Issued in gray stiff paper wraps printed in black and in dust jacket. Top edge unstained and all edges trimmed. Front: [a man hanging from gallows while reading a book. Two crows perched on the gallows and one on his book. The initials hof are on the bottom of the gallows] [printed at the bottom] SELECTED | WRITING   Spine: [printed downward] SELECTED WRITING   Back: Blank. Issued in white paper dust jacket printed in black and pink.

Contains: "The Baron and the Chemist"   (117-122)   Originally appeared in *The New Yorker*   February 26, 1938 and was not further collected.

B22   SATURDAY EVENING POST STORIES OF 1941   1942

POST STORIES | *OF 1941* | [black profile of a man in a circle] | WESLEY WINANS STOUT, *Editor* | *Associate Editors:* | A.W. NEALL, E. N. BRANDT, RICHARD THRUELSEN, | MARTIN SOMMERS, STUART ROSE, ALAN R. JACKSON | W. THORNTON MARTIN, *Art Editor* | L.B. KRITCHER, *Associate Art Editor* | BOSTON | LITTLE, BROWN AND COMPANY | 1942 [All enclosed in triple rule rectangle]

[i-vi], [1-3], 4-18, [19], 20-40, [41], 42-59, [60], 61-79, [80], 81-96, [97], 98-114, [115], 116-128, [129], 130-141, [142], 143-157, [158], 159-166, [167], 168-183, [184], 185-208, [209], 210-229, [230], 231-246, [247], 248-264, [265], 266-280, [281], 282-296, [297], 298-311, [312], 313-328, [329], 330-344, [345], 346-363, [364], 365-384, [385-386] pages; cream endpapers. 8 $^{1}/_{8}$" x 5$^{1}/_{2}$" Published May 6, 1942 at $2.50. Issued in blue cloth covered boards stamped in red. Top edge trimmed and unstained. Front and bottom edges trimmed. Front: *POST STORIES* | *OF 1941* | [embossed picture of man in circle]   Spine: *POST* | *STORIES* | *OF* | *1941* | *Little, Brown* | *and Company* Back: Blank.   Issued in cream paper dust jacket printed in red and black.

Contains: "Let There Be Honour"   (19-40)   which originally appeared in *The Saturday Evening Post*   November 8, 1941. (12-13)   Later collected in *Thirty Stories* and *Fifty Stories*.

B23   THE BEST AMERICAN SHORT STORIES 1942   1942

THE | [red] *Best* | AMERICAN | SHORT STORIES | 1942 | [decorative rule] | *and The Yearbook of the American Short Story* | [rule] | *Edited by* | MARTHA FOLEY | [1942 | [rule] | HOUGHTON MIFFLIN COMPANY • BOSTON [red publisher's device divides 1942, the rule and Houghton Mifflin Company Boston] | The Riverside Press Cambridge [i-ix], x-xii, [xiii], xiv-xv, [xvi], [1], 2-18, [19], 20-27, [28], 29-40, [41], 42-49, [50], 51-66, [67], 68-74, [75], 76-92, [93], 94-104, [105], 106-115, [116], 117-128, [129], 130-140, [141], 142-155, [156], 157-173, [174], 175-200, [201], 202-209, [210], 211-230, [231], 232-244, [245], 246-249, [250], 251-258, [259], 260-268, [269], 270-278, [279], 280-290, [291], 292-302, [303], 304-312, [313], 314-342, [343], 344-354, [355], 356-371, [372], 373-384, [385], 386-409, [410], 411-422, [423], 424-425, [426-427], 428 pages; cream endpapers. 8" x $5^1/_2$" Published September 10, 1942 at $2.75. Issued in orange cloth covered boards stamped in blue. Top edge unstained. Top and bottom edge trimmed and fore edge rough trimmed. Front: THE | *Best* | AMERICAN | SHORT STORIES | 1942 | [decorative rule] | and *The Yearbook of the American Short Story* | [rule]   Spine: THE | *Best* | AMERICAN | SHORT | STORIES | 1942 | [decorative rule] | *Foley* | [rule] | HOUGHTON | MIFFLIN CO. Back: Blank. Issued in a white paper dust jacket printed in red, blue, pink and white.

Contains: "Nothing Ever Breaks Except the Heart" (41-49) which first appeared in *The New Yorker* October 4, 1941. (18-21)   Later collected in *Nothing Ever Breaks Except the Heart and Other Stories.* Short biographical note. (423)

B24   THIS IS MY BEST   1942

America's 93 Greatest Living Authors Present | [script] This Is My Best | [leaf design] OVER 150 SELF-CHOSEN AND | COMPLETE MASTERPIECES, TOGETHER WITH | THEIR REASONS FOR THEIR SELECTIONS | [publisher's device] *Edited by Whit Burnett* | Burton C. Hoffman THE DIAL PRESS New York, 1942

[i-vi], vii-xiv, [1-2], 3-119, [120-122], 123-227, [228-230], 231-425, [426-428], 429-593, [594-596], 597-653, [654-656], 657-723, [724-726], 727-817, [818-820], 821-885, [886-888], 889-1017, [1018-1020], 1021-1169, [1170], 1171-1175, [1176], 1177-1180, [1181-1186] pages; cream endpapers $8^1/_2$" x $5^3/_4$" Published October 13, 1942 at $3.50. Issued in beige cloth covered boards stamped in gold. Top edge stained dark green and trimmed. Bottom edge trimmed, fore edge untrimmed. Front: [gold stamped publisher's device]. Spine: [thick rule] | [thin rule] | This Is | My Best | *Edited by* | *Whit Burnett* | [design] | THE DIAL PRESS | [thin rule] | [thick rule] all on a green rectangular background. Top fourth and bottom half of spine crossing green lines on beige spine. Issued in white paper dust jacket printed in red, black, white and yellow.

Contains: "They Weren't Going to Die" with an explanation of why she chose this story for inclusion in this anthology. (1005-1011). The story originally appeared in *The New Yorker* October 12, 1940.   (21-22) Collected in *Thirty Stories* and *Fifty Stories.*

B25   O. HENRY MEMORIAL AWARD PRIZE STORIES OF 1942   1942

O. HENRY MEMORIAL AWARD | *PRIZE STORIES* | OF | *1942* | [decorative rule] | SELECTED AND EDITED BY | HERSCHEL BRICKELL | ASSISTED BY MURIEL FULLER| [repeat decorative rule] | [publisher's device] | DOUBLEDAY, DORAN AND COMPANY, INC. | Garden City 1942 New York

[i-iv], v, [vi], vii-xvii, [xviii], [1-2], 3-30, [31-32], 33-48, [49-50], 51-71, [72-74], 75-88, [89-90], 91-102, [103-104], 105-113, [114-116], 117-124, [125-126], 127-136, [137-138], 139-158, [159-160], 161-168, [169-170], 171-191, [192-194], 195-203, [204-206], 207-215, [216-218], 219-227, [228-230], 231-237, [238-240], 241-256, [257-258], 259-272, [273-274], 275-297, [298-300], 301-312, [313-314], 315-330, [331-332], 333-346, [347-348], 349-356, [357-358] pages; cream endpapers. $7^3/_4$" x $5^1/_2$" Published November 6, 1942 at $2.50. Issued in red cloth covered boards stamped in gold.   Top edge stained red and trimmed. Bottom trimmed and fore edge rough trimmed. Front: Blank. Spine: O. HENRY | MEMORIAL | AWARD | PRIZE | STORIES | OF | 1942 | [decorative rule] | EDITED BY | HERSCHEL | BRICKELL | [repeat decorative rule] | [publisher's device] | DOUBLEDAY DORAN   Back: Blank. Issued in a cream paper dust jacket printed in black, gold, red, and white.

Contains: "Their Name Is Macaroni." (91-102) First appeared in *The New Yorker* January 3, 1942. (16-19) Later collected in *Thirty Stories* and *Fifty Stories*.   Short biographical note. (90)

B26   TWENTIETH CENTURY AUTHORS   [1942]

TWENTIETH CENTURY | AUTHORS | A Biographical Dictionary of Modern Literature | *Edited by* | STANLEY J. KUNITZ | *and* | HOWARD HAYCRAFT | COMPLETE IN ONE VOLUME WITH | 1850 BIOGRAPHIES AND | 1700 PORTRAITS | [publisher's device] | NEW YORK | THE H. W. WILSON COMPANY | NINETEEN HUNDRED FORTY-TWO

One blank leaf, [i-iv], v-vii, [viii], 1-1577, [1578-1582] pages; endpapers a montage of photographs of authors. $9^7/_8$" x $6^3/_4$" Published December 1, 1942 at $8.50. Top edge unstained and all edges trimmed. Issued in green cloth covered boards stamped in gold.   Front: Blank. Spine: [double rule] | TWENTIETH | CENTURY | AUTHORS | [short rule] | A BIOGRAPHICAL | DICTIONARY | [double rule] | KUNITZ | & | HAYCRAFT | [double rule] | [double rule] | THE H. W. WILSON | COMPANY | [double rule]   Back: Blank. No dust jacket seen.

Note: This is a revision and expansion of the 1933 *Authors Today and Yesterday* with a new and updated autobiography by Kay Boyle. See B9.

Contains: Autobiographical sketch. (173-174)

B27   THE BEST AMERICAN SHORT STORIES 1943   1943

THE | [red] *Best* | AMERICAN | SHORT STORIES | 1943 | [decorative rule] | *and*
The Yearbook of the American Short Story | [rule] | *Edited by* | MARTHA FOLEY |
[red publisher's device] | 1943 | [rule] | HOUGHTON MIFFLIN COMPANY •
BOSTON [a red publisher's device divides 19 from 43 MIFFLIN from
COMPANY] | The Riverside Press Cambridge

[i-ix], x-xi, [xii-xiii], xiv-xv, [xvi], [1], 2-9, [10], 11-22, [23], 24-40, [41], 42-46,
[47], 48-55, [56], 57-69, [70], 71-86, [87], 88-104, [105], 106-114, [115], 116-
121, [122], 123-134, [135], 136-143, [144], 145-165, [166], 167-186, [187], 188-
217, [218], 219-231, [232], 233-255, [256], 257-270, [271], 272-278, [279],
280-291, [292], 293-300, [301], 302-309, [310], 311-326, [327], 328-336, [337],
338-344, [345], 346-359, [360], 361-369, [370], 371-390, [391], 392-399. [400],
401-411, [412-413], 414-417, [418-423], 424-426, [427], 428 pages; cream endpapers. 8" x 5^1/$_2$" Published September 29, 1943 at $2.75. Top edge unstained.
All edges trimmed. Issued in rust colored cloth covered boards stamped in blue.
Front: THE | *Best* | AMERICAN | SHORT STORIES | 1943 | [decorative rule] |
and The Yearbook of the American Short-Story [rule]   Spine: THE | *Best* | AMER-
ICAN | SHORT | STORIES | 1943 | [decorative rule] | *Foley* | [rule]   Back: Blank.
Issued in white paper pictorial jacket printed in red, white, yellow, blue and green.

Contains: "Frenchman's Ship" (23-40) which first appeared in *The Saturday Evening
Post* (14-15, 84-90) November 21, 1942 and was later collected in *Nothing Ever
Breaks Except the Heart and Other Stories*. With biographical note (413)

B28   O. HENRY MEMORIAL AWARD PRIZE STORIES OF 1943   1943

Twenty-Fifth Anniversary Edition | O. HENRY MEMORIAL AWARD | *PRIZE*
STORIES | OF | *1943* | [horizontal decorative rule] | SELECTED AND EDITED
BY | HERSCHEL BRICKELL | ASSISTED BY | MURIEL FULLER | [horizontal
decorative rule] | [publisher's device] | Doubleday, Doran and Company, Inc. |
Garden City *1943* New York

[i-vi], vii-xxv, [xxvi], [1-2], 3-16, [17-18], 19-39, [40-42], 43-59, [60-62], 63-75,
[76-78], 79-88, [89-90], 91-103, [104-106], 107-126, [127-128], 129-139, [140-
142], 143-152, [153-154], 155-163, [164-166], 167-177, [178-180], 181-200,
[201-202], 203-212, [213-214], 215-219, [220-222], 223-231, [232-234], 235-
242, [243-244], 245-250, [251-252], 253-262, [263-264], 265-273, [274-276],
277-282, [283-284], 285-292, [293-294], 295-309, [310-312], 313-319, [320-
324] pages; cream endpapers. 7^3/$_4$" X 5^1/$_4$" Published November 19,1943 at
$2.50. Issued in blue cloth covered boards stamped in gold. Front: Blank. Spine:
[gold] O. HENRY | MEMORIAL | AWARD | PRIZE | STORIES | OF | 1943 |
[horizontal decorative rule] | EDITED BY | HERSCHEL | BRICKELL | [horizontal

decorative rule] | [publisher's device] | Doubleday, Doran   Back: Blank. Issued in white paper dust jacket printed in black, yellow and blue.

Contains: "The Canals of Mars"   (77-88)   which first appeared in *Harper's Bazaar* February 1943. (95-99)   Later collected in *Thirty Stories* and *Fifty Stories*.

B29   LITERATURE AND LIFE IN AMERICA   [1943]

[long decorative rule] LIFE-READING SERVICE | *Literature and Life* | *in America* | *by DUDLEY MILES and ROBERT C. POOLEY* | [repeat decorative rule inverted] | SCOTT, FORESMAN AND COMPANY | *Chicago   Atlanta   Dallas   New York*

[i], ii-xviii, 1-29, [30], 31-115, [116], 117-121, [122], 123-233, [234], 235-389, [390], 391-589, [590], 591-694, [695], 696-726 pages, coated paper color map of the United States after page 726; color photographic endpapers. 8 $^7/_8$" x 6 $^1/_8$" Published ca. July 1943 at $2.12. Issued in gray cloth covered boards printed in brown and yellow. Front: [brown liberty bell on a yellow rectangle composed of a series of vertical yellow lines] | [brown] *Literature and* | *Life in America* | [yellow] MILES [small brown semi-circle open end down] [yellow] POOLEY Spine: [brown rule] | vertical yellow decoration] | [printed downward] *Literature and Life in America* | [repeat vertical yellow decoration inverted] | [brown rule] | *Scott,* | *Foresman*   Back: Blank. No dust jacket seen.

Contains: "Hilaire and the Maréchal Pétard" (534-551) which originally appeared in *Harper's Magazine* August 1942.

B30   FOURTEEN OF THEM   [1944]

FOURTEEN | *of* THEM | *by* | *With a* John Hersey | *Foreword* Helen MacInnes | *by* John Cecil Holm | Mary Kurt Steel | Roberts   Faith Baldwin | Rinehart Clyde Brion Davis | Sarah Lorimer | Elizabeth Hollister Frost | Adela Rogers St. Johns | Margaret Widdermer | William Rose Benét | Helen Worden | Kay Boyle | Fannie Hurst | NEW YORK | TORONTO | FARRAR & RINEHART, INC.

[i-iv] + photographic plate, v-x, [1-2], 3-85, [86] pages; cream endpapers. 8 $^7/_8$" x 5 $^7/_8$" Published week of March 4, 1944 at $1.00. Issued in white paper covered boards printed in black. Top edge unstained. All edges trimmed. Front: [black and white picture with large tombstone printed   John J. Horan | Edwin T. Nee | Frank J. Johnson | Hubert J. Lynch | Henry Normansen | Irving Brundage | Walter J. Kupinski | John A. Lukacovic | Lawrence Daley | Joseph J. Kofka | Louis Rosenstein

| A. J. Rizzi | William T. Richards | John M. Azaltovic | Fourteen of them ....
Back: Blank.   Dust jacket unseen, probably issued without jacket.

Contains: "Anthony John Rizzi, Radioman, 3rd Class. U.S.N." (71-74)   Short biography of sailor from Tarrytown, New York who died in World War II. The fourteen biographies in this small book originally appeared in the Tarrytown Daily News November 5-20, 1943 Biographical note (81).

B31   THEY WERE THERE: THE STORY OF WORLD WAR II   [1944]
           AND HOW IT CAME ABOUT BY AMERICA'S
                  FOREMOST CORRESPONDENTS

THEY WERE THERE | THE STORY OF | WORLD WAR II AND HOW IT CAME ABOUT | BY AMERICA'S FOREMOST CORRESPONDENTS | EDITED BY CURT RIESS | G. P. PUTNAM'S SONS [publisher's device] NEW YORK

No i-ii [iii-vi], vii-xliii, [xliv], [1-2], 3-621, [622], 623-670 pages; cream endpapers printed in gray with all the contributor's names. $8^1/_2$" x $5^1/_2$" Published week of July 8, 1944 at $5.00. Issued in dark rust red cloth covered boards stamped in gold. Top unstained and all edges trimmed. Front: Blank. Spine: [double rule] |*THEY | WERE | THERE* | [double rule] | *Edited by* | *CURT RIESS* | [double rule] | PUTNAM   Issued in a white dust jacket printed in red and black.

Contains: "The Silent Women"   (228-231) originally appeared in *Vogue* April 1, 1942 (66-67, 95).

B32   THIRTEEN STORIES   [1944]

THIRTEEN STORIES | chosen by | WREY GARDINER | London | THE GREY WALLS PRESS | 4 Vernon Place, W. C. 1

[1-4], 5-84 pages; cream endpapers. $7^3/_{16}$" x $4^7/_8$" Published in March of 1944 at 6 shillings. Issued in tan cloth covered boards stamped in gold. Top edge unstained and all edges trimmed. Front: Blank. Spine: [stamped downward in gold] 13 STORIES [horizontal] GWP   Issued in a beige paper dust jacket printed in black and red.

Contains: "Wanderer"   (35-44) originally appeared in *Accent*   (85-91) Winter of 1942 and was uncollected.

Note: This story appeared in the United States approximately four months later in *American Writing 1943: The Anthology of the American Non-Commercial Magazine*, edited by Alan Swallow, Boston: Bruce Humphries, Inc. [1944]

B33   WRITERS AND WRITING   1946

WRITERS AND WRITING | by Robert van Gelder [preceding lines enclosed in ruled rectangle] | Charles Scribner's Sons   New York | 1946

one unpaginated leaf. [i-vi], vii-x, [xi-xii], 1-381, [382-386] pages; cream endpapers. 8" x 5$^1/_2$" Published July 15,1946 at $3.00. Issued in blue cloth covered boards stamped in gold. Top edge unstained and all edges trimmed. Front: *Writer's* | *and* | *Writing* [a gold rectangle begins centered on the s of *Writers* and encloses *and Writing* ending centered on the w of *Writers*. The rectangle is broken at the bottom by a feather pen.] | Robert van Gelder Spine: *Writers* | *and* | *Writing* | [device] | Robert | van Gelder | SCRIBNERS   Back: Blank.   Dust jacket: Issued in white paper dust jacket printed in gray and green.

Contains: An interview of Kay Boyle with Robert van Gelder (193-196) which originally appeared in *The New York Times Book Review*, August 3, 1941.

B34   ACCENT ANTHOLOGY   [1946]

Accent | ANTHOLOGY | Selections from *Accent*, | A Quarterly of New | Literature, 1940-1945 | *Edited   by* | KERKER QUINN *and* | CHARLES SHATTUCK | HARCOURT, BRACE AND COMPANY, NEW YORK

[i-iv], v-xiv, [1-2], 3-677, [678], 679-687, [688-690] pages; cream endpapers.   8" x 5$^1/_4$" Published August 19, 1946 at $4.00.   Issued in rust cloth covered boards stamped in gold. Top edge unstained all edges trimmed. Front: Blank. Spine: [stamped in gold on a black rectangle] *Accent* | ANTHOLOGY | *Edited by* | KERKER QUINN *and* | CHARLES SHATTUCK | HARCOURT, BRACE | AND COMPANY Back: Blank.   Issued in white paper dust wrapper printed in orange, black and white.

Contains: "Cairo Street" (44-50) which first appeared in *Accent*   Winter 1943 (95-99) and was uncollected.   Biographical note (680)

B35   O.HENRY MEMORIAL AWARD PRIZE STORIES OF 1946   1946

O. HENRY MEMORIAL AWARD | *PRIZE STORIES* | OF | *1946* | [decorative rule] | SELECTED AND EDITED BY | HERSCHEL BRICKELL | ASSISTED BY | MURIEL FULLER | [decorative rule] | [publisher's device] | DOUBLEDAY & COMPANY, INC. | Garden City 1946 New York

[i-iv], v-xxi, [xxii-xxiv], [1], 2-318, [319-320] pages; cream endpapers. 7$^3/_4$" x 5$^1/_2$" Published August 22, 1946 at $2.50. Issued in black cloth covered boards stamped in gold. Top edge unstained. Top and bottom edges trimmed. Front edge rough trimmed. Front: Blank. Spine: O. HENRY | MEMORIAL | AWARD | PRIZE |

STORIES | OF | 1946 | [decorative rule] | EDITED BY | HERSCHEL | BRICKELL | [decorative rule] | DOUBLEDAY   Back: Blank.   Issued in cream paper dust jacket printed in black, red, yellow and white.

Contains: "Winter Night"   (74-84) which first appeared in *The New Yorker* (19-23) January 19, 1946 and was later collected in *Thirty Stories* and *Fifty Stories*. Biographical note (306)

B36   PRIZE STORIES OF 1950 THE   1950
                       O. HENRY AWARDS

[double spread title page] prize | stories | of | 1950 | [publishers device] the | O. Henry Awards | [on verso] DOUBLEDAY & COMPANY, INC., GARDEN CITY, NEW YORK, 1950   [recto] SELECTED AND EDITED BY HERSCHEL BRICKELL

[one unnumbered leaf], [i-iv], v, [vi], vii-viii, [ix-xx], 1-325, [326-330] pages; cream endpapers. $8^1/_4$" x $5^1/_2$" Published September 21, 1950 at $3.50. Issued in black cloth covered boards printed in gold. Top edge unstained and all edges trimmed. Front: Blank. Spine: [printed downward] Prize Stories of 1950   THE O. HENRY AWARDS [top line] EDITED BY HERSCHEL BRICKELL [bottom line] | [horizontal] DOUBLEDAY Back: Blank. Issued in white paper dust jacket printed in blue, yellow, green, black and white.

Contains: "Summer Evening"   (89-101)   originally appeared in *The New Yorker* (20-24) on June 25, 1949 and was collected *The Smoking Mountain* and *Fifty Stories*. Biographical note (89)

B37   WORDS AND MUSIC: COMMENT BY   [ca. 1950-1951]
                       FAMOUS AUTHORS ABOUT THE
                       WORLD'S GREATEST ARTISTS

[no true title page]

1-3, [4], 5, [6], 7, [8], 9, [10], 11, [12], 13, [14], 15, [16], 17, [18], 19, [20], 21, [22], 23, [24], 25, [26], 27, [28], 29, [30], 31, [32], 33, [34], 35, [36], 37, [38], 39, [40], 41, [42], 43, [44], 45, [46], 47, [48], 49, [50], 51, [52], 53, [54], 55, [56], 57, [58], 59, [60], 61, [62], 63, [64], 65, [66], 67, [68], 69, [70], 71, [72], 73, [74], 75, [76], 77, [78], 79, [80], 81, [82], 83, [84], 85, [86], 87, [88], 89, [90], 91, [92] pages. $7^5/_8$" x 5"   Published ca. 1950/1951 and apparently distributed free by RCA Victor for promotional purposes. Issued in white paper stapled wrappers printed in black and gold. Top edge unstained and all edges trimmed. Front: Solid black printed in gold. WORDS | script] and | MUSIC | [in script snaking across the page] Comment by Famous Authors about the World's Greatest Artists [a white music symbol with the RCA Victor trade logo in a white circle] Spine: Blank. Back: [solid black with RCA Victor logo in the center] | [printed across the bottom in white] RCA VICTOR DIVISION | RADIO CORPORATION OF AMERICA • CAMDEN, NEW JERSEY

Contains: A short paragraph tribute to Blanche Thebom. (81)

B38   SATURDAY EVENING POST STORIES 1950   [1951]

THE SATURDAY EVENING | [in outline] POST | STORIES | 1950 | [publisher's device] RANDOM HOUSE • NEW YORK

[i-iv], v-vi, [1-2], 3-298, pages; cream endpapers. 8" x 5 $^3/_8$"   Published April 6, 1951 at $3.00. Issued in blue cloth covered boards stamped in white. Top edge stained black with all edges trimmed. Front: [Dark green printed on lime green rectangular paper paste on] Post | Stories | [elongated diamond shaped rule] | 1950 [also Random House blind stamped several times in script across the front] Spine: [printed downward] THE SATURDAY EVENING POST [Post is a white outline with blue cloth showing through] STORIES | [horizontal] 1950 | [publisher's device] | RANDOM | HOUSE   Back: Blank. Issued in white paper dust jacket printed in light and dark green and white.

Contains: "A Disgrace to the Family"   (274-298) originally appeared in *The Saturday Evening Post*   (22-23, 92-104) September 23, 1950. Later collected in *Nothing Ever Breaks Except the Heart and Other Stories* and *Fifty Stories*.

B39   AMERICAN NOVELISTS OF TODAY   [1951]

[The A in American is a very fancy script] AMERICAN NOVELISTS OF TODAY | [rule] | [in script] Harry R. Warfel | AMERICAN BOOK COMPANY | [in script] New York Cincinnati Chicago Boston | [in script] Atlanta Dallas San Francisco

[i-iv],v-vii, [viii], [1-2], 3-475, [476], 477-478, [479-480] pages; cream endpapers. 9 $^3/_{16}$" x 6 $^1/_8$" Published in 1951 at $6.50. Issued in blue cloth covered boards stamped in red and silver. Top edge unstained and all edges trimmed. Front: [The A in American the same as on the title page and in silver while the other letters are red] AMERICAN | [red] NOVELISTS | [red] OF TODAY | [silver in script] Harry R. Warfel Spine: [silver in script] Warfel | [red] AMERICAN | [red] NOVELISTS | [red] OF TODAY | [the rest in silver script] American | Book | Company   Dust jacket unseen.

Contains: Autobiographical statement (44-45)

B40   SATURDAY EVENING POST STORIES 1952   [1953]

THE SATURDAY EVENING | [in outline] POST | STORIES | 1952 | [publisher's device] | RANDOM HOUSE • NEW YORK

[one unnumbered leaf], [i-iv], v-vi, [1-2], 3-340, [341-344] pages; cream endpapers. 8" x 5 $^3/_8$" Published April 17, 1953 at $3.00. Issued in dark blue cloth covered boards stamped in silver. Top edge stained black with all edges trimmed. Front: [Black printed on pink square paper paste on] Post | Stories | [elongated diamond shaped rule] | 1952 [also Random House blind stamped several times in script across the front]   Spine: [printed downward] THE SATURDAY EVENING POST [Post is done in a white outline with blue cloth showing through] STORIES | [horizontal] 1952 | [publisher's device] | RANDOM | HOUSE   Issued in cream paper dust jacket printed in pink, black and white.

Contains: "Diagnosis of a Selfish Lady"   (133-150) which originally appeared in *The Saturday Evening Post*   (24, 119-124) April 5, 1952 and was uncollected.

B41   SATURDAY EVENING POST STORIES 1953   [1954]

THE SATURDAY EVENING | [in outline] POST | STORIES | 1952 | [publisher's device] | RANDOM HOUSE • NEW YORK

[i-iv], v-vi, [1-2], 3-344, [345-346] pages; cream endpapers. 8" x 5 $^3/_8$" Published April 12, 1954 at $3.00. Issued in gray cloth covered boards stamped in black. Top edge stained gold with all edges trimmed. Front: [black printed on dark gold square paper paste on]   Post | Stories | [elongated diamond shaped rule] | 1953 [also Random House blind stamped several times in script across the front]   Spine: [printed downward] THE SATURDAY EVENING POST [Post is done in a black outline with the gray cloth showing through] STORIES | [horizontal] 1953 | [publisher's device] | RANDOM | HOUSE Issued in a cream paper dust jacket printed in black, white and dark gold.

Contains "The Soldier Ran Away" (20-36) originally appeared in *The Saturday Evening Post*   (20-21,115-119) February 28, 1953. Later collected in *The Smoking Mountain.*

B42   SWORN STATEMENT OF KAY BOYLE FRANCKENSTEIN   [1954]

[Sworn statement of Kay Boyle Franckenstein: no title page]

[1], 2-32, [33-36] numbering includes covers; 9 $^1/_4$" x 6 $^1/_8$". White paper stapled wraps. Published ca. July 1954. Front: [beginning of letter to John W. Sipes with the Department of State from Joseph Franckenstein.] Back: [single rule] | | [device] 307

BAR PRESS INC., 54 LAFAYETTE ST., NEW YORK 13 —-WA. 5-3432-3. |
[4457-4467] Appendices B to F, under separate wraps 1-34, [35-36], 9 $^1/_4$" x 6 $^1/_8$".
White paper stapled wraps. Front: [double rule] APPENDICES B TO F, INCLU-
SIVE | TO | SWORN STATEMENTS | OF | JOSEPH M. FRANCKENSTEIN |
AND | KAY BOYLE FRANCKENSTEIN [double rule] | [device] 307 BAR PRESS
INC., 54 LAFAYETTE ST., NEW YORK 13 —-WA. 5-3432-3. Back: Blank.

Contains: Sworn statement by Kay Boyle that she was not and had never been a
communist. (19-32) Included in appendix B are the literary exhibits of Kay Boyle.
The short stories "Moscow" and "Siberia" which had both appeared previously and
the short story "Autobahn 1951" which apparently has never been published.

B43   SATURDAY EVENING POST STORIES 1954   [1955]

THE SATURDAY EVENING | [in outline] POST | STORIES | 1954 | [publisher's
device] | RANDOM HOUSE • NEW YORK

[i-iv], v-vi, [1-2], 3-341, [342-346] pages; cream endpapers. 8" x 5 $^3/_8$" Published
April 15, 1955 at $3.50. Issued in blue cloth covered boards printed in black and
white. Top edge stained black with all edges trimmed. Front: [white printed on
black square paper paste on] Post | Stories | [elongated diamond shaped rule] | 1954
[also Random House blind stamped several times in script across the front]   Spine:
[printed downward] THE SATURDAY EVENING POST [Post is done in a black
outline with the blue cloth showing through] STORIES | [horizontal] 1954 | [pub-
lisher's device] | RANDOM | HOUSE Back: Blank.   Issued in a white paper dust
jacket printed in yellow and black.

Contains: "Carnival of Fear"   (275-307). Originally appeared in *The Saturday
Evening Post* December 11 (20-21, 102-105) and December 18, 1954 (34-35, 50,
52-53) and was uncollected.

B44   BEST POEMS OF 1959   1961

BEST POEMS | of 1959 | BORESTONE MOUNTAIN | POETRY AWARDS |
1960 | *A Compilation of Original Poetry* | published in | *Magazines of the English-
speaking World* | *in 1959* | TWELFTH ANNUAL ISSUE | PACIFIC BOOKS,
PUBLISHERS • PALO ALTO, CALIFORNIA | 1961

[i-xii], [1-3], 4-116, pages; cream endpapers. 8 $^1/_2$" x 5 $^1/_2$"   Published in 1961 at
$3.50. Issued in beige cloth covered boards stamped in black. Top edge unstained
with all edges trimmed. Front: Blank. Spine: [printed downward] Best Poems of
1959 | [publishers device] Back: Blank. Issued in a white paper dust jacket printed
in white and two shades of red.

Contains: "A Poem of Gratitude: For Caresse" (22)   which originally appeared in *Poetry Magazine*, March 1959.   It was later collected in *Collected Poems*, 1962, *Testament for My Students and Other Poems*, 1970, and *Collected Poems of Kay Boyle*, 1991.

B45   A DIAMOND OF YEARS   1961

Edited by | *HELEN OTIS LAMONT* | *A DIAMOND* | *of Years* | [device] | *The Best of the* | *Woman's Home Companion* | *DOUBLEDAY & COMPANY, INC.* | *Garden City, New York, 1961*

[1-4], 5-6, [7], 8, [9], 10, [11-15], 16-26, [27], 28-64, [65-67], 68-87, [88], 89-111, [112], 113-120, [121], 122-134, [135-137], 138-170, [171-173], 174-181, [182], 183-204, [205], 206-217, [218], 219-222-, [223-225], 226-280, [281-283], 284-292, [293], 294-300, [301], 302-308, [309], 310-325, [326], 327-328, [329-331], 332-367, [368], 369-378, [379], 380-389, [390-393], 394-435, [436], 437-441, [442-445], 446-489, [490-493], 494-511, [512], 513-524, [525], 526-534, [535], 536-556, [557-559], 560-588, [589], 590-614, [615], 616-628, [629], 630-638, [639], 640 pages; cream endpapers. 8 $^1/_4$" x 5 $^1/_2$" Published July 7, 1961 at $6.95. Issued in lime green imitation cloth covered boards with black imitation cloth spine stamped in silver.   Front: Embossed red rose in the middle of the green. Spine: [printed downward] A *DIAMOND OF YEARS* [top line] | *The Best of the Woman's Home Companion* [second line] | *Doubleday* [bottom line]   Back: Blank.   Issued in a white paper dust jacket printed in black, red and green.

Contains: "Luck for the Road"   (567-588) which originally appeared in *Woman's Home Companion* in January 1944 (17, 38-45) and later collected in *Nothing Ever Breaks Except the Heart and Other Stories*.

B46   THE ARTISTS' AND WRITERS' COOKBOOK   [1961]

[all printing in purple] THE | ARTISTS' & WRITERS' | COOKBOOK [the preceding all enclosed in a black horizontal oval decorative design which extends out on both sides with two smaller ovals] | EDITED BY | BERYL BARR | AND | BARBARA TURNER SACHS | DESIGNED BY | NICOLAS SIDJAKOV | [horizontal ornament] | CONTACT | EDITIONS | SAUSALITO, CALIFORNIA | [repeat horizontal ornament]

[i-xx], 1-288, [289-308] pages; white endpapers. 9$^1/_2$" x 7 $^1/_4$". Published November 30, 1961 at $10.00. Issued in white imitation cloth covered boards printed in purple and olive green.   Front back and spine all printed with the names of the different contributors.   Issued in a dark gray slip case printed in black without a dust jacket.

Contains: A collaboration with Hilaire Hiler for a recipe (122-123). It also contains a recipe contribution of her own for Ratatouille Rowayton. (222-223).

B47   THE GERMANS: AN INDICTMENT   [1963]
                        OF MY PEOPLE

THE | GERMANS : | AN INDICTMENT OF | MY PEOPLE | [decorative rule] | *A Personal History & A Challenge* | *by* | GUDRUN TEMPEL | *Translated from the German by Sophie Wilkins* | WITH AN INTRODUCTION BY | KAY BOYLE | [publisher's device] | RANDOM HOUSE NEW YORK

[i-viii], xiv, [xv-xviii], [1-2], 3-43, [44-46], 47-71, [72-74], 75-81, [82-84], 85-96, [97-98], 99-105, [106-108], 109-113, [114-116], 117-143, [144-146], 147-172, [173-174] pages; cream endpapers. 8" x 5 $^1/_2$" Published April 8, 1963 at $3.95. Issued in maroon paper covered boards with black cloth spine stamped in silver. Top edge stained yellow with top and bottom edges trimmed. Fore edge rough trimmed. Front: [blind stamped] THE GERMANS *AN INDICTMENT OF MY PEOPLE* [with two blind stamped dots in the black cloth one above and one below the title] Spine: [printed downward] THE GERMANS: *An Indictment of My People* [top line] • • • • *by* GUDRUN TEMPEL [bottom line] | [publisher's device] | [horizontal] RANDOM | HOUSE   Back: Blank.   Issued in beige paper dust jacket printed in red and black.

Contains: An introduction by Kay Boyle. (vii-xv).

B48   THE BRIDGE OF SAN LUIS REY   [1963]

[orange] *Thornton Wilder* | [black] THE | BRIDGE | OF | SAN | LUIS | REY | [orange] *With a New Introduction by Kay Boyle* | [black publisher's device] Time Reading Program Special Edition | TIME INCORPORATED • NEW YORK

[i-vii], viii-xi, [xii-xiii], xiv-xvii, [xviii-xx], [1-3], 4-7, [8-11], 12-16, [17], 18-32, [33], 34-39, [40], 41-45, [46-50], 51-62, [63], 64-79, [80-83], 84-85, [86], 87-99, [100], 101-118, [119], 120-121, [122-125], 126-130, [131], 132-139, [140] pages. 8" x 5 $^3/_{16}$". Published in 1963 with no price marked. Issued in stiff yellow boards printed in green, pink, rose, gold and white. Top edge unstained and all edges trimmed. Front: [pink] THE BRIDGE OF SAN LUIS REY | [green] *Thornton Wilder*   Spine: [green printed downward] THE BRIDGE OF SAN LUIS REY *Thornton Wilder* Time Inc.

Contains: An introduction by Kay Boyle (xiii-xvii).

B49   AT LARGE   1963

a. First Edition:

AT LARGE | by | HERBERT KUBLY | *with a Foreword by* | KAY BOYLE |
LONDON | VICTOR GOLANCZ LTD | 1963

[1-9], 10-12, [13], 14-45, [46], 47-56, [57], 58-68, [69], 70-88, [89], 90-109,
[110], 111-115, [116], 117-134, [135], 136-151, [152], 153-165, [166], 167-175,
[176], 177-187, [188], 189-204, [205], 206-213, [214] 215-221, 222-224 pages;
cream endpapers. 8 $^1/_2$" x 5 $^3/_8$"   Published August 1963 at 21/- (shillings)
Issued in blue cloth covered boards stamped in gold. Top edge unstained and all
edges trimmed. Front: Blank. Spine: AT | LARGE | ★ | HERBERT KUBLY |
GOLLANCZ Back. Blank. Issued in white paper dust jacket printed in black and
green.

Contains: A foreword by Kay Boyle. (9-12)

b. First American Edition:

HERBERT | KUBLY | AT LARGE | *with a foreword* | *by* KAY BOYLE |
DOUBLEDAY & COMPANY, INC. | GARDEN CITY, NEW YORK | 1964

[i-ix], x-xiii, [xiv], [1], 2-38, [39], 40-51, [52-53], 54-66, [67], 68-90, [91], 92-114,
[115], 116-121, [122-123], 124-144, [145], 146-164, [165], 166-181, [182-183],
184-193, [194-195], 196-207, [208-209], 210-227, [228-229], 230-239, [240-
241], 242-250 pages with photographs between 58 and 59 and 178 and 179. Light
blue endpapers. 8 $^3/_{16}$" x 5 $^3/_8$" Published September 11, 1964 at $4.95.   Issued in
light blue cloth covered boards with black cloth spine printed in blue. Top edge
unstained and all edges trimmed.   Front: Blank.   Spine: [printed downward] AT
LARGE *Herbert Kubly* [horizontal] DOUBLEDAY Back: Blank. Issued in white
paper dust jacket printed in black, blue and red.

B50   THE WHISTLING ZONE   [1963]

THE | WHISTLING | ZONE | *by* | *Herbert Kubly* | SIMON AND SCHUSTER •
NEW YORK • 1963

[1-8], 9-68, [69-70], 71-255, [256-258], 259-348, [349-352] pages. 8 $^1/_8$" x 5 $^1/_2$"
The book was published September 11, 1963 at $4.95. This is the advance reading
copy. Issued in cream paper wrappers printed in blue. Front: ADVANCE
READING COPY | THE | WHISTLING | ZONE | *A novel by Herbert Kubly* | A
STATEMENT FROM KAY BOYLE: [statement follows] Spine: Blank. Back: [a
continuation of Kay Boyle's statement taking up entire back page]

Contains: Essentially a review of The Whistling Zone. A few lines from this
statement appeared as a dust jacket blurb on the published novel.

B51   THE MODERN SHORT STORY IN THE MAKING   [1964]

The | MODERN | SHORT | STORY | in the | MAKING | WHIT and HALLIE BURNETT / *Editors of* Story *Magazine* | HAWTHORNE BOOKS, INC | *Publishers* | *New York* / *London*

[1-4], 5, [6-7], 8-14, [15-16], 17-87, [88-90], 91-139, [140-142], 143-206, [207-208], 209-261, [262-264], 265-304, [305-306], 307-356, [357-358], 359-405, [406-408] pages; black endpapers. 9" x 5 $^7/_8$." Published October 19, 1964 at $6.95. Issued in light gray cloth covered boards printed in black. Top edge unstained and all edges trimmed. Front: [leaf design in lower right corner]   Spine: WHIT | and | HALLIE | BURNETT | THE | MODERN | SHORT | STORY | IN THE | MAKING | Twenty-two | writers' | short stories, | comments, | insights, | and | criticisms | HAWTHORN   Issued in mottled light gray paper dust jacket printed in black.

Contains: An interview. (192-194).   It also contains "Rest Cure" and short biography and background (185-192).

B52   CONTEMPORARY AMERICAN NOVELISTS   [1964]

Contemporary | American Novelists | EDITED BY | *Harry T. Moore* | Carbondale | SOUTHERN ILLINOIS UNIVERSITY PRESS

[i-vii], viii, [ix], x-xx, [1-3], 4-31, [32], 33-40, [41], 42-53, [54], 55-64, [65], 66-79, [80], 81-94, [95], 96-105, [106], 107-119, [120], 121-133, [134], 135-142, [143], 144-154, [155], 156-157, [158], 159-169, [170], 171-181, [182], 183-192, [193], 194-204, [205], 206-221, [222], 223-227, [228], 229-232, [233-236] pages; cream endpapers. 8 $^1/_4$" x 4$^3/_4$". Published October 19, 1964 at $4.50. Issued in maroon paper covered boards with gold cloth covered spine printed in black. Top edge stained gray with all edges trimmed.   Front: [a large C crossed lower left to upper right with a single rule and upper left to lower right with a doubled rule] Spine: [printed downward] Moore   Contemporary American Novelists   Southern Illinois [top line] University Press [bottom line]   Issued in white paper dust jacket printed in gray, red and rose.

Contains: "Introducing James Baldwin."   (155-157) An essay on James Baldwin.

B53   SEEDS OF LIBERATION   [1965]

SEEDS OF LIBERATION | *edited by Paul Goodman* | *George Braziller, New York*

[i-vii], viii-xiii, [xiv-xv], xvi-xviii, [1-3], 4-11, [12], 13-23, [24], 25-43, [44-47], 48-62, [63], 64-73, [74], 75-76, [77], 78-83, [84], 85-89, [90], 91-105, [106], 107-110, [111], 112-125, [126], 127-130, [131], 132-143, [144], 145-150, [151], 152-161,

[162], 163-164, [165], 166-171, [172-175], 176-180, [181], 182-183, [184], 185-191, [192], 193-200, [201], 202-247, [248], 249-261, [262], 263-269, [270], 271-277, [278], 279-281, [282], 283-286, [287], 288-299, [300], 301-305, [306], 307-316, [317], 318-324, [325], 326-335, [336], 337, [338], 339-345, [346], 347-349, [350], 351-353, [354], 355-367, [368-371], 372-374, [375], 376-379, [380], 381-387, [388], 389-395, [396], 397-413, [414], 415-419, [420], 421-432, [433], 434-444, [445]. 446-454, [455], 456-470, [471], 472-489, [490], 491-493, [494], 495-497, [498], 499-507, [508-511], 512-544, [545-547], 548-551, [552-558] pages; cream endpapers. 8 $^1/_4$" x 5 $^5/_8$". Published March 1965 at $7.50. Issued in bright green cloth covered boards stamped in black and gold. Top edge unstained with top and bottom edges trimmed and front edge rough trimmed. Front: Blank. Spine: [thin black rule] | [thick black rule] | [gold] SEEDS OF | LIBERATION | EDITED BY | PAUL GOODMAN | [thick black rule] | [thin black rule] | [gold] GEORGE | BRAZILLER   Back: Blank. Issued in white pictorial dust jacket printed in black, green.

Contains: " The Triumph of Principles"   (106-110)   which first appeared in the June 1960 issue of *Liberation.*

B54   BEST MODERN SHORT STORIES   [1965]

Best MODERN | SHORT | STORIES | Selected from | The Saturday Evening POST | CURTIS BOOKS | A Division of The Curtis Publishing Company | New York • Philadelphia | Distributed by DOUBLEDAY & COMPANY, INC.

[i-iv], v-vii, [viii], ix-xii, [xiii-ivx], 1-494, [495-498] pages; cream endpapers. 8$^1/_4$" x 5 $^1/_2$." Published September 3, 1965 at $5.95. Issued in black cloth covered boards stamped in gold. Top edge unstained and top and bottom edge trimmed. Front edge rough trimmed. Front: Blank. Spine: BEST | MODERN | SHORT | STORIES | [rule] | Selected from | The Saturday Evening | POST | CURTIS BOOKS | [rule] | DOUBLEDAY   Back: Blank. Issued in white paper dust jacket printed in green, blue, red, black and white.

Contains: "The Ballet of Central Park"   (236-249) which originally appeared in *The Saturday Evening Post* November 28, 1964 and was later collected in *Nothing Ever Breaks Except the Heart and Other Stories* and in *Fifty Stories.* also: a biographical note (487).

B55   THE LIFE OF DYLAN THOMAS   [1965]

a. First Edition:

THE LIFE OF | DYLAN | THOMAS | CONSTANTINE | FITZGIBBON | WITH FRONTISPIECE AND | 8 PAGES OF PLATES | LONDON | J. M. DENT & SONS LTD [i-vi], vii-ix, [x], 1-393, [394], 395-410, [411-412], 413-422, [423-430], 8 plates; cream endpapers. 8 $1/_4$" x 5 $3/_8$". Published in October 1965 at 42 shillings. Issued in black cloth covered boards stamped in gold. Top edge stained red and all edges trimmed. Front: Blank. Spine: *The Life of* | DYLAN | THOMAS | [large eight pointed asterisk] | CONSTANTINE | FITZGIBBON | DENT Back: Blank. Issued in white paper pictorial dust jacket printed in black and yellow.

Contains: An Excerpt for "Declaration for 1955" from *Nation*, January 29, 1955 about an evening with Dylan Thomas in an English pub.

b. First American Edition:

The Life of | DYLAN THOMAS | [series of six identical ornaments in a row] | by Constantine FitzGibbon | *with photographs* | [publisher's device] | *An Atlantic Monthly Press Book* | LITTLE, BROWN AND COMPANY • BOSTON • TORONTO

[i-vi], vii-ix, [x], xi, [xii], [1-2], 3-359, [360-362], 363-370, [371-372] pages; cream endpapers. 9 $1/_8$" x 6" Published October 25, 1965, 1965 at $7.95. Issued in black cloth covered boards stamped in gold. Top edge stained blue green and all edges trimmed. Front: [blind stamp of publisher's device] Spine: [three identical ornaments in a row] *The Life* | *of* | Dylan Thomas | [repeat ornaments] | CON-STANTINE | FITZGIBBON | *Atlantic* | LITTLE, BROWN Issued in white paper jacket printed in black.

B56   WRITE AND REWRITE A STUDY OF   [1967]
                      THE CREATIVE PROCESS

a. Meredith Press Edition:

write and rewrite | *a study of the creative process* | by John Kuehl | Also published under the title | *Creative Writing & Rewriting* | by Appleton-Century-Crofts | MEREDITH PRESS / New York

[i-iv], v-xii, [1-2], 3-18, [19-20], 21-48, [49-50], 51-67, [68], 69-96, [97], 98-129, [130], 131-166, [167-168], 169-232, [233], 234-263, [264], 265-287, [288], 289-308 pages; brown endpapers. 9 $1/_4$" x 6" Published September 13, 1967 at $6.95. Issued in black paper covered boards with brown cloth spine stamped in gold. Top edge unstained and all edges trimmed. Front: Blank. Spine: Edited | by | JOHN | KUEHL | [the following printed downward and on a black rectangle] WRITE & REWRITE | [printed horizontally in black] Meredith | Press Issued in white paper dust jacket printed in black, gray and two shades of brown.

Contains: Unpublished versions of select paragraphs from "The Ballet of Central Park" and an excerpt from a letter on the writing of this short story (21-48).

b. Appleton-Century-Crofts Edition:

John Kuehl | NEW YORK UNIVERSITY | *creative writing & rewriting* | *contemporary American novelists at work* | [seal] APPLETON-CENTURY-CROFTS / NEW YORK | DIVISION OF MEREDITH PUBLISHING COMPANY

B57   AUTHORS TAKE SIDES ON VIETNAM   [1967]

a. First Limited Edition:

[a short vertical rule to the left] AUTHORS | TAKE SIDES ON VIETNAM | Two questions on the war in Vietnam | answered by the authors of several nations | EDITED BY | CECIL WOOLF AND JOHN BAGGULEY | [publisher's device] | PETER OWEN • LONDON

[i-vi], vii-xii, 13-223, [224], 225-232 pages; cream endpapers.   8 $^3/_8$" x 5 $^3/_8$". Published September 18, 1967. Issued in dark purplish blue cloth covered boards stamped in gold.   Top edge stained gray with all edges trimmed. Front: Blank. Spine: [printed downward in gold] Authors Take Side on Vietnam   [top line] Edited by Cecil Woolf and John Bagguley [bottom line] | [printed horizontal] PETER OWEN   Issued in glassine dust jacket. Limited to 300 copies for presentation.

Contains: An untitled statement   pp. 19-21 by Kay Boyle protesting American involvement in the war in Vietnam.

b. First Trade Edition:

[a short vertical rule to the left] AUTHORS | TAKE SIDES ON VIETNAM | Two questions on the war in Vietnam | answered by the authors of several nations | EDITED BY | CECIL WOOLF AND JOHN BAGGULEY | [publisher's device] | PETER OWEN • LONDON

[i-vi], vii-xii, 13-223, [224], 225-232 pages; cream endpapers.   8 $^3/_8$" x 5 $^3/_8$". Published September 18,1967 at 37s 6d later raised to £2.   Issued in black cloth covered boards stamped in silver.   Top edge stained gray with all edges trimmed. Front: Blank. Spine: [printed downward in silver] Authors Take Side on Vietnam [top line] Edited by Cecil Woolf and John Bagguley [bottom line] | [printed horizontal] PETER OWEN   Issued in white paper dust jacket printed in black and red.

c. First American Edition:

AUTHORS | TAKE | SIDES | ON VIETNAM | Two Questions | on the War in Vietnam | Answered by the Authors | of Several Nations | Edited by | CECIL WOOLF and | JOHN BAGGULEY | [publisher's device]   SIMON AND SCHUSTER, NEW YORK

[1-13], 14-15, [16], 17-77, [78-79], 80-92, [93-96] pages. 11" x 8¹/₂" Published
October 31, 1967 at $1.95. Issued in white wrappers printed in red and black. All
edges trimmed. Front: [printed in white] Authors | Take | Sides | on | Vietnam [the
questions asked and the contributor's names are printed in red down the right and
left edge of the covers on both the front and the back]   Spine: [printed downward
in white] Authors Take Sides on Vietnam [printed downward in red] edited by Cecil
Woolf and John Bagguley Simon and Schuster

Note: Contributors to the American edition are different from that of the English,
but Kay Boyle is in both editions.

Contains: An untitled statement   (23-24) by Kay Boyle protesting American
involvement in the war in Vietnam.

B58   THE BEST AMERICAN SHORT STORIES 1967   1967

THE | [red] BEST | AMERICAN SHORT STORIES | [red] 1967 | & | the Yearbook
of | the American Short Story | EDITED BY | MARTHA FOLEY | AND | DAVID
BURNETT | HOUGHTON MIFFLIN COMPANY | BOSTON | 1967

[i-xi], xii-xiii, [xiv-xv], xvi, [xvii-xviii], [1], 2-12, [13], 14-23, [24-25], 26-36, [37],
38-65, [66-67], 68-83, [84-85] 86-99, [100-101], 102-134, [135], 136-150, [151],
152-160, [161], 162-174, [175], 176-185, [186-187], 188-192, [193], 194-209,
[210-211], 212-237, [238-239], 240-255, [256-257], 258-277, [278-279], 280-289,
[290-291], 292-301, [302-303], 304-313, [314-315], 316-331, [332-335], 336-339,
[340-343], 344-346, [347], 348-354, [355], 356-357, [358] pages; cream endpapers.
8 ³/₈" x 5 ⁵/₈". Published October 11, 1967 at $6.00. Issued in yellow cloth covered
boards stamped in black and gray. Top edge unstained and all edges trimmed. Front:
[gray] The | Best | American | Short | Stories | [black] 1967 Spine: [gray] The | Best
| Ameri- | can | Short | Stories | [black] 1967 | [gray] Edited by | Foley | and | Burnett
| H M Co. Issued in white paper dust jacket printed in black, gray and yellow.

Contains: "The Wild Horses"   (25-36) which originally appeared in The Saturday
Evening Post (60-65) April 9, 1966 and in Fifty Stories as "Seven Say You Can Hear
Corn Grow."

B59   100 YEARS OF THE AMERICAN FEMALE   [1967]
                   FROM HARPER'S BAZAAR

HARPER'S | BAZAAR | 100 years | of the | American | female | [rule] the sump-
tuous | the expensive | the precious | the moneyed | the luxe | the tasteful | the opu-
lent | and the | amusing | woman | from Bazaar | [rule] edited by | Jane Trahey |
[publisher's device] [vertical rule] Random House | New York

[i-iv], v-xii, [1], 2-5, [6-7], 8, [9-12],13-14, [15-16], 17-25, [26], 27-32, [33], 34-44, [45], 46-50, [51], 52-53, [54], 55-59, [60-61], 62-82, [83], 84-92, [93], 94, [95], 96, [97], 98-101, [102], 103-105, [106], 107-108, [109], 110, [111-112], 113-115, [116], 117, [118], 119, [120], 121-122, [123], 124, [125], 126-138, [139], 140-142, [143-144], 145, [146], 147-149, [150], 151-154, [155], 156, [157], 158-162, [163-164], 165-173, [174], 175-176, [177], 178, [179], 180, [181], 182-184, [185], 186-191, [192], 193-195, [196], 197-200, [201], 202, [203], 204, [205-206], 207-212, [213], 214, [215-216], 217-219, [220-221], 222, [223], 224-225, [226], 227-229, [230], 231-233, [234], 235-237, [238], 239-253, [254-255], 256, [257-258], 259, [260], 261, [262], 263-268, [269-270], 271, [272], 273, [274], 275-276, [277-278], 279, [280-281], 282, [283-284], 285-286, [287-288], 289-290, [291-292], 293-294, [295], 296, [297-298], 299, [300], 301, [302], 303-307, [308] pages with color plates between pages 28 & 29, 108 & 109, 204 & 205, 268 & 269 (2), 284 & 285 (2); navy blue endpapers. 12 $^1/_8$" x 9 $^1/_4$". Published October 17, 1967 at $20.00. Issued in light purple cloth covered boards stamped in black and silver. Top edge unstained and all edges trimmed. Front: HARPER'S | BAZAAR   Spine: [printed downward in black] HARPER'S [silver] BAZAAR [black] | [horizontal rule] | [black printed downward] EDITED BY [top line] JANE TRAHEY [bottom line] | [horizontal printed in black] | [publisher's device] | RANDOM | HOUSE   Back: Blank. Issued in white paper dust jacket printed in black and blue.

Contains: "Life Sentence" pp. 54-59 which originally appeared in *Harper's Bazaar* 42-43, 104-107 in June 1938. Was uncollected.

B60   THE AUTOBIOGRAPHY OF EMANUEL CARNEVALI   [1967]

the Autobiography | of | Emanuel Carnevali | *compiled & prefaced by* | *Kay Boyle* | Horizon Press New York

[1-7], 8-19, [20-22], 23-134, [135], 136-260, [261], 262-264 pages; dark gray endpapers. 9 $^3/_{16}$" x 6". Published October 30, 1967 at $5.95. Issued in white cloth covered boards printed in black. Top edge unstained with all edges trimmed. Front: [blind stamped] Emanuel Carnevali   Spine: the | Auto- | biography | of | Emanuel | Carnevali | *compiled* | *&* | *prefaced* | *by* | *Kay* | *Boyle* | Horizon | Press   Issued in white photographic dust jacket printed in black.

Contains: Preface (9-19) by Kay Boyle.

B61   TALKS WITH AUTHORS   [1968]

talks with | authors | edited by Charles F. Madden | *Carbondale and Edwardsville* | SOUTHERN ILLINOIS UNIVERSITY PRESS | FEFFER & SIMONS, INC. | *London and Amsterdam* [i-iv], v, [vi], vii, [viii-x], xi, [xii], xiii, [xiv], xv, [xvi], xvii, [xviii], xix, [xx], [1-2], pages 3 through 236 are numbered on odd numbered pages only with the exception of 12, 56, 152 and 180 which are numbered. Cream endpapers. 8 $^3/_{16}$" x 5" Published May 14, 1968 at $5.85. Issued in red cloth covered boards stamped in gold. Top edge unstained and all edges trimmed. Front: Blank. Spine: [printed downward] Talks with AUTHORS [horizontal] MADDEN | Southern | Illinois | University | Press Back: Blank. Issued in white paper dust jacket printed in black, white and gray.

Contains: A question and answer session held with Dr. James Livingston, Drury College; Dr. R.H. Jefferson, Jackson State College; Mrs. Moxye King, Langston University; Finley Campbell, Morehouse College; and Dr. Elizabeth Sewell, Tougaloo College held May 11, 1964. Also a biographical and bibliographical note (215-236).

B62   NANCY CANARD: BRAVE POET,   [1968]
               INDOMITABLE REBEL 1896-1965

Nancy Cunard: | *Brave Poet, Indomitable Rebel* | 1886-1965 | edited by hugh ford | *Chilton Book Company* | *Philadelphia New York London*

[i-vi], vii-xi, [xii], xiii-xiv, [xv-xxii], [1-2], 3-31, [32-34], 35-98, [99-100], 101-160, [161-162], 163-198, [199-200], 201-235, [236-238], 239-349, [350-352], 353-361, [362], 363-371, [372], 373-383, [384-386] pages; red endpapers with black dots getting smaller as the approach the bottom of the page. Photographs between pages 170 and 171. 9 $^1/_4$" x 6" Published on June 26, 1968 at $12.50. Issued in rose red cloth covered boards stamped in gold. Top edge unstained with all edges trimmed. Front: Blind stamp with a large N and C with a blind stamped period after the C. Spine: [printed downward in gold] *Nancy Cunard: Brave Poet, Indomitable Rebel* [top line] 1896-1965 edited by hugh ford • chilton 5357 [bottom line] Issued in white paper dust jacket printed in purple, black and orange with a photograph of Nancy Cunard on the front.

Contains: "Nancy Cunard." An article on Nancy Cunard (78-80).

B63   EDWARD DAHLBERG: AMERICAN   1968
               ISHMAEL OF LETTERS

[ink drawing of a flower] | [red] EDWARD DAHLBERG | [the rest in black] AMERICAN ISHMAEL OF LETTERS | *Selected Critical Essays with an Introduction* | *by* Harold Billings | ROGER BEACHAM · PUBLISHER AUSTIN 1968

[1-6], 7-10, [11], 12, [13-14], 15-25, [26], 27-49, [50], 51-53, [54], 55-87, [88], 89-109, [110], 111-115, [116], 117-133, [134], 135-147, [148], 149-167, [168], 169-175, [176] pages; cream endpapers.   9" x 6"   Published May 20, 1968 at $8.95. Issued in tan cloth covered boards stamped in black. Top edge unstained and all edges trimmed.   Front: [design] | AMERICAN ISHMAEL OF LETTERS Spine: [printed downward] EDWARD DAHLBERG   *Edited by Harold Billings* | [horizontal] Beacham   Issued in a cream paper dust jacket printed in black and rust red.

Contains: "A Man in the Wilderness." (159-162) A tribute to Edward Dahlberg which originally appeared in *The Nation*, May 29, 1967 (693-694).

B64   THE REMNANTS OF POWER   [1968]

THE | REMNANTS | OF POWER | The Tragic Last Years of | Adlai Stevenson | *by Richard J. Walton* | [publisher's device] | COWARD-McCANN, Inc. | NEW YORK

[1-6], 7-9, [10-12], 13-242, [243-244], 245-255, [256] pages; brownish yellow endpapers.   Photographs between pages 80 and 81.   8 $\frac{1}{4}$" x 5 $\frac{1}{8}$". Published October 29, 1968 at $5.95. Issued in blue cloth covered boards stamped in gold. Top edge unstained with top and bottom edges trimmed.   Front edge rough trimmed.   Front: [publisher's device stamped in gold in lower right hand corner] Spine: [printed downward] THE REMNANTS OF POWER [top line] *Richard J. Walton* [bottom line] | [design] | *COWARD McCANN*   Issued in a white paper dust jacket printed in blue, white and two shades of orange.

Contains: Excerpts from a letter to Adlai Stevenson (184-185).

B65   THE TRIAL OF HUEY NEWTON   [1968]

SELECTED ARTICLES | AND STATEMENTS | EDITED WITH | PREFA-TORY NOTES | Printed in U. S. A., December 31, 1968 | Published and edited by Mona Bazaar

182 unpaginated pages. 7" x 8 $\frac{1}{2}$". Published December 31, 1968. No price. Issued in black plastic spiral bound yellow wraps printed in black.   Top edge unstained with all edges trimmed.   Front: THE TRIAL OF HUEY NEWTON | Edited by Mona Bazaar | [photograph of Huey Newton giving the peace sign].

Contains: A collaboration with Mona Bazaar to write the introduction. She also collaborated with William Anderson and Eldridge Cleaver to write "Conspiracy and Violence in White America" and collaborated with William Anderson to write "The Prosecutor." She also contributed a piece called "Huey's Jury."   (unpaginated)

B66   A RETURN TO PAGANY   [1969]

[double spread title page] *A Return to* [design] PAGANY | [rule] | *The History,
Correspondence, and* | *Selections from a Little Magazine 1929-1932* | *Edited by*
STEPHEN HALPERT | *with* RICHARD JOHNS | *Introduction by* KENNETH
REXROTH | BEACON PRESS *Boston*

[i-xiii], xiv-xvi, [xvii], xviii, [xix-xx], [1-2], 3-45, [46-47], 48-99, [100-101], 102-
122, [123], 124-133, [134-135], 136-165, [166-167], 168-208, [209-210],
211-228, [229] 230-267, [268], 269-279, [280-281], 282-287, [288], 289-306,
[307], 308-340, [341], 342-372, [373-374], 375-380, [381], 382-431, [432-433],
434-455, [456-457], 458-483, [484-485], 486-519, [520-524] pages; dark blue
endpapers. 9 $^7/_8$" x 6 $^7/_8$". Published December 27, 1969 A $12.50. Top edge
unstained and all edges trimmed. Issued in dark blue paper covered boards with
reddish orange cloth spine printed in white. Front: Blind stamped castle on blue
boards. Spine: [printed downward] HALPERT • JOHNS *A Return to* PAGANY
BEACON PRESS Issued in white paper dust jacket printed in red, white and blue.

Contains: A facsimile of a previously unpublished letter written to Richard Johns,
dated January 9, 1931. (158-159)

B67   CONTEMPORARY POETS OF THE ENGLISH LANGUAGE [1970]

CONTEMPORARY POETS | OF THE | ENGLISH | LANGUAGE | WITH A
PREFACE BY | C. DAY LEWIS | EDITOR | ROSALIE MURPHY | DEPUTY
EDITOR | JAMES VINSON | ST JAMES PRESS | CHICAGO   LONDON

[i-iv], v-xvii, [xviii-xx], 1-1243, [1244] pages; white end papers.   9$^1/_2$" x 6 $^3/_4$".
Published in 1970 at $25.00. Issued in black cloth covered boards stamped in gold.
Top edge unstained and all edges trimmed. Front: Contemporary | Poets | of the |
English | Language   Spine: Contemporary | Poets | of the | English | Language | St
James Press. Dust jacket not seen.

Contains: A five-line statement by Kay Boyle about herself as a poet. (125)   Note:
Editions 2-5 contain the same statement.

B68   THIS IS MY BEST   [1970]

America's 85 Greatest Living Authors Present |THIS IS MY BEST | IN THE
THIRD QUARTER OF THE CENTURY | [rule] | Edited by Whit Burnett |
DOUBLEDAY & COMPANY, INC., GARDEN CITY, NEW YORK

[i-iv], v-viii, [ix], x-xii, [xiii], xiv-xx, [1-3], 4- 24, [25], 26-33, [34], 35-47, [48],
49-59, [60], 61-64, [65], 66-75, [76], 77-89, [90], 91-98, [99], 100-110, [111],

112-117, [118-121], 122-138, [139], 140-152, [153], 154-167, [168], 169-179, [180], 181-189, [190], 191-202, [203], 204-210, [211], 212-220, [221], 222-233, [234-237], 238-241, [242], 243-250, [251], 252-257, [258], 259-266, [267], 268-283, [284], 285-289, [290], 291-302, [303], 304-314, [315], 316-323, [324], 325-345, [346], 347-358, [359-361], 362-388, [389], 390-413, [414], 415-424, [425], 426-436, [437], 438-440, [441], 442-449. [450-453], 454-462, [463], 464-469, [470], 471-481, [482], 483-486, [487], 488-491, [492], 493-497, [498], 499-502, [503-505], 506-513, [514], 515-531, [532], 533-540, [541], 542-549, [550], 551-561, [562], 563-573, [574], 575-588, [589], 590-605, [606-609], 610-619, [620], 621-635, [636], 637-648, [649], 650-655, [656], 657-667, [668], 669-670, [671], 672-681, [682], 683-690, [691-693], 694-701, [702], 703-707, [708], 709-717, [718], 719-729, [730], 731-732, [733], 734-745, [746], 747-752, [753], 754-767, [768], 769-778, [779], 780-786, [787], 788-794, [795-797], 798-805, [806]; 807-823, [824], 825-840, [841], 842-857, [858]; 859-870, [871], 872-880, [881-883], 884-896, [897], 898-905. [906], 907-912, [913], 914-915, [916], 917-935, [936], 937-944, [945], 946-954, [955], 956-959, [960], 961-963, [964], 965-971, [972], 973-1040, [1041], 1042-1058, [1059], 1060 pages; grayish green end papers. 8 $^1/_8$" x 5$^1/_2$" Published September 17, 1970 at $10.00. Issued in light gray cloth covered boards printed in black and stamped in gold. Top edge unstained and all edges trimmed. Front : Blank. Spine: [printed downward] THIS IS MY BEST [top line printed in black] IN THE THIRD QUARTER OF THE CENTURY [second line printed in black] *Edited by Whit Burnett   Doubleday* [third line stamped in gold] Issued in white paper dust jacket printed in black, dark blue and grayish olive.

Contains: A note on "The Wild Horses" and the title change (Her original title had been "Seven Say You Can Hear Corn Grow") and why she chose the story for inclusion in this anthology. (562)   Also includes the story "The Wild Horses" (563-573) and biographical and bibliographical information. (978-979)   It was later collected in *Nothing Ever Breaks Except the Heart and Other Stories* and *Fifty Stories* under its original title "Seven Say You Can Hear Corn Grow."

B69   THE MAN OUTSIDE   [1971]

a. First Hard Cover Edition:

Wolfgang Borchert | [rule] | The Man Outside | [rule] | *Translated from the German by* | David Porter | *Foreword by* | Kay Boyle | *Introduction by* | Stephen Spender | *A New Directions Book*

[i-iv], v-xviii, [1-6], 7-35, [36-38], 39-50, [51-52], 53-76, [77-82], 83-135, [136-140], 141-167, [168-170], 171-234, [235-236], 237-270 pages; cream endpapers. 8" x 5 $^3/_8$". Published March 24, 1971 at $6.50. Issued in black cloth stamped in silver. Top edge unstained with all edges trimmed. Front: Blank. Spine: [printed downward in silver] Wolfgang Borchert THE MAN OUTSIDE *New Directions* Issued in a white paper photographic dust jacket printed in black.

Contains: A foreword by Kay Boyle (v-x).

a. First Paperback Edition:

Wolfgang Borchert | [rule] | The Man Outside | [rule] | *Translated from the German by* | David Porter | *Foreword by* | Kay Boyle | *Introduction by* | Stephen Spender | *A New Directions Book*

[i-iv], v-xviii, [1-6], 7-35, [36-38], 39-50, [51-52], 53-76, [77-82], 83-135, [136-140], 141-167, [168-170], 171-234, [235-236], 237-270 pages. 7 $^7/_8$" x 5 $^1/_8$". Published March 24, 1971 at $6.50. Issued in white stiff paper photographic wraps printed in black. Top edge unstained with all edges trimmed. Front: The Man Outside | Wolfgang | Borchert | [photograph of bombed ruins with sign stuck in the ruins] Spine: [printed downward in silver] Wolfgang Borchert THE MAN OUTSIDE NDP319 Back: A blurb about the book with photograph and design credits.

Contains: A foreword by Kay Boyle (v-x).

B70   MARK IN TIME PORTRAITS AND   [1971]
                    POETRY/SAN FRANCISCO

MARK IN TIME | PORTRAITS & POETRY / SAN FRANCISCO | PHOTOG-RAPHER: CHRISTA FLEISCHMANN COORDINATOR: ROBERT E. JOHNSON | EDITOR: NICK HARVEY PUBLISHER: GLIDE PUBLICA-TIONS, SAN FRANCISCO

[1-11], 12, [13-14], 15, [16], 17, [18-20], 21-22, [23-25], 26, [27-28], 29, [30-32], 33-34, [35-36], 37-38, [39], 40, [41-42], 43-44, [45-48], 49-50, [51], 52, [53-54], 55, [56], 57, [58-61], 62, [63], 64, [65], 66, [67-70], 71-72, [73-77], 78, [79-80], 81-82, [83-84], 85, [86], 87-88, [89-90], 91-92, [93], 94, [95-96], 97, [98], 99, [100-101], 102, [103], 104, [105-106], 107-108, [109-110], 111-112, [113-118], 119, [120], 121-122, [123], 124, [125], 126. [127-128], 129, [130-131], 132, [133-134], 135-136, [137], 138, [139-140], 141, [142], 143-144, [145], 146, [147-148], 149-150, [151], 152, [153-154], 155-156, [157-158], 159-160, [161-162], 163, [164], 165-166, [167], 168, [169-170], 171, [172], 173-189, [190-192] pages; purple endpapers. 9" x 9 $^1/_4$". Published June 21, 1971 at $10.95. Issued in brown cloth covered boards printed in very pale green. Top edge unstained with all edges trimmed. Front: MARK IN TIME | PORTRAITS & POETRY / SAN FRAN-CISCO Spine: [printed downward] MARK IN TIME PORTRAITS & POETRY / SAN FRANCISCO Back: Blank. Issued in a white paper photographic dust jacket printed in black and purple.

Contains: "To a Proud Old Woman Watching the Tearing Down of the Hurricane Shed." (72). Poem Collected in *This Is Not a Letter and Other Poems* and *Collected Poems of Kay Boyle.*

B71   ATTACKS OF TASTE   1971

[all of the following enclosed in a wide rust colored decorative band which is enclosed in a single black rectangular rule] [rust] ATTACKS | OF TASTE | [black horizontal ornament] | [black] *compiled and edited* | *by* | EVELYN B. BYRNE | & | OTTO M. PENZLER | ON TEENAGE READING: | *"You must remember that youngsters (as* | *youngsters for some reason never remem-* | *ber) have attacks of taste like attacks of* | *measles."* —*ARCHIBALD MACLEISH* | [in black outside the rectangle] | New York GOTHAM BOOK MART 1971

one leaf, [i-vi], vii, [viii-x including extra leaf], xi-xii, 1-49, [50-52], 53-63, [64-66] pages; rust colored endpapers. 9 $^1/_4$" x 6". Published December 25, 1971 at $15.00. Issued in beige cloth covered boards. Top edge unstained with all edges trimmed. Front: [white paste on label with text enclosed in a wide rust colored decorative band which is in turn enclosed in a black rectangular rule] [black horizontal ornament] | [rust] ATTACKS OF TASTE | [repeat ornament] *compiled and edited* | *by* | EVELYN B. BYRNE | & | OTTO M. PENZLER   Spine: [printed downward on white paste on label] [rust decoration] [black] ATTACKS OF TASTE [repeat rust decoration] [black] Evelyn B. Byrne & Otto M. Penzler [repeat rust decoration]. Issued in a plain white paper dust jacket with no printing.

Limitations statement: This first edition is limited to 500 copies numbered and signed by | the editors, of which 100 copies are for presentation & not for sale. | [ink number and signatures of Otto Penzler and Evelyn B. Byrne]

Contains: "Kay Boyle" A short piece by Kay Boyle about her early reading taste (7-8).

B72   ENOUGH OF DYING   [1972]

[Large peace sign] ENOUGH | OF | DYING! | VOICES FOR PEACE | *Edited by* KAY BOYLE | and | JUSTINE VAN GUNDY | [publisher's device] | A LAUREL ORIGINAL

[i-xvi], [1], 2-7, [8-11], 12-15, [16], 17, [18], 19, [20], 21-28, [29], 30-36, [37], 38-52, [53], 54-67, [68], 69-73, [74-77], 78-83, [84], 85-87, [88], 89-91, [92], 93-95, [96], 97-99, [100], 101-112, [113], 114-118, [119], 120-125, [126], 127-133, [134], 135-138, [139], 140, [141], 142-145, [146], 147-151, [152], 153-160, [161], 162-177, [178], 179-191, [192-195], 196-210, [211], 212-266, [267-269], 270, [271], 272-282, [283], 284-289, [290], 291-302, [303], 304-317, [318-319], 320-333, [334], 335-337, [338], 339-343, [344], 345-348, [349], 350-351, [352] pages. 7" x 4$^1/_4$". Published in February of 1972 at $1.25 by Dell Publishing Company Inc.. Issued in white wraps printed in yellow, red, black and white. All edges stained green.

Contains: Introduction by Kay Boyle (1-7) and reprints the short story "They Weren't Going to Die" from *Thirty Stories* published by Simon & Schuster, "The

Triumph of Principles" from *Seeds of Liberation*, New York: George Braziller, [1964], and "A Poem Dedicated to Terre des Hommes" from *Testament for My Students and Other Poems*.

B73   OPEN SECRETS: NINETY-FOUR WOMEN   [1972]
                      IN TOUCH WITH OUR TIME

Open Secrets | [rule] | *Ninety-four Women in Touch with Our Time* | *Barbaralee Diamonstein* | NEW YORK / THE VIKING PRESS

[i-vii], viii-xxxvi, [1-2], 3-474, [475-476] pages; cream endpapers.   9 $^1/_8$" x 6 $^1/_8$" Published February 28, 1972 at $10.00.   Issued in peach cloth covered boards with dark rust red cloth spine stamped in gold.   Top edge stained red with all edges trimmed.   Front: Blank.   Spine: [printed downward] *Open Secrets*   Viking [top line] | [rule] | BARBARALEE DIAMONSTEIN [bottom line]   Issued in a white paper dust jacket printed in black, red and yellow.

Contains: A written response from Kay Boyle to a fifty-four question questionnaire mailed out by the editor-compiler (23-27).

B74   THE CRITIC AS ARTIST: ESSAYS ON BOOKS   [1972]

a. First Hardcover Edition:

THE | CRITIC | AS | ARTIST | ESSAYS ON BOOKS 1920-1970 | *with some preliminary ruminations by H. L. Mencken* | Edited by Gilbert A. Harrison | [publisher's device] LIVERIGHT NEW YORK

One unpaginated leaf. [i-iv], v-x, [1-2], 3-394, [395-396] pages; red endpapers. 9" x 6".   Published in March 1972 at $12.00.   Issued in white cloth covered boards stamped in gold.   Front: Blank.   Spine: [printed downward] THE CRITIC AS ARTIST [top line] ESSAYS ON BOOKS 1920-1970 [bottom line] | edited by [top line] Gilbert A. Harrison [bottom line] | [the publisher's device printed horizontally] | LIVERIGHT   Issued in white paper dust jacket printed in black and red.

Contains: "The Unvanquished"   (38-41) a review of William Faulkner's "The Unvanquished"   which originally appeared in *The New Republic* as "Tattered Banners" (136-137) March 9, 1938.

b. First Paperback Edition:

THE | CRITIC | AS | ARTIST | ESSAYS ON BOOKS 1920-1970 | *with some preliminary ruminations by H. L. Mencken* | Edited by Gilbert A. Harrison | [publisher's device] LIVERIGHT NEW YORK

One unpaginated leaf. [i-iv], v-x, [1-2], 3-394, [395-396] pages; 9" x 5 $^3/_4$". Published in March 1972 at $3.95. Issued in white paper wrappers printed in black and red. Front: [printed in black] THE | CRITIC | AS | ARTIST [the A in artist extends up to include the same line as AS] | ESSAYS | ON BOOKS | 1920/1970 | with some preliminary ruminations by | H. L. MENCKEN | Edited by Gilbert A. Harrison | LIVERIGHT/L-60/$3.95 | [printed in red and interspersed among the title The Critic as Artist] Stanley Kauffmann | Katherine Ann Porter | Reed Whittemore] Malcolm Cowley Sherwood Anderson | Conrad Aiken | Philip Rahv | Kay Boyle | Leslie A. Fiedler Irving Howe | Robert Brustein Alfred Kazin | F. Scott Fitzgerald John Updike | Carl Van Doren | James Thurber | Quentin Anderson | Robert Penn Warren | Joseph Featherstone | Malcolm Muggeridge | Anatole Broyard | C. Vann Woodward | William Faulkner Spine: [printed downward in red] THE CRITIC AS ARTIST [top line] ESSAYS ON BOOKS 1920/1970 [bottom line in black] | edited by [top line in black] Gilbert A. Harrison [bottom line in black] | [the publisher's device printed horizontally] | LIVERIGHT | L-60

Contains: "The Unvanquished" (38-41) First book appearance of a review of William Faulkner's "The Unvanquished" which originally appeared in *The New Republic* as "Tattered Banners" pp. 136-137 March 9, 1938.

B75   THE LEFT BANK REVISITED   [1972]

THE LEFT BANK | REVISITED: | Selections from the | Paris *Tribune* 1917-1934 | [rule] | Edited with an Introduction | by Hugh Ford | Foreword by Matthew Josephson | The Pennsylvania State University Press | University Park and London

[i-xviii], xix-xxiv, [xxv-xxvi], 1-10, [11-12], 13-41, [42-44], 45-88, [89-90], 91-149, [150-152], 153-186, [187-188], 189-280, [281-282], 283-334 pages; bright yellow endpapers. Photographs between pages 134 and 135, 142 and 143. 8 $^7/_8$" x 5 $^7/_8$". Published August 23, 1972 at $12.50. Top edge unstained all edges trimmed. Issued in bright yellow cloth covered boards stamped in black and gold. Front: Blank. Spine: [horizontal in black] Ford | [printed downward in gold on black rectangle] THE LEFT BANK REVISITED | [horizontal in black] Penn State Issued in white paper dust jacket printed in black and brown.

Contains: "A New Mythology" (249-250) and "McAlmon's *Indefinite Huntress*" (276-277). "A New Mythology" appeared in the Paris *Tribune* March 10, 1929 and "McAlmon's *Indefinite Huntress*" appeared in the *Tribune* on December 17, 1932.

B76   SUNDOWN BEACH   [1973]

SUNDOWN BEACH | A PLAY | BY | BESSIE BREUER | WITH A FOREWORD BY | KAY BOYLE | Including the entire text of the play as it was given | by the Actor's

Studio in 1948 — the Studio's first | production; and a part of the play as it was originally | drafted by the author. | GRINDSTONE PRESS Brooklyn, New York

[i-v], vi-vii, [viii], ix, [x], xi-xii, 1-142, [143-144] pages.   8 $\frac{1}{2}$" x 5 $\frac{1}{2}$". Published in 1973 at $2.00.   Top edge unstained and all edges trimmed. Issued in white wraps printed in red white and black. Front: Photograph of Julie Harris in upper left hand corner. [under photograph in black] Julia Harris in SUNDOWN BEACH [printed in white in lower left hand corner] Bessie Breuer [printed in white bottom to top along front edge] SUNDOWN BEACH Spine: [printed downward in black] SUNDOWN BEACH   Bessie Breuer   Back: Photograph of Curtain call for Elia Kazan production of SUNDOWN BEACH. Blurbs by Kay Boyle, Julie Harris and Elia Kazan.

Contains: A foreword by Kay Boyle. (9)

B77   LAURENCE VAIL   [1974]

[no title page]

[1-8] pages.   Stapled pictorial wraps   11" x 8 $\frac{1}{2}$"   Published in January 1974 by Noah Goldowsky, Inc. Distributed by the gallery for a showing of Laurence Vail's sculptures.   15 photographs, two in color.

Contains: Excerpts from original manuscript dated May 1973 writing about Laurence Vail.

B78   JAMES STERN: SOME LETTERS FOR   1974
                       HIS SEVENTIETH BIRTHDAY

James Stern | [rule] | Some letters for his seventieth | birthday | Privately printed | Boxing Day 1974

[i-ii], 1-6, [7], 8-22, [23], 24-25, [26] pages. Pictorial Wraps.   Illustrations opposite pages 6 and 22.   9 $\frac{3}{4}$" x 6 $\frac{1}{4}$"   Published Boxing Day 1974 by John Byrne the compiler. Issued in dark green paper wraps. Front: [printed on a beige paper paste on] *J. A. S.*

Note: A copy inscribed by the compiler, John Byrne states printing was limited to 150 copies.

Contains: A letter from Kay Boyle to James Stern.

B79   PUBLISHED IN PARIS   [1975]

[design] | PUBLISHED | IN PARIS | American and British Writers, | Printers, and Publishers in | Paris, 1920-1939 | HUGH FORD | With a Foreword by | Janet

Flanner | [rule thickening slightly at the center] Macmillan Publishing Co., Inc. | NEW YORK

[one extra leaf], [i-viii], ix-xiv, [xv], xvi-xvii, [xviii], [1-2], 3, [4], 5-10, [11], 12-21, [22], 23-28, [29], 30-32, [33], 34-35, [36], 37-49, [50], 51, [52], 53-100, [101-102], 103-109, [110], 111-117, [118], 119-132, [133], 134-137, [138], 139-169, [170], 171, [172-173], 174-184, [185], 186-195, [196], 197-244, [245], 246-256, [257], 258-262, [263], 264-271, [272], 273-282, [283], 284-292, [293], 294-297, [298], 299-313, [314], 315-330, [331-332], 333-336, [337], 338-339, [340], 341-357, [358], 359-361, [362], 363-373, [374], 375-376, [377], 378-400, [401], 402-453, [454-360] pages; cream endpapers. 9 $^1/_8$" x 6" Published in September 1975 at $14.95. Top edge unstained and all edges trimmed. Issued in cream cloth covered boards printed in blue. Front: Blank. Spine: FORD | [rule] | [printed downward] Published in Paris | [rule] | [horizontal] MACMILLAN Back: [lower right corner] 53960 Issued in white paper pictorial dust jacket printed in black, blue and brown.

Contains: Excerpts from unpublished letters to Caresse Crosby and in particular a long excerpt on page 227. Hugh Ford gives no dates for these excerpts.

B80   SAMUEL BECKETT A COLLECTION   [1975]
OF CRITICISM

Samuel | Beckett | a collection of criticism edited by Ruby Cohn | [design] |Publisher's logo] | McGraw-Hill Book Company | New York • St. Louis • San Francisco • Auckland • Düsseldorf • Johannesburg | Kuala Lumpur • London • Mexico • Montreal • New Delhi • Panama • Paris | São Paulo • Singapore • Sydney • Tokyo • Toronto

[i-iv], v-xi, [xii], xiii-xvi, 1-13, [14], 15-19, [20], 21-31, [32], 33-94, [95], 96-119, [120], 121-135, [136], 137-138, [139-144] pages. 8" x 5 $^1/_4$". Published in August 1975 at $2.45. Issued in white wrappers printed in maroon, brown and black. Front: [upper right hand corner enclosed in a circle] $2.45 | [red] Samuel | Beckett | [brown] a collection of criticism edited by Ruby Cohn | [black] Contributions by | H. Porter Abbott ❑ Kay Boyle | Ruby Cohn ❑ Elin Diamond | John Fletcher ❑ Jan Hokenson | Ludovic Janvier ❑ Hugh Kenner | Dougald McMillan ❑ Alec Reid | Yasunari Takahashi ❑ Hersh Zeifman | *with a selected bibliography* | [red] Mc-Graw-Hill Paperbacks | [brown] Contemporary Studies in Literature | [red design] Spine: [red design] [printed downward in brown Samuel Beckett [red] edited by Cohn [black] Contemporary Studies in Literature [top line] McGraw-Hill Paperbacks $2.45 [bottom line]

Contains: "All Mankind Is Us" (15-19).

B81   BLACK SUN   [1976]

BLACK SUN | The Brief Transit and Violent | Eclipse of Harry Crosby | [rule] | [second slightly shorter rule] | [third rule slightly shorter than the second] | [fourth rule shorter than the third] | GEOFFREY WOLFF | [publisher's device] | [repeat descending order of rules except smaller than above] | Random House New York

[i-x], xi-xiii, [xiv-xvi], [1-2], 3-315, [316], 317-359, [360], 361-367, [368] pages; black endpapers. Photographs between pages 80 and 81 and between 240 and 241. 9 $^1/_4$" x 6" Published August 20, 1976 at $12.95. Top edges unstained and all edges trimmed. Issued in cream cloth covered boards stamped in gold. Front: [design enclosing the initials GW] Spine: [enclosed in double ruled rectangle with indented corners and printed downward] BLACK SUN | [three horizontal rules each shorter than the one above it] | [printed downward] GEOFFREY WOLFF | [horizontal publisher's device] | [horizontal] Random | House Issued in white paper dust jacket printed in black and reddish brown.

Contains: Excerpts from unpublished letters to Geoffrey Wolff January 23, 1973 (221-222 and 299-300); an excerpt from an unpublished and undated letter to Harry Crosby (251) and an excerpt from an unpublished introduction to Harry Crosby's *Shadows of the Sun* (299).

B82   FICTION! INTERVIEWS WITH NORTHERN   [1976]
                    CALIFORNIA NOVELISTS

a. First Edition:

Fiction! | Interviews with Northern | California Novelists | by Dan Tooker and | Roger Hofheins | Photographs by | Dan Tooker | HARCOURT BRACE JOVANOVICH, INC. / WILLIAM KAUFMANN, INC. | *New York • Los Altos*

[i-iv], v, [vi], vii-xii, [xiii-xiv], 1-13, [14], 15-35, [36], 37-53, [54], 55-69, [70], 71-85, [86], 87-99, [100], 101-109, [110], 111-123, [124], 125-147, [148], 149-165, [166], 167-179, [180], 181-191, [192], 193-197, [198-202] pages; white endpapers. 8" x 5 $^5/_8$" Published August 27,1976 at $8.95. Issued in red cloth covered boards stamped in silver. Top edge unstained and all edges trimmed. Front: Fiction! Spine: [printed downward] Fiction! | [horizontal rule] | [printed downward] Dan Tooker and [top line] Roger Hofheins [bottom line] | printed downward] HARCOURT BRACE JOVANOVICH, INC. | [top line] WILLIAM KAUFMANN, INC. [bottom line] Issued in white paper dust jacket printed in black, red and white.

Contains: An interview with Kay Boyle with photograph and bibliography (14-35).

b. First Paperback Edition:

Fiction! | Interviews with Northern | California Novelists | by Dan Tooker and | Roger Hofheins | Photographs by Dan Tooker | HARCOURT BRACE JOVANOVICH, INC. / WILLIAM KAUFMANN, INC. | *New York • Los Altos*

[i-iv], v, [vi], vii-xii, [xiii-xiv], 1-13, [14], 15-35, [36], 37-53, [54], 55-69, [70], 71-85, [86], 87-99, [100], 101-109, [110], 111-123, [124], 125-147, [148], 149-165, [166], 167-179, [180], 181-191, [192], 193-197, [198-202] pages.   8" x 5 $^5/_8$" Published August 27, 1976 at $3.95. Issued in white paper wrappers printed in red, white and black. Top edge unstained and all edges trimmed. Front: [black rule] | [white] Fiction! | Interviews with Northern | California Novelists | [black] by Dan Tooker and | Roger Hofheins | [rule] | Peter S. Beagle Kay Boyle | Don Carpenter Evan S. Connell, Jr. | Alfred Coppel Ernest J. Gaines | Leonard Gardner Herbert Gold | James Leigh Janet Lewis | Wallace Stegner Jessamyn West | [rule] | [white] Series One   Spine: [printed downward] Fiction! | [horizontal rule] | [printed downward] Dan Tooker and [top line] Roger Hofheins [bottom line] | printed downward] HARCOURT BRACE JOVANOVICH, INC. | [top line] WILLIAM KAUFMANN, INC. [bottom line]

Contains: An interview with Kay Boyle with photograph and bibliography (14-35).

B83   VETERANS OF THE ABRAHAM LINCOLN BRIGADE   [1977]

Bay Area Post | VETERANS of the ABRAHAM LINCOLN BRIGADE | 40th Anniversary Banquet | Honoring | *The Premature Anti-Fascist Women |* 1937 [three pointed star] 1977 | *Fredericka Martin, Chief Nurse in Spain, author, historian | Elena, estudiante y profesora linguistica espanola, "Espana Hoy" | * | Sarah Cunningham | John Randolph | Bay Area Progressive Music Association | Sunday Blue Dolphin Restaurant | February 6, 1977 San Leandro, California*

16 unnumbered pages. +covers. 8 $^1/_2$" x 6 $^1/_4$"   Published or issued February 6, 1977 at the banquet dinner a the Blue Dolphin Restaurant. Issued in stapled white paper wrappers printed in black.

Contains: Untitled tribute to the anti-fascist women fighting fascism in Spain. (unpaginated)

B84   A HASTY BUNCH   [1977]

a. First Edition:

A Hasty Bunch | [thick rule] | [thin rule] | *Short Stories |* By Robert McAlmon | Afterword by Kay Boyle | SOUTHERN ILLINOIS UNIVERSITY PRESS | Carbondale and Edwardsville | *Feffer & Simons, Inc.* | London and Amsterdam [i-vii], viii, [ix-x], 1-10, [11], 12-27, [28], 29-36, [37], 38-46, [47], 48-54, [55], 56-67, [68], 69-82, [83], 84-96, [97], 98-103, [104], 105-108, [109], 110-116, [117], 118-121, [122], 123-125, [126], 127-129, [130], 131-136, [137], 138-144, [145], 146-161, [162], 163-215, [216], 217-223, [224], 225-228, [229], 230-247, [248], 249-252, [253], 254-267, [268], 269-282, [283], 284-286, [287], 288-299, [300-302] pages; cream endpapers. 7 $^1/_4$" x 4 $^3/_4$". Published March 7, 1977 at $8.95. Issued in brown cloth covered boards stamped in gold. Top edge unstained with all edges trimmed. Front: Blank. Spine: Robert | McAlmon | [thick gold rule] | [thin gold rule] | A | Hasty | Bunch | [thin gold rule] | [thick gold rule] | Southern | Illinois | University | Press Back: Blank. Issued in plain brown paper dust jacket printed in black and two shades of brown.

Contains: An afterword by Kay Boyle (287-299).

b. First Paperback Edition:

A HASTY | BUNCH | by Robert McAlmon | Short Stories | *Afterword by* Kay Boyle | POPULAR LIBRARY • NEW YORK

[1-6], 7-83, [84], 85-107, [108], 109-111, [112], 113-125, [126], 127-139, [140], 141-181, [182], 183-207, [208], 209-251, [252], 253, [254-256] pages. 6 $^7/_8$" X 4 $^1/_8$" Published in 1971 at $1.95. Issued in white wraps with pictorial cover. All edges stained yellow. Front: [white] 0-445-04314-8 $1.95 | [yellow] A passion for naked truth – | [white] A HASTY | BUNCH | [yellow] by Robert McAlmon [montage of typewriter keys, male head profile looking right to left and other people in various poses printed in brown, yellow, green, red and white. Spine: [horizontal in blue] POPULAR | LIBRARY | FICTION | [printed downward in black] A HASTY BUNCH Robert McAlmon [downward in blue] 0-445-04314-8 $1.95

B85　　　　　　　　　FOUR VISIONS OF AMERICA　　　　　　[1977]

a. First Limited Edition:

[the following all enclosed in a single ruled rectangle] Four Visions | of | America | Erica Jong | Thomas Sanchez | Kay Boyle | Henry Miller | [publisher's device] | Capra Press | Santa Barbara

[1-9], 10-39, [40-42], 43-91, [92-93], 94-109, [110-112], 113-127, [128-130] pages; cream endpapers. 9" x 6". Published April 20, 1977 at $8.95. Issued in gray paper covered boards with red cloth spine stamped in silver. Top edge unstained with all edges trimmed. Front: Blank. Spine: [printed downward] FOUR VISIONS OF AMERICA: Jong, Boyle, Sanchez, Miller [publishers device] | [printed horizontally] CAPRA | PRESS Issued in white dust Jacket glazed in silver and printed in red and black with photographs of the four contributors.

Limitation Statement: FOUR VISIONS OF AMERICA | WAS DESIGNED BY NOEL YOUNG | SET IN JANSON BY CHARLES McADAMS, | PRINTED & BOUND BY R.R. DONNELLEY & SONS | IN CRAWFORDSVILLE, INDIANA. | 225 COPIES WERE NUMBERED AND SIGNED BY THE AUTHORS, MARCH 1977. [recto page] *This is copy no.* [number is stamped in red]

Contains: "Report from Lockup" (10-39). Describes her experiences in prison and the women with whom she shared the experience. Also gives a brief history of the American prison system.

b. First Trade Edition:

[the following all enclosed in a single ruled rectangle] Four Visions | of | America | Erica Jong | Thomas Sanchez | Kay Boyle | Henry Miller | [publisher's device] | Capra Press | Santa Barbara

The trade edition is identical to the limited with the lone exception being that the number and signature page is blank.

c. First Paperback Edition:

[the following all enclosed in a single ruled rectangle] Four Visions | of | America | Erica Jong | Thomas Sanchez | Kay Boyle | Henry Miller | [publisher's device] | Capra Press | Santa Barbara

[1-9], 10-39, [40-42], 43-91, [92-93], 94-109, [110-112], 113-127, [128] pages; cream endpapers. 9" x 6". Published April 20, 1977 at $3.95. Issued in white wrappers glazed in silver and printed in black. Top edge unstained with all edges trimmed. Front: Identical to hardcover dust jacket except printed all in black. Spine: Identical to hardcover dust jacket except printed all in black. Back: Identical to the hardcover edition except printed all in black.

B86   AMERICAN POETRY ARCHIVE   [1977]

american | poetry | archive | second series | 1977-78

[1-8], 9, [10-11], 12-83, [84-85], 86-104, [105], 106-111, [112] pages.   9" x 6" Published in 1977 as a catalogue for available and upcoming video tapes of writers and poets read from their works. Issued in white paper perfect bound wraps printed in black and blue. Front: american | poetry | archive | second series | 1977-78 [the printing is enclosed by a heavy white line running about one half inch from the top of the spine and down the fore edge returning along the bottom to the spine. Out side the white line is black and the line encloses a slanting blue and white background] Spine: [the design of the front covers extends around the spine] [printed downward] AMERICAN POETRY ARCHIVE Second Series 1977-78 Back: [no printing but the front back ground design continues around the spine and across the back]

Contains: An excerpt from the poem "A Message for Babette Deutsch." This title was later changed to "A Poem for Vida Hadjebi Tabriz" and this excerpt was altered considerably and in fact was not read on the tape the way it was written in the pamphlet.

B87   AN ILLUSTRATION IS WORTH A THOUSAND WORDS   [1978]

[single rectangular rule enclosing the following]   An Illustration | Is Worth a Thousand Words | [picture of a male and female dancer | [outside the rectangle] The School of Visual Arts in cooperation with The Master Eagle Family of Companies

48 unpaginated pages. 9" x 9" Published March or April 1978 and issued free in conjunction with a student art showing New York City, April 6 to May 23, 1978. Issued in white pictorial, stapled wrappers printed in black blues, red green and yellow. Front: The School of Visual Arts Presents | An Illustration | Is Worth a Thousand Words | [picture of a red automobile with the front end buried in a field] | Illustrator: Artie Horowitz | "Hello Auto Club? I'd like to speak to Emergency Road Service, but | first I have a question..." [signed by Dan Greenburg] | Writer: Dan Greenburg; Novels: *How to be a Jewish Mother* (1965) | *Kiss My Firm But Pliant Lips* (1968); *Scoring* (1973); *Something's There* (1976)

Contains: Kay Boyle's impressions of and a description of a painting by Dawn Kamfer. (31)

B88   THE NATIONAL BOOK AWARDS   [1978]

the | NATIONAL BOOK AWARDS | *for* | FICTION | [rule] | *an index to the* | *first twenty-five years* | JOSEPH F. TRIMMER | [rectangular design with a hand inside the rectangle holding a pen and below the wrist a capital G in script] | G. K. HALL & CO. | 70 LINCOLN STREET, BOSTON, MASS.

[i-vi], vii-xxv, [xxvi], 1-7, [8], 9-23, [24], 25-33, [34], 35-53, [54], 55-71, [72], 73-89, [90], 91-97, [98], 99-107, [108], 109-115, [116], 117-127, [128], 129-155, [156], 157-197, [198], 199-219, [220], 221-227, [228], 229-253, [254], 255-269, [270], 271-279, [280], 281-300, [301], 302-320, [321-326] pages; light brown endpapers. 9 $^1/_4$" x 6" Published in November 1978 at $35.00. Top edge unstained and all edges trimmed. Issued in maroon cloth covered boards stamped in gold. Front: [gold rectangular design with a hand inside the rectangle holding a pen and below the wrist a maroon capital G in script showing through the gold] Spine: [printed downward] *The National Book Awards for Fiction* [top line] *an index to the first twenty-five years* [bottom line] | [rule] | [printed downward] *Trimmer* Back: Blank. No dust jacket seen.

Contains: Excerpt from a letter in which Kay Boyle tells of the "unscrupulous" politicking between the National Book Award judges in promoting their choice. (xv) No date is given for the letter but it is noted that it was received March 30, 1973.

B89   WHILE THERE IS A SOUL IN PRISON   [1978]

while there is a | soul in prison... | STATEMENTS ON THE PRISON EXPERI-
ENCE | THE 1979 PEACE CALENDAR | AND APPOINTMENT BOOK |
[drawing of two hands breaking a rifle in half] | EDITED BY LARRY GARA |
WITH AND INTRODUCTION BY | KAY BOYLE | WAR RESISTERS
LEAGUE | NEW YORK

unpaginated. 8 $^3/_8$" x 5 $^1/_4$". Published in late 1978 at $3.50 and is not copyrighted.
Issued in white covers printed in red, black in spiral bound wraps. Front cover:
[printed in black] While there is a | soul in prison... | [drawing of arms holding up
broken chains] | The 1979 Peace Calendar

Contains: An Introduction by Kay Boyle. (Unpaginated)

B90   PRIZE STORIES 1981 THE O. HENRY AWARDS   1981

PRIZE STORIES 1981 | *The O. Henry Awards* | [decorative rule] | EDITED AND
WITH | AN INTRODUCTION | BY WILLIAM ABRAHAMS | DOUBLEDAY
& COMPANY, INC. | GARDEN CITY, NEW YORK | 1981

[1-5], 6, [7-9], 10-11, [12-15], 16-19, [20], 21-51, [52], 53-58, [59], 60-66,
[67], 68-80, [81], 82-93, [94], 95-104, [105], 106-116, [117], 118-126, [127],
128-137, [138], 139-153, [154]. 155-173, [174], 175-190, [191], 192-211, [212],
213-216, [217], 218-238, [239], 240-246, [247], 248-257, [258], 259-272, [273],
274-288, [289], 290-300, [301], 302-309, [310-312] pages; white endpapers. 8 $^1/_8$"
x 5 $^3/_8$". Published May 8, 1981 at $12.95. Issued in dark gray paper covered
boards with black cloth spine stamped in gold.   Front: Blank. Spine: [printed
downward] PRIZE STORIES 1981 [top line] The O. Henry Awards [bottom
line] | EDITED AND [top line] WITH AN INTRODUCTION BY [second
line] WILLIAM ABRAHAMS [third line] | [then printed horizontally]
Doubleday   Back: Blank. Issued in white paper dust jacket printed in beige, black
and purple.

Contains: "St. Stephen's Green" (59-66) which originally appeared in *The Atlantic
Monthly Magazine* June 1980 (41-44). Uncollected.

B91   SO LITTLE DISILLUSION   [1983]

[thin rule] | SO LITTLE | DISILLUSION | An American Correspondent | in Paris
and London | 1924-1931 | Edited by Elizabeth Benn Shinkman | [thin rule]

[1-10], 11-15, [16], 17-159, [160-162], 163-228, [229-230], 231-237, [238],
239, [240], pages; dark brown endpapers. 9" x 6"   Published 1983 at $14.95.

Issued in dark brown cloth covered boards stamped in gold. Top edge unstained and all edges trimmed. Front: SO LITTLE | DISILLUSION   Spine: [printed downward] SO LITTLE DISILLUSION   Shinkman [printed horizontal] EPM Back: Blank.   Issued in a white paper dust jacket printed in black, brown, gold and white.

Contains: An introductory note by Kay Boyle. (17-18)   Parts of which originally appeared in *Syracuse*, December 1959 (15-16, 33-37) in a slightly different form. The *Syracuse* article was the edited text of a speech she delivered at the Footprints Conference on the Syracuse University campus.

B92   WOMEN WRITERS OF THE WEST COAST   [1983]

Women Writers | of the West Coast | *Speaking of Their Lives and Careers* | EDITED AND INTRODUCED BY | Marilyn Yalom | PHOTOGRAPHS BY | Margo Davis | *Prepared under the auspices of the* | *Center for Research on Women* | *Stanford University* | Capra Press | SANTA BARBARA

[1-6], 7-9, [10], 11-19, [20], 21-28, [29-30], 31-39, [40], 41-55, [56], 57-66, [67-68], 69-78, [79-80], 81-90, [91-92], 93-102, [103-104], 105-120, [121-122], 123-141, [142-144] pages.   9 $^1/_4$" x 6 $^1/_4$"   Published in 1983 at $10.00. Issued in white photographic wrappers printed in brown and beige.   Front: *Women Writers* | OF THE WEST COAST | [photograph of woman sitting at a desk with her back to the viewer] | *Speaking of Their Lives and Careers* | MARILYN YALOM, EDITOR | MARGO DAVIS, PHOTOGRAPHER   Spine: [printed downward] *Women Writers* OF THE WEST COAST YALOM, DAVIS CAPRA PRESS   Back: Note about the book and the editor and photographer.

Contains: "Kay Boyle." A conversation between photographer Margo Davis and Kay Boyle with photograph of Kay Boyle and a selected bibliography (104-120).

B93   BEING GENIUSES TOGETHER   [1984]

a. First American Paperback:

Robert McAlmon | Being Geniuses | Together | 1920-1930 | *Revised with supplementary chapters* | *and an afterword by* | Kay Boyle | *1984* | *North Point Press* | *San Francisco*

One blank leaf. [i-xi], xii, [xiii-xiv], [1], 2-9, [10-11], 12-24, [25], 26-38, [39], 40-48, [49], 50-62, [63], 64-71, [72-73], 74-81, [82-83], 84-88, [89], 90-101, [102-103], 104-109, [110-111], 112-120, [121], 122-129, [130-131], 132-138, [139], 140-156, [157], 158-169, [170-171], 172-193, [194-195], 196-207, [208-209], 210-219, [220-221], 222-234, [235], 236-242, [243], 244-256, [257], 258-270,

[271], 272-282, [283], 284-301, [302-303], 304-309, [310-311], 312-332, [333], 334-343, [344-347], 348- 362, 363-368 pages.   8 $^1/_4$" x   5 $^3/_{16}$"   Published April 15,1984 at $13.50.   Issued in stiff white paper wraps in dust jacket.   Wrappers printed in silver gray with all edges   trimmed.   Front: BEING GENIUSES | TOGETHER 1920-1930 | Robert McAlmon | Revised with supplementary chapters and an afterword by | Kay Boyle   Spine: Being | Geniuses | Together | 1920- 1930 | ROBERT | McALMON | KAY | BOYLE | [Small arrow enclosed in small square]

Contains: A new afterword by Kay Boyle (333-343).

b. First English Paperback:

[the following enclosed in a ruled square broken at the top by a stylized fox head] BEING | GENIUSES | TOGETHER | 1920-1930 | Robert McAlmon | [outside of the square] *Revised, with supplementary chapters | and New Afterword by Kay Boyle* | THE HOGARTH PRESS | LONDON

[i-viii], [1], 2-9, [10-11], 12-24, [25], 26-38, [39], 40-48, [49], 50-62, [63], 64-71, [72-73], 74-81, [82-83], 84-88, [89], 90-101, [102-103], 104-109, [110-111], 112-120, [121], 122-129, [130-131], 132-138, [139], 140-156, [157], 158-169, [170-171], 172-193, [194-195], 196-207, [208-209], 210-219, [220-221], 222-234, [235], 236-242, [243], 244-256, [257], 258-270, [271], 272-282, [283], 284-301, [302-303], 304-309, [310-311], 312-332, [333], 334-343, [344-347], 348- 362 pages.   7 $^3/_4$" x   5"   Published in May 1984 at £4.95.   Top edge unstained with all edges trimmed. Issued in stiff white paper pictorial wraps printed in purple, black and blue.   Front: [stylized head of a fox] | [black and white photograph of Robert McAlmon] | Being Geniuses Together | [rule] 1920 [short rule] 1930 [rule] | ROBERT McALMON & KAY BOYLE | [black and white photograph of Kay Boyle] [the preceding on a blue decorative background]   Spine: [stylized head of a fox] | [printed downward in white on purple] Being Geniuses Together [top line] ROBERT McALMON & KAY BOYLE [bottom line]   Back: Notes about the book, Robert McAlmon and Kay Boyle printed in white on purple.

B94   CONTEMPORARY AUTHORS   [1984]
                       AUTOBIOGRAPHY SERIES

[script] Contemporary | [script] Authors | Autobiography Series | Dedria Bryfonski | Editor | Foreword by Alden Whitman | Author of *Come to Judgment* | [script] Volume 1| GALE RESEARCH COMPANY • BOOK TOWER • DETROIT, MICHIGAN 48226

[1-4], 5, [6], 7-11, [12], 13-14, [15-16], 17-79, [80], 81-95, [96], 97-125, [126], 127-137, [138], 139-159, [160], 161-175, [176], 177-199, [200], 202-235, [236], 237-281, [282], 283-305, [306], 307-323, [324], 325-403, [404-410], 411-431, [432] pages; purple endpapers.   10 $^7/_8$" x 8 $^3/_8$"   Published July 1984 at $70.00.

Issued in blue, pink, red, dark purple, light purple and black cloth covered boards printed in white. Front: [script] Contemporary | [script] Authors | Autobiography Series | [script] volume 1   Spine: [printed downward in script] Contemporary Authors [top line] | Autobiography Series [bottom line] | [printed horizontally] BRYFONSKI | [script] volume | 1 | GALE   Issued without a dust jacket.

Contains: "Kay Boyle: 1902-" an autobiographical sketch (97-125).

B95   SMOKE AND OTHER EARLY STORIES   [1985]

[double rectangular rule enclosing text] *SMOKE | and Other Early Stories | DJUNA BARNES | Edited, with an Introduction | by Douglas Messerli | Afterword by Kay Boyle | Virago |* [publisher's device]

[i-vii], viii-xix, [xx], [no pages 1-24], 25-96, [97-98], 99-119, [120], 121-134, [135], 136-157, [158], 159-184, [185-188] pages. 7 $^3/_4$" x 5". Published in February 1985 at £2.95. Issued in white pictorial wrappers printed in green and white. Top edge unstained with all edges trimmed.   Front: [lime green] Virago Modern Classics | [white rule] | [white] Djuna Barnes | [white rule] | Smoke and Other Early Stories | [picture of two women dressed in green and holding cards] Spine: [continuation from front cover of white rule] | [publisher's device] | [continuation of second white rule] | [printed downward in white] Smoke and Other Early Stories   Djuna Barnes   0 86068 586 1   Back: Description of *Smoke and Other Early Stories* with short biographical sketch about Djuna Barnes.

Contains: An afterword by Kay Boyle (181-184).

B96   BABYLON   1985

A NOVEL [series of little arrowheads] | BABYLON | [series of little arrowheads] RENÉ CREVEL | Illustrated by MAX ERNST | Translated and with an | Afterword by KAY BOYLE North Point Press *San Francisco* | 1985

[i-iv], v-vi, [1-2], 3-7, [8], 9-13, [14], 15-19, [20], 21-25, [26], 27-33, [34], 35-37, [38], 39-45, [46], 47-49, [50], 51-63, [64], 65-71, [72], 73-79, [80], 81-93, [94], 95-99, [100], 101-105, [106], 107-113, [114], 115-121, [122], 123-133, [134], 135-141, [142], 143-169, [170] pages; black endpapers. 9 $^1/_4$" x 5 $^3/_8$". Published June 15, 1985 at $15.50. Issued in dark gray cloth covered boards stamped in silver. Front: Blank. Spine: [printed downward] BABYLON | RENE [top line] | CREVEL [bottom line] | [series of little arrowheads pointing out from a center] | [publisher's device]   Issued in a white paper dust jacket printed in red, black and white.

Contains: "Afterword: A conversation with René Crevel" by Kay Boyle (157-169).

B97   BEST MINDS: A TRIBUTE TO ALLEN GINSBURG   1986

a. First Signed Limited Edition:

BEST MINDS | A TRIBUTE TO | ALLEN GINSBERG | EDITED BY BILL
MORGAN | & BOB ROSENTHAL | LOSPECCHIO PRESS | NEW YORK |
1986

[i-iv], v, [vi], vii-ix, [x], xi, [xii], xiii-xiv, [xv-xvi], 1-311, [312] pages; red endpapers.
10" x 6 $^3/_4$". Published June 3, 1986. Numbered edition $75.00. Lettered edition
$125.00. Issued in black cloth covered boards stamped in gold. Front: BEST
MINDS | [rule] | [fish design] Spine: [rule] | [printed downward] MORGAN AND
[top line] ROSENTHAL [bottom line] | BEST MINDS *A Tribute to Allen Ginsberg*
[printed horizontally] Lospecchio | [rule] Issued without dust jacket.

Limitation statement: This first printing of *Best Minds* is published on June 3rd,
1986 and is limited to an edition of | 226 copies, 200 of which are numbered and
signed by the editors and 26 of which are let- | tered A to Z and signed by the edi-
tors and Allen Ginsberg and contain an additional self- | portrait photograph by the
poet. In addition 500 contributors' copies in special binding have been printed 250
of which are numbered and 250 of which are hors commerce | copies for the writers
of these tributes

Contains: "A Tribute to Allen" by Kay Boyle (32).

b. First Trade Edition:

BEST MINDS | A TRIBUTE TO | ALLEN GINSBERG | EDITED BY BILL
MORGAN | & BOB ROSENTHAL | LOSPECCHIO PRESS | NEW YORK |
1986

[i-iv], v, [vi], vii-ix, [x], xi, [xii], xiii-xiv, [xv-xvi], 1-311, [312] pages; red end papers.
10" x 6 $^3/_4$". Published June 3, 1986 at $25.00. Issued in deep red cloth covered
boards stamped in gold. Front: BEST MINDS | [rule] | [fish design] Spine: [rule]
| [printed downward] MORGAN AND [top line] ROSENTHAL [bottom line] |
BEST MINDS *A Tribute to Allen Ginsberg* [printed horizontally] Lospecchio |
[rule]   Issued without dust jacket.

B98   WOMEN OF THE LEFT BANK PARIS, 1900-1940   [1986]

WOMEN OF THE | LEFT BANK | PARIS, 1900 – 1940 | SHARI BENSTOCK
| [stylized head of Texas longhorn steer] | UNIVERSITY OF TEXAS PRESS |
AUSTIN

[i-viii], ix-xi, [xii-xvi], [1-2], 3-140, [141-142], 143-307, [308-310], 311-477, [478],
479-518, [519-520] pages; white endpapers. Photographs between pages 142 and
143 and between pages 310 and 311. 9 $^1/_8$" x 6"   Published in December of 1986

at $26.95. Top edge unstained and all edges trimmed. Issued in black cloth covered boards stamped in gold. Front: Blank. Spine: BENSTOCK | [printed downward] WOMEN [then between women and left] OF [top line] THE [bottom line] LEFT BANK | [stylized head of Texas longhorn steer] | [horizontal] TEXAS Back: Blank. Issued in white paper dust jacket printed in black, red, yellow and green.

Contains: An excerpt from her interview with Leo Litwak, "Kay Boyle—Paris Wasn't Like That" which first appeared in *The New York Times Book Review*, July 15, 1984. (2)

B99   KAY BOYLE: ARTIST AND ACTIVIST   [1986]

Kay | Boyle Artist and Activist | [rule] | SANDRA WHIPPLE SPANIER | Southern Illinois University Press | Carbondale and Edwardsville

[i-x], xi-xvi, xvii-xviii, 1-221, [222-224], 225-249, [250], 251-261, [262] pages; purple endpapers. 9 $^{1}/_{4}$" x 6" Published August 16, 1986 at $22.50. Top edge unstained and all edges trimmed. Issued in purple cloth covered boards stamped in silver. Front: Blank. Spine: [printed downward] KAY BOYLE ARTIST AND ACTIVIST / SPANIER [printed horizontal] Southern | Illinois | University | Press Issued in white paper dust jacket printed in purple, black and white with photograph of Kay Boyle in upper right corner.

Contains: Excerpts from "Why Do Americans Live in Europe," *transition* 14, Fall 1928 (103); "Americans Abroad" with Laurence Vail, *Contempo* 3, March 15, 1933 (4, 6); "Homage to Harry Crosby," *transition* 14, June 1930 (221); "Writers Worth Reading," *Contempo* 2, July 5, 1932 (4), "Brighter Than Most," a review of *Robert McAlmon Expatriate, Publisher and Writer* in *Prairie Schooner* 34, Spring 1960 (1); "The Crosby's : An Afterword," *ICarbS 3*, 1977 (117-125); "Elizabeth Bowen," *The New Republic*, September 21, 1942 (355), a caption which appeared under a caricature Kay Boyle drew of herself for the *San Francisco Chronicle* September 15, 1968, an excerpt from "Kay Boyle's Bitter View of Johnson," interview in the *San Francisco Chronicle*, March 15, 1966, (15), "Kay Boyle Assesses San Francisco State" an interview with Bob Haesseler in the *San Francisco Chronicle*, November 16, 1968 (13), "Kay Boyle—A Study in Paradox" an interview with Blake Green in the *San Francisco Chronicle*, February 17, 1975 (12), "Kay Boyle: A Profile," interview with Charles Fracchia in San Francisco Review of Books 1, April 1976, (8), "Kay Boyle Dedicates Self to Human Dignity," with Kathy Drew in *Lost Generation Journal* 4, Winter 1976, (22), an interview with Sandra Whipple Spanier, July 22, 1979, May 20, 1982 and May 17, 1983.. Extensive quotes from unpublished letters of Kay Boyle to Robert Brown, Joan Boyle, Lola Ridge, Evelyn Scott, Katherine Evans Boyle, Edward Dahlberg, Caresse Crosby, Sandra Whipple Spanier, Doug Palmer, Kate Buss, Walter Lowenfels, Richard C. Carpenter, Ann Watkins, Edward Aswell and Edward Greenbaum.

B100   VOICES OF SURVIVAL IN THE NUCLEAR AGE   [1986]

VOICES OF | SURVIVAL | IN THE NUCLEAR AGE | *Conceived and Edited by* | Dennis Paulson | *Introduction by* | Carl Sagan | [Publisher's device] | Capra Press | SANTA BARBARA | 1986

[1-8], 9-288 pages. 9" x 6" Published October 1986 at $8.95. Top edge unstained and all edges trimmed. Issued in white paper wrappers printed in black, red, gray and white. Front: [white] VOICES OF | SURVIVAL | [gray] IN THE NUCLEAR AGE | [five rows of photographs of some of the contributors] | [white] 120 of Our World's Most Celebrated Men & Women Join Together In This | Unprecedented, Global Debate Addressing the Ultimate Issue of All Time! | CONCEIVED & EDITED BY DENNIS PAULSON | [gray] Introduction by Carl Sagan   Spine: [printed downward in white] VOICES OF SURVIVAL [gray] IN THE NUCLEAR AGE [black] CONCEIVED & EDITED BY [top line] | DENNIS PAULSON [bottom line] [horizontal publisher's device] CAPRA | PRESS Back: [excerpts from contributors]

Contains: "Kay Boyle" by Kay Boyle. (99-100)

B101   FOUR LIVES IN PARIS   [1987]

FOUR LIVES | IN PARIS [the preceding two lines enclosed in two rectangles, the outer thicker than the inner] | Hugh Ford | *With a Foreword by* | *Glenway Wescott* | NORTH POINT PRESS | *San Francisco 1987*

one unpaginated leaf, [i-vii], viii-ix, [x-xi], xii-xiv, [xv], xvi-xxiii, [xxiv], [1-3], 4-9, [10], 11-15, [16], 17-23, [24], 25-31, [32], 33-37, [38], 39-45, [46], 47-51, [52], 53-57, [58], 59-63, [64], 65-71, [72], 73-81, [82-83], 84-87, [88], 89-91, [92], 93-97, [98], 99-103, [104], 105-107, [108], 109-113, [114], 115-117, [118], 119-123, [124], 125-127, [128], 129-131, [132], 133-135, [136-137], 138-143, [144], 145-149, [150], 151-157, [158], 159-163, [164], 165-171, [172], 173-177, [178], 179-185, [186], 187-191, [192], 193-199, [200], 201-205, [206], 207-213, [214], 215-221, [222], 223-225, [226-227], 228-231, [232], 233-237, [238], 239-245, [246], 247-251, [252], 253-259, [260], 261-265, [266], 267-275, [276], 277-281, [282], 283-286, [287-294] pages; light brown endpapers. 9" x 6"   Published in February 1987 at $19.95. Top edge unstained all edges trimmed. Issued in brown cloth covered boards stamped in gold. Front: Blank. Spine: Ford | [printed downward] FOUR LIVES IN PARIS | [publisher's device] Back: Blank. Issued in white paper dust jacket printed in red, gray and black.

Contains: Numerous quotes from Kay Boyle and extracts from Kay Boyle's letters. However no specific letter or source is specified. Although it is never confirmed anywhere in the book one might assume that many of the quotes where no source or addressee is specified came from Hugh Ford's 1978 unpublished interview of Kay Boyle.

B102   A WOMAN ON PAPER   [1988]

a. First Hardcover Edition:

[all the following enclosed in rectangular box] | A WOMAN ON PAPER | [Georgia O'Keeffe's signature with rule on each side extending to sides of rectangle] | by Anna Pollitzer | Introduction by Kay Boyle | [rule extending to each side of rectangle broken in the middle by publisher's device] | A TOUCHSTONE BOOK | Published by Simon & Schuster Inc. | NEW YORK ❑ LONDON ❑ TORONTO ❑ SYDNEY ❑ TOKYO |

[i-ix], x-xx, [xxi], xxii, [xxiii], xxiv-xxv, [xxvi], [1], 2-3, [4-5], 6, [7], 8, [9], 10, [11], 12-13, [14], 15-16, [17], 18, [19], 20, [21], 22, [23], 24, [25], 26-33, [34], 35-41, [42-45], 46, [47], 48-49, [50-53], 54-56, [57], 58-66, [67], 68-70, [71-73], 74-78, [79], 80, [81-83], 84-85, [86-89], 90, [91], 92-93, [94-95], 96, [97-98], 99-102, [103-105], 106-110, [111], 112-113, [114-115], 116-118, [119], 120-131, [132-133], 134-135, [136-137], 138-143, [144-145], 146-161, [162-163], 164-165, [166-167], 168, [169-171], 172, [173], 174-175, [176-177], 178, [179], 180, [181], 182-184, [185], 186-189, [190], 191-193, [194], 195-199, [200-201], 202-204, [205-206], 207-210, [211], 212, [213-214], 215-217, [218-219], 220-221, [222-223], 224-226, [227-228], 229, [230-231], 232-234, [235], 236, [237], 238-239, [240-242], 243-244, [245], 246-247, [248-249], 250-253, [254-255], 256, [257], 258-262, [263], 264-267, [268-269], 270, [271], 272-276, [277], 278-279, [280], 281-290, [291-294] pages; beige endpapers. 9 $\frac{1}{4}$" x 7 $\frac{3}{8}$". Published July 1, 1988 at $24.95. Issued in beige paper covered boards with dark brown cloth spine stamped in gold.   Front: Blank. Spine: [printed downward] A WOMAN [top line] ON PAPER [bottom line] | [vertical rule] [in script signature] Georgia O'Keeffe [vertical rule] Anita [top line] Pollitzer [bottom line] | Simon and [top line] Schuster [bottom line   Issued in white paper dust jacket printed in black, reddish orange and cream with photograph of Georgia O'Keeffe on the cover and photograph of the author on the back.

Contains: "Heroines and Also Heroes" (ix-xx) an introduction by Kay Boyle.

b. First Paperback Edition:

[all the following enclosed in rectangular box] | A WOMAN ON PAPER | [Georgia O'Keeffe's signature with rule on each side extending to sides of rectangle] | by Anna Pollitzer | Introduction by Kay Boyle | [rule extending to each side of rectangle broken in the middle by publisher's device] | A TOUCHSTONE BOOK | Published by Simon & Schuster Inc. | NEW YORK ❑ LONDON ❑ TORONTO ❑ SYDNEY ❑ TOKYO |

[i-ix], x-xx, [xxi], xxii, [xxiii], xxiv-xxv, [xxvi], [1], 2-3, [4-5], 6, [7], 8, [9], 10, [11], 12-13, [14], 15-16, [17], 18, [19], 20, [21], 22, [23], 24, [25], 26-33, [34], 35-41, [42-45], 46, [47], 48-49, [50-53], 54-56, [57], 58-66, [67], 68-70, [71-73], 74-78, [79], 80, [81-83], 84-85, [86-89], 90, [91], 92-93, [94-95], 96, [97-98], 99-102, [103-105], 106-110, [111], 112-113, [114-115], 116-118, [119], 120-131,

[132-133], 134-135, [136-137], 138-143, [144-145], 146-161, [162-163], 164-165, [166-167], 168, [169-171], 172, [173], 174-175, [176-177], 178, [179], 180, [181], 182-184, [185], 186-189, [190], 191-193, [194], 195-199, [200-201], 202-204, [205-206], 207-210, [211], 212, [213-214], 215-217, [218-219], 220-221, [222-223], 224-226, [227-228], 229, [230-231], 232-234, [235], 236, [237], 238-239, [240-242], 243-244, [245], 246-247, [248-249], 250-253, [254-255], 256, [257], 258-262, [263], 264-267, [268-269], 270, [271], 272-276, [277], 278-279, [280], 281-290, [291-294] pages. $9\,^1/_8$" x $7\,^3/_8$ ".   Published simultaneously with hardcover at $12.95. Issued in white paper wrappers printed reddish orange, cream, gray and grayish green. Front cover: [photograph of Georgia O'Keeffe by Peter Juley] [reddish orange] A WOMAN | [cream irregular rule] | [reddish orange] ON PAPER | [Georgia O'Keeffe's signature in cream] | [the following in a cream rectangle at the bottom of the cover printed in grayish green] THE LETTERS & MEMOIRS OF | A LEGENDARY FRIENDSHIP | ANITA POLLITZER | [reddish orange irregular rule] | INTRODUCTION BY KAY BOYLE   Spine: [printed downward]   A WOMAN ON PAPER: | [in script signature] Georgia O'Keeffe ANITA POLLITZER [printed horizontally] TOUCHSTONE | [publisher's device] | SIMON AND | SCHUSTER

B103   LIVING IN WORDS: INTERVIEWS FROM   [1988]
                 THE BLOOMSBURY REVIEW

a. First Hardcover Edition:

Living in Words | Interviews from *The Bloomsbury Review* 1981-1988 | Edited by Gregory McNamee | Breitenbush Books | Portland, Oregon

[i-x], xi-xiii, [xiv], [1], 2-12, [13], 14-22, [23], 24-34, [35], 36-47, [48-49], 50-56, [57], 58-72, [73], 74-84, [85], 86-94, [95], 96-102, [103], 104-114, [115],116-124, [125], 126-141, [142-143], 144-156, [157], 158-169, [170], 171-173, [174-178] pages; grape endpapers. 9" x 6" Published in October 1988 at $15.95. Issued in black cloth covered boards stamped in silver. Front: Blank. Spine: • LIVING in WORDS • McNAMEE • BREITENBUSH •   Issued in white paper dust jacket printed in grape, brown, black and red.

Contains: "The Spirit of a Woman of Letters: Kay Boyle" an interview with Linda Ferguson (1-12).

b. First Paperback Edition:

Living in Words | Interviews from *The Bloomsbury Review* 1981-1988 | Edited by Gregory McNamee | Breitenbush Books | Portland, Oregon

[i-x], xi-xiii, [xiv], [1], 2-12, [13], 14-22, [23], 24-34, [35], 36-47, [48-49], 50-56, [57], 58-72, [73], 74-84, [85], 86-94,[95], 96-102, [103], 104-114, [115],116-124, [125], 126-141, [142-143], 144-156, [157], 158-169, [170], 171-173, [174-178] pages. 9" x 6" Published in October 1988 at $8.95.

B104   THE WRITER'S MIND: INTERVIEWS   [1989]
                 WITH AMERICAN AUTHORS

a. First Hardcover Edition:

The | WRITER'S | MIND | INTERVIEWS WITH | AMERICAN AUTHORS |
VOLUME I | *Edited by Irv Broughton* | *The University of Arkansas Press* | *Fayetteville*
London 1989

[i-viii], ix-xii], [1-2], 3-31, [32], 33-77, [78], 79-337, [338], 339-386, [387-388]
pages; beige endpapers. 9" x 6" Published in October 1989 at $22.00. Issued in
tan cloth covered boards printed in blue. Top edge unstained and all edges trimmed.
Front: Blank. Spine: BROUGHTON | [printed downward and underlined] THE
WRITER'S MIND [top line] INTERVIEWS WITH AMERICAN AUTHORS
[bottom line] | [horizontal roman numeral 1] | [horizontal] ARKANSAS | [device]
Issued in white paper dust jacket printed in dark bluish purple, light blue and tan.

Contains: "Kay Boyle." An interview with Irv Broughton. (105-130)

b. First Paperback Edition:

The | WRITER'S | MIND | INTERVIEWS WITH | AMERICAN AUTHORS |
VOLUME I | *Edited by Irv Broughton* | *The University of Arkansas Press* | *Fayetteville*
London 1989

[i-viii], ix-xii], [1-2], 3-31, [32], 33-77, [78], 79-337, [338], 339-386, [387-388]
pages; beige endpapers. 9" x 6" Published in October 1989 at $14.95. Issued in
white paper wrappers printed in bluish purple. light blue and tan. Top edge
unstained and all edges trimmed.   Front: [tan] THE WRITER'S MIND | [light
blue rule] [tan] INTERVIEWS WITH | AMERICAN AUTHORS | [light blue rec-
tangle outlined in white with a profile of a typewriter in tan] | [tan] VOLUME 1 |
[short blue rule] | EDITED BY IRV BROUGHTON   Spine: BROUGHTON |
[printed downward IN TAN and under-lined in blue] THE WRITER'S MIND
[top line] INTERVIEWS WITH AMERICAN AUTHORS [bottom line in tan] |
[horizontal roman numeral 1] | [horizontal] ARKANSAS | [device]

Contains: "Kay Boyle. An interview with Irv Broughton. (105-130)

B105   CARESSE CROSBY: FROM BLACK   1989
                 SUN TO ROCCASINIBALDA

[Caresse is in script with the C on the same line as CROSBY and curving up over
CROSBY] CROSBY | *From Black Sun to Roccasinibalda* | ANNE CONOVER |
[head of a ram with the ram's nose jutting down into next line] | CAPRA PRESS
[ram's nose separates Capra and Press] | SANTA BARBARA | 1989

[i-vi], vii, [viii], ix-xii, 1-104, [105-110], 111-232, [recto unnumbered], 223 [picks up on verso]-239, [240-243] pages, dark blue endpapers. 9" x 6" Published in October 1989 at $19.95. Issued in light green cloth covered boards stamped in blue. Top edge unstained and all edges trimmed. Front: Blank. Spine: [printed downward] [in script] Caresse [block] CROSBY ANNE CONOVER [horizontal] [ram's head] CAPRA | PRESS Issued in white paper dust jacket printed in black and two shades of green.

Contains: Excerpt from unpublished letter to Caresse Crosby dated April 11, 1930 (14) and an excerpt from "The Crosby's: An Afterword" which originally appeared in ICarbS 3.2 Spring/Summer 1977 (117-125).

B106   THE CHOICES WE MADE   [1991]

The | *25 Women and Men* | Choices | *Speak Out About* | We | *Abortion* | Made | Edited and with an Introduction by | *Angela* | *Bonavoglia* | [Random House logo] | Random House New York

[i-viii], ix-xiii, [xiv], xv, [xvi], xvii, [xviii], xix-xxxiii, [xxxiv], [1-2], 3-39, [40], 41-65, [66], 67-79, [80], 81-87, [88], 89-135, [136], 137-143, [144-146], 147-163, [164], 165-167, [168], 169-177, [178], 179-183, [184], 185-191, [192], 193-201, [202-206] pages; white endpapers. 9 $^1/_8$" x 6" Published January 22, 1991 at $19.95. Issued in light blue paper covered boards with dark blue cloth covered spine stamped in silver. Top edge unstained with all edges trimmed. Front: Blank. Spine: [printed downward] The Choices We Made Random [top line] House [bottom line] | [Random House logo] Issued in white paper dust jacket printed in dark blue, gray and salmon.

Contains: Kay Boyle's personal account of her two abortions, why she had them and her feelings about her decision (17-22).

B107   KAY BOYLE: A STUDY OF THE SHORT FICTION   [1992]

Kay | Boyle | _____ *A Study of the Short Fiction*_____ | *Elizabeth S. Bell* | *University of South Carolina at Aiken* | *TWAYNE PUBLISHERS • NEW YORK* | *Maxwell Macmillan Company • Toronto* | *Maxwell Macmillan International • New York Oxford Singapore Sydney*

[i-viii], ix-xiii, [xiv], [1-2], 3-85, [86-88], 89-126, [127-128], 129-153, [154], 155-173, [174-178] pages; white endpapers. 8 $^1/_2$" x 5 $^3/_8$" Published in 1992 at $22.95. Issued in black cloth covered boards stamped in gold. Top edge unstained and all edges trimmed. Front: Blank. Spine: [printed downward] KAY BOYLE [top line] *A Study of the Short Fiction* [bottom line] *Elizabeth S. Bell* [horizontal] TWAYNE

Back: ISBN 0-8057-8317-2 Issued in white paper dust jacket printed I lime green, gold and black.

Contains: An interview conducted in Kay Boyle's home December 12, 1978 by Elizabeth S. Bell (91-95), an interview conducted by Leo Litwak (96-100) which originally appeared in The New York Times July 15, 1984. (32-33) and several previously unpublished pieces: excerpt from a 1961 Speech, excerpt from an untitled speech (no date), "About These Stories," (12 December 1965), fragment of a class lecture (no date), criticism of student writing, 1941-1942, critique of student writing (no date) and a notebook entry: "Aglasterhausen" (12 March 1947) (119-126).

B108   METAMORPHOSIZING THE NOVEL   [1993]

Marilyn Elkins | Metamorphosizing | the Novel | Kay Boyle's | Narrative Innovations | [publisher's device] | PETER LANG | New York • San Francisco • Bern • Baltimore | Frankfurt am Main • Berlin • Wien • Paris

[i-viii], [1], 2-16, [17-19], 20-59, [60], 61, [62-63], 64-104, [105], 106-107, [108-109], 110-142, [143], 144-146, [147], 148-172, [173], 174-175, [176-177], 178-183, [184], 185, [186-187], 188-196, [197], 198-208 pages; white endpapers. 9" x 6" Published in 1993. Top edge unstained and all edges trimmed. Issued in red and black coated paper boards printed in white.   Front: [printed on a black background in white] W • R • I • T • I • N • G   A • B • O • U • T   W • O • M • E • N | Feminist Literary Studies | [printed in white and underline in black on a red background] Metamorphosizing | the Novel | [printed in white on red but without underlining] Kay Boyle's | Narrative Innovations | [printed in white on black] Marilyn Elkins   Spine: [printed downward in black] Elkins [printed downward in white] Metamorphosizing the Novel | [printed in black] 7 | [printed in white horizontally] [publisher's device] | LANG Back: A note about Kay Boyle and a note about Marilyn Elkins printed in white on red. Issued without a dust jacket.

Contains: Excerpts from letters to her aunt Nina Allender, Robert McAlmon, and Bessie Breuer.

B109   KAY BOYLE: AUTHOR OF HERSELF   [1994]

KAY | BOYLE |Author of | Herself | JOAN MELLEN | [design] | Farrar, Straus & Giroux | NEW YORK

one unpaginated leaf, [i-vii], viii-ix, [x-xvi], [1-3], 4-10, [11], 12-25, [26], 27-46, [47], 48-61, [62], 63-77, [78], 79-93, [94], 95-111, [112], 113-128, [129], 130-143, [144], 145-159, [160], 161-176, [177], 178-194, [195], 196-209, [210], 211-224, [225], 226-237, [238], 239-251, [252], 253-266, [267], 268-283, [284], 285-299,

[300], 301-313, [314], 315-328, [329], 330-341, [342], 343-355, [356], 357-369, [370], 371-384, [385], 386-399, [400], 401-414, [415], 416-427, [428], 429-442, [443], 444-456, [457], 458-468, [469], 470-480, [481], 482-497, [498], 499-511, [512], 513-525, [526], 527-538, [539], 540-552, [553-555], 556-628, [629], 630-641, [642-643], 644-650, [651], 652-670 pages; white end- papers.   9 $\frac{1}{4}$" x 6" Published in April 1994 at $35.00.   Top edge unstained and all edges trimmed. Issued in light gray paper covered boards with medium gray cloth covered spine stamped in silver.   Front: A capital K B blind stamped into the covers with a blind stamp design beneath the initials. Spine: KAY | BOYLE | Author of | Herself | JOAN MELLEN | [design] | FARRAR | STRAUS | GIROUX   Issued in white paper dust jacket printed in purple, blue and black with a photograph of Kay Boyle in profile.

Contains: Excerpts from unpublished letters to Milton Abernathy, Nina Allender, Howard Peterson Boyle, Jesse Peyton Boyle, Joan Boyle, Katherine Evans Boyle, Richard Brault, Robert Carlton Brown, Roger Burlingame, Harry Crosby, Caresse Crosby, Edward Dahlberg, James T. Farrell, Charles Henri Ford, Hugh Ford, John Glassco, Harry Goldcar, James Laughlin, David Lawson, Harold Loeb, Walter Lowenfels, Mabel Dodge Luhan, Robert McAlmon, "To Muddie," Howard Nemerov, Katherine Anne Porter, Ezra Pound, Virginia Rice, Lola Ridge, Evelyn Scott, Sandra Whipple Spanier, James Stern, Alfred Stieglitz' "Tante," Louise Theis, Kathe Vail, Ann Watkins, William Carlos Williams, et. al. It also contains unpublished interviews with Hugh Ford in 1978, Charles Amirkhanian: no date given, Katherine Heinemann: undated, Kay Bonnetti in March 1985, Erik Bauersfeld for KPFA undated, and Joan Mellon in August 1987. It also contains excerpts from a lecture at the San Francisco State University Poetry Center, 11 February 1987and excerpts from a speech given at Skidmore College in April 1977.

B110   RED SCARE: MEMORIES OF   [1995]
                        THE AMERICAN INQUISITION

[Letters outlined in black] RED | [Letters outlined in black] SCARE | *Memories of the | American Inquisition | An Oral History* | GRIFFIN FARIELLO | [publisher's device] W · W · NORTON & COMPANY | *New York   London*

[1-11], 12-14, [15], 16, [17], 18-19, [20-23], 24-26, [27], 28-44, [45-47], 48-73, [74], 75-80, [81], 82-126, [127], 128-143, [144], 145-174, [175], 176-198, [199], 200-235, [236], 237-254, [255], 256-314, [315], 316-361, [362], 363-374, [375], 376-401, [402], 403-418, [419], 420-468, [469], 470-506, [507], 508-520, [521], 522-543, [544], 545-548, [549], 550-556, [557], 558-575, [576] pages; white endpapers.   9 $\frac{1}{8}$" x 6"   Published in March of 1995 at $29.95. Top edge unstained and all edges trimmed. Issued in red paper covered boards with black cloth covered spine stamped in gold.   Front: Blank. Spine: FARIELLO | [printed downward letters out lined in gold] RED SCARE | NORTON   Issued in a white paper dust jacket printed in red, white, black and yellow.

Contains: An account of her and her husband's persecution by Joseph McCarthy and the State Department.

B111   EXILED IN PARIS   [1995]

[inside a rectangle] Exiled in Paris | [design] | *Richard Wright, James Baldwin,* | *Samuel Beckett, and Others* | *on the Left Bank* | JAMES CAMPBELL | SCRIBNER | New York London Toronto Sydney Tokyo Singapore

[i-vi], vii-xi, [xii-xiv], 1-251, [252], 253-271, [272-274], pages; cream endpapers. Photographs between pages 146 and 147. 9 $1/_4$" x 6" Published in 1995 at $25.00. Top edge unstained and all edges trimmed. Issued in beige speckled paper boards with black cloth covered spine stamped in gold. Front: Blank. Spine: [printed downward] Exiled in Paris   JAMES CAMPBELL   [design]   [horizontal] SCRIBNER Issued in a white paper dust jacket printed in red, blue, yellow, gold and black.

Contains: An excerpt from a letter from Kay Boyle to Richard Wright dated June 10, 1956 apparently warning him of a rumor circulating that he was working for the State Department or the FBI. (197)

B112   THIS MEADOW OF TIME: [1995]
                                A PROVENCE JOURNAL

THIS MEADOW *of* TIME | [rule] | *A Provence Journal* | *Frederick Smock* | Illustrated by | the author | [publishers device] The Sulgrave Press | Louisville, Kentucky   [all the preceding enclosed in a thin rectangular rule]

[1-8], 9-10, [11], 12-16, [17], 18-27, [28], 29-41, [42], 43-52, [53], 54-69, [70], 71-85, [86], 87-97, [98], 99-105, [106], 107-114, [115-116] pages; light blue endpapers. 7" x 5" Published in 1995 at $15.95. Issued in light blue cloth covered boards stamped in gold. Top edge unstained and all edges trimmed. Front: Blank. Spine: [printed downward] THIS MEADOW OF TIME   Smock   [publishers device]   Back: Blank.   Issued in a white paper dust jacket printed in black, blue yellow, green and red.

Contains: Excerpts from letters of Kay Boyle to Frederick Smock. (64, 65, 66, and 68)

B113   A LIVING OF WORDS   [1995]

A LIVING OF WORDS | *American Women in Print Culture* | Edited by | Susan Albertine | The University of Tennessee Press • Knoxville [i-xi], xii-xxi, [xxii], [1], 2-17, [18], 19-34, [35], 36-48, [49], 50-64, [65], 66-93, [94], 95-114, [115], 116-131, [132], 133-150, [151], 152-168, [169], 170-188, [189], 190-206, [207], 208-227, [228-229], 230-234, [235], 236-238, [239], 240-246, [247-250] pages; cream threaded paper endpapers.   9" x 6"   Published June 1995 at $38.00.   Issued in light purple cloth covered boards stamped in black.   Top edge unstained with all edges trimmed.   Front: Blank.   Spine: [printed downward] *Albertine* A Living in Words [top line]   American Women in Print Culture [bottom line] TENNESSEE   Issued in a white paper dust jacket printed in white and light and dark purple.

Contains: Excerpts from unpublished letters from Kay Boyle to Caresse Crosby dated January 14, 1930, September 26, 1930, October 1930, September 1931, September 3, 1931, June 11, 1933, January 10, 1942, January 27, 1956, October 3, 1961, July 29, 1961, July 21, 1967, and undated.

B114   DUCHAMP   [1996]

DUCHAMP | *A Biography* | CALVIN TOMKINS | A JOHN MACRAE BOOK HENRY HOLT AND COMPANY NEW YORK

[i-x], [1-2], 3-14, [15], 16-27, [28], 29-30, [31], 32-46, [47], 48-54, [55], 56-62, [63], 64, [65], 66-74, [75], 76, [77], 78-81, [82], 83-84, [85], 86-96, [97], 98-99, [100], 101-102, [103], 104-115, [116], 117-133, [134], 135-142, [143], 144, [145], 146-158, [159], 160-169, [170], 171-189, [190], 191-206, [207], 208-212, [213], 214-223, [224], 225-231, [232], 233-239, [240], 241-251, [252], 253-267, [268], 269-278, [279], 280-283, [284], 285-299, [300], 301-313, [314], 315-328, [329], 330-343, [344], 345-357, [358], 359-373, [374], 375-385, [386], 387, [388], 389-398, [399], 400-411, [412], 413-417, [418], 419-434, [435], 436-450, [451-453], 454-463, [464], 465, [466-467], 468-507, [508-509], 510, [511], 512-522, [523], 524, [525], 526-548, [549], 550 pages; white endpapers.   9 $^1/_8$" x 6 $^1/_8$" Published November 1996 at $35.00.   Top edge unstained and all edges trimmed. Issued in light gray paper covered boards and a black cloth covered spine stamped in silver.   Front: Blank.   Spine: CALVIN | TOMKINS | [printed downward] DUCHAMP [top line] *A Biography* [bottom line] | [horizontal] HENRY HOLT Issued in a white paper dust jacket printed in red and black.

Contains: Excerpts from an interview the author had with Kay Boyle. (284 and 326) No date is given for the interview.

B115   CRITICAL ESSAYS ON KAY BOYLE   [1997]

[rule broken in the middle by a solid diamond] | *Critical Essays on* | KAY BOYLE | [repeat same rule] |edited by | Marilyn Elkins | *G. K. Hall & Co.* | *An Imprint of*

Simon & Schuster Macmillan | *New York* | *Prentice Hall International* | *London Mexico City New Delhi Singapore Sydney Toronto*

[i-vi], vii-ix, [x], xi, [xii], xiii, [xiv], xv, [xvi], 1-24, [25-26], 27-85, [86-88], 89-311, [312], 313-316, [317-320] pages; white endpapers. 9 $\frac{1}{8}$" x 6" Published in 1997 at $48.00. Issued in dark blue cloth covered boards stamped in gold. Front: [gold rule broken in the middle by a gold diamond] | *Critical Essays on* | KAY BOYLE | [repeat same rule]   Spine: [printed downward] *Critical Essays on* KAY BOYLE ELKINS | [horizontal] G.K. | HALL | & CO. Issued without dust jacket.

Contains: Excerpts from the poems "Portrait" (228) which originally appeared in *Poetry* 29, February 1922 (122), from "Harbour Song" (229) which originally appeared in *Poetry* 25, February 1925 (250), from "Summer" (230) which originally appeared in *This Quarter* 1, 1925 (40-42), an excerpt from a letter she wrote to the editor (229) which appeared in *Poetry* 19, November 1921 (104-106) and an excerpt from the short story "Passeres' Paris" (230) which first appeared in *This Quarter* 1, 1925 (140).

C

Contributions to Newspapers and Periodicals

C1   "Reactionary Composers." *Poetry: A Magazine of Verse* 19.2 November 1921 (104-106) A letter to the editor.

C2   Unsigned review of *Mr. Antiphilos Satyr* by Remy de Gourmont. *Dial* 73.2 August 1922 (233)

C3   Unsigned review of *An Outline of Wells* by Sydney Dark. *Dial* 73.4 October 1922 (457)

C4   "Monody to the Sound of Zithers." *Poetry: A Magazine of Verse* 21.3 December 1922 (125) Collected in *Anthology of Magazine Verse for 1923* Edited by William Stanley Braithwaite.

C5   "Old Burden." *Forum* 69.1 January 1923 (1097) Uncollected poem.

C6   "Morning." *Broom* 4.2 January 1923 (121-122) Uncollected poem.

C7   "Shore." *Contact* o.s. #5 [New York] June 1923 Unpaginated. Uncollected poem.

C8   "Harbour Song i-v." *Poetry: A Magazine of Verse* 25.5 February 1925 (252-253) Uncollected poem.

C9   "Summer." *This Quarter* 1.1 Spring 1925 (40-42) Uncollected poem.

C10   "Passeres' Paris." *This Quarter* 1.1 Spring 1925 (140-143) Uncollected short story.

-1926-

C11   "Flight." *This Quarter* 1.2 [Milan] 1926 (167-171) Autumn\Winter 1925-1926 Uncollected short story.

C12   "Collation." *The Calendar of Modern Letters* 3.3 [London] October 1926 (171-174) Uncollected short story.

-1927-

C13   "Portrait." *Poetry: A Magazine of Verse* 29.5 February 1927 (250-251) Uncollected poem.

C14   "Depart." *Poetry: A Magazine of Verse* 29.5 February 1927 (250-251) Uncollected poem.

C15   "To a Seaman Dead on Land." *Poetry: A Magazine of Verse* 29.5 February 1927 (250-251) Uncollected poem.

C16   "To America." *This Quarter* 1.3 [Monte Carlo] April 1927 (109-110) Collected in *A Glad Day, Collected Poems* and *Collected Poems of Kay Boyle.*

C17   "For an American." *This Quarter* 1.3 [Monte Carlo] April 1927 (111-115) Collected in *A Glad Day, Collected Poems* and *Collected Poems of Kay Boyle.*

C18   "Poems." *This Quarter* 1.3 [Monte Carlo] April 1927 (116) Uncollected poem.

C19   "Carnival 1927." *This Quarter* 1.3 [Monte Carlo] April 1927 (117) Collected in *Collected Poems* and *Collected Poems of Kay Boyle.*

C20   "Comrade." *This Quarter* 1.3 [Monte Carlo] April 1927 (118) Uncollected poem.

C21   "Plagued by the Nightingale." *This Quarter* 1.3 [Monte Carlo] April 1927 (165-203) A work in progress.

C22   "Unrecommended List." *This Quarter* 1.3 [Monte Carlo] April 1927 (272-273) Uncollected miscellaneous prose.

C23   "Summer." *The Calendar of Modern Letters* 4.1 [London] April 1927 (38-43) Short story collected in *Short Stories* and *Wedding Day and Other Stories.*

C24   "Theme." *transition* No.1 April 1927 (31-35) Story collected in *Short Stories* and *Wedding Day and Other Stories.*

C25   "In the American Grain" by William Carlos Williams. *transition* No. 1 Paris April 1927 (139-141) A review by Kay Boyle. Collected in *Words That Must Somehow Be Said.*

C26   "Complaint." *transition* No. 2 May 1927 (142) Uncollected poem.

C27   "Portrait." *transition* No. 3 June 1927 (29-31) Short story later collected in *Short Stories* and *Wedding Day and Other Stories.*

C28   "And Winter." *transition* No. 5 August 1927 (114) Collected in *A Glad Day, Collected Poems* and *Collected Poems of Kay Boyle.*

C29   "Polar Bear and Others." *transition* No. 6 September 1927 (52-56) Short story collected in *Short Stories* and *Wedding Day and Other Stories.* Also included in the anthology *transition stories* New York: Walter V. McKee, 1929 (17-25).

C30   "Bitte nehmen Sie die Bluhmen." *transition* No. 9 December 1927 (88-93) Short story collected in *Short Stories* and *Wedding Day and Other Stories.*

-1928-

C31   "Mr. Crane and His Grandmother." *transition* No. 10 January 1928 (135-138) Review of Hart Crane's "White Buildings." Collected in *Words That Must Somehow Be Said.*

C32   "A Sad Poem." *transition* No. 10 January 1928 (109) Uncollected poem.

C33   "Written for Royalty." *transition* No. 13 Summer 1928 (60-64) Work in progress.

C34   "The United States." *transition* No. 13 Summer 1928 (186-187) Collected in *A Glad Day* and *Collected Poems of Kay Boyle.*

C35   "Letter to Archibald Craig." *transition* No. 13 Summer 1928 (188-190) Collected in *A Glad Day, A Testament for My Students* and *Collected Poems of Kay Boyle* as "A Letter to Francis Picabia". Also included in *Collected Poems of Kay Boyle* is a poem titled "A Letter to Archibald Craig" which is very similar but has apparently been entirely rewritten.

C36   "Why Do Americans Live in Europe." *transition* No.14 Fall 1928 (102-103) Miscellaneous prose.

C37   "Vacation Time." *transition* No. 14 Fall 1928 (143-145) Story collected in *Short Stories* and *Wedding Day and Other Stories.*

-1929-

C38   "Mr. Benét Looks at the Civil War." *transition* No. 15 (169-170) February 1929 Review of "John Brown's Body" by Stephen Vincent Benét.

C39   "A Confession to Eugene Jolas." *Blues* 1.6 July 1929 (140-143) A poem collected in *A Glad Day* and in *Collected Poems of Kay Boyle*.

C40   "A New Mythology." *Paris Tribune* March 10, 1929 Reprinted in *The Left Bank Revisited: Selections from the Paris Tribune 1971-1934* University Park: and London: The Pennsylvania State University Press, [1972] (249-250).

C41   "Proclamation." *transition* Nos. 16/17 June 1929 (13) A joint effort signed by Kay Boyle and others.

C42   "On the Run." *transition* Nos. 16/17 June 1929 (83-85) Short story collected in *Wedding Day and Other Stories* .

C43   "Dedicated to Guy Urquart." *transition* No. 18 November 1929 (85) Collected in *A Glad Day* and *Collected Poems*. The title was changed to "Dedicated to Robert McAlmon" and it was collected in *A Testament For My Students and Other Poems* and *Collected Poems of Kay Boyle*.

C44   "Prayer." *transition* No. 18 November 1929 (85) Uncollected poem.

C45   "Mr. Knife and Miss Fork by Rene Crevel." Translated by Kay Boyle. *transition* No. 18 November 1929 (242-251) This was separately published by The Black Sun Press, Paris, 1931.

-1930-

C46   "A Paris Letter for Charles Henri Ford." *Blues* 2.8 Spring 1930 (32-33) Open letter.

C47   "Homage to Harry Crosby." *transition* No. 19/20 June 1930 (221-222) Miscellaneous prose.

C48   "The Only Bird that Sang." *transition* No. 19/20 June 1930 (261-263) Collected in *A Glad Day*, *Collected Poems*, *A Testament for My Students and Other Poems* and *Collected Poems of Kay Boyle*.

C49   "Episode in the Life of an Ancestor." *Hound and Horn* 4.1 Fall 1930 (33, 42) Story collected in *Wedding Day and Other Stories*, *Thirty Stories* and *Fifty Stories*.

C50   "A Valentine for Harry Crosby." *Blues* 2.9 Fall 1930 (35-37) Collected in *A Glad Day*, *Collected Poems* and *Collected Poems of Kay Boyle*.

C51   "Letters to a Lady." *Bulletin of the Women's Club* 4 November 1930.

C52   "Kroy Wen." *Front* 1.1 [The Hague] December 1930 (25-30) Story collected in *The First Lover and Other Stories, Thirty Stories* and *Fifty Stories*.

C53   "A Statement for El Greco and William Carlos Williams." *Morada* No. 5 December 1930 (21-25) Poem collected in *A Glad Day, Collected Poems* and *Collected Poems of Kay Boyle*.

-1931-

C54   "Hunt." *The Nation* 132.3426 March 4, 1931 (245) Collected in *A Glad Day, Collected Poems* and *Collected Poems of Kay Boyle*.

C55   "Letters to a Niece." *Bulletin of the Women's Club* 4 April 1931.

C56   "Career." *The Nation* 132.3432 April 15, 1931 (414) Collected in *A Glad Day* and *Collected Poems of Kay Boyle*.

C57   "Rest Cure." *Story Magazine* 1.1 April/May 1931 (1-17) Short story collected in *The First Lover and Other Stories, Thirty Stories* and *Fifty Stories*.

C58   "The First Lover." *Harper's Magazine* 163.973 June 1931 (33-36) Short story collected in *The First Lover and Other Stories* and *Life Being the Best and Other Stories*.

C59   "His Idea of a Mother." *Scribner's* 90.1 July 1931 (73-77) Short story collected in *The First Lover and Other Stories* and *Life Being the Best and Other Stories*.

C60   "Kroy Wren." *The New Yorker* 7.23 July 25, 1931 (13-15) Short story collected in *The First Lover and Other Stories, Thirty Stories* and *Fifty Stories*.

C61   "His Idea of a Mother." *The Adelphi* 2.6 September 1931 (488-495) Short story collected in *The First Lover and Other Stories* and *Life Being the Best and Other Stories*.

C62   "One of Ours." *The New Yorker* 7.35 October 17, 1931 (17-19) Short story collected in *The First Lover and Other Stories*.

C63   "Christmas Eve." *The New Yorker* 7.45 December 26, 1931 (13-15) Uncollected short story.

C64   Autobiographical sketch. *Wilson Bulletin for Librarians* 6.4 September 1931 (326)

-1932-

C65 *Comment.* Unknown story, unknown volume or date. Acknowledgments for included stories in *The First Lover and Other Stories* list *Comment* but the compiler was unable to locate this publication or which story it had published.

C66 Autobiographical sketch. *Wilson Bulletin for Librarians* 6.5 January 1932 (329)

C67 "Glad Day for L.V." *transition* No. 21 March 1932 (157-158) Poem. Title changed to "A Glad Day for Laurence Vail" and collected in *A Glad Day, Collected Poems, Collected Poems of Kay Boyle* and *Testament for My Students and Other Poems.*

C68 "In Defense of Homosexuality." *New Review* 2.5 [Paris] April 1932 (24-25) Poem collected in *A Glad Day, Testament for My Students and Other Poems* and *Collected Poems of Kay Boyle.*

C69 "Black Boy." *The New Yorker* 8.13 May 14, 1932 (15-17) Short story collected in *The First Lover and Other Stories, Thirty Stories* and *Fifty Stories.*

C70 "The Man Who Died Young." *The Yale Review* n.s. 21.4 June 1932 (785-809) Short story collected in *The First Lover and Other Stories.*

C71 "To the Pure." Scribner's 91.6 June 1932 (341-344) Short story collected in *The First Lover and Other Stories* and *Life Being the Best and Other Stories.*

C72 "Writer's Worth Reading." *Contempo* 2.4 [Chapel Hill] July 5, 1932 (4) Miscellaneous prose.

C73 "Friend of the Family." *Harper's Magazine* 165.988 September 1932 (396-401) Short story collected in *The First Lover and Other Stories, Thirty Stories* and *Fifty Stories.*

C74 "Three Little Men." *Criterion* 12.46 October 1932 (17-23) Short story collected in *The First Lover and Other Stories.*

C75 "Lydia and the Ring Doves." *Vanity Fair* 39.3 November 1932 (36, 62, 66) Short story collected in *The First Lover and Other Stories.*

C76 "American Periodicals." Letter to the editor. *New English Weekly* 2.7 December 1, 1932 (167-168)

C77 "The Art Colony." *The New Yorker.* 8.43 December 10, 1932 (17-19) Short story collected in *The First Lover and Other Stories* and *Life Being the Best and Other Stories.*

C78   "I Can't Get Drunk." *Contempo* 3.3 [Chapel Hill] December 15, 1932 (1, 4) Short story collected in *The First Lover and Other Stories* and *Life Being the Best and Other Stories.*

C79   "McAlmon's Indefinite Huntress." Paris Tribune December 17, 1932. Reprinted in *The Left Bank Revisited: Selections from the Paris Tribune 1917-1934* (276-277).

-1933-

C80   "Black Boy." *The Adelphi* 5.5 February 1933 (327-331) Short story collected in *The First Lover and Other Stories*, *Thirty Stories* and *Fifty Stories.*

C81   A review of *Americans Abroad. Contempo* 3.7 Chapel Hill March 15, 1933 (1, 4-5) With Laurence Vail.

C82   "Convalescence." *Story Magazine* 2.12 April 1933 (34-40) Short story collected in *The White Horses of Vienna and Other Stories* and *Life Being the Best and Other Stories.*

C83   "The Sky is Woven of the Winds Four Directions." *Seed* 1 London April/July 1933 (3-7) Uncollected poem.

C84   "White as Snow." The New Yorker 9.25 August 5, 1933 (20-22, 26-28) Short story collected in *The White Horses of Vienna and Other Stories, Thirty Stories* and *Fifty Stories.*

C85   "Flight of Fish." *The Nation* 137.3554 August 16, 1933 (190) Uncollected poem.

C86   "Flying Foxes and Others." The Nation 137.3563 October 18, 1933 (444-445) Uncollected poem.

C87   "Life Being the Best." *Harper Magazine* 167.1002 November 1933 (727-738) Short story collected in *The White Horses of Vienna and Other Stories* and *Life Being the Best and Other Stories.*

C88   "White as Snow." The Adelphi n.s. 7.2 November 1933 (80-88) Short story collected in *The White Horses of Vienna and Other Stories, Thirty Stories* and *Fifty Stories.*

C89   "Keep Your Pity." *The Brooklyn Daily Eagle* November 26, 1933 Short story collected in *The White Horses of Vienna and Other Stories, Thirty Stories* and *Fifty Stories.*

C90   "Peter Foxe." Harper's Bazaar. 66.2654 December 1933 (50-51, 118, 120) Short story collected in *White Horses of Vienna and Other Stories* and *Life Being the Best and Other Stories.*

-1934-

C91   "Natives Don't Cry." *The American Mercury* 31.123 March 1934 (309-315) Short story collected in *The White Horses of Vienna and Other Stories, Thirty Stories* and *Fifty Stories.*

C92   "Keep Your Pity." *Lovat Dickson* 3.3 London September 1934 (320-339) Short story collected in *The White Horses of Vienna and Other Stories, Thirty Stories* and *Fifty Stories.*

C93   "Career." *Direction* 1.1 Autumn 1934 (1-4) Short story collected in *The White Horses of Vienna and Other Stories* and *Life Being the Best and Other Stories.*

C94   "Maiden, Maiden." *Harper's Bazaar* 67.2666 December 1934 (60, 109-117) Short story collected in *The White Horses of Vienna and Other Stories, Thirty Stories* and *Fifty Stories.*

-1935-

C95   "Maiden, Maiden." *Harper's Bazaar.* [London] January 1935 (32) Short story collected in *The White Horses of Vienna and Other Stories, Thirty Stories* and *Fifty Stories.* (Not seen but according to *Best British Short Stories of 1936.* Edited by Edward J. O'Brien.)

C96   "First Offense." *The New Yorker* 10.47 January 5, 1935 (19-20) Short story collected in *The White Horses of Vienna and Other Stories.*

C97   "A Waterfront for Allan Ross MacDougall." *Direction* 1.2 January-March 1935 (94-95) Poem collected in *A Glad Day* and *Collected Poems of Kay Boyle.*

C98   "The White Horses of Vienna." *Harper's Magazine* 170.1019 April 1935 (580-589) Short story collected in *The White Horses of Vienna and Other Stories, Thirty Stories* and *Fifty Stories.*

C99   "Count Lothar's Heart." *Harper's Bazaar* 68.2671 May 1935 (84-85+) Short story collected in *The White Horses of Vienna and Other Stories, Thirty Stories* and *Fifty Stories.*

C100   "I'm Ready to Drop Dead." *The New Yorker* 11.21 July 6, 1935 (23)
Reprinted in *Fun in Bed Series 4 Just What the Doctor Ordered.* New York:
Simon and Schuster, 1938.

C101   "Winter in Italy." *The New Yorker* 11.41 November 23, 1935 (15-16) Short
story collected in *The White Horses of Vienna and Other Stories* and *Life Being
the Best and Other Stories.*

C102   "Major Alshuster." *Harper's Magazine* 172.1027 December 1935 (10-18)
Short story collected in *The White Horses of Vienna and Other Stories, Thirty
Stories* and *Fifty Stories.*

C103   "Astronomer's Wife." *London Mercury* 33.194 December 1935 (169-173)
Short story collected in *The White Horses of Vienna and Other Stories* and *Life
Being the Best and Other Stories.*

C104   "Venezuela." *The Dubuque Dial* No. 4 December 1935 (103) Short story
collected in *365 Days.*

C105   "Portugal." *The Dubuque Dial* No. 4 December 1935 (103) Short story
collected in *365 Days.*

C106   "March the Eleventh (Tasmania)." *Caravel* No. 4 1935 (16-17) Short story
collected in *365 Days.*

C107   "July the Twenty Seventh (Austria)." *Caravel* No. 4 1935 (16-17) Short story
collected in *365 Days.*

-1936-

C108   "Security." *The New Yorker* 11.50 January 25, 1936 (15-17) Short
story collected in *The White Horses of Vienna and Other Stories* and *Fifty
Stories.*

C109   "Natives Don't Cry." *Fortnightly* n.s. 139.2 February 1936 (199-208) Short
story collected in *The White Horses of Vienna and Other Stories, Thirty Stories*
and *Fifty Stories.*

C110   "Your Body is a Jewel Box." *New Writers* 1.2 February 1936 (3-14) Short
story collected in *The White Horses of Vienna and Other Stories, Thirty Stories*
and *Fifty Stories.*

C111   "Rondo at Carraroe." *The Spectator* 156.5618 February 28, 1936 (340-341)
Short story collected in *The White Horses of Vienna and Other Stories* and
Fifty Stories.

C112   "How Birdie's Girl Was Won." *Harper's Magazine* 172.1030 March 1936 (393-400) Short story collected in *Thirty Stories* and *Fifty Stories*.

C113   "January the Eighth (Derry)." *Caravel* No. 5 March 1936 (unpaginated) Short story collected in *365 Days*.

C114   "Volunteer." *The New Yorker* 12.13 May 16, 1936 (25-26) Uncollected short story.

C115   "The Intruders." *Signatures* 1.1 Spring 1936 (28-41) by count but magazine is unpaginated) A work in progress later to become *Death of a Man*.

C116   "Friend of the Family." *London Mercury* 34.199 May 1936 (19-25) Short story collected in *Wedding Day and Other Stories, Thirty Stories and Fifty Stories*.

C117   "Career." *The Spectator* 157.5638 July 17, 1936 (94-95) Short story collected in *The White Horses of Vienna and Other Stories* and *Life Being the Best and Other Stories*.

C118   "Winter in Italy." *The New Statesman and Nation* n.s 12.292 September 21,1936 (426-427) Short story collected in *The White Horses of Vienna and Other Stories* and *Life Being the Best and Other Stories*.

C119   "Lydia and the Ring Dove." *London Mercury* 34.203 September 1936 (404-411) Short story collected in *The First Lover and Other Stories*.

C120   "Education." *The New Yorker* 12.35 October 17, 1936 (23-24) Miscellaneous prose.

C121   "Major Alshuster." *London Mercury* 35.206 December 1936 (140-151) Short story collected in *The White Horses of Vienna and Other Stories, Thirty Stories*, and *Fifty Stories*.

-1937-

C122   "The King of the Philistines." *The New Yorker* 13.4 March 13, 1937 (22-29) Miscellaneous prose.

C123   "The Herring Piece." *The New Yorker* 13.8 April 10, 1937 (24-28) Short story collected in *Thirty Stories* and *Fifty Stories*.

C124   "A Communication to Nancy Cunard." *New Republic* 91.1175 June 9, 1937 (126-127) Poem Collected in *A Glad Day, Collected Poems* and *Collected Poems of Kay Boyle*.

C125 "Lydia and the Ring Dove." *Fiction Parade* 5.3 July 1937 (275-282) Short story collected in *The First Lover and Other Stories*.

C126 "Katherine Mansfield: A Reconsideration." *New Republic* 92.1194 October 20, 1937 (309) A review of *The Short Stories of Katherine Mansfield*. Collected in *Words That Must Somehow Be Said*.

-1938-

C127 "The Baron and the Chemist." *The New Yorker* 14.2 February 26, 1938 (19-20) Uncollected short story.

C128 "Tattered Banners." *New Republic* 94.1214 March 9, 1938 (136-137) A review of William Faulkner's *The Unvanquished*. Collected in *Words That Must Somehow Be Said*.

C129 "Angels for Djuna Barnes." *Delta* 2.2 April 1938 (3-4) A poem collected in *A Glad Day* and *Collected Poems of Kay Boyle*.

C130 Response to questionnaire sent to a representative list of writers regarding the Spanish Civil War. *New From Spain* April 13, 1938 (8)

C131 "A Complaint for M and M." *transition* No. 27 Paris April/May 1938 (34-35) A Poem Collected in *A Glad Day* and in *Collected Poems of Kay Boyle* as "A Complaint for Mary and Marcel."

C132 "The Story I Wanted to Tell You." *transition* No. 27 April/May 1938 (34) Uncollected short story.

C133 "Your Love Song." *transition* No. 27 April/May 1938 (39-40) Uncollected poem.

C134 "Life Sentence." *Harper's Bazaar* 71.2710 June 1938 (42-43, 104-107) Uncollected short story.

C135 "The Bridegroom's Body." *Southern Review* 4.1 Summer 1938 (58-100) Short novel later published in the book *The Crazy Hunter*.

C136 "Big Fiddle." *The Phoenix* (Part 1) 1.3 Autumn 1938 (112-146) (part 2) 2.1 Spring 1939 (28-51) (part 3) 2.2 September 1939 (27-59) Short novel later published in the book *The Crazy Hunter*.

C137 "The Taxi Ride." *Seven* No. 2 Autumn 1938 (16-21) Uncollected short story.

C138 "War in Paris." *The New Yorker* 14.41 November 26, 1938 (18-20) Uncollected short story.

C139   "Ben." *The New Yorker* 14.45 December 24, 1938 (15-16) Short story collected in *Thirty Stories* and *Fifty Stories*.

-1939-

C140   "World Tour: For Nancy Cunard." *Seven* No. 4 Tauton, England Spring 1939 (2-3) Poem later collected in *New Directions in Prose and Poetry* and *Collected Poems of Kay Boyle*.

C141   "Anschluss." *Harper's Magazine* 178.1067 April 1939 (474-483) Short story later collected in *Nothing Ever Breaks Except the Heart and Other Stories*.

C142   "Listen Munich." *The New Yorker* 15.27 August 19,1939 (17-19) Uncollected short story.

C143   "Second Generation." *Seven* No. 6 Tauton, England Autumn 1939 (3-4) Uncollected short story.

C144   "Listen Munich." *John O'London Weekly* 41.1066 September 15, 1939 (793-794) Uncollected short story.

C145   "Mrs. Carrigan's Daughter." *Kingdom Come* 1.1 November 1939 (9-10) Uncollected short story.

C146   "Ben." *John O'London Weekly* 42.1077 December 1, 1939 (251-252) Short story collected in *Thirty Stories* and *Fifty Stories*.

C147   "The Crows." *Kingdom Come* 1.2 December/January 1939/1940 (44) Uncollected short story.

-1940-

C148   "Poor Monsieur Panalitus." *The New Yorker* 15.49 January 20, 1940 (19-22) Uncollected short story.

C149   Letter to the editor. *Partisan Review* 7.1 January/February 1940 (79) (With a response by Dwight MacDonald.)

C150   "Diplomat's Wife." *Harper's Bazaar* 73.2733 (48-49, 110+) February 1940 Collected in *Thirty Stories* and *Fifty Stories*.

C151   "Germans." *Kingdom Come* 1.3 Spring 1940 (79) Uncollected short story.

C152   "Effigy of War." *The New Yorker* 16.15 May 25, 1940 (17-19) Collected in *Thirty Stories* and *Fifty Stories*.

C153   "A Blackout." *Harper's Bazaar* 73.2739 July 1940 (63, 64) Uncollected short story.

C154   "Major Engagement in Paris." *The American Mercury* 50.200 August 1940 (450-456) Short story collected in *Thirty Stories* and *Fifty Stories*.

C155   "The Most Unforgettable Character I Ever Met." *Reader's Digest* 37.221 September 1940 (46-50).

C156   "They Weren't Going to Die." *The New Yorker* 16.35 October 12, 1940 (21-22) Short story collected in *Thirty Stories* and *Fifty Stories*.

C157   "T'en Fais Pas." *Harper's Bazaar* 73.2745 December 1940 (122) Uncollected short story.

-1941-

C158   "Men." *Harper's Bazaar* 74.2747 February 1941 (45, 102, 105) Short story collected in *Thirty Stories* and *Fifty Stories*.

C159   "Defeat." *The New Yorker* 17.14 May 17, 1941 (18-22) Short story collected in *Thirty Stories* and *Fifty Stories*.

C160   "Rest Cure." *Story Magazine* 18.89 May/June 1941 (15-20) Short story collected in *The First Lover and Other Stories, Thirty Stories* and *Fifty Stories*.

C161   "An Interview with Kay Boyle, Expatriate" by Robert Van Gelder. *The New York Times Book Review* 46.31 August 3, 1941 (2, 19).

C162   "Les Six Enfants." *Harper's Bazaar* 74.2757 October 1941 (73, 122) Uncollected article.

C163   "Nothing Ever Breaks Except the Heart." *The New Yorker* 17.34 October 4, 1941 (18-21) Short story collected in *Nothing Ever Breaks Except the Heart and Other Stories*.

C164   "Two and Carry One." *The New Republic* 105.18 November 3, 1941 (597-598) Book reviews of *On Troublesome Creek* by James Still, *Anything Can Happen by* Edward Newhouse, and *The Penguin New Writing 6* edited by John Lehmann.

C165   "Let There Be Honour." *The Saturday Evening Post* 214.19 November 8, 1941 (12-13, 104-105) Short story collected in *Thirty Stories* and *Fifty Stories*.

C166 "Full Length Portrait." *The New Republic* 105.21 November 24, 1941 (707-708) Reviews of four books *A Curtain of Green* by Eudora Welty, *House of Fury* by Felice Swados, *Strangers Are Coming* by I. A. R. Wylie, and *Saratoga Trunk* by Edna Ferber.

C167 "The Aliens." The New York Times Book Review 46.52 December 28, 1941 (12) Letter to editor.

-1942-

C168 "Their Name Is Macaroni." *The New Yorker* 17.47 January 3, 1942 (16-19) Short story collected in *Thirty Stories* and *Fifty Stories*.

C169 "Les Six Enfants." *Senior Scholastic* 39.16 January 19, 1942 (17-18) Uncollected article.

C170 "The New Novels." *The New Republic* 106.4 January 26, 1942 (124-125) Reviews of four books: *The Real Life of Sebastian Knight* by Vladimir Nabokov, *Victory Was Slain* by Hilde Abel, *The Ivory Mischief* by Arthur Meeker, Jr. and *Dragon's Teeth* by Upton Sinclair.

C171 Letter to the editor. *The New Republic* 106.10 March 9, 1942 (335) Letter in response to a letter in the same edition of *The New Republic* complaining about her review of *Victory Was Slain* by Hilde Abel.

C172 "Europe's Women — Fiercely Silent." *Vogue* 99.7 April 1, 1942 (66-67, 95) Uncollected article.

C173 "Men at Work." *The New Republic* 106.15 April 13, 1942 (513-514) Review of *The Undiscoverables* by Ralph Bates.

C174 "Hollywood Paris." *The Nation* 154.17 April 25, 1942 (490-491) Review of *The Last Time I Saw Paris* by Elliot Paul.

C175 "The Steel of Victory." *The Nation* 154.21 May 23, 1942 (604-605) Review of *The Edge of the Sword* by Vladimir Pozner.

C176 "The Eternal Train." *Harper's Bazaar* 75.2766 June 1942 (40, 46-47) Uncollected short story.

C177 "The Statue's Face." *Mademoiselle* 15.3 July 1942 (30-31, 60-65) Article.

C178 "Hilaire and the Maréchal Pétard." *Harper's Magazine* 185.1107 August 1942 (284-296) Short story collected in *Thirty Stories*.

C179 "If You Wanted to Learn to Write." *Harper's Magazine* 185.1107 August 1942 (284-296) Article.

C180 "Elizabeth Bowen." *The New Republic* 107.12 September 21, 1942 (355-356) Review of *Bowen's Court* by Elizabeth Bowen. Collected in *Words That Must Somehow Be Said.*

C181 "This They Carried with Them." *Harper's Bazaar* 75.2770 October 1942 (100-101, 136-138) Short story collected in *Thirty Stories* and *Fifty Stories* as "This They Took with Them."

C182 "Frenchman's Ship." *The Saturday Evening Post* 215.21 November 21, 1942 (14-15, 84-90) Story collected in *Nothing Ever Breaks Except the Heart and Other Stories* and also appearing in *The Best American Short Stories 1943*, Boston: Houghton Mifflin, 1943.

C183 "Wanderer." *Accent* 2.2 Winter 1942 (85-91) Short story which later appeared in *American Writing 1942: The Anthology and Yearbook of the American Non-Commercial Magazine*, Boston: Bruce Humphries, Inc, 1944 and *Anchor at Sea*, New York: The Swallow Press and William Morrow, 1947.

-1943-

C184 "The Canals of Mars." *Harper's Bazaar* 77.2774 February 1943 (56-57, 102, 104) Short story collected in *Thirty Stories* and *Fifty Stories*. Also appeared in the *O. Henry Memorial Award Stories of 1943*, Garden City: Doubleday and Company, 1943 and *It's a Woman's World*, New York: McGraw-Hill, 1944.

C185 "The Little Distance." *The Saturday Evening Post* 215.36 March 6, 1943 (22-23, 74-78) Short story collected in *Nothing Ever Breaks Except the Heart and Other Stories.*

C186 "Occupied France." *The New York Times Book Review* 48.18 May 2, 1943 (8, 18) Review of *First Harvest* by Vladimir Pozner.

C187 "The Fall of France." *The New York Times Book Review* 48.19 May 9, 1943 (5) Review of *A French Officer's Diary* by D. Barlone.

C188 "The Sword of Fighting France." *The New York Times Book Review* 48.22 May 30, 1943 (5, 17) Review of *The Fighting French* by Raoul Aglion.

C189 "The Loneliest Man in the US Army." *Woman's Home Companion* 70.7 July 1943 (26-27, 64) Short story collected in *Thirty Stories* and *Fifty Stories.*

C190 "World Harmony." *The Saturday Evening Post* 216.17 October 23, 1943 (4) Article.

C191 "Avalanche." *The Saturday Evening Post* (part 1) 216.17 October 23, 1943 (9-11, 80, 83, 87-89) (part 2) 216.18 October 30, 1943 (28-29, 80-82, 84-

85) (part 3) 216.19 November 6, 1943 (28-29, 76, 78-80, 83) (part 4) 216.20 November 13, 1943 (28-29, 35, 37, 39, 41, 43) (part 5) 216.21 November 20, 1943 (32, 34, 100, 102, 104, 107-108, 110-111) (part 6) 216.22 November 27, 1943 (32, 35, 52, 55, 57-58, 60, 63) (part 7) 216.23 December 4, 1943 (32, 34, 72, 74, 76, 78-79). Serialization of the novel *Avalanche* occurring in seven consecutive issues.

C192   "Anthony John Rizzi, Radioman 3rd Class, U.S.N. " Short biography of sailor from Tarrytown, New York who died in World War II. *Tarrytown Daily News* November 5-20, 1943.

C193   "Last Aviator Left Flying." *American Magazine* 136.6 December 1943 (44-45, 114-118) Uncollected short story.

C194   "Cairo Street." *Accent* 3.2 Winter 1943 (95-99) Story which also appeared in *The Accent Anthology*, New York: Harcourt, Brace and Company, 1946.

-1944-

C195   "Defeat." *Modern Reading* No. 10 London 1944 (13-21) Short story. For other appearances see C159.

C196   "Luck for the Road." *Woman's Home Companion* 71.1 January 1944 (17, 38-45) Short story collected in *Nothing Ever Breaks Except the Heart and Other Stories*. Also appeared in *A Diamond of Years: The Best of Woman's Home Companion,* Garden City: Doubleday and Company, 1961.

C197   "The French Retreat." *The New York Times Book Review* 49.6 February 6, 1944 (12) A review of *War Diary* by Jean Malaquais.

C198   "A Good German in a Poetic Setting." *The New York Times Book Review* 49.9 February 27, 1944 (5, 22) Review of *The Silence of the Sea* by Vercors.

C199   "Souvenir City." *Harper's Bazaar* 78.2787 March 1944 (120-121, 170-172) Article.

C200   "Defeat." *Senior Scholastic* 44.14 May 8, 1944 (21-22) Short story. For other appearances see C159.

C201   "Where the National Hero Is an Outlaw." *The New York Herald Book Review* 20.43 June 18, 1944 (1-2) Review of *Army of Shadows* by Joseph Kessel.

C202   "Biography of a Misunderstood Leader." *The New York Times Book Review* 49.30 July 23, 1944 (7) Review of *The Truth About DeGaulle* by Andre Riveloup.

C203 "The Ships Going to Glory." *The Saturday Evening Post* 216.6 Aug 5, 1944 (26-27, 62, 64, 66) Uncollected short story.

C204 "The Poetry of Walter Mehring." *The New York Times Book Review* 49.36 September 3, 1944 (4) Review of *No Road Back* by Walter Mehring (poems).

C205 "Notebook of Paris a Decade Ago." *New York Herald Tribune Weekly Book Review* 21.4 September 17, 1944 (2) Review of *Fair Fantastic Paris* by Harold Ettlinger.

C206 "Canard by Cannell." (Letter to the editor) *The Nation* 159.13 September 23, 1944 (363-364)

C207 Letter also signed by Janet Flanner, Elsa Maxwell, Solita Solano, and Mary Reynolds. *The Nation* 159.13 September 23, 1944 (363).

C208 "Through Four Years' Darkness." *New York Herald Tribune Weekly Book Review* 20.44 October 29, 1944 (5) Review of *Imaginary Interviews* by Andre Gide.

C209 "Vocabulary of Courage." *Harper's Bazaar* 78.2794 October 1944 (65) Article.

C210 "Dossier on Petain." *The Nation* 159.25 December 16, 1944 (748, 750) Letter to the editor.

C211 "Battle of the Sequins." *The Nation* 159.26 December 23, 1944 (770-771) Article collected in *Words That Must Somehow Be Said*.

-1945-

C212 "Reaping Enemy Harvest." *New York Herald Tribune Weekly Book Review* 21.20 January 7, 1945 (10) Review of *I Lied to Live* by Alexander Janta.

C213 Letter to the editor. *The Nation* 160.2 January 13, 1945 (55-56) same signers as C207.

C214 "The Spirit of France." *The New York Times Book Review* 50.8 February 25, 1945 (6) Review of *The Speeches of Charles DeGaulle*.

C215 "Introduction to a Poem in Flight." *Portfolio: An International Quarterly* Volume 1 Summer 1945 (Leaf two with photograph of Kay Boyle on leaf three).

C216 "An Open Letter to René Crevel." *Portfolio: An International Quarterly* Volume 1 Summer 1945 (Leaf six) Accompanies her translation of an excerpt from Crevel's *Babylon*. (Chapter 6: The Child Approaching Womanhood).

C217   "Hotel Behind the Lines." Part I. *The Nation* 160.23 June 9, 1945 (642-645) Part II. *The Nation* 160.24 June 16, 1945 (668-670) Story collected in *Nothing Ever Breaks Except the Heart and Other Stories* and *Fifty Stories*.

C218   "The Jew Is a Myth." *The Nation* 161.15 October 13, 1945 (368, 372) Review of *Stepchildren of France* by Charles Jean Odic. Collected in *Words That Must Somehow Be Said*.

C219   Letter to the editor. *The Nation* 161.17 October 27, 1945 (443).

C220   "Stranger in the Snow." *Mademoiselle* 22.2 December 1945 (131, 211-213) Article.

-1946-

C221   "Winter Night." *The New Yorker* 21.49 January 19, 1946 (19-23) Short story collected in *Thirty Stories* and *Fifty Stories*. Also appeared in *O. Henry Memorial Award Stories of 1946,* Garden City: Doubleday and Company, 1946, *Masters and Masterpieces of the Short Story*, New York: Rinehart, Holt and Winston, 1960, *American Short Stories to the Present*, Chicago: Scott, Foreman, 1964, *Introduction to the Short Story*, Rochelle Park, New Jersey: Hayden, 1972, *The Age of Anxiety: Modern American Stories*, Boston: Allyn & Bacon, 1972, *Women and Fiction*, New York: Penguin, 1975, and *Great American Short Stories*, Pleasantville, New York: Reader's Digest Association, 1979.

C222   "A Frenchman Must Die." *The Saturday Evening Post* (part 1) 218.32 February 9, 1946 (9-11, 110, 112, 114-116) (part 2) 218.33 February 16, 1946 (30-31, 106, 108, 110, 112, 114) (part 3) 218.34 February 23, 1946 (34, 52, 54, 56, 58) (part 4) 218.35 March 2, 1946 (32, 56-57, 59-60, 62) (part 5) 218.36 March 9, 1946 (34, 115-117, 119) (part 6) 218.37 March 16, 1946 (34, 129-130, 132, 134, 136) (part 7) 218.38 March 23, 1946 (34, 94-95, 97-98) (part 8) 218.39 March 30, 1946 (32, 106, 108, 110, 113) Serialization of the novel appearing in eight consecutive issues.

C223   "How America Lives: Family with Nine Kids." *Ladies Home Journal* 63.3 March 1946 (165-170+) Article.

C224   "Military Zone." *Portfolio: An International Quarterly* Volume 3 Spring 1946.

C225   "Meet a United Nations Family in the USA." *Ladies Home Journal* 63.12 December 1946 (181-186, 244-248) Article.

-1947-

C226 "The Miracle Goat." *Woman's Home Companion* 74.1 January 1947 (24-25, 83-85) Uncollected short story.

C227 "A Farewell to New York." *The Nation* 164.10 March 8, 1947 (271-272) Article collected in *Words That Must Somehow Be Said.*

C228 "Monument to Hitler." *The Nation* 164.15 April 12, 1947 (417-419) Article.

C229 "Kay Boyle Challenges *New Masses* review." *New Masses* 63.3 April 15, 1947 (21-22) Letter to the editor.

C230 "Isabelita Has Lost Her Reason." *New Statesman and Nation* 33.845 May 17, 1947 (352) Article.

C231 "Isabelita Has Lost Her Reason." *The Nation* 164.21 May 24, 1947 (628-629) Article.

C232 "Army of Occupation." *The New Yorker* 23.16 June 7, 1947 (29-34) Short story collected in *Nothing Ever Breaks Except the Heart and Other Stories* and *Fifty Stories.*

C233 "Faces of Spain." *The Nation* 165.2 July 12, 1947 (35-38) Article.

C234 "Protest for Isabelita." *The Nation* 165.4 July 26, 1947 (110) Letter to the editor.

C235 "One Small Diamond Please." *Woman's Home Companion* 74.8 August 1947 (26-27, 113-117) Uncollected short story.

C236 "Isabelita's Trial." *The Nation* 165.15 October 11, 1947 (393-394) Letter to editor.

C237 "Dream Dance." *The Saturday Evening Post* 220.24 December 13, 1947 (32-33) Uncollected short story.

-1948-

C238 "The Searching Heart." *Woman's Home Companion* 75.1 January 1948 (18-19+) Uncollected short story.

C239 "French Harvest." *Tomorrow* 7.9 May 1948 (5-12) Short story collected in *Nothing Ever Breaks Except the Heart and Other Stories* and *Fifty Stories.*

C240 "Passport to Doom." *The Saturday Evening Post* 220.46 May 15, 1948 (20-24+) Later appeared as "Decision" in *Three Short Novels.*

C241   "Evening at Home." *The New Yorker* 24.33 October 9, 1948 (26-32) Short story later collected in *Nothing Ever Breaks Except the Heart and Other Stories* and *Fifty Stories*.

-1949-

C242   "The Criminal." *The New Yorker* 25.2 March 5, 1949 (27-32) Collected in *The Smoking Mountain* and *Fifty Stories*.

C243   "Begin Again." *The New Yorker* 25.11 May 7, 1949 (32-34) Collected in *The Smoking Mountain*.

C244   "Summer Evening." *The New Yorker* 25.18 June 25, 1949 (20-24) Short story collected in *The Smoking Mountain* and *Fifty Stories*.

C245   "Adam's Death." *The New Yorker* 25.29 September 10. 1949 (29-34) Short story collected in *The Smoking Mountain* and *Fifty Stories*.

C246   "Fife's House." *The New Yorker* 25.34 October 15. 1949 (32-36) Short story collected in *The Smoking Mountain* and *Fifty Stories*.

C247   "Frankfurt in Our Blood." *The Nation* 169.16 October 15, 1949 (364-366) Short story collected in *The Smoking Mountain* and in *Words That Must Somehow Be Said*.

-1950-

C248   "Travel in Spain." *The New Republic* 122.22 May 29, 1950 (4) Letter to the editor.

C249   "The Lovers of Gain." *The Nation* 170.25 June 24, 1950 (615-618) Short story collected in *Nothing Ever Breaks Except the Heart and Other Stories* and *Fifty Stories*.

C250   "News in Frankfurt." *The New Republic* 123.4 July 24, 1950 (4) Letter to the editor.

C251   "A Reporter in Germany—The People with Names." *The New Yorker* 26.29 September 9, 1950 (37, 77) Article.

C252   "A Disgrace to the Family." *The Saturday Evening Post* 223.13 September 23, 1950 (22-23, 92, 104) Story collected in *Nothing Ever Breaks Except the Heart and Other Stories* and *Fifty Stories*. Also appeared in *The Saturday Evening Post Stories* 1950, New York: Random House, 1950.

-1951-

C253   "Home." *Harper's Magazine* 202.1208 January 1951 (78-83) Short story collected in *The Smoking Mountain.*

C254   "The Lost." *Tomorrow* 10.7 March 1951 (10-17) Short story collected in *The Smoking Mountain* and *Fifty Stories.*

C255   "Cabaret." *Tomorrow* 10.8 April 1951 (10-17) Short story collected in *The Smoking Mountain* and *Fifty Stories.*

C256   "Aufwiedersehn Abend." *Harper's Magazine* 202.1211 April 1951 (57-67) Short story collected in *The Smoking Mountain* and *Fifty Stories.*

C257   "Talk with Kay Boyle." with Harvey Breit. *The New York Times Book Review* 56.17 April 29, 1951 (26)

C258   "Some of the Authors of 1951 Speaking for Themselves." *The New York Herald Tribune Book Review* 28.8 October 7, 1951 (6, 28) Autobiographical sketch.

C259   "Hans Jahn Fights Rearmament." *The Nation* 173.24 December 15, 1951 (519-521) Article.

-1952-

C260   "Diagnosis of a Selfish Lady." *The Saturday Evening Post* 224.40 April 5, 1952 (24, 119-124) Short story which also appeared in *The Saturday Evening Post Stories 1952*, New York: Random House, 1952.

-1953-

C261   "The Soldier Ran Away." *The Saturday Evening Post* 225.35 February 28, 1953 (20-21, 115-119) Short story collected in *The Smoking Mountain.*

C262   "The Daring Impersonation." *The Saturday Evening Post* 226.6 & 7 August 8, 1953 (17-19, 69-70, 74, 76) and August 15, 1953 (36-37, 96-99, 101) Uncollected short story.

C263   "Farewell to Europe." *The Nation* 177.24 December 12, 1953 (526-528) Article collected in *Words That Must Somehow Be Said.*

-1954-

C264   "Fear." *New Statesman and Nation* 48.1229 September 25, 1954 (352+) Uncollected short story.

C265   "October 1954." *The Nation* 179.18 October 30, 1954 (383) A poem collected in *Collected Poems* and *Collected Poems of Kay Boyle*.

C266   "Carnival of Fear." *The Saturday Evening Post* 227.24 & 25 December 11, 1954 (20-21, 102-105) and December 18, 1954 (34-35, 50, 50-53) Short story also appearing in *Saturday Evening Post Stories 1954*, New York: Random House 1954.

-1955-

C267   "A Declaration for 1955." *The Nation* 180.5 January 29, 1955 (102-104) Article. Collected in *Words That Must Somehow Be Said*.

C268   "A Puzzled Race." *The Nation* 180.23 June 4, 1955 (481-483) Short story collected in *Nothing Ever Breaks Except the Heart and Other Stories* and *Fifty Stories*.

C269   "Spain Divided." *The Nation* 180.24 June 11, 1955 (506-507) Review of *The Cypresses Believe in God* by Jose Maria Gironella.

C270   "The Kill." *Harper Magazine* 211.1263 August 1955 (43-51) Uncollected short story.

C271   "They Sing of Love— A German Vignette." *The Nation* 181.11 September 10, 1955 (224-225) Article.

C272   "A Fanciful French Village and Five Typical Children." *New York Herald Tribune Book Review* 32.11 October 23, 1955 (15) Review of *The Headland* by Carol Brink.

-1956-

C273   "Evidence of Conscience." *The Nation* 182.15 April 14, 1956 (316-318) Review of *They Fell from God's Hands* by Hans Werner Richter, *The Burnt Offering* by Albrecht Goes and *The Revolt of Gunner Asch* by Hans Helmut Kirst.

C274   "Education on the East Front." *The Nation* 183.2 July 14, 1956 (43-44) Review of *Cross of Iron* by Willi Heinrich and *The Train Was on Time* by Heinrich Böll.

C275   "The New Emigration." *The Nation* 183.12 September 22, 1956 (246) Poem collected in *Collected Poems* and *Collected Poems of Kay Boyle*.

C276   "Breach of Satire." *The Nation* 183.21 November 24, 1956 (462-463) Review of *The Tribe That Lost Its Head* by Nicholas Monsarrat.

C277 "The Intellectuals Are Failing America." *The Saint Louis Post Dispatch* 78.332 December 2, 1956 Between Bookends Section II (1) Article.

-1957-

C278 "Spring." *Ladies Home Journal* 74.3 March 1957 (211) Poem collected in *Collected Poems* and *Collected Poems of Kay Boyle*.

C279 "Creative Writing." *The Dolphin* [of the Thomas School] March 9, 1957 (1-2) Article.

C280 "So Slowly We Move." *The Nation* 184.18 May 4, 1957 (390-393) Article.

C281 "Wit, Humor— and a Dash of Kafka." *The New York Times Book Review* 62.19 May 12, 1957 (30) Review of *Tiger in the Kitchen* by Villy Sorenson.

C282 "The Far East and Fiction." *American Scholar* 26.2 Spring 1967 (222-228) Review of *The Setting Sun* by Osamu Dazai, *The Frontiers of Love* by Diana Chang and *The Sound of Waves* by Yukio Mishima.

C283 "The Doctor's Daughter." *New York Times Book Review* 62.31 August 4, 1957 (17) Review of *Missy* by Dorothy James Roberts.

C284 "Living Up to the Part." *The New York Times Book Review* 62.40 October 6, 1957 (4) Review of *The Actress* by Bessie Breuer.

C285 "No Time to Listen." *The Nation* 185.16 November 16, 1957 (341-342) Article collected in *Words That Must Somehow Be Said*.

C286 "City of Invisible Men." *The Nation* 185.21 December 21, 1957 (475-476) Article.

-1958-

C287 "The Imposed Revolution." *The Nation* 186.1 January 4, 1958 (14-15) Review of *Forced to Remember* by John D. Montgomery.

C288 "The Long Dead Fathers." *The Progressive* 22.9 September 1958 (35-37) Article.

C289 "Penchants of the Prettiest Girl." *Saturday Review of Literature* 41.47 November 22, 1958 (19) Review of *The Visitor* by Mary McMinnies.

-1959-

C290   "Poem of Gratitude—for Caresse." *Poetry* 93.6 March 1959 (376) A poem collected in *Collected Poems, Testament for My Students and Other Poems,* and *Collected Poems of Kay Boyle.*

C291   "Dreams Dreamed." *Saturday Review of Literature* 42.14 April 4, 1959 (24) A poem collected in *Collected Poems of Kay Boyle.*

C292   "Big Books on the Bonn Side." *Saturday Review of Literature* 42.22 May 30, 1959 (21-22) Review of *The Forsaken Army* by Heinrich Gerlach, *The Seventh Day* by Hans Helmut Kirst and *Tidings* by Ernst Wiechert.

C293   "In Memoriam, Bob Brown." *The Village Voice* 4.44 August 26, 1959 (4) Editorial.

C294   "The Seventh Day." *Venture* 3.3 Fall 1959 (62-63) Review of *The Seventh Day* by Hans Helmut Kirst.

C295   "The Aesthetics of the Future." *Syracuse* 2.2 December 1959 (32-35) Article.

-1960-

C296   "Two Twilights for William Carlos Willliams." *Poetry, A Magazine of Verse* 95.6 March 1960 (356) Poem collected in *Collected Poems* and *Collected Poems of Kay Boyle.*

C297   "A Dialogue of Birds for Howard Nemorov." *Poetry* 95.6 March 1960 (357) Poem collected in *Collected Poems* and *Collected Poems of Kay Boyle.*

C298   "Nazi Affiliation Charged." *The New York Times* 109.37299 March 8, 1960 (32) Letter to the editor.

C299   "Has Germany Changed?" *Foreign Policy Bulletin* 39.15 April 15, 1960 (117-118) Article.

C300   "Brighter Than Most." *Prairie Schooner* 34.1 Spring 1960 (1-4) Review of *Robert McAlmon: Expatriate Publisher and Writer* by Robert E. Knoll.

C301   "The Triumph of Principals." *Liberation* 5.4 June 1960 (10-11) Article collected in *Words That Must Somehow Be Said.*

C302   "Swastikas Out of Sight Are Not Out of Mind." *The New York Times Book Review* 65.24 June 12, 1960 (6) Review of *The Fear Makers* by Wilfrid Schilling.

C303 "The Compassion and Creative Fury of Bertolt Brecht." *New York Herald Tribune Weekly Book Review* 36.46 June 19, 1960 (5) Review of *Brecht: The Man and His Work* by Martin Eslin.

C304 "What Did Friedenberg Say?" *The New Republic* 143.1 & 2 July 11, 1960 (31) Letter to the editor with response from Daniel Friedenberg.

C305 "Paintings in Flight." *Mark* [Norwalk, CN] 7 July 30, 1960 (9-10) Poem.

C306 "Hitler's Inferno." *New York Post Weekend Magazine* Section 2 October 16, 1960 (11) Review of *The Rise and Fall of the Third Reich* by William L. Shirer.

C307 Letter. *The New York Herald Tribune* October 16, 1960.

C308 "Kaufman and the Germans." *The New Republic* 143.18 October 24, 1960 (23) Letter to the editor.

-1961-

C309 "Poem for a Painter Who Drinks Wine." *The Nation* 192.2 January 14, 1961 (38) Poem collected in *Collected Poems* and *Collected Poems of Kay Boyle*.

C310 "Two Poems for a Poet." *Poetry* 97.5 February 1961 (300-301) Poem collected in *Collected Poems* and *Collected Poems of Kay Boyle*.

C311 "Nemerov's Poetry." *The Nation* 192.6 February 11, 1961 (opposite 109) Letter to the editor.

C312 "Addendum." *New York Times Book Review* 67.8 February 19, 1961 (32) Letter to the editor.

C313 "Print from a Lucite Block." *Outsider* 1.1 New Orleans Fall 1961 (85) Poem collected in *Collected Poems* and *Collected Poems of Kay Boyle*.

-1962-

C314 "Seascape for an Engraver." *Poetry* 99.4 January 1962 (214) Poem collected in *Collected Poems* and *Collected Poems of Kay Boyle*.

C315 "Rendezvous." *Poetry* 99.4 January 1962 (215-216) Poem collected in *Collected Poems* and *Collected Poems of Kay Boyle*.

C316 "January Twenty Ninth, 1962." Liberation 7.1 March 1962 (8)

C317   "Life With Penn's Coeds." *Philadelphia Sunday Bulletin Magazine* March 25, 1962 (7) Article.

C318   "Conscience Perished Too." *The New York Times Book Review* 67.20 May 20, 1962 (5) Review of *Anything But a Hero* by Rudolph Lorenzen.

C319   "The Room, the Siege, the Escape of a Versatile Man." *Contact* 3.2 June 1962 (25-29) Article on the artist Arthur Deshaies.

C320   "Every 'Heil!' Was a Cry of Revenge." *The New York Times Book Review* 67.29 July 22, 1962 (7) Review of *The Sins of the Fathers* by Christian Geisler.

C321   "An Exile Who Couldn't Return." *The New York Times Book Review* 67.31 August 5, 1962 (5, 25) Review of *McAlmon and the Lost Generation* by Robert E. Knoll.

C322   "The Writer in Our Time." *News* [MacDowell Colony] September 1962 (1-2) Article.

C323   "Washed up on the Unknown Shore of Life." *The New York Time Book Review* 67.37 September 16, 1962 (5) Review of *The Few and the Many* by Hans Sahl.

C324   "I Remember Philadelphia." *Philadelphia Sunday Bulletin Magazine* October 21, 1962 (6-7) Article.

C325   "Kostelanetz." *The New Republic* 147.26 December 29, 1962 (30) Letter to the editor.

C326   "The Tin Drum." *The Griffin* 12. 1962 (7-8) Review of *The Tin Drum* by Günter Grass.

-1963-

C327   "Story of a Man: His Bitter Ordeal." *Cosmopolitan* 154.1 January 1963 (33) Reviews of *The Street Where the Heart Lies* by Ludwig Bemelmans and *The Sand Pebbles* by Richard Kenna and *That Summer in Paris* by Morley Callaghan.

C328   "Should Be Considered Extremely Dangerous." *Story Magazine* 36.138 Issue 1 January/ February 1963 (54-71) Story collected in *Nothing Ever Breaks Except the Heart and Other Stories*.

C329   "Where There Is Always Spring." *Glamour* 49.1 March 1963 (148-149, 206-208) Article.

C330   "A Biography of Lou Andreas Salome." *The New York Times Book Review* 68.14 April 7, 1963 (44) A review of *My Sister, My Spouse* by H.F. Peters.

C331   "Never Stop Learning." *The New Haven Register* 151.110 April 21, 1963 (3) An interview with unnamed interviewer.

C332   "The Vanishing Short Story." *Story Magazine* 36.141 Issue 4 July/August 1963 (108-119) Article about the short story.

C333   "No Other Place to Be." *Liberation* 8.7 September 1963 (9)

C334   "Stiff Upper Lip." *New York Herald Tribune Book Week* 1.2 September 22, 1963 (5) Review of *Going to the River* by Constantine FitzGibbon.

C335   "Tragedy Became Commonplace." *The New York Times Book Review* 68.40 October 6, 1963 (5) Review of *Other Winters—Other Springs* by F. Sandstrom.

C336   "Skiing." *Glamour* 50.3 November 1963 (130, 174-175) Article.

C337   *"The Time Is Now, the Place Is Here."* *The New York Times Book Review* 68.47 November 24, 1963 (38) Review of *Herdo's Children* by Ilse Aichinger.

-1964-

C338   "A Cry in the Dusk of Nightmare." *The New York Times Review of Books* 69.3 January 19, 1964 (5) Review of *Blood from the Sky* by Piotr Rawicz.

C339   "The Teaching of Writing." *NEA Journal* 53.3 March 1964 (11-12) Article. Collected in *Words That Must Somehow Be Said.*

C340   "Raymond Whearty." *Genesis West* 2.2 & 3 Winter/Spring 1964 (113-114) Introduction to Whearty's short story "The LaSalle to Kingston and Animals."

C341   "A Voice from the Future." *Holiday Magazine* 36.4 (12, 16-20, 22) October 1964 Article.

C342   "Mid-Education." *The New York Times Book Review* 69.42 October 18, 1964 (36) Letter in response to a review of *Compulsory Mid-Education* by Paul Goodman.

C343   "The Ballet of Central Park." *The Saturday Evening Post* 237.42 November 28, 1964 (44-48, 50-51) Story collected in *Nothing Ever Breaks Except the Heart and Other Stories* and *Fifty Stories.*

-1965-

C344   "World Tour." Liberation 9.11 February 1965 (21) Poem collected in *Testament for My Students and Other Poems* and *Collected Poems of Kay Boyle.*

C345   "3 Novelists Speak of Involvement in Art." with Betty Burroughs. *The Evening Journal* (Wilmington, Delaware) February 18, 1965 (3)

C346   "World Tour." *Liberation* 10.1 March 1965 (43) See C344.

C347   "Mississippi's Record." *The New York Times* 114.39143 March 26, 1965 (34) Letter to the editor.

C348   "In Defense of the Boar." *The Nation* 200.24 June 14, 1965 (629) Letter to the editor.

C349   "One Sunny Morning." *The Saturday Evening Post* 238.13 July 3, 1965 (61-62, 64) Short story collected in *Nothing Ever Breaks Except the Heart and Other Stories.*

C350   "A Short Poem in Color." *Southern Review* n.s. 1.3 Summer 1965 (606) Poem collected in *Testament for My Students and Other Poems* and *Collected Poems of Kay Boyle.*

C351   "A Poem for Arthur." *Southern Review* n.s 1.3 July 1965 (607) Poem collected in *Testament for My Students and Other Poems* and *Collected Poems of Kay Boyle.*

C352   "A Square Dance for a Square." *Southern Review* n.s. 3.1 July 1965 (608-611) Poem collected in *Testament for My Students and Other Poems* and *Collected Poems of Kay Boyle.*

-1966-

C353   "Hart Crane." *The New York Review of Books* 6.5 March 31, 1966 (30-31) Letter to the editor praising Edward Dahlberg's review of Hart Crane's Letters. The review appeared in the January 20 edition of *The New York Review of Books.*

C354   "The Wild Horses." *The Saturday Evening Post* 239.8 April 9, 1966 (60-65) Included *in The Best American Short Stories 1967,* Boston: Houghton Mifflin Company, 1967 and *This is My Best,* Garden City: Doubleday and Company, 1970.

C355   "You Don't Have to Be a Member of the Congregation." *Liberation* 11.2 April 1966 (26-28) Short story collected in *Nothing Ever Breaks Except the Heart and Other Stories.*

C356 "One Sunny Morning." *Solidarity* 1 April/June 1966 (98-102)

C357 "Fire in the Vineyards." *The Saturday Evening Post* 239.14 July 2, 1966 (76-77, 79-81) Short story collected in *Nothing Ever Breaks Except the Heart and Other Stories* and *Fifty Stories*.

C358 "The Battle of the Pagoda." *Liberation* 11.5 August 1966 (28-29) Article.

C359 "A Poem About the Jews." *The Harvard Advocate* 100.3 & 4 Fall 1966 (21-23) Poem collected in *Testament for My Students and Other Poems* and *Collected Poems of Kay Boyle*.

C360 "Kay Boyle's Bitter View of Johnson." *The San Francisco Chronicle* 102.258 September 15, 1966 (15) Interview.

C361 "Assignment in Cambodia." *The Progressive* 30.11 November 1966 (17-20) Article.

C362 "Dedication to Terre des Hommes." *The Catholic Worker* 33.3 December 1966 (8) Poem collected in *Testament for My Students and Other Poems* and *Collected Poems of Kay Boyle*.

C363 "A Poem of Love." *Love (Incorporating Hate)* 1966 (25) A Poem collected in *Testament for My Students and Other Poems* and *Collected Poems of Kay Boyle*.

-1967-

C364 "On Black Power." *Liberation* 11.10 January 1967 (23) Uncollected poem.

C365 "Man in the Wilderness." *The Nation* 204.22 May 29, 1967 (693-694) Review of *Epitaphs of Our Times: The Letters of Edward Dahlberg* and *The Edward Dahlberg Reader* edited by Paul Carroll. Collected in *Words That Must Somehow Be Said*.

C366 "Thunderstorm in South Dakota." *Southern Review* n.s. 3.4 October 1967 (951) Poem collected in *Testament for My Students and Other Poems* and *Collected Poems of Kay Boyle*.

C367 "Seeing the Sights of San Francisco." *The Progressive* 31.12 December 1967 (19-21) Article collected in *Words that Must Somehow Be Said*.

C368 "Letter from Joyce." *Tri Quarterly* No.8 Winter 1967 (195-197) Introduction to letter from James Joyce.

C369 "A Poem About Black Power." *Journal of Contemporary Revolution* 2.1 Winter 1967/1968. (28) See C364.

-1968-

C370   Letter. *The Nation* 206.8 February 19, 1968 (250) Letter to the editor.

C371   "Defense Fund." *The New Republic* 158.10 March 9, 1968 (36-37) Letter to the editor also signed by Herbert Gold, Jessica Mitford and Mark Schorer.

C372   "For Marianne Moore's Birthday, November 15, 1967." *Twigs IV* (Pikeville College) 1968 (4) Poem collected in *Collected Poems of Kay Boyle*.

C373   "A Poem in One Sentence." *Twigs IV* (Pikeville College) 1968 (5) Poem collected in *Collected Poems of Kay Boyle*.

C374   "Notes on Jury Selection in the Huey Newton Trial." *The Progressive* 32.10 October 1968 (29-35) Article about jury selection at Newton's trial.

C375   "Policemen as Suicides." *The Progressive* 32.10 October 1968 (30) Note on police suicides.

C376   "For James Scheville, on the Occasion of His Arrest." *Poem* 3 & 4 November 1968 (1) Poem collected in *Testament for My Students and Other Poems* and *Collected Poems of Kay Boyle*.

C377   "Kay Boyle Assesses San Francisco State." *The San Francisco Chronicle* 104.313 November 16, 1968 (13) An interview with Bob Haesler.

C378   "Kay Boyle Replies." Correction from Kay Boyle. *The Progressive* 32.12 December 1968 (43) Letter to the editor.

C379   "Langston Hughes, (1902-1967) Commemorative Tribute." *Proceedings of the American Academy of Arts and Letters and the National Institute of Arts and Letters* Second Series Number 15 1968 (118-120) Tribute to Langston Hughes.

-1969-

C380   "Pickets on the Long March." *The Nation* 208.8 February 24, 1969 (226) Letter to the editor also signed by Leo Litwak, Ray B. West, Jr. and Herbert Wilner.

C381   "Bohemian Journey to a State of Mind." *San Francisco Sunday Examiner and Chronicle This World* 32.38 March 2, 1969 (34, 39) Review of *The Overland Journey of Joseph Frankl: The First Bohemian to Cross the Plains to the California Gold Fields*.

C382   "The Syllabic Sound Refused to Stay Still." *San Francisco Sunday Examiner and Chronicle This World* 32.50 May 25, 1969 (39, 41) A review of *Violence and Glory: Poems 1962-1968* by James Schevill.

C383 "Nothing New Here About Paris of the 20s." A review of *Americans in Paris* by George Wickes *Chicago Sun Times Book Week* 22.51 September 21, 1969 (4) Book review.

C384 "The Lost Dogs of Phnom Penh." *Lace Curtain* No. 1 Winter 1969/1970 (8) Poem collected in *Testament for My Students and Other Poems* and *Collected Poems of Kay Boyle*.

C385 "The Collapse of the Third Republic by William Shirer." *The New York Times Book Review* 74.51 December 21, 1969 (17) Letter to the editor.

-1970-

C386 "Testament for My Students." *Southern Review* 6.1 January 1970 (149-154) Poem Collected in *Testament for My Students and Other Poems* and *Collected Poems of Kay Boyle*.

C387 "A Day on Alcatraz with the Indians." *The New Republic* 162.3 January 17, 1970 (10-11) Article collected in *Words That Must Somehow Be Said*.

C388 "Indians on the Rock." *The Nation* 210.2 January 19, 1970 (34) Letter to the editor.

C389 "Excerpt from *The Long Walk at San Francisco State.*" *Evergreen Review* 14.76 March 1970 (21-23, 69-80) Excerpt from an essay published in whole in the book *The Long Walk at San Francisco State and Other Essays* New York: Grove Press, 1970 and collected in *Words That Must Somehow Be Said*.

C390 "The Voice of the Poet Speaks Quickly." *San Francisco Sunday Examiner and Chronicle* 1970.14 *This World* April 4, 1970 (31) Article.

C391 "Jazz Is the Pulse of Harper's Poetry Review." *San Francisco Sunday Examiner and Chronicle* 1970.21 *This World* May 24, 1970 (31) Review of *Dear John, Dear Coltrane* by Michael S. Harper.

C392 "No One Can Be All Things to All People." *Evergreen Review* 14.81 August 1970 (62-66) Article about Huey Newton.

C393 "A Man in the Wilderness." *Tri Quarterly* No. 19 Fall 1970 (66-69) Article about Edward Dahlberg.

C394 "Power to the People." *New York Times* 120.41174 October 17, 1970 (28) A response to this letter by Richard Pipes a professor of history at Harvard which appeared in the November 1, 1970 issue on page 14 of section IV.

C395   "On Taking Up Residence in Virginia-For James Joyce and James Liddy." *Hart.* Ca. 1970-1971 (16) Poem collected in *This Is Not a Letter and Other Poems* and *Collected Poems of Kay Boyle.*

-1971-

C396   "So Vividly Alive." *Philadelphia Sunday Bulletin Books and Art Section* January 10, 1971 (3) Article.

C397   "Exposure." *The Nation* 212.2 January 11, 171 (24) Letter to the editor.

C398   "The Long Walk at San Francisco State- A Rebuttal." *San Francisco Sunday Examiner and Examiner and Chronicle* 1971.7 *This World* February 14, 1971 (39) Letter to the editor.

C399   "Branded for Slaughter-for Shawn Wong." *Anteus* 3 Spring 1971 (75-76) Poem collected in *Collected Poems of Kay Boyle.*

C400   "The Winter Soldiers: Section of Unfinished Poem." *Cargoes* 54.2 Hollins College Exam Book (45-46) Spring 1971 Unfinished and uncollected.

C401   "Was the Issue Black Studies?" *Ararat* 12.3 Summer 1971 (40-42) Review of *Blow It Up* by Dikran Karagueuzian.

C402   "Introduction to a *Modern History of Germany.*" *Prose* 3 Fall 1971 (5-18) Article.

C403   "Writers in Metaphysical Revolt." *Conference of College Teachers of English of Texas* 36. [no number] September 1971 (6-12)

C404   "A New Name for Peace." *Liberation* 16.4 September 1971 (28-30) Appeared later as the Introduction to *Enough of Dying*, New York: Dell Publishing, 1972.

C405   "This is Not a Letter." *Twigs* 7 1971 (1-2) A poem collected in *This is Not a Letter and Other Poems* and *Collected Poems of Kay Boyle* in a slightly different form.

C406   "For an Historian Following an Operation on His Eyes." *Twigs* 7 1971 (3-5) Uncollected poem.

C407   "The Lyman's Family's Holy Siege of America." Part 1 by David Felton. *Rolling Stone* Issue 98 December 23, 1971 (40-60) Article includes excerpts from an interview with Kay Boyle by David Felton.

-1972-

C408 "The Lyman's Family's Holy Siege of America." Part 2 by David Felton. *Rolling Stone* Issue 99 January 6, 1972 (40-60) Article includes excerpts from an interview with Kay Boyle by David Felton.

C409 "Saluting Kings and Presidents." *The Nation* 214.6 February 7, 1972 (184-187) Review of *Stories, Fables and Other Diversions* by Howard Nemerov.

C410 "For an Historian Following an Operation on His Eyes." *The Mark Twain Journal* 16.3 Winter 1972 (25) Uncollected poem.

C411 "Our Lower Depths." *Mercury Book Review* December 6, 1972 (12-13) Review of *Absolutely Nothing to Get Alarmed About* by Charles Wright.

-1973-

C412 "A Fictional Triumph of the Survival Struggle." *San Francisco Sunday Examiner and Chronicle* 1973.5 *This World* February 4, 1973 (40, 45) A review of *The Cell* by Horst Bienek.

C413 "Excerpts from a Novel in Progress." *ICarbS* 1.1 Fall 1973 (3-9) Excerpts from *The Underground Woman.*

-1974-

C414 "A Dialogue with Victor Ourin." *Pembroke Magazine* 5 March 1974 (3-4) Uncollected poem.

C415 "Some Thoughts on Writing." *New School Letter on Human Conflict* Mar 11, 1974 (1) Article.

C416 "Nancy Cunard." *The Nation* 218.17 April 27, 1974 (514) Letter to the editor.

C417 "On the Death of My Student, the Poet Serafin." *Wind* No. 11 Spring 1974 (10-12) Poem collected in *Collected Poems of Kay Boyle.*

C418 "A Poem for Rosemary and Timothy Leary." *New School Letter on Human Conflict* May 28, 1974 (2) Uncollected poem.

C419 "Nolo Contendere." *Anteus* 13 & 14 Spring and Summer 1974 (253-265) Uncollected short story.

C420   "Introduction—A selection of Young Filipino Poets." *American Poetry Review* 3.4 July/August 1974 (47-48)

C421   "I Am Furious-Yellow." *Rolling Stone* 13.168 August 29, 1974 (64-65) Review of *AIIIEEEEE: An Anthology of Asian-American Writers.*

C422   "Kay Boyle: From a New Novel." *Pacific Sun Literary Quarterly* No volume or issue number. Week of November 14-20, Final quarter 1974 (4) Excerpt from *The Underground Woman.*

C423   "The Journal as a Highway." *Pacific Sun Literary Quarterly* No volume or issue number Week of November 14-20 Final Quarter 1974 (5) Review of *Long Distance* by Penelope Mortimer.

-1975-

C424   "The New Mission of an Elegant Protester." An interview with Mildred Hamilton. *The San Francisco Sunday Examiner and Chronicle* 1975.3 January 19, 1975 Sunday Scene (7)

C425   "Boyle Boils." *Zenger: Associated Students of San Francisco State* April 2, 1975 (2) Letter to the editor with accompanying response from the lady who interviewed her. (See Zenger March 19, 1975)

C426   "The Crime of Attica." *The New Republic* 172.11 March 15, 1975 (23-25) Review of *A Time to Die* by Tom Wicker and collected in *Words That Must Somehow Be Said.*

C427   "A Talk Given Here and There." *Aisling* 1 Summer 1975 (8-13) Article.

C428   "New Printer, New Writers and a New Literature." *New York Times Book Review* 80.7 September 14, 1975 (6) A review of *Published in Paris* by Hugh Ford.

C429   "I'm Not Solzhenitsyn." *Pacific Sun Literary Quarterly* 13.34 Week of August 21-27, 1975 Fall 1975 (6-7, 17) Review of *Cry of the People and Other Poems* by Kim Chi Ha.

C430   "A Poem for the Students of Greece." *The New York Quarterly* No. 17 1975 (44-46) Poem collected in *Collected Poems of Kay Boyle.*

-1976-

C431   "Sisters of the Princess." *CAIFI News Letter* (Committee for Artistic and Intellectual Freedom in Iran) March 1976 (11) Article.

C432 "Sisters of the Princess." *The Nation* 222.9 March 6, 1976 (261-262) Article collected in *Words That Must Somehow Be Said*.

C433 "Kay Boyle: A Profile." *The San Francisco Review of Books* 1.12 April 1976 (7-9) An interview with Charles Fracchia.

C434 "Dialogue with Indian Women." *Pacific Sun Literary Quarterly* 14.10 Week of May 5-12, 1976 (7) Review of *Indian Women of the Western Morning* by John Upton Terrell and Donna M. Terrell.

C435 "Poets." *Pacific Sun Literary Quarterly* 14.11 Week of May 21-27, 1976 (7)

C436 "The Genius of Robert McAlmon." *Pembroke Magazine* 7 1976 (324-327) Article.

-1977-

C437 "An Open Letter to Vida Hadjebi Tabrizi." *CAIFI Newsletter* (Committee for Artistic and Intellectual Freedom in Iran) March 1977 (8-10) Letter.

C438 "March in the Cove." *Perma Frost* 1.1 April 1977 (8)

C439 "The Crosbys: An Afterword." *ICarbS* 3.2 Spring/Summer 1977 (117-125). Article.

C440 A blurb about Laurel Lee's *Walking Through the Fire* appearing in a Dutton advertisement. *New York Times Book Review* 82.24 June 12, 1977 (6)

C441 "Alexander Berkman: A Memory." *Phoenix* 6. 1 & 2 Summer/Autumn 1977 (158-171) Article about Alexander Berkman.

-1978-

C442 "For Paul Jacobs." *San Francisco Review of Books* 3.1 March 1978 (23) Uncollected poem to Paul Jacobs.

C443 "When Writers Give Themselves Away." *The San Francisco Chronicle* 114.50 March 15, 1978 (15) A sketch of herself with a short note on how she thinks others view her with a note by Merla Zellerbach.

C444 "From: A Book on Irish Women." *Gallimaufry* No. 13 Summer 1978 (126-129) From a work in progress.

C445 "Conquered People Are Afraid to Be Themselves." *KPFA Folio* July/August 1978 (6) Article.

C446   Book review. *The New Republic* 179.18 October 28, 1978 (36-38) *Review of Lucky Eyes and a High Heart: The Life of Maud Gonne* by Nancy Cardoza. Collected *Words That Must Somehow Be Said.*

C447   "No on 6: A Personal Opinion." *New West* 3.23 November 6 1978 (56-61) Opinion.

-1979-

C448   Book review. *San Francisco Review of Books* 4.7 March 1979 (12) Review of *Figures of Thought* by Howard Nemerov.

C449   "A Poem for George Mascone, Assassinated November 27, 1978." *Letters Magazine* [Maine Writers Workshop] April 1979 (2-3) Uncollected poem.

C450   "Strictly San Francisco." *San Francisco Review of Books* 5.2 July 1979 (5) Review of *Awake in the River* by Janice Mirikitani.

C451   "Two on Harrison on Didion." *The Nation* 229.16 November 17, 1979 (482) Letter to the editor.

-1980-

C452   "St. Stephen's Green." *Atlantic Monthly* 245.6 June 1980 (41-44) Also appeared in *Prize Stories 1981 The O. Henry Awards*, Garden City: Doubleday & Company, 1981.

C453   "PW Interviews Kay Boyle." with Patricia Holt. *Publisher's Weekly* 218.16 October 17, 1980 (8-9)

C454   "A Friend and Fighter Is Moving on with Leah Garchik." *San Francisco Sunday Examiner and Chronicle* 1980.42 October 19, 1980. (9) Interview.

-1981-

C455   "The Spirit and Candor of a Grand Lady of Letters." *Bloomsbury Review* 1.2 January/February 1981 (15, 17-18) An interview with Linda Ferguson.

C456   "Muriel Rukeyser 1913-1980." *Proceedings of the American Academy and Institute of Arts and Letters* Second Series Number 31, 1981 (81-85) Tribute to Muriel Rukeyser.

-1982-

C457   "Excerpt from a Long Poem in Progress." *Conjunctions* No. 2 Spring and Summer 1982 (113-114) Excerpt from a poem for Samuel Beckett. Later completed and collected in *Collected Poems of Kay Boyle.*

C458   "What Parents Do Not Know Yet." *Pearl* No. 9 Spring 1982 (May 5, 1982) (12) Poem later collected in *This is Not a Letter and Other Poems* and *Collected Poems of Kay Boyle.*

C459   "Creed." *Pearl* No. 9 Spring 1982 (May 5, 1982) (13) Uncollected poem with note from the author that the poem was written in 1918.

C460   "Dining Out." *Pearl* No. 9 Spring 1982 (May 5, 1982) (13) Uncollected poem with note by the author that a the poem was written in 1920.

C461   "The Uneasiness of Autobiography." *Willow Springs* Number 10 Spring 1982 (33-37) Article.

C462   Sections of a Poem in Progress. "For Samuel Beckett." *Willow Springs* Number 10 Spring 1982 (38-39) Later completed and collected in *The Collected Poems of Kay Boyle.*

C463   Letter. *Sagetrieb* 1.2 Fall 1982 (320) Excerpt from a letter to Donald Powell about Emanuel Carnevali dated January 15, 1982.

-1983-

C464   "Kay Boyle: An Eightieth Birthday Interview." with David R. Mesher. *Malahat Review* No. 65 July 1983 (82-95)

C465   "A Poem for the Teesto Dine of Arizona." *Malahat Review* No. 65 July 1983 (96-97) Poem collected in *This Is Not a Letter and Other Poems* and *Collected Poems of Kay Boyle.*

C466   "Reincarnation." *Rolling Stock* No. 5 1983 (3) Excerpt from "For Samuel Beckett."

-1984-

C467   "Kay Boyle: Paris Wasn't Like That." *The New York Times Book Review* 84.29 July 15, 1984 (1, 32- 34) An interview with Leo Litwak.

-1985-

C468   "The Men in My Family." *The Berkeley Monthly* 16.2 November 1985 Article.

-1987-

C469   "Pound in Rapallo." *New York Review of Books* 34.8 May 7, 1947 (47) Article.

C470 "Transylvania, February 18." *The American Voice* No. 7 Summer 1987 (22-23) Story originally published in *365 Days* New York: Harcourt, Brace and Company, 1936.

C471 "Over Russia August 10." *The American Voice* No. 7 Summer 1987 (23-24) See C470 for previous publication.

C472 "New Zealand October 16." *The American Voice* No. 7 Summer 1987 (24-26) See C470 for previous publication.

-1988-

C473 "A Lesson in Anatomy." *Exquisite Corpse* 6. 10, 11 & 12 October through December 1988 (1) Collected in *Collected Poems of Kay Boyle.*

C474 "On the Run." *Twentieth Century Literature.* 34.3 Fall 1988 (258-260)

C475 "Why Are We Here?." *Twentieth Century Literature.* 34.3 Fall 1988 (261-262)

C476 "For Marianne Moore's Birthday, November 15, 1967." *Helicon Nine* No. 19 (29)

-1991-

C477 "Rest Cure." *Story Magazine* 39.2 Spring 1991 (26-33) See C57. Short story.

-1992-

C478 "Career." *Alchemy* XXVII 1992 (6) Short story.

C479 "Poem for a Painter Who Drinks Wine." *Alchemy* XXVII (7) Poem.

C480 "Poem for a Painter Bent on Suicide." *Alchemy* XXVII (8) Poem.

D

Broadsides

D1 "The Lost Dogs of Phnom Penh" Two Windows Folio II [Berkeley: Two Windows Press, 1968] 17" x 13" 6 leaves. Leaves unpaginated 15" x 11$^1/_4$" This poem first appeared in *Lace Curtain* 1, Winter 1969/1970.

D2 "A Poem for February First 1975" [San Francisco: The Quercus Press, 1975] 23" x 12" First appearance.

D3 "A Poem for Muriel Rukeyser" [Chicago]: Lovell and Whyte, [1979] 34" x 23" Illustrated by John Sandford.

D4 "Advice to the Old (Including Myself)" Beyond Rice: A Broadside Series. San Francisco: Mango Publications and Noro Press, 1979 11$^3/_4$ x 9$^1/_2$" With cover sheet +Table of contents +credit and acknowledgments +13 unpaginated leaves. 11" x 8$^1/_2$" Edition of 600 out of which 52 were signed by the artists and writers. Issued at $6.00.

D5 "After the Earth Quake" Portfolio. [Port Townsend, Washington]: Copper Canyon Press, 1983] 11$^1/_2$" x 7$^1/_2$" Also includes Michael McClure, Linda Bragg, and Howard Nemerov.

D6 "September 24, Marseilles." [n.p.]: Lovell and White, [n.d.] 35" x 23" $^1/_{75}$ copies.

E

Translations by Kay Boyle

E1   DON JUAN   [1932]

First Edition:

DON JUAN | BY JOSEPH DELTEIL | *Translated from the French by* KAY BOYLE | Illustrated by CHARLES SANDFORD | [design] | NEW YORK | JONATHAN CAPE & HARRISON SMITH

Collation: [i-xii], xiii-xvii, [xviii-xxii], [1-3], 4-28, [29-30], 31-36, [37-39], 40-42, [43-44], 45-63, [64-67], 68-84, [85-86], 87-88, [89-91], 92-102, [103-104], 105-110, [111-112], 113-115, [116-119], 120-122, [123-124], 125-146, [147-149], 150-166, [167-168], 169-174, [175-176], 177, [178-181], 182-206 pages; cream endpapers. $7 \, ^3/_8$" x $4 \, ^7/_8$"   [A-M] ^{8} [N]^{10}

Contents: (i) fly title; (ii) publisher's information; (iii) blank; (iv) illustration; (v) title page; (vi) copyright page; (vii) [dedication] To the great Barbey | the great Huysmans | the great Bloy; (viii) blank; (ix) PRÉFACE | *Man is an animal seeking God* | J.D.; (x) blank; (xi) "Il m'évoqua Pascal...." | Barrès; (xii) blank; (xiii-xvii) translator's fore-word; (xviii) blank; (ixx) contents; (xx) blank; (xxi) list of illustrations; (xxii) blank; (1) [chapter title]: ODOR DI FEMINA; (2) blank; (3-28) text; (29) illustration; (30) blank; (31-36) text; (37) [chapter title]: FLESH IN TORMENT, (38) blank, (39-42) text; (43) illustration; (44) blank; (45-63) text; (64) blank; (65) [chapter title]: HEART IN TORMENT; (66) blank; (67-84) text; (85) illustration; (86) blank; (87-88) text; (89) [chapter title]: SOUL IN TORMENT; (90) blank; (91-102) text; (103) illustration; (104) blank; (105-110) text; (111) illustration; (112) blank; (113-115) text; (116) blank; (117) [chapter title]: REVOLUTION; (118) blank; (119-122) text; (123) illustration; (124) blank; (125-146) text; (147) [chapter title]: THE RETURN TO THE FOLD; (148) blank; (149-166) text; (167) illustration; (168) blank; (169-174) text; (175) illustration; (176) blank; (177) text; (178) blank; (179) [chapter title: ODOUR OF SANCTITY; (180) blank; (181-206) text.

Copyright page: COPYRIGHT, 1931, BY JONATHAN CAPE AND | HARRISON SMITH, INC. | [circle with a dot in the center] | FIRST PUBLISHED, 1931 | [repeat circle with dot] | PRINTED IN THE UNITED STATES OF AMERICA | BY THE VAIL-BALLOU PRESS, BINGHAMPTON, NEW | YORK AND BOUND BY THE J. F. TAPLEY COMPANY | [repeat circle with dot]

Binding: Dark blue cloth covered boards stamped in gold. Top edge stained black and all edges trimmed. Front: DON JUAN | JOSEPH DELTEIL | [design] Spine: [design] | [rule] | DON | JUAN | [circle with dot in the center] | DELTEIL

| [rule] | [design] | [Jonathan Cape logo]   NOTE: A variant binding with BLACKFRIAR | PRESS substituted for the Cape and Smith logo at the bottom of the spine.

Dust jacket: Gray paper printed in black, blue and beige.   Front: [beige on black background] DON JUAN | [illustration of man in period dress; heart design and ten beige asterisks] | JOSEPH DELTEIL | THE AUTHOR OF JOAN D'ARC   Spine: DON | JUAN | [white dot] | DELTEIL | [heart design] | [four beige asterisks] | JONATHAN CAPE | HARRISON SMITH   Back : List of other books by Jonathan Cape and Harrison Smith.   Front flap: Story plot. [price in lower right corner]: $2.50   Back flap: Description of *Traitor or Patriot: The Life and Death of Roger Casement* by Denis Gwynn.

Published April 6th, 1931 at $2.50.

E2   MR. KNIFE, MISS FORK   [1932]

First Edition:

a: Edition of 200 Copies:

Mr. Knife [red] | [upright knife and fork] | Miss Fork [red] | by | RÉNE CREVEL [red] | Translated by Kay Boyle [black] | Illustrated by [red] | MAX ERNST [red] | The Black Sun Press [black] | Rue Cardinale [black] | Paris [black] | MCMXXXI [red]

Collation: [i-vi], 1-38, [39-46] pages; blue endpapers. Pages numbered in red.   7" x 4 $^3/_4$"   [1-7]^4 with first and last leaves pasted to endpapers

Contents: (i-ii) blank; frontispiece covered by glassine sheet; (iii) fly title; (iv) blank; (v) title page; (vi) blank; (1-38) text; (39-40) blank; (41) [limitation statement]: This edition of Mr. Knife, Miss Fork | being a fragment of the novel Babylone | by René Crevel translated into English | by Kay Boyle and illustrated with nine- | teen photograms by Max Ernst | printed at the Black Sun Press, Paris | September 1931, is limited to 50 | numbered copies on Hollande paper signed | by the authors, 200 copies on finest bristol | paper and also 5 special copies, each copy | containing four of the original drawings. | [numbered stamped in]; (42-44) blank; (45) a list of other books for sale by Black Sun Press.

Illustrations: Covered by a glassine sheet with illustration title in red are placed before the fly title and directly after pages 2, 4, 6, 10, 12, 14, 16, 18, 20, 22, 24, 26, 28, 30, 32, and 34.

Copyright page: None

Binding: Blue buckram covered boards stamped in gold.   Front and back with identical gold floral design with gilt rule borders.   Spine: [rule] | [rule] | [design] |

[triple rule] | [design: knife and fork] | [triple rule] | [design] | [rule] | [rule] Issued in a gold trimmed slip case.

b. Signed Edition:

The signed edition is the same as above except bound in black cloth covered boards with black endpapers. The front covers are stamped with a gold floral design, gold and blue ruled borders and a red gold center design. The back is similar but without red and blue stamp. These copies are numbered in pencil and signed on the fly title.

Published in September 1931

E3a   DEVIL IN THE FLESH   1932

First Edition:

Devil | in the Flesh | by | Raymond Radiguet | translated by Kay Boyle | introduction | by Aldous Huxley | PARIS | Crosby Continental Editions | 2, Rue Cardinale | 1932

Collation: [i-iv], v-viii, [no 1-8], 9-35, [36], 37-47, [48], 49-69, [70], 71-85, [86], 87-107, [108], 109-119, [120], 121-135, [136], 137-155, [156], 157-199, [200], 201, [202], 203-213, [214], 215-217, [218], 219-229, [230], 231-237, [238], 239-253, [254-256] pages. $6^{1}/_{2}$" x $4^{1}/_{2}$" $[1]^8$ 2-16^8

Contents: (i) half title page; (ii) blank; (iii) title page; (iv) blank; (v-viii) introduction; (9-35) text; (36) blank; (37-47) blank; (48) blank; (49-85) text; (86) blank; (87-107) text; (108) blank; (109-119) text; (120) blank; (121-135) text; (136) blank; (137-155) text; (156) blank; (157-199) text; (200) blank; (201) text; (202) blank; (203-213) text; (214) blank; (215-217) text; (218) blank; (219-229) text; (230) blank; (231-237) text; (238) blank; (239-253) text; (254) blank; (255) publisher's statement; (256) PUBLISHED BY | THE BLACK SUN PRESS | 2, RUE CARDINALE | PARIS | [short rule] | PRINTED BY | f. PAILLART | PARIS — ABBEVILLE | [short rule] | JANUARY 1932.

Copyright page: See contents page 256

Binding: Cream paper wraps printed in red.   Top edge unstained and all edges trimmed.   Front: World-wide Master-pieces in English | Devil | in the Flesh | by | Raymond Radiguet | translated by Kay Boyle | [Crosby Continental logo] | Crosby Continental Editions | Paris   Spine: No. 2 | Devil | in the | Flesh | [Crosby Continental logo] | Radiguet | 10 fr.   Back: Not to be introduced | into the British Empire and U.S.A. | Sole distributors Hachette, Paris   Front flap: A note about the previous appearance of Hemingway's *The Torrents of Spring* and a note about Crosby Continental Editions by Aldous Huxley.   Back flap: A note about future Crosby Continental Editions.

Published in January 1932 at 10 francs.

E3b   THE DEVIL IN THE FLESH   1932

First American Edition:

BY R. RADIGUET | *Foreword by Aldous Huxley* | *Translated by Kay Boyle* | The | DEVIL | in the | FLESH | 1932 | *Crosby Continental Editions, Paris* | HARRISON SMITH • NEW YORK   [all the preceding enclosed in a wavy rectangle]

Collation: [i-vi], vii-x, [no 1-10], [11-12], 13-43, [44], 45-95, [96], 97-105, [106], 107-119, [120], 121-129, [130], 131-135, [136], 137-139, [140], 141-159, [160], 161-171, [172], 173-179, [180], 181-195, [196], 197-205, [206], 207-228, [229-230] pages; cream end papers.   7 $^3/_8$" x 5"   [A^8- O^8]   Signatures are incorporated into the front pastedown and free end paper and also into the rear pastedown and rear free endpaper.

Contents: (i) half title page; (ii) *Harrison Smith, Inc. – 17 E. 49th St. – New York;* (iii) title page; (iv) copyright page; (v) FOREWORD; (vi) blank; (vii-x) foreword by Aldous Huxley; (11) fly title page; (12) blank; (13-43) text; (44) blank; (45-95) text; (96) blank; (97-105) text; (106) blank; (107-119) text; (120) blank; (121-129) text; (130) blank; (131-135) text; (136) blank; (137-139) text; (140) blank; (141-159) text; (160) blank; (161-171) text; (172) blank; (173-179) text; (180) blank; (181-195) text; (196) blank; (197-205) text; (206) blank; (207-228) text; (229-230) blank.

Copyright page: *Copyright, 1932, by Harrison Smith, Inc.* | *First published in the United States in 1932* | *Printed in the United States of America*

Binding: Light blue green cloth covered boards printed in black. Top edge unstained and all edges trimmed. Front: Blank.   Spine: The | DEVIL | in the | FLESH | R. RADIGUET   Back: Blank.

Dust jacket: Yellow paper printed in black and red.   Front: RAYMOND RADIGUET'S | The | Devil | in the | Flesh | TRANSLATION BY KAY BOYLE | FOREWORD BY ALDOUS HUXLEY   [There is a wide red stripe down the middle of the yellow jacket with a woman's hair and extending from the left and a devil's tail and cloven hoof extending from the right]   Spine: RAYMOND | RADIGUET | THE | DEVIL | IN THE | FLESH | [Harrison Smith design]   [wide red strip down the spine from top to bottom with two thin red lines on each side]   Back: Blurbs for other books published or to be published by Harrison Smith.   Front flap: Story plot for *Devil in the Flesh.* [price In lower right corner] $2.50.   Back flap: Story plot for Ward Greene's *Weep No More.*

Published the week of February 27, 1932 at $2.50.

E3c   DEVIL IN THE FLESH   1948

Second American Edition:

Devil | in the Flesh | by | Raymond Radiguet | translated by Kay Boyle | introduction | by Aldous Huxley | Black Sun Press | 1948

Collation: [i-iv], v-viii, [no 1-8], 9-35, [36], 37-47, [48], 49-69, [70], 71-85, [86], 87-107, [108], 109-119, [120], 121-135, [136], 137-155, [156], 157-213, [214], 215-217, [218], 219-229, [230], 231-237, [238], 239-253, [254] pages; $6^1/_4$" x $4^1/_2$" [A-H]^{16} endpapers are incorporated into the signatures with the first page of A being the front pastedown and the last page of H being the back pastedown.

Contents: (i) half title page; (ii) photograph from the movie; (iii) title page; (iv) copyright page; (v-viii) introduction; (9-35) text; (36) photograph from the movie; (37-47) text; (48) photograph from the movie; (49-69) text; (70) photograph from the movie; (71-85) text; (86) photograph from the movie; (87-107) text; (108) photograph from the movie; (109-119) text; (120) photograph from the movie; (121-135) text; (136) photograph from the movie; (137-155) text; (156) photograph from the movie; (157-213) text; (214) photograph from the movie; (215-217) text; (218) photograph from the movie; (219-229) text; (230) photograph from the movie; (231-237) text; (238) photograph from the movie; (239-253) text; (254) blank.

Copyright page: *Copyright assigned 1948 to Caresse Crosby* | Published by The Black Sun Press | All Rights Reserved | Printed in the United States of America

Binding: Red cloth covered boards stamped in gold. Top edge unstained and all edges trimmed. Front: Gold stamped face of the Devil. Spine: Devil | in the | Flesh Back: Blank.

Dust jacket: White paper printed in red. Front: World-wide Masterpieces in English | Devil | in the Flesh | *Le Diable au Corps* | by | Raymond Radiguet | translated by Kay Boyle | [Crosby Continental Editions logo] | Crosby Continental Editions | Paris | The Black Sun Press | Washington   Spine: [printed downward] *Devil in the Flesh*   Back: Photograph from the movie in red tones. Front flap: The Only Complete Illustrated Edition | Price $1.50 Back flap: Blank.

E3d   DEVIL IN THE FLESH   1948

Third American Edition:

Devil | in the Flesh | by | Raymond Radiguet | translated by Kay Boyle | introduction | by Aldous Huxley | Black Sun Press | 1948 | 2008 Q Street, N.W., Washington, D.C.

Collation: [i-iv], v-viii, [no 1-8], 9-35, [36], 37-47, [48], 49-69, [70], 71-85, [86], 87-107, [108], 109-119, [120], 121-135, [136], 137-155, [156], 157-213, [214], 215-217, [218], 219-229, [230], 231-237, [238], 239-253, [254-256] pages; $6^1/_4$" x $4^1/_2$"   [A-H][16]

Contents: (i) half title page; (ii) blank; (iii) title page; (iv) copyright page; (v-viii) introduction; (9-35) text; (36) blank; (37-47) text; (48) blank; (49-69) text; (70) blank; (71-85) text; (86) blank; (87-107) text; (108) blank; (109-119) text; (120) blank; (121-135) text; (136) blank; (137-155) text; (156) blank; (157-213) text; (214) blank; (215-217) text; (218) blank; (219-229) text; (230) blank; (231-237) text; (238) blank; (239-253) text; (254) blank.

Copyright page: *Copyright 1932, Harrison Smith, Inc.* | *Copyright assigned 1948 to Caresse Crosby* | Published by The Black Sun Press | All rights Reserved | Printed in the United States of America | by The Polygraphic Company of America

Binding: White paper wraps printed in red.   Top edge unstained and all edges trimmed.   Front: World-wide Masterpieces in English | Devil | in the Flesh | *Le Diable au Corps* | by | Raymond Radiguet | translated by Kay Boyle | [Crosby Continental Editions logo] | Crosby Continental Editions | Paris | The Black Sun Press | Washington   Spine: Devil | in | the | Flesh | Radiguet | 1948 Back: Blank.

E3e   THE DEVIL IN THE FLESH   [1949]

Second American Paperback Edition:

Devil in the Flesh | by | Raymond Radiguet | translated by Kay Boyle | introduction by | Aldous Huxley | [publishers logo] A SIGNET BOOK | Published by THE NEW AMERICAN LIBRARY

Collation: [1-8], 9-144 pages.   7" x $4^1/_4$"

Contents: (1) half title page; (2) blank; (3) title page; (4) copyright page; (5-7) introduction; (8) blank; (9-144) text.

Copyright page: COPYRIGHT, 1932, BY CARESS CROSBY | *Crosby Continental Editions 1932-1948,* | *copyright of all rights reserved* | *by Caress Crosby* | *Published as a SIGNET BOOK* | *by arrangement with Caresse Crosby* | FIRST PRINTING, NOVEMBER, 1949 | The picture of Raymond Radiguet, on page v, | is by courtesy of the Paris Theatre, New York | City — where the American premiere of *Devil* | *in the Flesh* was held. | [the following enclosed in a rectangular ruled box] *SIGNET BOOKS are published by* | *The New American Library of World Literature, Inc.* | *245 Fifth Avenue, New York 16, New York* | [the following line outside of the rectangle] PRINTED IN THE UNITED STATES OF AMERICA

Binding: White paper pictorial wraps printed in brown, black, blue yellow and white. Front: [printed in black on a yellow panel across the top] 750 | Temptation • Passion • Tenderness | [Signet logo] | the following printed in white on the picture panel. The picture is of a young boy on a bed with a woman] DEVIL IN THE FLESH | [printed in yellow] Raymond Radiguet | [printed in white on a black band across the bottom] SIGNET BOOKS | Complete and unabridged   Spine: [printed horizontal on dark yellow band] 750 | [printed downward on lighter yellow than above] DEVIL IN THE FLESH   Raymond Radiguet   Back: Excerpts from some reviews and a short blurb about Raymond Radiguet.

E3f   THE DEVIL IN THE FLESH   [1949]

First English Edition:

RAYMOND RADIGUET | THE | DEVIL IN | THE FLESH | *translated by Kay Boyle* | *with an introduction by* | *Aldous Huxley* | GREY WALLS PRESS

Collation: [1-8], 9-167, [168] pages; cream endpapers. 7 $^1/_8$" x 4 $^3/_4$"   [A]^8 B-H^8 J-K^8 L^4

Contents: (1) half title page; (2) blank; (3) title page; (4) copyright page; (5-7) Introduction; (8) blank; (9-167) text; (168) blank.

Copyright page: *English translation | first published in 1932 | by the Black Sun Press, Paris. | This edition published in 1949 | by the Grey Walls Press Limited, | 7 Crown Passage, Pall Mall, London, S.W. 1 | Printed in Great Britain | by C.W.S. Printing Works, | Longsight, Manchester* | AUSTRALIA | *The Invincible Press* | *Sydney, Melbourne, Brisbane, Adelaide* | NEW ZEALAND | *The Invincible Press, Wellington* | SOUTH AFRICA | *M. Darling (Pty.) Ltd., Capetown*

Binding: Pink cloth covered boards stamped in gold. Top edge unstained with all edges trimmed. Front: Blank.   Spine: THE | DEVIL | IN | THE | FLESH | *RAYMOND* | *RADIGUET* | [design] | *G.W.P.* Back: Blank.

Dust jacket: White paper pictorial jacket printed in red, yellow and white. Front: THE | DEVIL | IN THE | FLESH [the preceding letters in black with yellow highlight stripe] | *RAYMOND* | *RADIGUET* [red] [all the preceding enclosed in a white shield-like design edged in yellow. [at the top of the shield the busts of two ladies facing each other and the bottom of the shield the head of a man looking straight ahead. Spine: RAYMOND | RADIGUET [black] | THE | DEVIL | IN | THE | FLESH [enclosed in similar but smaller shield with same lettering as the front with a cup at the head of the shield and the head of a woman facing outward at the bottom] | *G. W. P.* [white outlined letters with red showing through. Back: Blurb about the book *Marie Donadieu* by Charles Louis Philippe. Front flap: Blurb

about *The Devil in the Flesh*   Price in lower right corner: 8s, 6d. | net   Back flap:
Catalogue No. R6729   [lower left corner]

E4a   BABYLON   1985

First Edition:

A NOVEL >>>>>>>>>>>>>>>>>>>>>>>>> | BABYLON | >>>>>>>>>>>>>>>>>>
RÉNE CREVEL | Illustrated by MAX ERNST | Translated and with an | Afterword
by KAY BOYLE | North Point Press *San Francisco* | 1985

Collation: [i-iv], v-vi, [1,2], 3-7, [8], 9-13, [14], 15-19, [20], 21-25, [26], 27-33,
[34], 35-37, [38], 39-45, [46], 47-49, [50], 51-63, [64], 65-71, [72], 73-79, [80],
81-93, [94], 95-99, [100], 101-105, [106], 107-113, [114], 115-121, [122], 123-
133, [134], 135-141, [142], 143-169, [170] pages; gray endpapers. 9 $\frac{1}{8}$" x 5 $\frac{3}{8}$"

Contents: (i) [publisher's logo in upper right corner; (ii) blank; (iii) title page; (iv)
copyright page; (v-vi) preface; (1) fly title; (2) illustration; (3-7) text; (8) illustration;
(9-13) text; (14) illustration; (15-19) text; (20) illustration; (21-25) text; (26) illustration; (27-33) text; (34) illustration; (35-37) text; (38) illustration; (39-45) text;
(46) illustration; (47-49) text; (50) illustration; (51-63) text; (64) illustration; (65-
71) text; (72) illustration; (73-79) text; (80) illustration; (81-93) text; (94) illustra-
tion; (95-99) text; (100) illustration; (101-105) text; (106) illustration; (107-113)
text; (114) illustration; (115-121) text; (122) illustration; (123-133) text; (134)
illustration; (135-141; (142) illustration; (143-169) text; (170) blank.

Copyright page: Originally published in French as *Babylone*, 1927; | translation pub-
lished by arrangement with | Éditions Jean-Jacques Pauvert, Paris. | Translation and
Afterword copyright © 1985 | by Kay Boyle, | Chapter one, "Mr. Knife, Miss Fork,"
was | originally published by Black Sun Press in a | limited edition in 1931. | Max
Ernst' s photograms are printed with | the permission of Dallas Ernst. | Printed in
the United States of America. | Library of Congress Catalogue Number: 84—62302
| ISBN: 0—86547—191—6

Binding: Dark Gray cloth covered boards stamped in silver. Front: Blank. Spine:
[printed downward] BABYLON   RENE [over] CREVEL   [design] [publisher's
logo]

Dust jacket: White paper printed in red white and black. Front: [printed in white]
RENÉ CREVEL <<<<<<>>>>>> A NOVEL | [printed in red] BABYLON | [printed
in white] Translated and with an Afterword by KAY BOYLE | Illustrated by MAX
ERNST | [the rest of the front is covered with three telephone poles with multiple
cross bars which are filled with birds] Spine: [printed downward in red] Babylon |
[printed downward in white] RENÉ [printed downward in white and under René]
CREVEL [printed in red the same series of opposing arrows like on the front] Back:
[picture of René Crevel with a short biographical note. Front flap: Story plot. Back

flap: Short biographical note about Kay Boyle and other books published by North Point Press.

Note: Kay Boyle claimed to have collaborated with Laurence Vail in translating *Bubu of Montparnasse* by Charles-Louis Philippe with a preface by T. S. Eliot. Paris: Crosby Continental Editions, 1932   218 pages, which was also published in a revised edition by Avalon Press, inc., New York, 1945.

F

Translations of Kay Boyle's Works

F1   *Avant-Hier* (*Year Before Last*) Paris: Calman Levy, 1937 Translated into French by Marie Louise Soupault.

F2   *Lawine* (*Avalanche*) Amsterdam: G. W. Breughel, [n.d.] 239 pages. Translated into Dutch by C. Houwaard.

F3   *Avalanche* Rio de Janeiro: O Cruzeiro, S.A. 1946 wraps 186 pages. Translated into Portuguese by Maluh Ouro Prêto.

F4   *La Nuit de Lundi* (*Monday Night*) Paris: Le Club Francais du Livre, 1952 257 pages. Translated into French by René Guyonnet.

F5   *Generation ohne Abshied* (*Generation Without Farewell*) Bern: Scherz, [ca. 1962] 268 pages Translated into German by Egon Strohm.

F6   *La verdad increible* (*Breaking the Silence*) Buenos Aires: Instituto Judio-Argentino de Cultura e Informacion, 1963   Translated into Spanish by Natalio Mazur.

F7   *Relambrando a Historia* (*Breaking the Silence*) Rio de Janeiro: Instituto Brasileiro Judaico de Cultura e Divulgcao, 1964   14 leaves stapled at the center.

F8   *Quatre Visions de l'Amérique* (*Four Visions of America*) Paris: Éditions Buchet/Chastel, [1978]   Wraps. 192 pages.   Translated into French by Fabrice Hélion.

F9   *Relatos (Falsamente) Inocentes* (*Life Being the Best and Other Stories*) Barcelona: Icaria Editorial, S. A., [1988] wraps 174 pages.   Translated into Spanish by Gloria Uyá with an introduction by Sandra Whipple Spanier.

F10   *Der rauchende Berg* (*The Smoking Mountain*). Frankfurt am Main: Neue Kritik, [1991] 254 pages   Translated into German by Hannah Harders.

F11   *Eisbaren und andere: Erzählungen* (excerpts from *Wedding Day and Other Stories* and *The First Lover and Other Stories*) [Frankfurt am Main]: Verlag Neu Kritik, [1992]   224 pages   Translated into German by Hannah Harders.

F12   *Das Schweigen der Nachtigall* (*Plagued by the Nightingale*) [Frankfurt am Main]: Verlag Neue Kritik, [1993]   256 pages   Translated into German by Hannah Harders.

F13   *Das Jahr davor*   (Year Before Last)   [Frankfort am Main]: Verlag Neue Kritik, [1994]   276 pages   Translated into German by Hannah Harders.

F14   *Die weisen Pferde von Wien*   (*The White Horses of Vienna*)   [Frankfurt am Main]: Verlag Neue Kritik, [1995]   Translated into German by Hannah Harders.

F15   *Das kleine Kamel*   (*The Youngest Camel*)   [Frankfurt am Main]: Fisher Taschenbuch Verlag, [1998]   110 pages.   Translated into German by Alissa Walser and illustrated by Sabine Wilharm.

F16   *Meine nächste Braut (My Next Bride)* [Frankfurt am Main]: Verlag Neue Kritik, [2000]   277 pages.   Translated into German by Hannah Harders.

G

Dust Jacket Blurbs

G1   *Memory of Love* by Bessie Breuer. New York: Simon and Schuster, 1935

G2   *The Last Optimist* by J. Alvarez Del Vayo. New York: The Viking Press, 1950

G3   *The Dark and the Light* by Elio Vittorini. New York: A New Directions Book, [1960]

G4   *The Messenger* by Charles Wright. New York: Farrar, Straus & Giroux, [1963]

G5   *The Whistling Zone* by Herbert Kubly. New York: Simon & Schuster, 1963 The book has a fairly long blurb, but the advanced reading copy (wraps) has an almost two page long statement from which the blurb was taken.

G6   *January* by David Shapiro. New York: Holt, Rinehart and Winston, [1965]

G7   *Mark Twain and the Three R's* edited with an introduction by Maxwell Geismer, Indianapolis/New York: The Bobbs-Merrill Company, Inc., [1973]

G8   *Absolutely Nothing to Get Alarmed About* by Charles Wright. The dust jacket on the uncorrected page proof has a short blurb by Kay Boyle about Charles Wright's novel *The Messenger* part of which appeared on the jacket of that novel. The final book, however, has a blurb for *Absolutely Nothing to Get Alarmed About*.

G9   *A Memory and Other Stories* by Mary Lavin. Boston: Houghton Mifflin, 1973

G10   *Aiiieeeee!* edited by Frank Chin, Jeffrey Paul Chan, Lawson Fusao Inada, Shawn Hsu Wong. Garden City, New York: Anchor Press/Doubleday, 1975

G11   *The Woman Warrior* by Maxine Hong Kingston. New York: Alfred A. Knopf, 1976

G12   *Homebase* by Shawn Wong. New York: I. Reed Books, [1979]

G13   *The Princess of 72nd Street* by Elaine Kraf. New York: A New Directions Book, [1979]

G14   *Island: Poetry and History of Chinese Immigrants on Angel Island 1910-1940* by Him Mark Lai, Genny Lim and Judy Yung. San Francisco: HOC DOI, [1980]

G15   *Love Medicine* by Louise Erdrich. New York Holt, Rinehart and Winston, [1984]

G16   *The Chinaman Pacific* & *Frisco R.R. Co.* by Frank Chin. Minneapolis: Coffee House Press, 1988

G17   *Tracks* by Louise Erdrich. New York: Henry Holt and Company, [1988]

G18   *Samuel Beckett's Wake and Other Uncollected Prose* by Edward Dahlberg. [Elmwood Park, Il]: Dalkey Archives Press, [1989]

G19   *Take One as Needed* by Oscar London, M.D., W.B.D. Berkeley, California: Ten Speed Press, [1989]

G20   *Post Adolescence: A Selection of Short Fiction* by Robert McAlmon. Albuquerque: University of New Mexico Press, [1991]

G21   *Concrete Music* by F.D. Reeve. Amherst: Pyncheon House, [1992]

H

Appearances in Anthologies

H1   *Anthology of Magazine Verse for 1923 and Yearbook of American Poetry.* Edited by William Stanley Braithwaite. Boston: B. J. Brimmer Company, 1923.
Contains: First book appearance of "Monody to the Sound of Zithers." (47) see B1.

H2   *The Second American Caravan: A Yearbook of American Literature.* Edited by Alfred Kreymborg, Lewis Mumford and Paul Rosenfeld. New York: The Macaulay Company, 1928.
Contains: First book appearance of "A Christmas Carol for Emanuel Carnevali" and "Madame Tout Petit." (307-311) see B2.

H3   *transition* [sic] *Stories: Twenty-Three Stories from "transition."* Edited by Eugene Jolas and Robert Sage. New York: Walter V. McKee, 1929.
Contains: First book appearance of "Polar Bears and Others." (17-25) see B3.

H4   *The Best Short Stories of 1931 and the Yearbook of the American Short Story.* Edited by Edward J. O'Brien. New York: Dodd, Mead & Company, 1931.
Contains: First book appearance of "Rest Cure." (47-54) see B5.

H5   *Readies for Bob Brown's Machine* by A. Lincoln Gillespie, Jr., John A. Farrell, Alfred Kreymborg, John Banting, Axton Clark, Kay Boyle, B.C. Hagglund, K.T. Young, Carlton Brown, Laurence Vail, Charles Beadle, Lloyd Stern, Clare L. Brackett, Manuel Komroff, Charles Henri Ford, Nancy Cunard, Daphne Carr, Norman MacLeod, Donal MacKenzie, Paul Bowles, Eugene Jolas, Peter Neagoè, Ezra Pound, Richard Johns, Filippo Tommaso Marinetti, Robert McAlmon, George Kent, Rose Brown, Gertrude Stein, Rue Menken, Herman Spector, Samuel Putnam, Hilaire Hiler, Sydney Hunt, Hiler, pere, Theodor Pratt, J. Jones, Walter Lowenfels, James T. Farrell, Wambly Bald, Jay du Von and William Carlos Williams, Cagnes-sur-Mer: Roving Eye Press, 1931.
Contains: First book appearance of "Change of Life" and "Landscape for Wyn Henderson." (37-41) see B6.

H6   *O. Henry Memorial Award Prize Stories of 1932.* Edited by Blanch Colton Williams. Garden City, New York: Doubleday, Doran & Company, 1932.
Contains: First book appearance of "The First Lover" (71-76) with biographical note. (70) see B7.

H7   *An Anthology of the Younger Poets.* Edited by Oliver Wells. Philadelphia: The
      Centaur Press, 1932.
      Contains: First book appearance of "A Comeallye for Robert Carlton
      Brown" and "A Statement." (85-95) see B8.

H8   *Americans Abroad: An Anthology.* Edited by Peter Neagoé. The Hague:
      Sevire Press, 1932. Contains: "A Comeallye for Robert Carlton Brown."
      (37-41) see B9.

H9   *Capajon: Fifty-Four Short Stories Published 1921-1933.* with an introduction
      by Edward Garnett. London: Jonathan Cape, [1933].
      Contains: "Summer." (118-123)

H10   *A Story Anthology 1931-1933.* Edited by Whit Burnett and Martha Foley.
      New York: The Vanguard Press, 1933.
      Contains: "Rest Cure." (45-53)

H11   *Short Story Hits, 1932: An Interpretive Anthology.* Edited by Thomas H.
      Uzzell. New York: Harcourt Brace and Company, [1933].
      Contains: "To the Pure" (229-237) with critical notes (290) and technical
      analysis. (321-322)

H12   *Twentieth Century Short Stories.* Selected by Sylvia Chatfield Bates. Boston:
      Houghton Mifflin Company, [1933].
      Contains: "First Lover" (321-327) with short biographical note. (320)

H13   *Editor's Choice.* Edited by Alfred Dashiell. New York: G.P. Putnam's Sons,
      [1934].
      Contains: "Black Boy" (170-176) with critical note. (176)

H14   *Short Stories of Today.* Edited by Raymond Woodbury Pence. New York: The
      Macmillan Company, 1934.
      Contains: "Friend of the Family." (30-38)

H15   *O. Henry Memorial Award Prize Stories of 1935.* Edited by Harry Hanson.
      Garden City, New York: Doubleday, Doran & Company, 1935.
      Contains: First book appearance of "The White Horses of Vienna" (3-20)
      with biographical introduction. (2) see B10.

H16   *A Book of Contemporary Short Stories.* Edited by Dorothy Brewster. New
      York: The Macmillan Company, 1936.
      Contains: "Rest Cure" (35-44) with introductory note. (34)

H17   *New Directions in Prose and Poetry.* Edited by James Laughlin, IV. Norfolk:
      New Directions, 1936.
      Contains: "January the Twenty-Fourth, New York," "February the Ninth,
      USA," and "May the Twenty-Third, USA." (Unpaginated)

H18 *365 Days*. Edited by Kay Boyle, Laurence Vail and Nina Conarain. New York: Harcourt Brace and Company, [1936].
Contains: Ninety-six short pieces under her own name and apparently several others under pseudonyms. see B12.

H19 *Neue Amerika: Zwansig Erzähler der Gegenwart*. Herausgegeben und eingeleitet von Kurt Ullrich. Berlin: S. Fischer Verlag, 1937. wraps.
Contains: "Dein Leib ist ein Juwelenschrein" ("Your Body is a Jewel Box") (65-86) with biographical sketch. (65) Translated by Mildred Harnacke-Fish.

H20 *New Directions in Prose and Poetry 1937*. Norfolk, Connecticut: New Directions, [1937].
Contains: First book appearance of "Funeral in Hungary." (79-80) see B13.

H21 *50 Best American Short Stories, 1915-1939*. Edited by Edward J. O'Brien. Boston: Houghton Mifflin Company, 1939.
Contains: "Rest Cure" (403-412) with biographical note. (860)

H22 *New Directions in Prose & Poetry 1939*. Norfolk, Connecticut: New Directions, [1939].
Contains: First book appearance of "World Tour." (63-65) see B15.

H23 *O. Henry Memorial Award Prize Stories of 1939*. Edited by Harry Hanson. New York: Doubleday, Doran & Company, 1939.
Contains: First book appearance of "Anschluss" (79-102) with introductory note. (78) see B16.

H24 *Short Stories: A Collection of Types of the Short Story*. Edited by William Thompson Hastings, Benjamin Crocker Clough, and Kenneth Oliver Mason. Revised edition. Boston: Houghton MifflinCompany, [1939].
Contains: "Art Colony." (402-408)

H25 *Tellers of Tales: 100 Short Stories from The United States, England, France, Russia, and Germany*. Selected and with an Introduction by W. Somerset Maugham. New York: Doubleday, Doran and Company, 1939.
Contains: "Convalescence." (1505-1518)

H26 *The Best Short Stories, 1940*. Edited by Edward J. O'Brien. Boston: Houghton Mifflin Company, 1940.
Contains: "Anschluss." (1-19)

H27 *O. Henry Memorial Award Prize Stories of 1940*. Edited by Harry Hanson. New York: Doubleday, Doran & Company, 1940.
Contains: First book appearance of "Poor Monsieur Panalitus" (59-60) with introductory note. (58) see B18.

H28   *Short Stories from the New Yorker.* No stated editor. New York: Simon &
       Schuster, 1940.
       Contains: "Black Boy" and "Kroy Wen." (42-47)

H29   *O. Henry Memorial Award Prize Stories of 1941.* Edited by Herschel Brickell.
       Garden City, New York: Doubleday, Doran and Company, Inc., 1941.
       Contains: First book appearance of "Defeat" (3-13) with biographical note.
       (2) see B19.

H30   *Vertical: A Yearbook for Romantic-Mystic Ascensions.* Edited by Eugene Jolas.
       New York: The Gotham Book Mart Press, [1941].
       Contains: First book appearance of "Two Fragments from an Aviation Epic."
       (20-29) see B20.

H31   *Post Stories of 1941.* Edited by Wesley Winans Stout. Boston: Little, Brown
       and Company, 1942.
       Contains: First book appearance of "Let There Be Honour." (19-40) see B22.

H32   *American Harvest: Twenty Years of Creative Writing in the United States.*
       Edited by Allen Tate and John Peale Bishop. New York: L.B. Fisher, [1942].
       Reprinted Garden City: Doubleday and Company, [1943].
       Contains: "Defeat" (339-349) with biographical note. (541)

H33   *The Best American Short Stories 1942 and the Yearbook of the American Short
       Story.* Edited by Martha Foley. Boston: Houghton Mifflin Company, [1942].
       Contains: First book appearance of "Nothing Ever Breaks Except the Heart"
       (41-49) with biographical note. (423) see B23.

H34   *This Is My Best.* Edited by Whit Burnett. New York: The Dial Press, 1942.
       Contains: First book appearance of "They Weren't Going to Die" with an
       article by her about why she chose this story for inclusion in this anthology.
       (1005-1011) see B24.

H35   *O. Henry Memorial Award Prize Stories of 1942.* Edited by Herschel Brickell.
       Garden City, New York: Doubleday, Doran and Company, Inc., 1942
       Contains: First book appearance of "Their Name Is Macaroni" (91-102)
       with introductory note. (90) see B25.

H36   *The Best American Short Stories 1943 and the Yearbook of the American Short
       Story.* Edited by Martha Foley. Boston: Houghton Mifflin Company, [1943].
       Contains: First book appearance of "Frenchman's Ship" (23-40) with
       biographical note. (413) see B27.

H37   *Literature and Life in America.* Edited by Dudley Miles and Robert C.
       Pooley, Chicago: Scott Foreman, and Company, [1943].
       Contains: First book appearance of "Hilaire and the Maréchal Pétard."
       (534-551) see B29.

H38   *O. Henry Memorial Award Prize Stories of 1943.* Edited by Herschel Brickell. Garden City, New York: Doubleday, Doran and Company, Inc., 1943. Contains: First book appearance of "The Canals of Mars." (77-88) see B28.

H39   *Fourteen of Them.* by John Hersey, Helen McInnes, John Cecil Holm, Kurt Steel, Faith Baldwin, Clyde Brion Davis, Sarah Lorimer, Elizabeth Hollister Frost, Adela Rogers St. Johns, Margaret Widdemer, William Rose Benét, Helen Worden, Kay Boyle, Fannie Hurst, with a foreword by Mary Roberts Rinehart. New York and Toronto: Farrar & Rinehart, [1944]. Contains: First book appearance of "Anthony John Rizzi, Radioman, 3rd Class, U.S.N." (71-74) with biographical note. (81) see B30.

H40   *Thirteen Stories* chosen by Wrey Gardiner. London: The Grey Walls Press, [1944]. Contains: First book appearance of "Wanderer." (35-44) see B32.

H41   *American Writing 1943: The Anthology and Yearbook of the American Non-Commercial Magazine.* Edited by Alan Swallow. Boston: Bruce Humphries, Inc. Publishers, [1944] Contains: "Wanderer." (19-27)

H42   *It's a Woman's World: A Collection of Stories from Harper's Bazaar.* Edited by Mary Louise Aswell. New York and London: Whittlesey House/McGraw-Hill Book Company, Inc., [1944]. Contains: "The Canals of Mars." (107-116)

H43   *New Road: 1944: New Directions in European Art and Letters* Edited by Alex Comfort and John Bayliss. London: The Grey Walls Press, [1944]. Contains: "A Communication to Nancy Cunard." (223-226)

H44   *The Story Pocket Book.* Edited by Whit Burnett. New York: Pocket Books, Inc., [1944]. Wraps. Contains: "Rest Cure." (296-305)

H45   *The PL Book of Modern American Short Stories.* Edited by Nicholas Moore. London: Editions Poetry, [1945]. Contains: "His Idea of a Mother." (142-148)

H46   *Primer for White Folks.* Edited by Bucklin Moon. Garden City: Doubleday, Doran & Company, 1945. Contains: "White as Snow." (224-232)

H47   *Time to Be Young: Great Stories of the Growing Years.* Edited by Whit Burnett. Philadelphia and New York: J.B. Lippincott, [1945]. Contains: "Black Boy" (212-216) with biographical note. (435)

H48   *Accent Anthology: Selections from Accent, a Quarterly of New Literature, 1940-1945.* Edited by Kerker Quinn and Charles Shattuck. New York: Harcourt, Brace and Company, [1946].
Contains: First book appearance of "Cairo Street" (44-50) with biographical note. (680) see B34.

H49   *A New Anthology of Modern Poetry: Revised Edition.* Edited by Seldon Rodman. New York: Random House, [1946]. Also in Modern Library Giant.
Contains: "Spiritual for Nine Voices" from "A Communication to Nancy Cunard." (113-114)

H50   *O. Henry Memorial Award Prize Stories of 1946.* Edited by Herschel Brickell. Garden City, New York: Doubleday & Company, Inc., 1946.
Contains: First book appearance of "Winter Night" (74-84) with biographical note. (306) see B35.

H51   *The Saturday Evening Post Stories. 1942-1945.* Introduced by Ben Hibbs editor of the Saturday Evening Post. New York: Random House, [1946].
Contains: "Frenchman's Ship." (62-80)

H52   *Taken at the Flood: The Human Drama as Seen by the Modern American Novelist.* Collected and arranged by Ann Watkins. New York and London: Harper and Brothers, Publishers, [1946].
Contains: "The Family of the Victim" from *Monday Night* (313-326) with critical note. (313)

H53   *Anchor in the Sea: An Anthology of Psychological Fiction.* Edited by Alan Swallow. New York: The Swallow Press and William Morrow & Company, 1947.
Contains: "Wanderer." (24-35) also wraps: Denver: Alan Swallow, [1947] (123-134); New York: The Swallow Press and William Morrow & Company, 1947. (24-35)

H54   *The Pocket Book of O. Henry Prize Stories.* Edited with an introduction by Herschel Brickell. New York: Pocket Books, [1947].
Contains: "The White Horses of Vienna." (333-351)

H55   *Spearhead: 10 Years' Experimental Writing in America.* No stated editor. [New York]: A New Directions Book, [1947].
Contains: "A Complaint for Mary and Marcel," A Communication to Nancy Cunard," and "Angels for Djuna Barnes" (405-414) with biographical note. (15)

H56   *The College Short Story Reader.* Edited by Harry W. Hastings. New York: Odyssey Press, [1948].
Contains: "First Lover." (42-48)

H57   *Junges Amerika: Preisgekrönte stories aus den USA* Berlin und München:
      Heinz Ullstein-Helmut Kindler, 1948. Translated by Hansi Bochow-
      Blüthgen with an introduction by Hellmuth Jaesrich.
      Contains: "Winterabend" ("Winter Evening") (85-98) with capsule biogra-
      phical sketch. (367-368)

H58   *The Art of Modern Fiction.* Edited by Ray B. West, Jr. and Robert Wooster
      Stallman. New York: Rinehart & Company, 1949.
      Contains: "His Idea of a Mother." with questions and exercises. (293-298)
      and with biographical note. (637)

H59   *55 Short Stories from the New Yorker.* No stated editor. New York: Simon &
      Schuster, 1949.
      Contains: "Defeat." (11-19)

H60   *The Great American Horse Omnibus from Homer to Hemingway.*
      Edited by Thurston Macaulay. Chicago: Ziff-Davis Publishing Company,
      1949.
      Contains: Excerpt from "The White Horses of Vienna." (138-140)

H61   *Transition Workshop.* Edited by Eugene Jolas. New York: The Vanguard
      Press, [1949].
      Contains: "Theme" (44-47) and "And Winter" (203) with biographical
      note. (400)

H62   *15 Stories and Suggestions for Teaching 15 Stories.* Edited by Herbert Barrows.
      Boston: D.C. Heath & Company, Inc., 1950.
      Contains: "Keep Your Pity." (23-26)

H63   *Modern Short Stories: A Critical Anthology.* Edited by Robert B. Heilman.
      New York: Harcourt, Brace and Company, [1950].
      Contains: "Effigy of War" with an introductory note and a comment.
      (155-163)

H64   *Prize Stories of 1950 the O. Henry Awards.* Edited by Herschel Brickell.
      Garden City, New York: Doubleday & Company, 1950.
      Contains: First book appearance of "Summer Evening" (89-101) with
      introductory note. (89) see B36.

H65   *Reading Fiction: A Method of Analysis with Selections for Study.* By Fred B.
      Millett. New York: Harper and Brothers, [1950].
      Contains: "Art Colony" with a short explication and story questions.
      (135-143)

H66   *Current American Thinking and Writing 2nd Series.* New York: Appleton-
      Century-Crofts, 1951.

Contains: "Lovers of Gain." Note: Not seen. This according to Roberta Sharp: "A Bibliography of Works by and about Kay Boyle." *Bulletin of Bibliography and Magazine Notes* October/December 1978

H67   *Modern Short Stories.* Edited by Marvin Felheim, Franklin B. Newman, and William R. Steinhoff. New York: Oxford University Press, [1951]. Contains: "Natives Don't Cry." (290-299)

H68   *The Saturday Evening Post Stories 1950.* New York: Random House, [1951]. Contains: First book appearance of "A Disgrace to the Family." (274-298) see B38.

H69   *American Short Stories: 1820 to the Present.* Edited by Eugene Current-Garcia and Walton Potriack. Chicago: Scott, Foreman & Company, [1952]. Revised edition [1964]. Contains: "Winter Night" with capsule biography. (559-569) Revised edition wraps. (496-507)

H70   *The Best American Short Stories 1952 and the Yearbook of the American Short Story.* Edited by Martha Foley. Boston: Houghton Mifflin Company, 1952. Contains: "The Lost" (31-48) with biographical note. (373)

H71   *The Best of the Best Short Stories 1915 to 1950.* Edited by Martha Foley. Boston: Houghton Mifflin Company, 1952. Contains: "Nothing Ever Breaks Except the Heart." (31-38)

H72   *The Best of the Nation* New York: The Nation Associates, Inc. [1952]. wraps. Contains: "The Lovers of Gain." (33-38)

H73   *Nine Short Novels.* Edited by Richard M. Ludwig and Marvin B. Perry Jr.. Boston: D.C. Heath and Company, [1952]. Contains: "The Crazy Hunter" (96-172) with biographical and critical introduction. (xv-xviii)

H74   *Reading Modern Fiction: Thirty Stories with Study Aids.* Selected and edited by Winifred Lynskey. New York: Charles Scribner's Sons, [1952. *Reading Modern Fiction: Twenty-Nine Stories* Second edition with study aids revised. [1957]. *Reading Modern Fiction: Thirty-One Stories* 3rd edition revised with critical aids [1962] *Reading Modern Fiction: 31 Stories with Critical Aids,* Fourth Edition expanded and revised: New York: Charles Scribner's Sons, [1968.] wraps. Contains: "They Weren't Going to Die" with a comment and questions for students. (43-49)

H75 *An Anthology of Stories from the Southern Review.* Edited by Cleanth Brooks and Robert Penn Warren. Baton Rouge: Louisiana State University Press, [1953].
Contains: "The Bridegroom's Body." (193-235)

H76 *The Saturday Evening Post Stories 1952.* New York: Random House, [1953].
Contains: First book appearance of "Diagnosis of a Selfish Lady." (133-150) see B40.

H77 *Short Stories in Context.* Edited by Woodburn O. Ross and A. Dayle Wallace. New York: American Book Company, [1953].
Contains: "The First Lover" with a capsule biography and questions for the student. (212-220)

H78 *First Prize Stories, 1919-1954 from the O. Henry Memorial Awards.* Introduction by Harry Hanson. Garden City: Hanover House, [1954].
Contains: "The White Horses of Vienna." (271-283) and "Defeat" (344-351) with introductory note.

H79 *The Saturday Evening Post Stories 1953.* New York: Random House, [1954].
Contains: First book appearance of "The Soldier Ran Away." (20-36) see B41.

H80 *A Treasury of Mountaineering Stories.* Edited by Daniel Talbot. New York: G.P. Putnam's Sons, [1954].
Contains: "Maiden, Maiden." (93-113)

H81 *Women on the Wall.* New York: Pyramid Books, [1954]. Paperback original. Edited by Marshall McClintock
Contains: "Your Body Is a Jewel Box." (54-70)

H82 *The Saturday Evening Post Stories 1954.* New York: Random House, [1955].
Contains: First book appearance of "Carnival of Fear." (275-307) see B43.

H83 *Masters and Masterpieces of the Short Story.* Edited by Joshua McClennen. New York: Holt, Rinehart, and Winston, [1960]. wraps
Contains: "Winter Night." (64)

H84 *Vanity Fair: A Cavalcade of the 1920s and 1930s.* Edited by Cleveland Amory and Frederic Bradlee. New York: The Viking Press, [1960].
Contains "Lydia and the Ring Doves." (221-222)

H85 *A Diamond of Years: The Best of the Woman's Home Companion.* Edited by Helen Otis Lamont. Garden City, New York: Doubleday & Company, 1961.

Contains: First book appearance of "Luck for the Road." (567-588) see B45.

H86   *Stories of Modern America*. Edited by Herbert Gold and David L. Stephenson. New York: St. Martin's Press, 1961.
Contains: "Winter Night" with a note, editor's analysis and questions. (45-55)

H87   *Lesbian Love in Literature* edited by Stella Fox. New York: Avon Book Division, [1962].
Contains: An excerpt from *Monday Night* . (Chapter 14 pp. 7-16)

H88   *Modern Short Stories: The Fiction of Experience*. Edited by M. X. Lesser and John N. Morris. New York: McGraw-Hill Book Company, 1962.
Contains: "Your Body Is a Jewel Box." (317-331)

H89   *First Prize Stories 1919-1963 from the O. Henry Memorial Awards*. Introduction by Harry Hanson. Garden City: Doubleday & Company, Inc., [1963].
Contains: "The White Horses of Vienna" with note (271-283) and "Defeat" (344-351) with introductory note. (271)

H90   *Introduction to Literature: Stories/Poems/Plays* Edited by Lynn Altenbernd and Leslie L. Lewis. New York: The Macmillan Company, [1963]. 2nd edition [1969] enlarged and revised. wraps.
Contains: "The White Horses of Vienna." (413-421)

H91   *When Women Look at Men: An Anthology*. Edited by John A. Kouwenhoven and Janice Farrar Thaddeus. New York: Harper & Row, Publishers, [1963].
Contains: "Effigy of War." (17-23)

H92   *The Modern Short Story in the Making*. Edited by Whit and Hallie Burnett. New York and London: Hawthorne Books, Inc. [1964].
Contains: "Rest Cure" (185-192) with short biography and interview. (192-194) see B51.

H93   *Best Modern Short Stories Selected from The Saturday Evening Post*. New York: Curtis Books/A Division of The Curtis Publishing Company, [1965].
Contains: "The Ballet of Central Park" (236-249) with a biographical note. (487) see B54.

H94   *Fifty Best American Short Stories: 1915-1965*. Edited by Martha Foley. Boston: Houghton Mifflin Company, 1965. Reprinted New York Avenel Books, [1986].
Contains: "Nothing Ever Breaks Except the Heart" (270-277) with an introductory note. (270)

H95   *50 Great American Short Stories*. Edited and with an introduction by Milton Crane. New York: Bantam Books, [1965]. Wraps.
Contains: "Friend of the Family" (349-356) with selected bibliography. (501)

H96   *Great Short Stories of the World*. Edited by Whit and Hallie Burnett. London: Souvenir Press, [1965].
Contains: "Rest Cure." (55-61)

H97   *Introduction to the Short Story*. Edited by Robert W. Boynton and Maynard Mack. Rochell Park, NJ: Hayden Book Company, 1965. Second edition [1978]. Wraps. (191-202)
Contains: "Winter Night" with exercises.

H98   *The Realm of Fiction: 61 Short Stories* edited by James B. Hall. New York: McGraw-Hill Book Company, [1965].
Contains: "Astronomer's Wife." (367-372) 2nd edition drops "Astronomer's Wife" and adds "Black Boy" see H110.

H99   *Story Jubilee*. Edited by Whit and Hallie Burnett. Garden City: Doubleday and Company, 1965.
Contains: "Rest Cure" with note (55-62) and with critical notes. (61-62)

H100 *Studies in Fiction*. Edited by Blaze O. Bonazza and Emil Roy. New York: Harper & Row, Publishers, [1965]. wraps (305-319) 2nd Edition: New York: Harper & Row, Publishers, [1971] wraps with questions for discussion. (207-225)
Contains: "The White Horses of Vienna."

H101 *First Prize Stories 1919-1966 from the O. Henry Memorial Awards*. Introduced by Harry Hanson. Garden City: Doubleday and Company, [1966].
Contains: "The White Horses of Vienna" with note (271-283) and "Defeat" (344-351) with introductory note. (271)

H102 *Sometimes Magic: A Collection of Outstanding Stories for the Teenage Girl*. Introduction by Hallie Burnett and afterword by Jean Crabtree. New York: Platt and Monk, Publishers, [1966].
Contains: "White as Snow" with short biographical note. (50-62)

H103 *The Best American Short Stories 1967 and the Yearbook of the American Short Story*. Edited by Martha Foley and David Burnett. Boston: Houghton Mifflin Company, 1967.
Contains: First book appearance of "The Wild Horses" (25-36) with biographical note. (335) see B58.

H104   *100 Years of the American Female from Harper's Bazaar.* Edited by Jane Trahey. New York: Random House, [1967].
Contains: First book appearance of "Life Sentence." (54-59) see B59.

H105   *The Shape of Fiction: British and American Short Stories.* Edited by Leo Hamalian and Frederick R. Karl. New York: McGraw-Hill Book Company, [1967].
Contains: "Effigy of War." (61-68) 2nd edition [1978] same contents. (144-152)

H106   *Write and Rewrite: A Study of the Creative Process* by John Kuehl. New York: Meredith Press, [1967] Also published as *Creative Writing and Rewriting,* New York: Appleton-Crofts, [1967].
Contains: "The Ballet of Central Park" with explication and commentary. (21-48)

H107   *Microcosm: An Anthology of the Short Story.* Selected and Edited by Donna Gerstenberger and Frederick Garber. San Francisco: Chandler Publishing Company, [1969].
Contains: "Rest Cure" with short note. (28-35)

H108   *The World of Short Fiction.* Edited by Robert C. Albrecht. New York: The Free Press, [1969].
Contains: "The White Horses of Vienna." (153-168)

H109   *Fifty Years of the American Short Story from the O. Henry Awards 1919-1970.* Edited and with an introduction by William Abrahams. Garden City: Doubleday and Company, 1970. 2 volumes.
Contains: "The White Horses of Vienna." (volume 1 pg 116-129)

H110   *The Realm of Fiction: 65 Short Stories.* Edited by James B. Hall. New York: McGraw Hill Book Company, [1970]. 2nd edition
Contains: "Black Boy." (374-378) The 1st edition contains "Astronomer's Wife." see H98.

H111   *This is My Best in the Third Quarter of the Century.* Edited by Whit Burnett. Garden City: Doubleday and Company, [1970].
Contains: "The Wild Horses." with an explanation by Kay Boyle why she chose this story to be included (562-573) and with biographical and bibliographical note. (978-979)

H112   *Rediscoveries: Informal Essays in Which Well-Known Novelists Rediscover Neglected Works of Fiction by One of Their Favorite Authors.* Edited with an introduction by David Madden. New York: Crown Publishers, [1971].
Contains: Foreword to "The Man Outside." (75-86)

H113 *Studies in the Short Story.* Edited by Virgil Scott. New York: Holt, Rinehart and Winston, 1971.
Contains: "Astronomer's Wife" and "Effigy of War."

H114 *The Age of Anxiety: Modern American Stories.* Edited by C. Jeriel Howard and Richard Francis Tracz. Boston: Allyn & Bacon, [1972]. wraps.
Contains: "Winter Night" (201-209) and with study questions on page 209.

H115 *Enough of Dying: Voices for Peace.* Edited by Kay Boyle and Justine Van Gundy. [New York]: Dell Publishing Company, [1972]. wraps.
Contains: "They Weren't Going to Die," "The Triumph of Principles" and "A Poem Dedicated to Terre des Hommes."

H116 *Feminine Plural: Stories by Women About Growing Up* edited by Stephanie Spinner. New York: The Macmillan Company, [1972].
Contains: "Your Body Is a Jewel Box" (173-194) with biographical note. (237)

H117 *The Women Poets in English: An Anthology.* Edited with introduction by Ann Stafford. New York: McGraw-Hill Book Company, 1972.
Contains: "Thunderstorms" (227) and "New Emigration." (227-228)

H118 *Images of Women in Literature.* Edited by Mary Anne Ferguson. Boston: Houghton Mifflin Co., [1973].
Contains: "His Idea of a Mother" with short introductory note. (115-120) 2nd Edition [1977] (119-124) Wraps. Kay Boyle is excluded in the third edition.

H119 *No More Masks: An Anthology of Poems by Women* edited by Florence Howe and Ellen Bass. Garden City, New York: Anchor Press/Doubleday Anchor Books, [1973]. wraps
Contains: "A Communication to Nancy Cunard" (74-78); "The Invitation in It" from "American Citizen" (79); "For Marianne Moore's Birthday" (80); "For James Baldwin" (81-82) with capsule biography. (371)

H120 *Rising Tides: 20th Century American Women Poets.* Edited by Laura Chester and Sharon Barba, Introduction by Anaïs Nin. New York: Washington Square Press, [1973]. wraps
Contains: A note (47), "For Marianne Moore's Birthday" (48), "Excerpt from American Citizen" (48-49) and "October 1954." (50).

H121 *Fiction 100: An Anthology of Short Stories.* Edited by James H. Pickering. New York: Macmillan and Company, [1974]. wraps
Contains: "Astronomer's Wife" with questions for study (93-96) biographical note. (1030)

H122   *Little Victories Big Defeats*. Compiled by Georgess McHargue. New York: Delacorte Press, [1974].
Contains: "You Don't Have to Be a Member of the Congregation." (11-18)

H123   *200 Years of Great American Short Stories*. Edited by Martha Foley. Boston: Houghton Mifflin Company, 1975.
Contains: "Seven Say You Can Hear Corn Grow" (903-913) with short biographical sketch.

H124   *Women and Fiction: Short Stories by and about Women*. Edited by Susan Cahill. [New York]: A Mentor Book, [1975].
Contains: "Winter Night" with note (85-95) and with biographical note. (85)

H125   *Women and Men, Men and Women: An Anthology of Short Stories* edited by William Smart. New York: St. Martin's Press, [1975]. wraps
Contains: "Astronomer's Wife." (277-281)

H126   *First Flowering: The Best of the Harvard Advocate*. Edited by Richard M. Smoley. Reading, MA: Addison Wesley Publishing Company, [1977].
Contains: "A Poem About the Jews." (296-298)

H127   *The Norton Anthology of Short Fiction* edited by R. V. Cassill. New York: W.W. Norton & Company, [1977].
Contains: "Rest Cure" (121-127) with questions for study. (127)

H128   *The Poetry Anthology 1912-1977: Sixty-five Years of America's Most Distinguished Magazine*. Edited by Daryl Hine and Joseph Parisi. Boston: Houghton Mifflin Company, 1978. wraps.
Contains: "Monody to the Sound of Zithers" (84) and "To a Seaman Dead on Land." (100)

H129   *Great American Short Stories*. Selected by the editors of *The Reader's Digest*. Pleasantville, NY: The Reader's Digest Association, [1979].
Contains: "Winter Night" (395-405) with biographical note. (631)

H130   *Prize Stories of 1981: The O. Henry Awards*. Edited by William Abrahams. Garden City, New York: Doubleday & Company, 1981.
Contains: First book appearance of "St. Stephens Green" (59-66) with introductory note. (59) see B90.

H131   *The Treasury of American Short Stories*. Edited by Nancy Sullivan. Garden City: Doubleday and Company, [1981].
Contains: "Nothing Ever Breaks Except the Heart." (317-323)

H132   *Fictions* edited by Joseph F. Trimmer and C. Wade Jennings. San Diego: Harcourt Brace Jovanovich, Publishers, [1985]. wraps.

Contains: "Astronomer's Wife" with introductory note about Kay Boyle and questions for discussion. (153-157)

H133   *The Norton Anthology of Literature by Women.* Edited by Sandra Gilbert and Susan Gubar. New York: W. W. Norton & Company, [1985].
Contains: "Winter Night" (1695-1703) with short biography.

H134   *New Directions in Prose and Poetry.* Edited by James Laughlin. [New York]: A New Directions Book, [1986].
Contains: "January 24th, New York" with short biography. (48-51)

H135   *The World of the Short Story: A 20th Century Collection.* Edited by Clifton Fadiman. Boston: Houghton Mifflin Company, 1986.
Contains: "Men" with an introductory note about Kay Boyle. (272-282)

H136   *American Poetry Since 1970: Up Late.* Selected and introduced by Andrei Codrescu. New York: Four Walls Eight Windows, [1987].
Contains: "Poets." (xxix-xxx) with biographical note. (571)

H137   *Reading Fiction: An Anthology of Short Stories* edited by Robert DiYanni. New York: Random House School Division, [1988]. wraps.
Contains: "Winter Night" (147-156) with capsule biography. (505).

H138   *The Dolphin's Arc: Poems on Endangered Creatures of the Sea.* Edited by Elisavietta Ritchie. College Park, Maryland: SCOP Publications, Inc., [1989]. wraps.
Contains: "Reincarnation." from "A Poem to Samuel Beckett" (131) with biographical note. (157)

H139   *Wave Me Goodbye: Stories of the Second World War* edited by Ann Boston. [New York]: Viking, [1989].
Contains: "Defeat." (17-26)

H140   *In transition: A Paris Anthology, Writings and Art from transition Magazine 1927-1930.* [New York]: Doubleday, [1990].
Contains: "Vacation Time" (48-49), "On the Run" (49-51), "Letter to Archibald Craig" (52-53) and "The United States (for William Carlos Williams)." (54-55).

H141   *San Francisco Stories: Great Writer's on the City,* edited by John Miller. San Francisco: Chronicle Books, [1990]. wraps.
Contains: "Seeing the Sights of San Francisco" (251-258) with biographical note. (291)

H142   *The World of Fiction* edited by David Madden. Fort Worth: Holt, Rinehart & Winston, Inc., [1990]. wraps.

Contains: "Rest Cure" (147-152) with questions and writing suggestions. (1090-1091)

H143   *Writer's on World War II.* Edited by Mordecai Richler. New York: Alfred A. Knopf, 1991.
Contains: Opening pages of "Defeat" (70-71) with introductory note. (70)

H144   *That Kind of Woman.* Edited by Bronte Adams and Trudi Tate. New York: Carroll & Graf Publishers, [1992].
Contains: "Wedding Day." (43-49)

H145   *The Before Columbus Foundation Fiction Anthology.* Edited by Ishmael Reed, Kathryn Trueblood and Shawn Wong. New York: W. W. Norton & Company, [1992].
Contains: Chapters 4, 5, and 6 from *The Underground Woman,* (540-566) and a note about Kay Boyle by Shawn Wong. (537-539)

H146   *The Story and Its Writer: An Introduction to Short Fiction* Edited by Ann Charters. Boston: Bedford Books of St. Martin's Press, [1995]. 4th edition wraps (not in previous editions)
Contains: "Black Boy" (179-183) with introductory note about Kay Boyle. (179)

I

Books about Kay Boyle or that
Significantly mention Kay Boyle

I 1   *Twentieth Century Short Stories* selected by Sylvia Chatfield Bates. Boston:
       Houghton Mifflin Company, [1933].
       Contains: Short biographical note (320) also the short story "First Lover"
       (321-327)

I 2   *Creating the American Novel* by Harlan Hatcher. New York: Farrar,
       Incorporated, [1935].
       Contains: "Poetic Versus Hardboiled Realism" an article on her early work.
       (258-260)

I 3   *The School of Femininity: A Book for and about Women as They Are Interpreted
       Through Feminine Writers of Yesterday and Today* by Margaret Lawrence. New
       York: Frederick A. Stokes, 1936 Reprinted: Port Washington, New York:
       Kenniket Press, 1966.
       Contains: "Helpmeets" an article about *Year Before Last* (278-280).

I 4   *We Moderns* New York: The Gotham Book Mart, [1939].
       Contains: A paragraph of critical praise for Kay Boyle by Peter Neagoé.
       (14-15).

I 5   *Contemporary American Authors* by Fred B. Millett. New York: Harcourt,
       Brace and Company, 1940.
       Contains: Short biographical sketch and bibliography. (256-257)

I 6   *Current Biography: Who's New and Why 1942* edited by Maxine Block. New
       York: The W. H. Wilson Company, 1942
       Contains: A short biography of Kay Boyle. (101-104) taken from *Current
       Biography* 3.6 June 1942

I 7   *The Private Reader: Selected Articles and Reviews.* [New York]: Henry Holt
       and Company, [1942].
       Contains: "Under the Swastika" by Mark Van Doren a review of *Death of a
       Man.* (241-244)

I 8   *Twentieth Century Authors* edited by Stanley J. Kunitz and Howard
       Haycroft. New York: The H.W. Wilson Company, 1942.
       Contains: A capsule biography (173-174) First supplement 1955 (109-110)

I 9   *American Authors and Books 1640-1940* edited by W.J. Burke and Will D.
       Howe. New York: Gramercy Publishing, 1943.

Contains: Capsule bibliography. (82-83) New York: Crown Publishers, [1962] edited by W.J. Burke and Will D. Howe; augmented and revised by Irving R. Weiss. Short bibliography (82). see I43.

I 10   *Bessie Graham's Bookman's Manual: A Guide to Literature* 6th edition revised and edited by Hester R. Hoffman. New York: R. R. Bowker Company, 1948 Contains: a list of books in print with a short note. (701) 7th edition revised and enlarged by Hester R. Hoffman. 1954.
Contains: A short bibliography with note. (737) 8th edition revised and enlarged by Hester R. Hoffman. [1958] Contains same as 7th edition (879)

I 11   *The Oxford Companion to American Literature* edited by James D. Hart. London, New York and Toronto: Oxford University Press, [1941].
Contains: A capsule biography and bibliography. (86-87); 2nd edition New York and Oxford [1948] (86-87); 3rd edition 1956 (86-87); 4th edition [1965] (99); 5th edition [1983] (91-92) 6th edition with additions and revisions by Phillip W. Leininger New York/Oxford: Oxford University Press 1995, (82)

I 12   *The Reader's Encyclopedia* edited by William Rose Benét. New York: Thomas Y. Crowell, [1948].
Contains: a short paragraph about Kay Boyle. (135) 2nd edition [1965] (127)

I 13   *Classics and Commercials: A Literary Chronicle of the Forties* by Edmund Wilson. New York: Farrar, Straus, and Company, [1950].
Contains: "Kay Boyle and the *Saturday Evening Post*" a review of *Avalanche*. (128-132)

I 14   *Reading Fiction*: A Method of Analysis with Selections for Study by Fred B. Millett. New York: Harper & Brothers, Publishers, [1950]
Contains: "Art Colony" with short explication and questions about the story. (135-142).

I 15   *Suggestions for Teaching Fifteen Stories*. Boston: Heath & Company, 1950
Contains: An article about "Keep Your Pity" by Herbert Barrows (23-26).

I 16   *American Novelists of Today* by Harry R. Warfel. New York: American Book Company, [1951].
Contains: Biographical sketch. (44-46).

I 17   *Study Aids for Teachers of Modern Short Stories* edited by Marvin Felheim, Franklin Newman and William Steinhoff. New York: Oxford University Press, 1951.
Contains: An article on "Natives Don't Cry" (42-44).

I 18   *Cavalcade of the American Novel* by Edward Wagenknecht. New York: Holt, Rinehart & Winston, [1952].
        Contains: A capsule biography and bibliography. (467)

I 19   *The Short Story in America, 1900-1950* by Ray B. West. Chicago: Henry Renery, 1952.
        Contains: "Fiction and Reality: The Traditionalists" (59-84)

I 20   *Short Stories in Context* edited by Woodburn O. Ross and A. Dayle Wallace. New York: American Book Company, [1953].
        Contains: Capsule biography with notes about her work and questions for the student about "The First Lover" (217-220) Also includes "The First Lover." (212-217).

I 21   *Cassell's Encyclopaedia of Literature* (in two volumes) edited by S.H. Steinberg. New York: Funk and Wagnalls, [1954]. Volume 2 see I47.
        Contains: Short note about Kay Boyle (1717)

I 22   *Concise Dictionary of American Literature* edited by Robert Fulton Richards. New York: Philosophical Library, [1955].
        Contains: Capsule biography and bibliography. (18)

I 23   *The Twenties: American Writing in the Postwar Decade* by Frederick J. Hoffman. New York: The Viking Press, [1955] Reprinted by: New York: The Free Press, [1965] wraps.
        Contains: Short biographical note (455) and slight mention throughout.

I 24   *Who's Who of American Women: A Biographical Dictionary of Notable Living American Women Writers.* Volume 1 (1958-1959) Chicago: The A.N. Marquis Company, [1958].
        Contains: Capsule biography (153)

I 25   *A Library of Criticism: Modern American Literature* compiled and edited by Dorothy Nyren. New York: Frederick Ungar Publishing Company, [1960]
        Contains: Excerpts from the following: "Too Good to Be Smart" a review of *Wedding Day and Other Stories* by Gerald Sykes. *The Nation,* December 24, 1930; "Example to the Young" by Katherine Anne Porter a review of *Wedding Day and Other Stories* and *Plagued by the Nightingale. The New Republic* April 22, 1931; "Kay Boyle: Experimenter" by Evelyn Harter. *The Bookman,* June/July 1932; "The Romantic Temper" by Myra Marini a review of *Year Before Last. The New Republic,* July 13, 1932; "Style Without Design" by Harry Seidel Canby a review of *Gentlemen, I Address You Privately. The Saturday Review of Literature,* November 4, 1933; "Exiles" by Robert Cantwell a review of *Gentlemen, I Address You Privately. The New Republic,* December 13, 1933; "In Favor of Best Sellers" by Mary M. Collum a review of *Monday Night. Forum,* October 1938; "Improvisations

of Reality" by Phillip Rahv a review of *The Crazy Hunter*. *The Nation*, March 23, 1940; "Kay Boyle's Coincidence and Melodrama" by Struthers Burt a review of *Avalanche*. *The Saturday Review*, January 15, 1944; "Foreign Legion in Colorado" by Nathan L. Rothman a review of *His Human Majesty*. *The Saturday Review*, April 9, 1949; Biographical sketch by Harry R. Warfel. *American Novelists of Today*, New York: The American Book Company, [1951]; and "Kay Boyle:" by Richard C. Carpenter. *English Journal*, November 1953. (72-75) 2nd Edition edited by Dorothy Nyren [1961] (72-75) 3rd Edition [1964] compiled and edited by Dorothy Nyren (72-75) 4th Edition [1969] compiled and edited by Dorothy Nyren Curley, Maurice Kramer, and Elaine Fiolka Kramer. Adds "Poetry Chronicle" by Richard Howard a review of *Collected Poems* Poetry July 1963, "Kay Boyle: The Figure in the Carpet" by Richard C. Carpenter. *Critique* Winter 1964-1965; and "Aristocrat of the Short Story" by Maxwell Geismer a review of *Nothing Ever Breaks Except the Heart*. *New York Times Book Review* July 10, 1968 (141-146) with bibliography (449)

I 26   *The Reader's Guide and Bookman's Manual: A Guide to the Best in Print in Literature, Biographies, Dictionaries, Encyclopedias, Bibles, Classics, Drama, Poetry, Fiction, Science, Philosophy, Travel and History* 9th edition revised and enlarged by Hester R. Hoffman. New York: R. R. Bowker Company, 1960 see I29.
Contains: Capsule bibliography with short note. (995)

I 27   *McAlmon and the Lost Generation: A Self Portrait* edited with commentary by Robert Knoll. Lincoln, Nebraska: University of Nebraska Press, 1962.
Contains: Significantly mentions Kay Boyle throughout.

I 28   *The Reader's Encyclopedia of American Literature* edited by Max J. Herzberg. New York: Thomas Y. Crowell, [1962].
Contains: A capsule biography and bibliography. (102)

I 29   *The Reader's Advisor: An Annotated Guide to the Best in Print in Literature, Biographies, Dictionaries, Encyclopedias, Bibles, Classics, Drama, Poetry, Fiction, Science, Philosophy, Travel and History* revised and enlarged by Hester R. Hoffman. 10th edition New York: R. R. Bowker Company, 1964.
Contains: Capsule bibliography with note. (1113)

I 30   *Story Jubilee* edited by Whit and Hallie Burnett. Garden City: Doubleday and Company, 1965.
Contains: A short note about Kay Boyle and "Rest Cure" (61-62) "Rest Cure" is also included. (55-61)

I 31   *Teacher's Manual for The Realm of Fiction: 61 Stories* by James B. Hall. Princeton: McGraw-Hill Book Company, 1965.
Contains: An article about "Astronomer's Wife" (41-42)

I 32   *Encyclopedia of World Literature in the Twentieth Century* edited by Wolfgang
        Bernard Fleischman. New York: Frederick Ungar Publishing Company,
        [1967] volume 1 A-F.
        Contains: A Capsule biography and bibliography. (159) Revised edition
        [1981] edited by Leonard C. Klein and contains capsule bibliography and
        an article about Kay Boyle by Joanne McCarthy. (312-313).

I 33   *Write and Rewrite: A Study of the Creative Process* edited by John Kuehl. New
        York: Meredith Press, 1967. (also published by Appleton-Croft in 1967
        under the title *Creative Writing and Rewriting: Contemporary American
        Novelists at Work.*)
        Contains: A study of "The Ballet of Central Park" contrasting different
        drafts of selected passages with the final version with concluding commen-
        tary. (21-48)

I 34   *The Reader's Advisor: A Guide to the Best in Literature* edited by Winfred F.
        Courtney. Revised and enlarged 11th edition. New York and London: R.R.
        Bowker Company, 1968 Volume 1. See I50.
        Contains: Capsule bibliography with a note about her work. (485)

I 35   *Kay Boyle: From the Aesthetics of Exile to the Polemics of Return* by Frank
        Gado. DA 29.4485A (Duke) 1969.
        Contains: Doctoral dissertation.

I 36   *Two Hundred Contemporary Authors* edited by Barbara Harte and Carolyn
        Riley. Detroit: Gale Research Company, [1969].
        Contains: Capsule biographical and bibliographical information. (51)

I 37   *Contemporary Poets of the English Language* edited by Rosalie Murphy
        Chicago and London: St. Martin's Press, [1970]. From 2nd edition on called
        simply *Contemporary Poets*.
        Contains: Capsule bibliography with comment by Kay Boyle. 2nd edition
        edited by James Vinson, New York: St. James Press and London: St. James
        Press, [1975] capsule biography and bibliography with a comment by Kay
        Boyle and article by Gaynor Bradish. (159-161). 3rd edition New York: St.
        Martin's Press, [1980] edited by James Vinson with a capsule biography and
        bibliography and a short article about Kay Boyle's poetry by Gaynor F.
        Bradish, (152-154); 4th edition edited by James Vinson & D. L.
        Kirkpatrick, New York: St. Martin's Press, [1985] (79-80); 5th edition
        Chicago & London, St. James Press, [1991] edited by Tracy Chevalier with
        capsule biography and bibliography and a short article about Kay Boyle by
        Gaynor Brandish. (89-90)

I 38   *A Dictionary of Literature in the English Language from Chaucer to 1940*
        Volume one. Compiled and edited by Robin Myers. Oxford, London,

Edingburgh, New York, Toronto, Sydney, Paris, Braunsweig: Permagon Press, [1970].
Contains: Capsule note and bibliography (101-102)

I 39   *Longman's Companion to Twentieth Century Literature* edited by A. C. Ward. Harlow, Essex Longman.2nd edition A.C. Ward [1975] (84) 3rd edition A. C. Ward and revised by Maurice Hussey [1981] (84) 4th edition, [1984]. Contains: Capsule biography.

I 40   *Age of the Modern and Other Literary Essays* by Harry T. Moore. Carbondale and Edwardsville: Southern Illinois University Press, [1971]. Contains: "Kay Boyle's Fiction" a review of *Generation Without Farewell*. (32-36)

I 41   *Instructor's Manual for Studies in the Short Story* edited by Virgil Scott. New York: Holt, Rinehart and Winston, 1971. Contains: A study of "Astronomer's Wife" and "Effigy of War."

I 42   *The Penguin Companion to World Literature* edited by Malcolm Bradbury, Eric Mattram and Jean Franco. New York: McGraw-Hill Book Company, [1971]. Contains: A capsule biography and bibliography. (39)

I 43   *American Authors and Books: 1640 to the Present Day* edited by W.J. Burke and Will D. Howe. Revised by Irving Weiss and Anne Weiss. New York: Crown Publishers, [1972]. Contains: Capsule bibliography (71)

I 44   *Contemporary Novelists* edited by D.L. Kirkpatrick. New York: St. Martin's Press, [1972]. Contains: An excerpt from Kay Boyle's "Triumph of Principals" *Liberation*, June 1960 and *The Seeds of Liberation* edited by Paul Goodman, New York: George Braziller, [1964] and an original article about Kay Boyle by Jacqueline Hoefer. (154-155); 2nd edition; London: St. James Press & New York: St. Martin's Press, [1976] Capsule biography and bibliography and same article by Jacqueline Hoefer. (161-165) 3rd edition: New York: St. Martin's Press, [1982] same as first and 2nd editions (88-90) 4th edition 1986 same as 1st, 2nd & 3rd editions. (118-120) 5th edition Chicago & London: St. James Press, [1991], same as 2nd, 3rd and 4th editions, (125-127)

I 45   *The Critic as Artist: Essays on Books, 1920-1970* edited by Gilbert A. Harrison. New York: Liveright, [1972]. Contains: "Kay Boyle: Example to the Young" by Katherine Anne Porter. (277-281)

I 46   *The American Short Story* by Arthur Ross. Norman: University of Oklahoma Press, [1973].
Contains: Information about Kay Boyle and her work. Also in wraps. (285-287)

I 47   *Cassell's Encyclopedia of World Literature* Edited by J. Buchanan-Brown. Revised and enlarged in three volumes New York: William Morrow and Company, [1973] see I 21.
Contains: Short note Volume 2. (200)

I 48   *Contemporary Literary Criticism* edited by Carolyn Riley. Vol. 1 Detroit: Gale Research Company, [1973].
Contains: Excerpts from "A Question of Fiction" by Betty Hoyenga from *Prairie Schooner* Winter 1966-1967 and "Plastic Possibilities" by M.L. Rosenthal in *Poetry Magazine* November 1971. (42)

I 49   *Directory of American Poets* New York: American Fiction Writers, [1973].
Contains: Address of her agent and a list of a few of her works. (2) 1975 Edition (47).

I 50   *The Reader's Advisor: A Layman's Guide to Literature* edited by Sarah L. Prahken. 12th edition New York & London: R.R. Bowker Company, [1974].
Contains: Short paragraph about her work. (589)

I 51   *Contemporary Authors* edited by Clare D. Kinsman. vol.13-16 first revised Detroit: Gale Research Company, [1975].
Contains: Capsule biography with notes on her work. (99-100)

I 52   *Published in Paris: American and British Writers, Printers, and Publishers, 1920-1939* by Hugh Ford. New York: Macmillan Publishing Company, [1975].
Contains: Considerable information about her life in Paris during these years.

I 53   *Black Sun: The Brief and Violent Transit of Harry Crosby* by Geoffrey Wolfe. New York: Random House, [1976].
Contains: Significant mention of Kay Boyle throughout the book.

I 54   *Contemporary Literary Criticism* edited by Carolyn Riley and Phyllis Carmel Mendelson. vol. 5 Detroit: Gale Research Company, [1976].
Contains: "Kay Boyle's Fiction" by Harry T. Moore *Kenyon Review* Spring 1960 and his book *Age of the Modern*, Carbondale: Southern Illinois University Press, 1971; "Life with Daughter" by Peter S. Prescott in *Newsweek*, January 13, 1975 (67); a review of *The Underground Woman* by J.D. O'Hara in *The New York Times Book Review*, February 2, 1975; review

of *The Underground Woman* by Doris Grumbach in *The New Republic* February 8, 1975 and a review of *The Underground Woman* by Phillip Corwin in *The Nation*, March 22, 1975. (65-67)

I 55   *Directory of American Fiction Writers.* New York: Poets and Writers, Inc. [1976].
Contains: Address for her agent and a list of a few of her works. (25)

I 56   *The International Authors and Writers Who's Who* edited by Ernest Kay. Cambridge, England: Melrose Press, 1976 7th edition.
Contains: Capsule biography and bibliography. (66) not in editions 8, 9, or 10. 11th edition Cambridge: International Biographical Centre, [1989] contains short biography and bibliography. (97) 12th edition Cambridge: International Biographical Centre, [1991] Capsule biography and bibliography. (98)

I 57   *Who's Who in Twentieth Century Literature* by Martin Seymour Smith. New York: Holt, Rinehart and Winston, [1976].
Contains: Capsule biography and note on her work. (51-52)

I 58   *Women and Literature: An Annotated Bibliography of Women Writers.* [Cambridge, MA]: Women and Literature Collective, [1976].
Contains: Short biography of Kay Boyle with very brief story plots for *Plagued by the Nightingale* and *Thirty Stories.* (19) and a brief description of *The Underground Woman.* (54)

I 59   *The International Who's Who in Poetry 1977-1978* 5th edition edited by Ernest Kay. Cambridge, England: International Biographical Centre, [1977].
Contains: Capsule biography. (63)

I 60   *American Women Writers: A Critical Reference Guide from Colonial Times to the Present in Four Volumes* edited by Lina Mainiero. New York: A Frederick Ungar Book, [1979].
Contains: Volume 1 "Kay Boyle" by Joanne McCarthy (207-209) Volume 5 supplement [1994] capsule bibliography with article about Kay Boyle's work by Joanne McCarthy. (38-40)

I 61   *Great Writers of the English Language: Novelists and Prose Writers* edited by James Vinson. New York: St. Martin's Press, [1979].
Contains: Capsule biography and bibliography with an article about Kay Boyle by Jacqueline Hoefer. (145-148)

I 62   *Dictionary of Literary Biography: American Writers in Paris, 1920-1939* edited by Karen Lane Rood. Detroit: Gale Research, Inc [1980] volume 4.
Contains: Capsule bibliography and an article "Kay Boyle" by David Koch. (46-56)

I 63   *A Directory of American Poets and Fiction Writers*, New York: Poets and Writers, Inc.,1980-81.
Contains: Agents address and some publications. (110); 1983-84 (115); 1985-86 (128); 1987-88 (134); 1989-90 1991-92 (148); 1993-1994 (138)

I 64   *Literary San Francisco: A Pictorial History from the Beginning to the Present Day* by Lawrence Ferlinghetti and Nancy J. Peters. San Francisco: City Lights Books and Harper and Row, Publishers, [1980].
Contains: Paragraph about Kay Boyle and her life with photographs. (210-211)

I 65   *Novels and Novelists* by Martin Seymour Smith. New York: St. Martin's Press, [1980].
Contains: A short paragraph about Kay Boyle. (104)

I 66   *Contemporary Literary Criticism* edited by Sharon R. Gunton. Vol. 19 Detroit: Gale Research Company, [1981].
Contains: "Example to the Young" by Katherine Anne Porter a review of *Wedding Day and Other Stories* from *New Republic* April 22, 1931; "Kay Boyle and *The Saturday Evening Post*" a review of *Avalanche* by Edmund Wilson from *The New Yorker* January 15, 1944; "The Mature Craft of Kay Boyle" by Struthers Burt, a Review of *Thirty Stories* in *Saturday Review of Literature*, November 30, 1946; "Foreign Legion in Colorado" by Nathan L. Rothman a review of *His Human Majesty* from *Saturday Review of Literature*, April 9, 1949; "Kay Boyle" by Richard C. Carpenter in *College English* November 1953 (81-87); "Love Poems" by Robert Knoll a review of *Collected Poems* from *Prairie Schooner* Spring 1963; "Kay Boyle: The Figure in the Carpet" by Richard C. Carpenter from *Critique: Studies in Modern Literature*, Winter, 1964-1965; "Distant Landscapes" by Earl Rovit, a review of *Fifty Stories* from *The Nation*, September 27, 1980 and "Moving and Maturing" by Vance Bourjaily a review of *Fifty Stories* from The *New York Times Book Review*, September 28, 1980. (61-66)

I 67   *Critical Survey of Short Fiction* edited by Frank N. Magill. Englewood Cliffs: New Jersey: Salem Press, [1981] volume 3.
Contains: An article about the short fiction of Kay Boyle by Sandra Whipple Spanier. (994-1003)

I 68   *Dictionary of Literary Biography* edited by James J. Martine. Detroit: Gale Research Company, 1981 Volume 9.
Contains: Capsule biography and bibliography and article about Kay Boyle by Byron K. Jackson. (83-92)

I 69   *Interviews and Conversations with 20th Century Authors Writing in English: An Index* by Stan A. Verna. Methuchen, New Jersey & London: The Scarecrow Press, 1982.

Contains: A list of Kay Boyle interviews (22). Series II 1986 (31) Series III 1990 (38)

I 70   *Contemporary Authors: Autobiography Series* volume 1 edited by Dedria Bryfonski. Detroit: Gale Research Company, [1984].
Contains: Autobiographical essay with bibliography. (97-125)

I 71   *Critical Survey of Long Fiction* edited by Frank N. Magill. Englewood Cliffs, New Jersey: Salem Press, [1983] volume 1.
Contains: An article about Kay Boyle's novels by Janet Polansky. (270-281)

I 72   *Sylvia Beach and the Lost Generation: A History of Literary Paris in the Twenties and Thirties* by Noel Riley Fitch. New York and London: W. W. Norton Company, [1983].
Contains: Mention of Kay Boyle throughout.

I 73   *The American Short Story: 1900-1945 A Critical History* edited by Philip Stevick. Boston: Twayne Publishers, [1984].
Contains: Notes on Kay Boyle's short stories. (115-118)

I 74   *Articles on Women Writers 1976-1984 a Bibliography* edited by Narda Lacey Schwartz. Santa Barbara, California and Oxford, England: ABC-CLIO, [1985].
Contains: A bibliography of articles about Kay Boyle (29)

I 75   *The New Guide to Modern World Literature* edited by Martin Seymour Smith. [New York]: Peter Bedrick Books, [1985].
Contains: A short paragraph about Kay Boyle and her work. (126-127)

I 76   *The Norton Anthology of Literature by Women* edited by Sandra M. Gilbert and Susan Gubar. New York: W. W. Norton and Company, [1985].
Contains: Capsule biography and "Winter Night" (1694-1703)

I 77   *Twentieth Century American Literature* edited by Harold Bloom, New York: Chelsea House Publishers, 1985 Volume I.
Contains: Capsule biography and notes on her work; "Too Good to Be Smart" a review of *Wedding Day and Other Stories* by Gerald Sykes, *The Nation*, December 24, 1930; "Kay Boyle and *The Saturday Evening Post*" by Edmund Wilson, *The New Yorker*, January 15, 1944; a review of *Collected Poems* by Richard Howard, *Poetry Magazine*, July 1963; "Aristocrat of the Short Story" by Maxwell Geismer, a review of *Nothing Ever Breaks Except the Heart*, *The New York Times Book Review*, July 10, 1966; the introduction to *Fifty Stories* by David Daiches in *Fifty Stories*, GC: Doubleday & Company, 1980; "Example to the Young" by Katherine Anne Porter a review of *Wedding Day and Other Stories* and *Plagued by the Nightingale*, *The New Republic*, April 22, 1931 and *The Critic As Artist*, New York: Liveright,

[1972], and "Kay Boyle's Fiction" by Harry T. Moore a review of *Generation Without Farewell, Kenyon Review*, Spring 1960 and *Age of the Modern*, Carbondale: Southern Illinois University Press, [1971]. (560-566)

I 78   *The Cambridge Handbook of American Literature* edited by Jack Salzman. Cambridge, London, New York, New Rochelle, Melbourne, Sydney: Cambridge University Press, [1986].
       Contains: Capsule biography. (30)

I 79   *Dictionary of Literary Biography* edited by Peter Quartermain. Detroit: Gale Research Company, [1986] Volume 48.
       Contains: Short biography and bibliography and an article about Kay Boyle by Joanne McCarthy (45-52)

I 80   *Kay Boyle: Artist and Activist* by Sandra Whipple Spanier. Carbondale: Southern Illinois University Press, 1986.

I 81   *Women of the Left Bank: Paris 1900-1940* by Shari Benstock. Austin: University of Texas Press, [1986].
       Contains: Significant mention of Kay Boyle throughout.

I 82   *Benet's Reader's Encyclopedia* with no stated editor. This is the 3rd edition of *The Reader's Encyclopedia* edited by William Rose Benét. New York: Harper & Row, Publishers, [1987].
       Contains: A capsule biography (119-120)

I 83   *The First Wave: Women Poets in America 1915-1945* by William Drake. New York: Macmillan Publishing Company and London: Collier-Macmillan Publishers, [1987].
       Contains: Mention throughout with capsule biography (292-293)

I 84   *Four Lives in Paris* by Hugh Ford. San Francisco: North Point Press, 1987.
       Contains: Biographical sketch of Kay Boyle. (137-225).

I 85   *Geniuses Together* by Humphrey Carpenter. London: Unwin Hyman. [1987].
       Contains: Significant mention of Kay Boyle throughout.

I 86   *Reference Guide to American Literature* edited by D.L. Kirkpatrick. Chicago and London: St. James Press, [1987].
       Contains: A capsule biography with article about Kay Boyle by Jacqueline Hoefer. 2nd edition [1987] (101-102)

I 87   *Who's Who in U.S. Writers, Editors and Poets: A Biographical Directory 1986-1987* edited by Curt Johnson. Highland Park, IL: December Press, [1986-1987].
       Contains: Capsule biography (56); [1988] edition (73)

I 88   *The Cambridge Guide to Literature in English* edited by Ian Ousby.
Cambridge: Cambridge University Press, [1988].
Contains: Capsule biography. (115)

I 89   *Short Story Writers and Their Work: A Guide to the Best* by Brad Hooper.
Chicago and London: American Library Association, 1988.
Contains: Short paragraph on Kay Boyle's story writing. (39)

I 90   *Cyclopedia of World Authors II*, Volume One edited By Frank N. Magill.
Pasadena, California and Englewood Cliffs, New Jersey: Salem Press, [1989].
Contains: Capsule biography with list of works and bibliographical
reference by Joseph Rosenblum (228-230)

I 91   *Dictionary of Literary Biography* edited by Bobby Ellen Kimball. Detroit:
Gale Research Company, [1989] Volume 86.
Contains: Bibliography and an article about Kay Boyle by Elizabeth Bell.
(31-42)

I 92   *Who's Who in Writers, Editors and Poets* edited by Curt Johnson. Highland
Park, IL: December Press, [1992] Fourth edition.
Contains: Capsule biography and bibliography. (63)

I 93   *Contemporary Authors* edited by Hal May and James G. Lesniak. Vol. 29 new
revision series. Detroit: Gale Research Company, [1990].
Contains: Capsule biography and bibliography with a short article about
Kay Boyle's work. (60-62)

I 94   *Contemporary Literary Criticism* edited by Roger Matuz. Vol. 58 Detroit:
Gale Research Company, [1990].
Contains: a short bio of Kay Boyle; "Kay Boyle" by Richard C. Carpenter
from *College English*, November 1953; "Behind the Facade" by James Kelly
a review of *Seagull on the Step* from *Saturday Review of Literature*, May 14,
1955; "Hope Out of France" by Paul Engle a review of *Seagull on the Step*
from *The New Republic*, May 16, 1955; "There is No Armistice" by Virgilia
Peterson a review of *Generation Without Farewell* from *The New York Times
Book Review*, January 17, 1960; a review of *Generation Without Farewell* by
Melvin Maddocks from the *Christian Science Monitor*, January 21, 1960;
"Two Poets and their Muses" a review of *Collected Poems* by David Ray from
The New Republic, November 10, 1962; A Review of *Collected Poems* by
Richard Howard from *Poetry Magazine*, July 1963; "Aristocrat of the Short
Story" by Maxwell Geismer review of *Nothing Ever Breaks Except the Heart
and Other Stories* from *The New York Times Book Review*, July 10, 1966;
"Where Have All of the Children Gone?" by Theodore L. Gross a review of
Nothing Ever Breaks Except the Heart and Other Stories from *Saturday Review
of Literature* July 16, 1966; "I Poems and You Poems" by Robert S. French a
review of *Testament for My Students and Other Poems* from *The Nation*, June

8, 1970; "Generous Hope and Living Without Hope" by Chad Walsh a review of *Testament for My Students and Other Poems* from *The Washington Post Book World*, November 15, 1970; an interview with David Mesher from *Malahat Review*, July 1983; "Kay Boyle: From the Left Bank to the New Left" by Robert W. Smith a review of *Words That Somehow Must Be Said* from *The Washington Post Book World* July 14, 1985; "60 Years of Passion and Compassion" by Hugh Ford a review of *Words That Somehow Must Be Said* from *The New York Times Book Review, August* 25, 1985; "Virtues of Dissent" by Anne Chisholm a review of *Words That Somehow Must Be Said* from *The Times Literary Supplement,* September 27, 1985; "Take the Old Fury in Your Empty Arms" by David Dwyer a review of *This is Not a Letter and Other Poems* from *The American Book Review*, November/December 1986; "Refusal to Mourn" by Rachel Hadas a review of *This Is Not a Letter and Other Poems* from *Parnassus: Poetry in Review*, Fall/Winter 1988; a review of *This Is Not a Letter and Other Poems* by Ann Hornaday from *The New York Times Book Review*, July 3, 1988; "*My Next Bride*: Kay Boyle's Text of the Female Artist" by Deborah Denenholz Morse and "Tails, You Lose: Kay Boyle's War Fiction" by Edward Uehling from *Twentieth Century Literature* 34.3 Fall 1988. (63-83)

I 95   *A Feminist Companion to Literature in English* edited by Virginia Blain, Patricia Clements, and Isobel Grunly. New Haven and London: Yale University Press, [1990].
Contains: Article about Kay Boyle and her work. (126-127)

I 96   *Short Story Criticism* edited by Thomas Votteler. Detroit, New York, and Washington, D.C.: Gale Research Inc., [1990] volume 5.
Contains: A capsule bibliography and a short article about her work; an excerpt from "The Somnambulist" a review of *Short Stories* by William Carlos Williams, *transition* Fall 1929; an excerpt from "Example to the Young" a review of *Wedding Day and Other Stories* and *Plagued by the Nightingale* by Katherine Anne Porter, *New Republic* April 22, 1931 and *The Critic As Artist: Essays on Books*, New York: Liveright, 1972; an excerpt from a review of *Wedding Day and Other Stories* by Richard Strachey in *The New Statesman and Nation* September 24, 1932; an excerpt from "The Mature Craft of Kay Boyle" a review of *Thirty Stories* by Struthers Burt in *The Saturday Review of Literature*, November 30, 1946; an excerpt from a review of *Thirty Stories* by Rosemary Paris in *Furioso* Summer 1947; an excerpt from a review of *The Smoking Mountain* by Robert Alter in *Critique* winter 1963/1964; an excerpt from "Kay Boyle: The Figure in the Carpet" by Richard C. Carpenter in *Critique* Winter 1964/1965; an excerpt from "The Heart is Not Enough" a review of *Nothing Ever Breaks Except the Heart and Other Stories* by W.J. Stucky in *Critique* 9.2 1967; an excerpt from "Dead Landscapes" a review of *Fifty Stories* by Earl Rovit in *The Nation* September 27, 1980; an excerpt from "Moving and Maturing" a review of *Fifty Stories*

by Vance Bourjaily in *The New York Times Book Review* September 28, 1980; an excerpt from *Kay Boyle: Artist and Activist*, Carbondale: Southern Illinois University Press, 1986 by Sandra Whipple Spanier; "Revolution, the Woman, and the Word: Kay Boyle" by Suzanne Clark in *Twentieth Century Literature* 34.3 Fall 1988; and "Tails, You Lose: Kay Boyle's War Fiction" by Edward M. Uehling in *Twentieth Century Literature* 34.3 Fall 1988. (51-77)

I 97   *Benét's Reader's Encyclopedia of American Literature* edited by George Perkins, Barbara Perkins and Phillip Leiniger. [New York]: Harper Collins Publishers, [1991].
Contains: Capsule biography and bibliography. (115-116)

I 98   *Literary Exile in the Twentieth Century* edited by Meredith Tucker. New York, Westport, CN, and London: Greenwood Press, [1991].
Contains: Capsule biography. (130-131)

I 99   *Major Twentieth Century Writers, A Selection of sketches from Contemporary Authors* edited by Bryan Ryan. Detroit/New York/ London: Gale Research, Inc., [1991].
Contains: Short biography and bibliography with a critical comment about Kay Boyle and her work. (357-359)

I 100   *Sentimental Modernism: Women Writers and the Revolution of the Word* by Suzanne Clark. Bloomington & Indianapolis: Indiana University Press, [1991].
Contains: "Revolution, the Woman, and the Word: Kay Boyle" (127-152)

I 101   *The Bloomsbury Guide to Women's Literature* edited by Claire Buck. New York: Prentice Hall General Reference, [1992].
Contains: Capsule biography and bibliography (363)

I 102   *Contemporary Authors* edited by Donna Olendorf. Vol. 140 Detroit: Gale Research Company, [1993].
Contains: Obituary. (48)

I 103   *Current Biography Year Book* edited by Judith Graham. New York The W.H. Wilson Company, [1993].
Contains: An obituary (623) taken from *The New York Times*, December 29, 1992 (A-13L).

I 104   *Dictionary of Literary Biography: Yearbook 1993* edited by James W. Hipp. Detroit and London: Gale Research, Inc [1994]. Capsule bibliography with an obituary by Elizabeth Bell. (261-269).

I 105   *Metamorphosizing the Novel: Kay Boyle's Narrative Innovation* by Marilyn Elkins. New York: Peter Lang, [1993].

I 106 *Great Women Writers: The Lives and Works of 135 of the Worlds' Most Important Women Writers, from Antiquity to the Present* edited by Frank N. Magill. New York: Henry Holt and Company, [1994].
Contains: Kay Boyle's achievements, biography and analysis. (43-46).

I 107 *Kay Boyle: Author of Herself* by Joan Mellon. New York: Farrar, Straus, & Giroux, 1994.

I 108 *Larousse Dictionary of Writers* edited by Rosemary Goring. [Edinburgh]: Larousse, [1994].
Contains: Short paragraph. (119).

I 109 *Reference Guide to Short Fiction* edited by Noelle Watson. Detroit, London & Washington, D.C.: St. James Press, [1994].
Contains: A Capsule biography and bibliography and an article about Kay Boyle by Marilyn Elkins, (86-87), an article by R.V. Cassill about "The White Horses of Vienna" (970-971) and an article by Paul Sladky about "Astronomer's Wife." (626)

I 110 *The Remarkable Lives of 100 Women Writers and Journalists* by Brooke Bailey. Holbrook, Massachusetts: Bob Adams, [1994].
Contains: Biographical sketch. (32-33)

I 111 *The Oxford Companion to Women's Writing in the United States* edited by Cathy N. Davidson and Linda Wagner-Martin, editors-in-chief. New York/Oxford: Oxford University Press, 1995.
Contains: Capsule biography by Marilyn Elkins. (131)

I 112 *A Reader's Guide to the Twentieth Century Novel* edited by Peter Parker. New York: Oxford University Press, 1995.
Contains: Story plot for *Plagued by the Nightingale* (144) and a capsule biography (680).

I 113 *Resources for Teaching The Story and Its Writer: An Introduction to Short Fiction* prepared by Ann Charters and William E. Sheidley. Boston: Bedford Books of St. Martin's Press, [1995].
Contains: Article on "Black Boy" with questions for discussion and topics for writing. (36-38)

I 114 *The Story and Its Writer: An Introduction to the Short Story* edited by Ann Charters. Boston: Bedford Books of St. Martin's Press, [1995].
Contains: Note about Kay Boyle (179) with the short story "Black Boy" (179-183)

I 115 *Critical Essays on Kay Boyle* edited by Marilyn Elkins. New York: G. K. Hall & Co. An Imprint of Simon & Schuster Macmillan, [1997].
Contains: A group of reviews of Kay Boyle's works and critical essays about her works. 316 pages.

J

Articles About Kay Boyle and Reviews of Her Works

-1929-

J1   A review of *Short Stories* by Eugene Jolas. *transition* # 16/17 June 1929 (336)

J2   "The Somnambulist" by William Carlos Williams. A review of *Short Stories*. *transition* #18 Fall 1929. (147-151)

J3   A review of *Short Stories* by Charles Henri Ford. *Blues* 2.7 Fall 1929 (45) 60w

-1930-

J4   "Kay Boyle's Experiments." A review of *Wedding Day and Other Stories*. *The New York Times Book Review*. 35.46 November 16, 1930. (8) 550w

J5   "Shapes of Feeling." A review of *Wedding Day and Other Stories* by Margaret Cheney Dawson. *New York Herald Tribune Books*. 7.10 November 16, 1930. (6) 600w

J6   A review of *Wedding Day and Other Stories*. *The Boston Transcript*. 101.277 November 29, 1930. (3) 300w

J7   "Say It with Books." A note about *Wedding Day and Other Stories*. *The Saturday Review of Literature* 7.21 December 13, 1930 (455)

J8   "Too Good to Be Smart" by Gerald Sykes. A review of *Wedding Day and Other Stories*. *The Nation*. 131.3416 December 24, 1930 (711-712) 550w

-1931-

J9   A review of *Wedding Day and Other Stories*. *Book Review Digest* 26.11 January 1931.

J10   "Perpetuating the Family" by Margaret Cheney Dawson. A review of *Plagued by the Nightingale*. *New York Herald Tribune Books*. 7.26 March 8, 1931. (7) 500w

J11   A review of *Plagued by the Nightingale* by R.M.C. *The New Yorker* 7.7 April 4, 1931 (85) 70w

J12   "Kay Boyle's Novel" by Charles Hansen Towne. A review of *Plagued by the Nightingale*. *The New York Times Book Review* 36.14 April 5, 1931 (7, 20) 550w

J13   A review of *Plagued by the Nightingale* by W.E.H. *The Boston Transcript* 102.88 April 15, 1931 (3) 600w

J14   "Example to the Young" by Katherine Anne Porter. A review of *Wedding Day and Other Stories* and *Plagued by the Nightingale*. *The New Republic* 66.855 April 22, 1931 (279-280) 700w

J15   Note about *Plagued by the Nightingale*. The New Yorker 7.11 May 2, 1931 (75)

J16   A review of *Don Juan* by Joseph Delteil as translated by Kay Boyle. Review by Robert M. Coates. *The New Yorker* 7.11 May 2, 1931 (80)

J17   "Notes on Fiction." A review of *Plagued by the Nightingale*. *The Nation* 132.3435 May 6, 1931 (509) 300w

J18   A review of *Don Juan* by Joseph Delteil as translated by Kay Boyle. *The New York Times Book Review* 36.21 May 24, 1931 (23)

J19   A review of *Plagued by the Nightingale*. *Booklist* 27.10 June 1931 (453)

J20   A review of *Plagued by the Nightingale*. *Book Review Digest* 27.4 June 1931

J21   "Library of the Quarter" by Helen MacAffee. A review of *Plagued by the Nightingale*. *Yale Review* 20.4 Summer (June) 1931 (viii) 200w

J22   A review of *Plagued by the Nightingale* by L.A.G. Strong. *The Spectator* 147.5377 July 18, 1931 (94) 250w

J23   "New Novels" by Viola Meynell. A review of *Plagued by the Nightingale*. *The New Statesman and Nation* 2.23 August 1, 1931 (144) 650w

J24   "New Novels." A review of *Plagued by the Nightingale*. *London Times Literary Supplement* 30.1540 August 6, 1931 (608) 400w

J25   A review of *Plagued by the Nightingale* by H.C. Harwood. *Saturday Review* (London) 152.3954 August 8, 1931 (185) 450w

J26   "Books of the Day" by O.M. A review of *Plagued by the Nightingale*. *The Manchester Guardian* #26502 August 14, 1931 (5)

J27   "Critics Commentary." A review of *Plagued by the Nightingale*. *Time and Tide* 12.33 August 15, 1931 (968) 80w

J28   "The Curse." A review of *Plagued by the Nightingale*. *John O'London Weekly* 25.646 September 5, 1931 (759) 250w

J29   A review of *Plagued by the Nightingale* by E.B.C. Jones. *The Adelphi* 3.1 October 1931 (68)

J30   "Kay Boyle: Artist" by Oakley Johnson. A review of *Wedding Day and Other Stories*. *Scribner's* 90.4 October 1931 (14)

-1932-

J31   "Precocious Lovers." A review of *Devil in the Flesh* as translated by Kay Boyle. *The New York Times Book Review* 37.10 March 6, 1932 (18-19) 400w

J32   "The Young Classic" by Ben Ray Redmon. A review of *Devil in the Flesh* by Raymond Radiguet. (translated by Kay Boyle) *New York Herald Tribune Books* 8.27 March 13, 1932 (2)

J33   "Wedding Bells for Kay Boyle and Laurence Vail" by Wambly Bald. *The Paris Tribune* March 22, 1932

J34   "Laurence Vail and Kay Boyle Wed in Simple Ceremony" by Wambly Bald [unsigned] *The Paris Tribune* April 3, 1932.

J35   "Relentless Beauty" by Margaret Cheney Dawson. A review of *Year Before Last*. *New York Herald Tribune Books* 8.41 June 19, 1932 (3) 650w

J36   "The Spirit at Bay." A review of *Year Before Last*. *The New York Times Book Review* 37.26 June 26, 1932 520w

J37   A review of *Year Before Last*. *The Boston Transcript* 103.152 June 29, 1932 (2) 220w

J38   "Kay Boyle: Experimenter" by Evelyn Harter. *The Bookman* 75.3 June/July 1932 (249-253)

J39   A review of *Year Before Last* by Geoffrey Stone. *The Bookman* 75.3 June/July 1932 (318) 800w

J40   A review of *Year Before Last* by E. B.C. Jones. *The Adelphi* 4.4 July 1932 (718-720)

J41   "Kay Boyle Writes Novel of Quality Too Rarely Found" by Waverly Root. A review of *Year Before Last*. *Paris Tribune* July 4, 1932.

J42   A review of *Year Before Last* by Gerald Bullett. *The New Statesman and Nation* 4.72 n.s. July 9, 1932 (43) 350w

J43   "Inescapable End" by Gladys Graham. A review of *Year Before Last*. *The Saturday Review of Literature* 8.52 July 9, 1932 (827) 600w

J44   "Fiction" by L.A.G. Strong. A review of *Year Before Last*. *The Spectator* 149.5428 July 9, 1932 (58) Incorrectly reviewed as *Day Before Yesterday*.

J45   "Turns with a Bookworm" by I.M.P. A review of *Year Before Last*. *New York Herald Tribune Books* 8.44 July 10, 1932 (9) 100w

J46   "The Romantic Temper" by Myra Marini. A review of *Year Before Last*. *The New Republic* 71.919 July 13, 1932 (242) 500w

J47   "American Exile" by Robert Cantwell. A review of *Year Before Last*. *The Nation* 135.3498 July 20, 1932 (60-61) 650w

J48   A review of *Year Before Last* by Alvah Bessie. *Scribner's* 92.2 August 1932 (5)

J49   A review of *Year Before Last*. *London Times Literary Supplement* 31.1592 August 4, 1932 (558) 180w

J50   "Reading Kay Boyle." An editorial. *Contempo* 2.6 August 31, 1932 (2)

J51   A review of *Year Before Last*. *Book Review Digest* 28.7 September 1932

J52   A review of *Year Before Last* by Eric Linklater. *The Listener* 8. September 21, 1932 (428)

J53   "New Novels" by Richard Strachey. A review of *Wedding Day and Other Stories*. *The New Statesman and Nation* 4.83 September 24, 1932 (347)

J54   A review of *Wedding Day and Other Stories*. *London Times Literary Supplement* 31.1600 September 29, 1932 (692) 280w

J55   A review of *Wedding Day and Other Stories* by E.B.C. Jones. *The Adelphi* 5.1 October 1932 (73-74)

J56   A review of *Wedding Day and Other Stories* by Helen Moran. *The London Mercury* 26.156 October 1932 (565)

J57   Article by H.E. Bates *John O'London's Weekly* 28.704 October 8, 1932 (51) 110w

J58   A review of *Year Before Last* by Ted Wilson. *Contempo* 3.1 October 25, 1932 (5)

J59   "The Library of the Quarter: Outstanding Novels" by Helen MacAfee. A review of *Year Before Last*. *The Yale Review* 22.1 Autumn 1932 (iv) 280w

J60   A review of *Year Before Last*. *Booklist* 29.3 November 1932 (73)

-1933-

J61   A review of *First Lover and Other Stories* by Margaret Cheney Dawson. *New York Herald Tribune Books* 9.28 March 19, 1933 (9) 650w

J62   "Books" by RMC (Robert M. Coates). A review of *The First Lover and Other Stories*. *The New Yorker* 9.6 March 25, 1933 (55) 60w

J63   "Kay Boyle As Experimenter in Words and Episodes" by Karl Schriftsgiesser. A review of *First Lover and Other Stories*. *The Boston Transcript* 104.70 March 25, 1933 (1) 600w

J64   Mention of *The First Lover and Other Stories* by R.M.C. *The New Yorker* 9.6 March 25, 1933 (55)

J65   "Artistic Fiction" by Gladys Graham. A review of *The First Lover and Other Stories*. *The Saturday Review of Literature* 9.36 March 25, 1933 (501) 600w

J66   "The Short Stories of Kay Boyle" by Louis Kronenberger. A review of *The First Lover and Other Stories* with photo. *New York Times Book Review* 38.13 March 26, 1933 (7) 750w

J67   "Shorter Notices," A review of *The First Lover and Other Stories*. *The Nation* 136.3537 April 19, 1933 (453) 250w

J68   A review of *The First Lover and Other Stories*. (note only) *Scribner's* 93.5 May 1933 (5)

J69   A review of *The First Lover and Other Stories*. *Forum and Century* 89.5 May 1933 (vi) (70w)

J70   A review of *The First Lover and Other Stories*. *Book Review Digest* 29.3 May 1933

J71   "Kay Boyle" by Hazel Hawthorne. A review of *The First Lover and Other Stories*. *The New Republic* 74.961 May 3, 1933 (342) 320w

J72   A review of *The First Lover and Other Stories*. *Contempo* 3.9 May 15, 1933 (7)

J73   "Books of the Fall" by Amy Loveman. A note about *Gentlemen, I Address You Privately*. *The Saturday Review of Literature* 10.13 October 14, 1933 (188)

J74   A review of *Gentlemen, I Address You Privately*. *The Kirkus Review* 1.20 November 1, 1933 (174) 170w

J75   "Books of the Times" by John Chamberlain. A review of *Gentlemen, I Address You Privately*. *The New York Times* (daily) 83.27677 November 3, 1933 (17) 600w

J76   A review of *Gentlemen, I Address You Privately* by Clifton Fadiman. *The New Yorker* 9.38 November 4, 1933 (66-67)

J77   "Style Without Design" by Henry Seidel Canby. A review of *Gentlemen, I Address You Privately*. *The Saturday Review of Literature* 10.4 November 4, 1933 (233) 850w

J78   "Kay Boyle's Story of a Moral Crisis" by Louis Kronenberger. A review of *Gentlemen, I Address You Privately*. *The New York Times Book Review* 38.46 November 12, 1933 (9) 850w

J79   "Leading Recent Fiction" by Margaret Cheney Dawson. A review of *Gentlemen, I Address You Privately*. *New York Herald Tribune Books* 10.10 November 12, 1933 (28) 750w

J80   "Shorter Notices." A review of *Gentlemen, I Address You Privately*. *The Nation* 137.3569 November 29,1933 (630) 240w

J81   A review of *Gentlemen, I Address You Privately*. *Book Review Digest* 29.10 December 1933

J82   "Exiles" by Robert Cantwell. A review of *Gentlemen, I Address You Privately*. *The New Republic* 77.993 December 13, 1933 (136-137) 850w

-1934-

J83   "The Pamphlet Poets" by T.C. Wilson. A review of *A Statement*. *Poetry, A Magazine of Verse* 43.4 January 1934 (225)

J84   A review of *Gentlemen, I Address You Privately* by Alvah Bessie. *Scribner's* 95.1 January 1934 (2)

J85   "Kay Boyle's Queer Folk" by Herschel Brickell. A review of *Gentlemen, I Address You Privately*. *The North American Review* 237.1 January 1934 (93) 350w

J86   A review of *Gentlemen, I Address You Privately* by Edwin Muir. *The Listener* 11.265 February 7, 1934 (256) 350 w

J87   "Fiction" by Bonamy Dobrée. A review of *Gentlemen, I Address You Privately*. *The Spectator* 152.5511 February 9, 1934 (208)

J88   "Some New Novels" by C.E. Bechhoffer Roberts. A review of *Gentlemen, I Address You Privately*. *The New English Weekly* 4.18 February 17, 1934 (427-428) 250w

J89   "Paris American" by John Brophy. A review of *Gentlemen, I Address You Privately*. *John O'London Weekly* February 17, 1934 30.775 (766) 380w

J90   A review of *Gentlemen, I Address You Privately* by Peter Quenell. *The New Statesman and Nation* 7.156 n.s. February 17, 1934 (231-232) 200w

J91   "New Fiction" by Richard Rheidol. A review of *Gentlemen, I Address You Privately*. *Time and Tide* 15.7 February 17, 1934 (216-217) 350w

J92   A review of *Gentlemen, I Address You Privately* by Helen Moran. *The London Mercury* 29.173 March 1934 (465)

J93   "New Novels." A review of *Gentlemen, I Address You Privately*. *London Times Literary Supplement* 33.1680 April 12, 1934 (260)

J94   A review of *Gentlemen, I Address You Privately* by E. B.C. Jones. *The Adelphi* 8.2 May 1934 (155)

J95   A review of *Gentlemen, I Address You Privately* by M.G. *Dublin Magazine* 9.3 n.s July/September 1934 (86-87)

J96   A note about *My Next Bride*. *The Library Journal* 59.15 September 1, 1934 (676) 50w

J97   "Burton Rascoe's Review of the Fall Books." A brief review of *My Next Bride*. *The New York Herald Tribune Books* 11.3 September 23, 1934 (4) 40w

J98   A review of *My Next Bride*. *The Kirkus Review* 2.19 October 15, 1934 (291) 100w

J99   "Books and Things" by Lewis Gannett. A review of *My Next Bride*. *New York Herald Tribune* (daily) 94.32134 November 8, 1934 (25) 650w

J100 "Remember Your Alice?—The Vegetarian Novel—The Women Who Did" by Clifton Fadiman. A review of *My Next Bride*. *The New Yorker* 10.39 November 10, 1934 (90-91)

J101 "Books of the Times" by Robert Van Gelder. A review of *My Next Bride*. *The New York Times* (daily) 84.28049 November 10, 1934 (13) 680w

J102 "The Intense Art of Kay Boyle" by Elizabeth Hart. A review of *My Next Bride*. *New York Herald Tribune Books* 11.10 November 11, 1934 (4) 850w

J103   "Miss Boyle's Irony" by Edith Walton. A review of *My Next Bride*. *New York Times Book Review* 39.45 November 11, 1934 (6) 800w

J104   "Kay Boyle Writes Best Novel of Real Imaginary Character" by Waverly Root. A review of *My Next Bride*. *Paris Tribune* (Chicago) November 12, 1934

J105   "The New Books." A review of *My Next Bride* by G.S. *The Saturday Review of Literature* 11.19 November 24, 1934 (318) 200w

J106   A review of *My Next Bride* by Helen MacAfee. *The Yale Review* 24.2 December (Winter) 1934 (vi) 250w

J107   Mention by William Plommer of *Gentlemen, I Address You Privately*. *The Bookman* (London) 87.519 December 1934 (149)

J108   A review of *My Next Bride*. *Book Review Digest* 30.10 December 1934

J109   A review of *My Next Bride* by H.A. Mason. *Forum and Century* 92.6 December 1934 (ix) 70w

J110   A review of *My Next Bride*. *Christian Century* 51.49 December 5, 1934 (1564) 70w

J111   "Kay Boyle's Story of Expatriates in Paris." A review of *My Next Bride*. *The Springfield Republican* 57.14 December 9, 1934 (7e) 220w

J112   "Who's Loony Now?" by T. S. Mathews. A review of *My Next Bride*. *The New Republic* 81.1045 December 12, 1934 (136) 370w

J113   "The Romance of Paris" by Mary McCarthy. A review of *My Next Bride*. *The Nation* 139.3625 December 26, 1934 (746) 400w

-1935-

J114   "Extraordinarily Alive" by Grace Flandrau. A review of *My Next Bride*. *Scribner's* 97.2 February 1935 (2-3)

J115   "New Fiction" by C.E. Bechhofer Roberts. A review of *My Next Bride*. *Time and Tide* 16.6 February 9, 1935 (196) 80w

J116   "Fiction" by William Plommer. A review of *My Next Bride*. *The Spectator* 154.5564 February 15, 1935 (259) 600w

J117   A review of *My Next Bride* by Richard Church. *John O'London Weekly* 32.827 February 16, 1935 (775) 200w

J118 "New Novels" by Cyril Connolly. A review of *My Next Bride*. *The New Statesman and Nation* 9.208 n.s. February 16, 1935 (216) 300w

J119 "Refugees in Paris" by M.H. A review of *My Next Bride*. *The Manchester Guardian* #27596 February 22, 1935 (5) 250w

J120 A review of *My Next Bride* by Edwin Muir. *The Listener* 13.320 February 27, 1935 (384) 350w

J121 A review of *My Next Bride*. *The London Mercury* 31.185 March 1935 (501)

J122 A review of *My Next Bride* by George Sutherland Fraser. *Life and Letters* 11.63 March 1935 (739-741)

J123 A review of *My Next Bride* by E.B.C. Jones. *Adelphi* 10.1 April 1935 (58) 500w

J124 A review of *My Next Bride* by Osbert Burdett. *English Review* 60.4 April 1935 (497) 60w

J125 A review of *My Next Bride*. *London Times Literary Supplement* 34. 1731 April 4, 1935 (229-230)

J126 A review of *My Next Bride* by H.A. Mason. *Scrutiny* 4.1 June 1935 (74-76) 750w

J127 "The Phoenix Nest" by William Rose Benét. A note about *The White Horses of Vienna and Other Stories*. *The Saturday Review of Literature* 12.6 June 8, 1935 (129)

J128 "Footnotes to Romans a Clef" by Earl Walbridge. A note about *My Next Bride*. *The Saturday Review of Literature* 12.8 June 22, 1935 (12)

-1936-

J129 A note about *The White Horses of Vienna and Other Stories*. *The Library Journal* 61.1 (32) 30w

J130 A review of *The White Horses of Vienna and Other Stories*. *The Kirkus Review* 4.3 February 1, 1936 (39) 50w

J131 "The Lost Speakers" by Achibald MacLeish. A poem for Kay Boyle. *The Saturday Review* 13.15 February 8, 1936 (6)

J132 "Also Out This Week." A review of *The White Horses of Vienna and Other Stories*. *The New Yorker* 11.52 February 8, 1936 (71) 90w

J133   "Kay Boyle's Stories" by Nathan Rothman. A review of *The White Horses of Vienna and Other Stories*. *The Saturday Review* 13.15 February 8, 1936 (6) 600w

J134   "Kay Boyle's Stories" by Edith H. Walton. A review of *The White Horses of Vienna and Other Stories*. *The New York Times Book Review* 41.6 February 9, 1936 (7) 1000w

J135   "The Style of Miss Kay Boyle" by Elizabeth Hart. A review of *The White Horses of Vienna and Other Stories*. *New York Herald Tribune Books* 12.23 February 9, 1936 (5) 1500w

J136   "Kay Boyle Shows Her Power Once More" by Russell W. Seaver. A review of *The White Horses of Vienna and Other Stories*. *The Boston Transcript* 107.39 February 15, 1936 (3) 450w

J137   A review of *The White Horses of Vienna and Other Stories* by R.A. C.. *The Springfield Republican* 58.24 February 16, 1936 (7e) 550w

J138   "Slot Machine: Peephole." A review of *The White Horses of Vienna and Other Stories*. *Time Magazine* 27.7 February 17, 1936 (70) 220w

J139   "The New Fiction" by Frances Valensi. A review of *The White Horses of Vienna and Other Stories*. *The New Republic* 86.1108 February 26, 1936 (89) 380w

J140   A review of *The White Horses of Vienna and Other Stories*. *Book Review Digest* 32.1 March 1936

J141   "Beauty and the Beast" by Mark Van Doren. A Review of *The White Horses of Vienna and Other Stories*. *The Nation* 142.3687 March 4, 1936 (286, 288) 480w

J142   "What Is It All About?" by Sylvia Pass. A review of *The White Horses of Vienna and Other Stories*. *The Christian Century* 53.10 March 4, 1936 (368) 180w

J143   A review of *The White Horses of Vienna and Other Stories* by Paul Hoffman. *The Atlantic Monthly* 157.4 April 1936 (in Atlantic Bookshelf) 110w

J144   A review of *The White Horses of Vienna and Other Stories* by J.H. *The Churchman* vol. 150 April 15, 1936 (18) 30w

J145   Photograph in Books to Be Published Section. *The New York Times Book Review* 41.38 September 20, 1936 (8)

J146   A review of *365 Days* by Graham Bell. *The New Statesman and Nation* 12.292 n.s. September 26, 1936 (440) 180w

J147   A review of *365 Days* by Edwin Muir. *The Listener* 16.403 September 30, 1936 (644) 300w

J148   A note about *The Death of a Man. The Library Journal* 61.15 (645) 30w

J149   A review of *Death of a Man* by Helen Moran. *The North American Review* 242.2 Winter 1936 (443-445) 900w

J150   A review of *Death of a Man* by Helen MacAfee. *The Yale Review* n.s 26.2 Winter 1936 (x)

J151   "Miss Kay Boyle" by A. C. Boyd. A review of *Death of a Man. The London Mercury* 34.204 October 1936 (562)

J152   A review of *Death of a Man. The Kirkus Review* 4.19 October 1, 1936 (422) 100w

J153   "Fiction" by Peter Burra. A review of *Death of a Man. The Spectator* 157.5649 October 2, 1936 (560) 320w

J154   "New Novels" by J.D. Beresford. A review of *Death of a Man. The Manchester Guardian* #28096 October 2, 1936 (7) 300w

J155   A review of *Death of a Man. London Times Literary Supplement* 35.1809 October 3, 1936 (788-789) 300w

J156   "New Novels" by Edith Shackleton. A review of *Death of a Man. Time and Tide* 17.40 October 3, 1936 (1352) 240w

J157   A review of *Death of a Man* by Richard Church. *John O'London Weekly* 36.913 (90) 500w

J158   "Books of the Times" by Robert Van Gelder. A review of *Death of a Man. New York Times* (daily) 86.28747 October 8, 1936 (21) 800w

J159   "Short Stories" by Graham Greene. A review of *365 Days. The Spectator* 157.5650 October 9, 1936 (604, 606) 130w

J160   A review of *Death of a Man. The New Yorker* 12.34 October 10, 1936 (72)

J161   "Kay Boyle's Sketch of a Likeable Nazi" by Henry Seidel Canby. A review of *Death of a Man. The Saturday Review of Literature* 14.24 October 10, 1936 (12) 450w

J162   *"Death of a Man* Powerful Book of Love Abroad" by F.B. A review of *Death of a Man. The Chicago Tribune* October 10, 1936 (16) 320w

J163   "Kay Boyle's Profound and Poetic Story" by Geoffrey Parsons. A review of *Death of a Man. New York Herald Tribune Books* 13.6 October 11, 1936 (3) 850w

J164   "Kay Boyle's New Novel" by Alfred Kazin. A review of *Death of a Man. The New York Times Book Review* 41.41 October 11, 1936 (6-7) 900w

J165   "Nazi Idyll." A review of *Death of a Man. Time Magazine* 28.15 October 12, 1936 (87) 400w

J166   "Fact and Fiction." A review of *365 Days. London Times Literary Supplement* 35.1811 October 17, 1936 (838) 550w

J167   Review of *Death of a Man* by Edwin Muir. *The Listener* 16.406 October 21, 1936 (786) 750w

J168   "The Brown Blouses of Vienna" by Otis Ferguson. A review of *Death of a Man. The New Republic* 89.1142 October 21, 1936 (322) 900w

J169   "Under the Swastika" by Mark Van Doren. A review of *Death of a Man. The Nation* 143.17 October 24, 1936 (494) 850w

J170   A review of *Death of a Man. Book Review Digest* 32.9 November 1936

J171   "Kay Boyle's Novel *'Death of a Man'* in Austrian Tirol." A review of *Death of a Man. The Springfield Republican* 59.9 November 1, 1936 (7e) 500w

J172   "Romance in the Heart of Austrian Mountains" by Florence Milner. A review of *Death of a Man. The Boston Transcript* 107.262 November 7, 1936 (8) 1050w

J173   A review of *Death of a Man* by E.S.H. *The Churchman* vol. 150 November 15, 1936 (13) 20w

J174   "Politics of Love" by Andrew Corry. A review of *Death of a Man. Commonweal* 25.4 November 20, 1936 (111) 300w

J175   A review of *365 Days* by Margaret Cheney Dawson. *New York Herald Tribune Books* 13.12 November 22, 1936 (13) 600w

J176   A review of *365 Days. Book Review Digest* 32.10 December 1936

J177   "The Book Forum" by Mary M. Colum. A review of *Death of a Man. Forum* 96.6 December 1936 (ix) 200w

J178   A review of *Death of a Man* by Q.D. Leavis. *Scrutiny* 5.3 December 1936 (299) 150w

J179   "Cross Section of a Year" by Louis Kroneneberger. A review of *365 Days*. *The New York Times Book Review* 41.49 December 6, 1936 (34) 750w

J180   "Word Game" by Carlton Brown. A review of *365 Days*. *The New Republic* 89.1149 December 9, 1936 (183) 350w

J181   "Daily Themes: Kay Boyle and Others Provide *365 Days*.'" A review of *365 Days*. *The Springfield Republican* 59.16 December 27, 1936 (7e) 180w

-1937-

J182   "Notes on Recent Novels" by Henry Smith. A review of *Death of a Man*. *The Southern Review* 2.3 January 1937 (577)

J183   "The Library of the Quarter: Outstanding Novels" by Helen MacAfee. A review of *Death of a Man*. *The Yale Review* 26.2 January 1937 (x) 130w

J184   A review of *Death of a Man*. *Booklist* 33.5 January 1937 (156)

J185   "Books in Brief." A review of *365 Days*. *The Christian Century* 54.1 January 6, 1937 (23) 200w

J186   "From Many Worlds" by L.A. Pavey. A review of *The White Horses of Vienna and Other Stories*. *The London Times Literary Supplement* 36.1824 January 16, 1937 (43) 380w

J187   "New Novels" by Peter Quenell. A review of *The White Horses of Vienna and Other Stories*. *The New Statesman and Nation* 13.308 n.s. January 16, 1937 (86-88) 380w

J188   "Unusual Short Stories" by L.A. Pavey. A review of *The White Horses of Vienna and Other Stories*. *The Sunday Times* [London] #5936 January 17, 1937 (11)

J189   "New Novels" by Wilfrid Gibson. A review of *The White Horses of Vienna and Other Stories*. [London] *The Observer* January 17, 1937 (6) 150w

J190   "Fiction" by Peter Burra. A review of *The White Horses of Vienna and Other Stories*. *The Spectator* 158.5665 January 22, 1937 (138) 1200w

J191   A review of *The White Horses of Vienna and Other Stories* by Richard Church. *John O'London Weekly* 36.928 January 22, 1937 (708) 100w

J192   "New Novels" by John Brophy. A review of *The White Horses of Vienna and Other Stories*. *Time and Tide* 18.4 January 23, 1937 (108-110) 90w

J193   "Idiots and Shirts" by C.E. Bechhoffer Roberts. A review of *The White Horses of Vienna and Other Stories*. *The New English Weekly* 10.16 January 28, 1937 (318) 270w

J194   "American Novels" by Benedict Thielen. A review of *Death of a Man*. *The Atlantic Monthly* 159.2 February 1937 (Atlantic Bookshelf) 300w

J195   "Miss Kay Boyle" by V.E. Brooks. A review of *The White Horses of Vienna and Other Stories*. *The London Mercury* 35.208 February 1937 (425) 220w

J196   A review of *The White Horses of Vienna and Other Stories* by Edwin Muir. *The Listener* 17.421 February 3, 1937 (240) 200w

J197   "Short Stories" by Thomas Moult. A review of *The White Horses of Vienna and Other Stories*. *The Manchester Guardian* #28205 February 9, 1937 (5) 350w

J198   "In and Around the Bullseye." A review of *The White Horses of Vienna and Other Stories*. *Punch* Vol. 192 February 10, 1937 (168)

J199   "New Short Stories: American and British." A review of *The White Horses of Vienna and Other Stories*. *The Times* [London] #47613 February 19, 1937 (19) 130w

J200   A review of *The White Horses of Vienna and Other Stories* by Maurice L. Richardson. *English Review* 64.3 March 1937 (383) 170w

J201   "Kay Boyle: An Appreciation" by Katherine F. Hirsh. *Reading and Collecting* 1.4 March 1937 (8)

J202   A review of *Death of a Man* by Desmond Hawkins. *The Criterion* 16.64 April 1937 (500)

J203   "New Novels" by Cyril Connolly. A review of *The First Lover and Other Stories*. *The New Statesman and Nation* 14.347 n.s. October 16, 1937 (606-607) 70w

J204   A review of *The First Lover and Other Stories* by Doreen Wallace. [London] *The Sunday Times* #5975 October 17, 1937 (9)

J205   A review of *The First Lover and Other Stories*. *John O'London Weekly* 38.967 October 22, 1937 (166) 100w

J206   "Fiction" by Kate O'Brien. A review of *The First Lover and Other Stories*. *The Spectator* 159.5704 October 22, 1937 (700)

J207   "The New Novels." A review of *The First Lover and Other Stories*. *The London Times Literary Supplement* 36.1864 October 23, 1937 (780)

J208   "Short Stories" by Thomas Moult. A review of *The First Lover and Other Stories*. *The Manchester Guardian* October 26, 1937 (7) 330w

J209   "New Short Stories" by J.S. A review of *The First Lover and Other Stories*. [London] *The Times* #47828 October 29, 1937 (10) 170w

J210   A review of *The First Lover and Other Stories*. *The London Mercury* 37.217 November 1937 (93)

J211   A review of *The First Lover and Other Stories* by Edwin Muir. *The Listener* 18.461 November 10, 1937 (1039) 250w

J212   "Short Stories" by Tullis Clare. A review of *The First Lover and Other Stories*. *Time and Tide* 18.46 November 13, 1937 (1520-1522) 160w

J213   A review of *365 Days* by Weldon Kees. *The Prairie Schooner* 11.4 Winter 1937 (319-320)

-1938-

J214   A review of *The White Horses of Vienna and Other Stories* and *365 Days* by Howard Baker. *The Southern Review* 3.3 January 1938 (588-589)

J 215   A review of *The First Lover and Other Stories* by T. de V. W. *Dublin Magazine* n.s 13.1 January/March 1938 (79-80)

J216   "Short Stories" by David Gillespie. A review of *The First Lover and Other Stories*. *Left Review* 3.13 February 1938 (821) 500w

J217   "Fiction Chronicle" by A. Desmond Hawkins. A review of *The First Lover and Other Stories*. *The Criterion* 17.68 April 1938 (500)

J218   A review of *Monday Night*. *The Kirkus Review* 6.13 July 1, 1938 (261) 140w

J219   "Books of the Times" by Ralph Thompson. A review of *Monday Night*. *The New York Times* (daily) 87.29405 July 28,1938 (17) 875w

J220   "Walpurgisnacht" by Basil Davenport. A review of *Monday Night*. *The Saturday Review* 18.14 July 30, 1938 (13) 650w

J221   A review of *Monday Night*. *The New Yorker* 14.24 July 30, 1938 (48) 60w

J222   "M. Sylvestre" by Louis Kronenberger. A review of *Monday Night*. *The Nation* 147.5 July 30, 1938 (111) 700w

J223   "The Tormented People of Kay Boyle" by Alfred Kazin. A review of *Monday Night*. *The New York Times Book Review* 43.31 July 31, 1938 (7) 950w

J224   "Kay Boyle: Nine Years." A review of *Monday Night*. *Newsweek* 12.5 August 1, 1938 (29) 400w

J225   "The Lost, to the Lost" by Otis Ferguson. A review of *Monday Night*. *The New Republic* 95.1235 August 3, 1938 (369) 900w

J226   "An Exercise in Horror" by William Soskin. A review of *Monday Night*. *New York Herald Tribune Books* 14.49 August 7, 1938 (4) 1250w

J227   "Flashes of Dementia." A review of *Monday Night*. *Time Magazine* 32.6 August 8, 1938 (51) 330w

J228   A review of *Monday Night* by Philip Hartung. *Commonweal* 28.17 August 19, 1938 (432-433) 300w

J229   "Outstanding Novels" by Ralph Thompson. A review of *Monday Night*. *The Yale Review* n.s. 28.1 Autumn 1938 (viii) 160w

J230   A review of *Monday Night*. *Scribner's Magazine* 104.3 September 1938 (53)

J231   A review of *Monday Night*. *Book Review Digest* 34.7 September 1938

J232   "New Novels" by J.S. A review of *Monday Night*. [London] *The Times* #48113 September 30, 1938 (7) 50w

J233   "The International vs. the Local Outlook" by Mary M. Colum. A review of *Monday Night*. *Forum* 100.4 October 1938 (162-167) 1250w

J234   "Four New Novels" by Charles Marriott. A review of *Monday Night*. *The Manchester Guardian* October 4, 1938 (7) 250w

J235   A review of *Monday Night* by Richard Church. *John O'London Weekly* 40.1017 (71-72) 200w

J236   "New Novels" by L.A.G. Strong. A review of *Monday Night*. *Time and Tide* 1941 October 8, 1938 (1396) 130w

J237   "Books in Brief." A review of *Monday Night*. *The Christian Century* 55.41 October 12, 1938 (1233-1234) 200w

J238   A review of *Monday Night* by Edwin Muir. *The Listener*. 20.509 October 13, 1938 (795) 350w

J239   "Recent Fiction" by Dylan Thomas. A review of *Monday Night*. *The New English Weekly* 14.1 October 13, 1938 (11-12) 200w

J240   "Other New Novels." A review of *Monday Night*. *The London Times Literary Supplement* 37.1915 October 15, 1938 (665) 300w

J241   A review of *A Glad Day* by Louise Bogan. *The New Yorker* 14.36 October 22, 1938 (95-97) 270w

J242   A review of *Monday Night* by Kathleen J. Raine. *Life and Letters* 19.15 November 1938 (103-104)

J243   "An Unhabitual Way" by Babette Deutsch. A review of *A Glad Day*. *The Nation* 147.20 November 12, 1938 (514-515) 500w

J244   "Books in Brief." A review of *A Glad Day*. *The Boston Transcript* 109.277 November 26, 1938 (2) 100w

J245   A review of *A Glad Day* by Selden Rodman. *Common Sense* 7.12 December 1938 (26) 300w

J246   "Poetical Experimentalism" by Ruth Lechlitner. A review of *A Glad Day*. *New York Herald Tribune Books* 15.14 December 4, 1938 (35)

J247   "Nine and Two." A review of *A Glad Day*. *Time Magazine* 32.26 December 26, 1938 (41-43) 100w

-1939-

J248   "Poets of the European Sickness" by Richard Eberhardt. A review of *A Glad Day*. *The Virginia Quarterly Review* 15.1 January 1939 (148-149)

J249   A review of *A Glad Day*. *Book Review Digest* 34.11 January 1939

J250   "Six American Poets" by Dudley Fitts. A review of *A Glad Day*. *The Saturday Review* 19.11 January 7, 1939 (10-11) 150w

J251   A review of *A Glad Day* by Winifred Bryher. *Life and Letters* 20.18 February 1939 (117-124)

J252   "Group of Poets" by Muriel Rukeyser. A review of *A Glad Day*. *The New Republic* 98.1266 March 8, 1939 (144-145)

J253   A quote by Delmore Schwartz from the preface of *365 Days*. *The Southern Review* 4.2 Spring 1939 (351)

J254   "Collection of Kay Boyle's Poems by Willard Trask. A review of *A Glad Day*. *The New York Times Book Review* 44.28 July 9, 1939 (14) 400w

J255   A review of *Monday Night* by George Sutherland Fraser. *Seven* Number 5 Summer 1939 (34-39)

J256   A review of *The Youngest Camel*. *The Kirkus Review* 7.12 June 15, 1939 (241) 70w

J257   "Fine Workmanship" by Reuel Denny. A review of *A Glad Day*. *Poetry, a Magazine of Verse* 54.6 September 1939 (347-349)

J258   A review of *The Youngest Camel* by Anne Caroll Moore. *The Horn Book Magazine*. 15.5 September/October 1939 (295) 60w

J259   "Golden Hoofs and Ice Cream." A review of *The Youngest Camel*. *Time Magazine* 34.10 September 4, 1939 (52) 350w

J260   A review of *The Youngest Camel* by Ellen Lewis Buell. *The New York Times Book Review* 44.37 September 10, 1939 (12) 420w

J261   A review of *The Youngest Camel*. *Book Review Digest* 35.8 October 1939

J262   "Books for Young People" by May Lamberton Becker. A review of *The Youngest Camel*. *New York Herald Tribune Books*. 16.6 October 8, 1939 (8) 600w

J263   A review of *The Youngest Camel* by Alice M. Jordan. *The Horn Book Magazine* 15.6 November/December 1939 (380-381) 70w

J264   A review of *Monday Night*. *The London Mercury* 39.229 November 1939 (99)

J265   A review of *The Youngest Camel* by Margaret Fishback. *The Atlantic Monthly* 164.5 November 1939 (Atlantic Bookshelf) 110w

J266   A review of *Monday Night* by R. W. Stewart. *Library Journal* 64.19 November 1, 1939 (870) 160w

J267   A review of *The Youngest Camel*. Note only. *The New Republic* 101.1302 November 15, 1939 (122) 40w

J268   A brief note about *The Youngest Camel* by Rosemary Carr Benet. *The Saturday Review* 21.4 November 18, 1939 (22) 20w

J269   A review of *The Youngest Camel* by Lena Barksdale. (one sentence only). *The Nation* 149.22 November 25, 1939 (588)

J270   A review of *The Youngest Camel* by Clifton Fadiman. *The New Yorker* 15.41 November 25, 1939 (85) 120w

J271   A review of *The Youngest Camel* by Eleanor Farjeon. *The Listener* 22.568 November 30, 1939 (v) in the Children's Book Supplement. Just a short note.

J272   A review of *The Youngest Camel* by Annabel Williams-Ellis. *The Spectator* 163.5815 December 8, 1939 (842) 30w

J273   A review of *The Youngest Camel* by H.E. Bates. *The New Statesman and Nation* 18.459 n.s. December 9, 1939 (844) 70w

J274   "Private and Public Verse" by Clarence Millspaugh. A review of *A Glad Day*. *The Kenyon Review* 1.1 Winter 1939 (87-89)

J275   "Nine Poets" by Richard P. Blackmur. A review of *A Glad Day*. *The Partisan Review* 6.2 Winter 1939 (108-115) 200w

-1940-

J276   "Two Years of Poetry "by Morton Dauwen Zabel. A review of *A Glad Day*. *The Southern Review* 5.3 January 1940 (568)

J277   A review of *The Crazy Hunter*. *The Kirkus Review* 8.1 January 1, 1940 (5) 150w

J278   "Books: The American Scene" by David Daiches. A review of *The Crazy Hunter*. *The Partisan Review* 7.3 (244-247) January/February 1940 130w

J279   A note about *The Crazy Hunter*. *The Library Journal* 65.3 February 1, 1940 (120) 20w

J280   "A Reader's Almanac" by Virginia Kirkus. A note about *The Crazy Hunter*. *The Saturday Review of Literature* 21.15 February 3, 1940 (14)

J281   "New Novels" by J.S. A review of *The Crazy Hunter*. [London] *The Times* #48559 March 8, 1940 (40) 120w

J282   A review of *The Crazy Hunter* by Clifton Fadiman *The New Yorker* 16.4 March 9, 1940 (76-77) 360w

J283   "Three Short Novels" by Olga Owens. A review of *The Crazy Hunter*. *The Boston Transcript* 111.58 March 9, 1940 (1) 700w

J284   "The Pale Fraternity of Death" by William Soskin. A review of *The Crazy Hunter*. *New York Herald Tribune Books* 16.28 March 10. 1940 (2) 1050w

J285   "Recent and Readable." A review of *The Crazy Hunter*. *Time Magazine* 35.11 March 11, 1940 (87-88) 100w

J286   "Four Novels" by Wilfrid Gibson. A review of *The Crazy Hunter*. *The Manchester Guardian* March 15, 1940 (5) 450w

J287   "Springs of Tragedy." A review of *The Crazy Hunter*. *The London Times Literary Supplement* 39.1989 March 16, 1940 (133) 800w

J288   A review of *The Crazy Hunter* by Anthony West. *The New Statesman and Nation* 19.473 n.s. March 16, 1940 (371-372) 100w

J289   "Among the New Books" by Christopher Stull. A review of *The Crazy Hunter*. *The San Francisco Examiner* 150.62 March 17, 1940 *This World* (23)

J290   "Three Unusual Stories by Kay Boyle" by Peter Monroe Jack. A review of *The Crazy Hunter*. *The New York Times Book Review* 45.11 March 17, 1940 (5) 900w

J291   A review of *The Crazy Hunter* by Edwin Muir. *The Listener* 23.584 March 21, 1940 (597) 1000w

J292   "Psychology and Symbolism" by Harry Thornton Moore. A review of *The Crazy Hunter*. *The Saturday Review* 21.22 March 23, 1940 (10) 400w

J293   "Improvisations of Reality" by Phillip Rahv. A review of *The Crazy Hunter*. *The Nation* 150.12 March 23, 1940 (396) 480w

J294   "New Novels" by Lettice Cooper. A review of *The Crazy Hunter*. *Time and Tide* 21.12 March 23, 1940 (321) 200W

J295   "New Novels" by Frank Swinnerton. A review of *The Crazy Hunter*. [London] *The Observer* March 24, 1940 (5) 130w

J296   A review of *The Crazy Hunter* by Philip T. Hartung. *Commonweal* 31.23 March 29, 1940 (497-498) 370w

J297   "Fiction" by Kate O'Brien. A review of *The Crazy Hunter*. *The Spectator* 164.5831 March 29, 1940 (457) 800w

J298   "Books of the Times" by Charles Poore. A review of *The Crazy Hunter*. *The New York Times* (daily) 89.30016 March 30, 1940 (13) 525w

J299   A review of *The Crazy Hunter*. *Book Review Digest* 36.2 April 1940

J300   "Stories by Kay Boyle" by B.G. A review of *The Crazy Hunter*. *New Masses* 35.2 April 2, 1940 (30)

J301   "Fiction" by Otis Ferguson. A review of *The Crazy Hunter*. *The New Republic* 102.15 April 8, 1940 (480) 550w

J302   "Stories" by Rayner Heppenstall. A review of *The Crazy Hunter*. *The New English Weekly* 16.25 April 11, 1940 (371)

J303   A review of *The Crazy Hunter* by H.E. Bates. *John O'London Weekly* 43.1097 April 19, 1940 (90 100w)

J304   A brief review of *The Crazy Hunter*. *College English* 1.8 May 1940 (721)

J305   A review of *The Crazy Hunter*. *The Christian Century* 57.22 May 29, 1940 (706) 70w

J306   "The New Novels" by Wallace Stegner. A review of *The Crazy Hunter*. *The Virginia Quarterly Review* 16.3 Summer 1940 (459-463)

J307   "Outstanding Novels" by Robert Littell. A review of *The Crazy Hunter*. *The Yale Review* n.s. 29.4 Summer 1940 (xii) 80w

J308   "Poets and Psychologists" by Mary M. Colum. A review of *The Crazy Hunter*. *Forum* 103.6 June 1940 (324)

-1941-

J309   "They Break the Clipper Record" Photograph of the Vail family with text. *The New York World Telegram* 74.12 July 15, 1941 (13)

J310   "Kay Boyle and Six Children Back Home Again" by Agnes Adams. *The New York Post* no v. or issue # July 31 1941 (11)

J311   "From Mont Blanc to Matanack by Clipper: The Vail Children Wish They Had Snow for Skiing." *The Providence Sunday Journal* August 3, 1941

J312   [Kay Boyle] Wins O. Henry Prize for Short Story. *The New York Times* (daily) 91.30603 November 7, 1941 (20)

-1942-

J313   "Kay Boyle Returns." A photograph of Kay Boyle by George Platt Lynes. *Town and Country* 97.4232 January 1942 (62)

J314   "Biographical Note" *Senior Scholastic* 39.16 19-24 January 1942 (180)

J315   Review of *Primer for Combat*. *The Kirkus Review* 10.18 September 15, 1942
         (455) 140w

J316   Photograph. *The New York Times Book Review* 47.38 September 20, 1942
         (12)

J317   A review of *Primer for Combat* by S.E. Sherman. *Library Journal* 67.17
         October 1 1942 (844) 100w

J318   "An Almanac for Fall Reading" by Amy Loveman. A note about
         Primer for Combat. *The Saturday Review of Literature* 25.43 October 24,
         1942 (11)

J319   A review of *Primer for Combat*. *Newsweek* 20.18 November 2, 1942 (72)

J320   "Books of the Times" by Orville Prescott. A review of *Primer for Combat*.
         The New York Times (daily) 92.30963 November 2, 1942 (19) 900w

J321   "What Comes With Defeat" by Marianne Hauser. A review of *Primer for
         Combat*. *The New York Times Book Review* 47.45 November 8, 1942 (6)
         1000w

J322   "Lost Worlds" by Malcolm Cowley. A review of *Primer for Combat*. *The New
         Republic* 107.19 November 9,1942 (614-615) 330w

J323   A review of *Primer for Combat* by Clifton Fadiman. *The New Yorker* 18.39
         November 14, 1942 (78) 90w

J324   "The Last Time She Saw France" by Rosemary Benet. A review of *Primer for
         Combat*. *New York Herald Tribune Books* 19.12 November 15, 1942 (4)
         1000w

J325   A review of *Primer for Combat*. *Booklist* 39.5 November 15, 1942 (102)

J326   A review of *Primer for Combat*. *Book Review Digest* 38.10 December 1942

J327   A review of *Primer for Combat* by Raoul de Roussy de Sales. *The Atlantic
         Monthly* 170.6 December 1942 (152) 500w

J328   "Clamor for Combat" by Jean Connolly. A review of *Primer for Combat*. *The
         Nation* 155.25 December 19, 1942 (689-690) 600w

J329   "Fresh Snow on the Summits" by I.S. A review of *Primer for Combat*. *The
         Christian Science Monitor* 35.26 December 26, 1942 (11) Weekly Magazine
         Section 360w

J330   "Biography" *Current Biography* 3.6 June 1942 (102) edited by Maxine
         Block

-1943-

J331   A review of *Primer for Combat* by Beatrice Gross. *Common Sense* 12.1
        January 1943 (462) 380w

J332   "Two New Novels" by Gertrude Buckman. A review of *Primer for Combat*.
        The *Sewanee Review* 51.2 April/June 1943 (341-345)

J333   A review of *Primer for Combat* by J. Hampson. *The Spectator* 171.6015
        October 8, 1943

J334   A review of *Primer for Combat* by Phillip Toynbee. *The New Statesman and
        Nation* 26.660 October 16, 1943 (254) 130w

J335   A review of *Primer for Combat* by K. John. *The Illustrated London News*
        113.2948 October 23, 1943 (471) 450w

J336   A family photograph with caption by Louise Dahl-Wolf. *Harper's Bazaar*
        77.2783 November 1943 (63)

J337   A review of *Avalanche*. *The Kirkus Review* 11.21 November 1, 1943 (492)
        270w

J338   "Women Interpret Women" by George Herbert Clark. A review of *Primer
        for Combat*. *The Virginia Quarterly Review* 19.1 Winter 1943 (139-144)

J339   A review of *Primer for Combat* by Ray B. West, Jr. *The Rocky Mountain
        Review* (now *Western Review*) 7.2 Winter 1943 (16)

J340   A review of *Primer for Combat* by Robert Littell. *The Yale Review* 32.2
        Winter 1943 (7) 160w

J341   A review of *Primer for Combat* by Charles Neider. *Accent* 3.2 Winter 1943
        (122)

-1944-

J342   A review of *Avalanche* by Ethel S. Brown. *Library Journal* 69.1 January 1,
        1944 (30) 30w

J343   "France: Strong, Exciting and Unconquerable" by Rose Feld. A review of
        Avalanche. *New York Herald Tribune Weekly Book Review* 20.20 January 9,
        1944 (5) 850w

J344   "Kay Boyle's Avalanche Can Be Variously Read" by E.M.B. A review of
        Avalanche. *The Springfield Republican* 66.18 January 9, 1944 (7e) 470w

J345   A review of *Avalanche. Best Sellers* 3.20 January 15, 1944 (149) 200w

J346   "Kay Boyle's Coincidence and Melodrama" by Struthers Burt. A review of *Avalanche. The Saturday Review* 27.3 January 15, 1944 (6) 1100w

J347   "Kay Boyle and the Saturday Evening Post" by Edmund Wilson. A review of *Avalanche. The New Yorker* 19.47 January 15, 1944 (66+) 1500w

J348   A review of *Avalanche. Booklist* 40.9 January 15, 1944 (183)

J349   "Alpine Adventure" by Catherine Maher. A review of *Avalanche. The New York Times Book Review* 49.3 January 16, 1944 (4-5) 480w

J350   "French Girl Learns Man She Loves Flouts Germans" by Irene Elwood. A review of *Avalanche. The Los Angeles Times* January 16, 1944 Books and Authors section

J351   "Pot-Boyler." A review of *Avalanche. Time Magazine* 43.3 January 17, 1944 (96, 98, 100) 400w

J352   "Hollywood Thriller." A review of *Avalanche. Commonweal* 39.14 January 21, 1944 (357) 330w

J353   "Italicized Passages" by Diana Trilling. A review of *Avalanche. The Nation* 158.4 January 22, 1944 (104) 120w

J354   "Avalanche: The Book Versus the Critics" by Elizabeth Bullock. A review of *Avalanche. The Chicago Sun Book Week* 1.26 January 23, 1944 (2) 1100w

J355   "Love in the Underground." A review of *Avalanche. Newsweek* 23.4 January 24, 1944 (72, 74) 400w

J356   "Alpine Adventure" by M.W.S. A review of *Avalanche. The Christian Science Monitor* 36.55 January 31, 1944 (18) 600w

J357   A review of *Avalanche. The Cleveland Open Shelf* January 1944 (4)

J358   A review of *Avalanche. Book Review Digest* 40.1 March 1944

J359   A review of *Avalanche* by N.E. Monroe. *The Catholic World* 158.948 March 1944 (600-601) 300w

J360   "Ski Trooper Husband Aided Kay Boyle's Book" by Douglas Gilbert. (with photograph) *The New York World-Telegram* 77.46 August 24, 1944 (15)

J361   "The War Years" by Margaret C. Scoggin. A review of *Avalanche. The Horn Book Magazine* 20.5 September /October 1944 (399-400)

J362   A review of *Avalanche*. *Booklist* 41.3 October 15, 1944 (63)

J363   "Fiction" by Kate O'Brien. A review of *Avalanche*. *The Spectator* 173.6078 December 22, 1944 (584) 600w

J364   "New Novels" by Wilfrid Gibson. A review of *Avalanche*. *The Manchester Guardian* December 29, 1944 (3) 150w

J365   "New Novels" by Walter Allen. A review of *Avalanche*. *Time and Tide* 25.53 December 30, 1944 (1152) 250w

J366   A review of *American Citizen* by F. Cudworth Flint. *The New York Times Book Review* 49.52 December 31, 1944 (4) 750w

-1945-

J367   "Smugglers of Men." A review of *Avalanche*. *The London Times Literary Supplement* 44.2240 January 6, 1945 (5) 360w

J368   A review of *Avalanche* by K. John. *The Illustrated London News* 116.3011 January 6, 1945 (26) 100w

J369   "Writer to Writer, Kay Boyle Speaks of a Mate in Service" by Leo Kennedy. A review of *American Citizen*. *The Chicago Sun Book Week* 2.24 January 7, 1945 (4) 360w

J370   A review of *American Citizen*. *Book Review Digest* 40.12 February 1945

J371   A review of *Avalanche* by Henry Reed. *The New Statesman and Nation* 29.730 February 17, 1945 (112) 220w

J372   A review of *Avalanche* by Edwin Muir. *The Listener* 33.839 February 8, 1945 (162) 400w

J373   A review of *American Citizen* by Jeremy Ingalls. *Poetry* 65.6 March 1945 (333-335)

J374   A review of *A Frenchman Must Die*. *Kirkus Review* 13.23 December 1, 1945 (534) 130w

-1946-

J375   "Under-cover Stuff" by Bernadine Kielty. A note on Kay Boyle. *The Ladies Home Journal* 63.3 March 1946 (5)

J376 "New Novels of the Spring Season" by Rose Feld. A review of *A Frenchman Must Die*. *New York Herald Tribune Weekly Book Review* 22.32 March 31, 1946 (10) 700w

J377 "Maqui Leader's Long Search for an Underground Quisling" by David Karno. A review of *A Frenchman Must Die*. *The Chicago Sun Book Week* 3.36 March 31, 1946 (6) 270w

J378 A review of *A Frenchman Must Die*. *Booklist* 42.14 April 1, 1946 (247)

J379 "Manhunt" by Lawrence Lee. A review of *A Frenchman Must Die*. *The New York Times Book Review* 51.14 April 7, 1946 (43) 370w

J380 A review of *A Frenchman Must Die* by Helen L. Butler. *Best Sellers* 6.2 April 15, 1946 (17-18)

J381 "The War After the War" by Robert Pick. A review of *A Frenchman Must Die*. *The Saturday Review* 29.16 April 20, 1946 (16) 650w

J382 A review of *A Frenchman Must Die*. *Book Review Digest* 42.3 May 1946

J383 A review of *Thirty Stories*. *Kirkus Review* 14.18 September 15, 1946 (465) 160w

J384 "Kay Boyle: Journalist" by Eugene Jolas. *The New York Times Book Review* 51.47 November 24, 1946 (8)

J385 "New Novels" by Charles Marriott. A review of *A Frenchman Must Die*. *The Manchester Guardian* November 29, 1946 (3) 80w

J386 "Love and Intrigue." A review of *A Frenchman Must Die*. *The Times Literary Supplement* 45.2339 November 30, 1946 (589) 480w

J387 A review of *A Frenchman Must Die* by K. John. *The Illustrated London News* 119.3110 November 30, 1946 (632) 150w

J388 "The Mature Craft of Kay Boyle" by Struthers Burt. A review of *Thirty Stories*. *The Saturday Review* 29.48 November 30, 1946 (11) 1100w

J389 A review of *Thirty Stories* by J.V. *The San Francisco Chronicle* 163.139 December 1, 1946 Christmas Book Section (32) 250w

J390 "Author's Preference." A review of *Thirty Stories*. *The Chicago Sun Book Week* 4.19 December 1, 1946 (42) 90w

J391 "Stories to Remember" by Edith Mirrielees. A review of *Thirty Stories*. *The New York Times Book Review* 51.48 December 1, 1946. (9, 72) 1000w

J392 "Short Story Technician" by Richard Match. A review of *Thirty Stories*. *New York Herald Tribune Weekly Book Review* 23.15 December 1, 1946 (6) 650w

J393 "Fiction" by Walter Allen. A review of *A Frenchman Must Die*. *The Spectator* 177.6180 December 6, 1946 (622) 100w

J394 A review of *A Frenchman Must Die* by Henry Reed. *The Listener* 36.935 December 12, 1946 (856) 450w

J395 "Tour in Technicolor" by Margaret Barrett. A review of *Thirty Stories*. *New Masses* 62.1 December 31, 1946 (23-24)

-1947-

J396 A review of *Thirty Stories*. *Book Review Digest* 42.11 January 1947

J397 A review of *Thirty Stories*. *Booklist* 43.8 January 1, 1947 (132)

J398 A review of *A Frenchman Must Die* by Tullis Clare. *Time and Tide* 28.3 January 18, 1947 (83) 150w

J399 "Fiction Chronicle" by Elizabeth Hardwick. A review of *Thirty Stories*. *The Partisan Review* 14.2 March/April 1947 (196-200)

J400 "Reply to Kay Boyle" by Margery Barrett concerning her review of December 31, 1946. *New Masses* 63.3 April 15, 1947 (21-22)

J401 A review of *1939*. *The Kirkus Review* 15.9 May 1, 1947 (245) 170w

J402 A review of *Thirty Stories* by Rosemary Paris. *Furioso* 2.4 Summer 1947 (81-82)

J403 A review of *1939*. *Kirkus Review* 15.24 December 15, 1947 (683) 170w Same review appeared earlier, May 1, 1947.

-1948-

J404 "Two Cards at a Time" by Nona Balakian. A review of *1939*. *The New York Times Book Review* 53.7 February 15, 1948 (22) 650w

J405 "The Man Without a Country" by Florence Haxton Bullock. A review of *1939*. *New York Herald Tribune Weekly Book Review* 24.26 February 15, 1948 (4) 700w

J406 "Avalanche in the Haute-Savoie" by Walter Havighurst. A review of *1939*. *The Saturday Review* 31.9 February 28, 1948 (12) 550w

J407   "Intensity in the Alps." A review of *1939*. *Time Magazine* 51.9 March 1, 1948 (92) 270w

J408   A review of *1939*. *Booklist* 44.14 March 1, 1948 (233)

J409   "Choice of Love or War" by Joseph Hallock. A review of *1939*. *New York Herald Tribune Weekly Book Review* 24.29 March 7, 1948 (3)

J410   "Briefly Noted." A review of *1939*. *The New Yorker* 24.3 March 13, 1948 (109-110) 120w

J411   "The Sitzmark" by Edward Weeks. A review of *1939*. *The Atlantic Monthly* 181.4 April 1948 (108) 420w

J412   A review of *1939*. *Book Review Digest* 44.2 April 1948

J413   "New Novels" by Paul Bloomfield. A review of *1939*. *The Manchester Guardian* July 16, 1948 (3) 210w

J414   "Fiction" by Robert Kee. A review of *1939*. *The Spectator* 181.6265 July 23, 1948 (122-124) 220w

J415   "Fiction of the War" by K. John. A review of *1939*. *The Illustrated London News* 123.3197 July 31, 1948 (138)

J416   "Personal Conflicts." A review of *1939*. *London Times Literary Supplement* 47.2427 August 7, 1948 (441) 180w

J417   A review of *Thirty Stories* by George D. Painter. *The Listener* 40.1023 September 2, 1948 (353) 400w

-1949-

J418   A review of *His Human Majesty*. *Booklist* 45.12 February 15, 1949 (201)

J419   A review of *His Human Majesty*. *Kirkus Review* 17.5 March 1, 1949 (117) 160w

J420   A review of *His Human Majesty* by Robert E. Kingery. *Library Journal* 74.7 April 1, 1949 (546) 80w

J421   "Foreign Legion in Colorado" by Nathan L. Rothman. A review of *His Human Majesty*. *The Saturday Review* 32.15 April 9, 1949 (13) 850w

J422   "In and Out of Books" by Ralph Thompson. A review of *His Human Majesty*. *The New York Times Book Review* 54.15 April 10, 1949 (8) 250w

J423 "The War in Colorado" by Nona Balakian. A review of *His Human Majesty*. *The New York Times Book Review* 54.15 April 10, 1949 (21) 500w

J424 "Kay Boyle Writes a Novel of War, Men and the Colorado Mountains" by Carolyn Stull. A review of *His Human Majesty*. *The San Francisco Sunday Examiner and Chronicle This World* 12.49 April 10, 1949 (22) 950w

J425 "Capturing the Well Nigh Inexpressible" by Florence Haxton Bullock. A review of *His Human Majesty*. *New York Herald Tribune Weekly Book Review* 25.34 April 10, 1949 (5) 800w

J426 A review of *His Human Majesty*. *Booklist* 45.16 April 15, 1949 (281)

J427 "Romance and Poetry in Kay Boyle's Novel." A review of *His Human Majesty*. *The Chicago Sunday Tribune Magazine of Books* 108.16 April 17, 1949 Part 4 (3)

J428 "Ski Troops in the Rockies" by Jex Martin, Jr. A review of *His Human Majesty*. *The Chicago Sun* 2.72 April 26, 1949 (45) 350w

J429 A review of *His Human Majesty*. *The New Yorker* 25.10 April 30, 1949 (95) 180w

J430 A review of *His Human Majesty*. *Book Review Digest* 45.3 May 1949

J431 "A Group of Late Spring Novels" by Ruth Chapin. A review of *His Human Majesty*. *The Christian Science Monitor* 41.135 May 5, 1949 (11) 450w

J432 A review of *His Human Majesty* by Peter White. *Commonweal* 50.6 May 20, 1949 (155-156) 350w

J433 "New Books" by Marguerite Page Corcoran. A review of *His Human Majesty*. *The Catholic World* 169.1012 July 1949 (317) 350w

J434 A review of *His Human Majesty* by Howard Troyar. *The Antioch Review* 9.3 Fall 1949 (409-414)

-1950-

J435 "New Novels" by John Richardson. A review of His *Human Majesty*. *The New Statesman and Nation* 39.1006 June 17, 1950 (693-694) 380w

-1951-

J436 A review of *The Smoking Mountain*. *Booklist* 47.16 April 15, 1951 (285)

J437   "Averted Hearts" by Louise Field Cooper. A review of *The Smoking Mountain*. *The Saturday Review* 34.16 April 21, 1951 (17-18) 700w

J438   "On an Author" by John K. Hutchens. *New York Herald Tribune Book Review* 27.36 April 22, 1951 (3)

J439   "Another Face of Germany" by Virgilia Peterson. A review of *The Smoking Mountain*. *New York Herald Tribune Book Review* 27.36 April 22, 1951 (8) 800w

J440   "Vignettes of Postwar Germany" by Carolyn Stull. A review of *The Smoking Mountain*. *The San Francisco Sunday Examiner and Chronicle* This World 14.51 April 22, 1951 (20) 600w

J441   "On the Books of an Author" by John Hutchins. *The New York Times Book Review* 56.16 April 22, 1951 (3)

J442   "In Germany the Ruins Still Smolder" by Harry T. Moore. A review of *The Smoking Mountain*. *The New York Times Book Review* 56.16 April 22, 1951 (5) 650w

J443   "Briefly Noted." A review of *The Smoking Mountain*. *The New Yorker* 27.11 April 28, 1951 (103-104) 50w

J444   "Mind, Spirit of the German People Today" by Mildred Walker. A review of *The Smoking Mountain*. *The Chicago Sunday Tribune* 110.17 April 29, 1951 Magazine of Books (5) 410w

J445   "Books and Things" by Lewis Gannett. A review of *The Smoking Mountain*. *New York Herald Tribune* (daily) 111.38151 April 30, 1951 (15)

J446   A review of *The Smoking Mountain* (note only). *Booklist* 47.17 May 1, 1951 (310)

J447   A review of *The Smoking Mountain*. *Book Review Digest* 47.4 June 1951

J448   A review of *The Smoking Mountain* by L.S. Mann. *The Springfield Republican* 73.41 June 24, 1951 (11d) 250w

J449   A review of *The Smoking Mountain*. *The US Quarterly Book Review* 7.3 September 1951 (241-242) 250w

-1952-

J450   A review of *Plagued by the Nightingale*. *Dublin Magazine* n.s 27.1 January/March 1952 (79-80)

J451   A review of *The Smoking Mountain. Adelphi* 28.3 May 1952 (652-653) 400w

J452   "Search in Limbo" by Anthony Powell. A review of *The Smoking Mountain. The Times Literary Supplement* May 9, 1952 (309)

J453   A review of The *Smoking Mountain* by Anthony Calder-Marshall. *The Listener* 47.1211 May 15, 1952 (805) 200w

J454   "New Short Stories" by Angus Wilson. A review of *The Smoking Mountain. The New Statesman and Nation* 43.1111 June 21, 1952 (738) 300w

J455   A review of *The Smoking Mountain. Dublin Magazine* n.s. 27.4 October/December 1952 (71-72)

-1953-

J456   "Kay Boyle" by Richard Carpenter. *English Journal* 42.8 November 1953 (425-430)

J457   "Kay Boyle" by Richard Carpenter. *College English* 15.2 November 15, 1953 (81-87)

-1955-

J458   A review of *The Seagull on the Step. Kirkus Review* 23.2 January 15, 1955 (47-48) 170w

J459   A review of *The Seagull on the Step* by Reed A. Hoey. *Library Journal* 80.5 March 1, 1955 (560) 140w

J460   "The Gulf Between" by Sidney Alexander. A review of *The Seagull on the Step. The New York Times Book Review* 60.19 May 8, 1955 (5) 550w

J461   "Vibrant, Rich Tale of France" by Richard Sullivan. A review of *The Seagull on the Step. The Chicago Sunday Tribune* 114.19 May 8, 1955 Magazine of Books (3) 370w

J462   "Kay Boyle's Craft and Magic in a Moving Novel of Post War France" by Virgilia Peterson. A review of *The Seagull on the Step. New York Herald Tribune Book Review* 31.39 May 8, 1955 (1) 750w

J463   "Love Letters to France" by Lewis Gannett. A review of *The Seagull on the Step. New York Herald Tribune* (daily) 115.39621 May 9, 1955 (15)

J464   "Behind the Facade" by James Kelly. A review of *The Seagull on the Step*. *The Saturday Review* 38.20 May 14, 1955 (16) 700w

J465   A review of *The Seagull on the Step* by Doris D. Maguire. *Best Sellers* 15.4 May 15, 1955 (39) 400w

J466   A review of *The Seagull on the Step*. *Booklist* 51.18 May 15, 1955 (388)

J467   "Hope out of France" by Paul Engle. A review of *The Seagull on the Step*. *The New Republic* 132.20 May 16, 1955 (38-39) 900w

J468   A review of *The Seagull on the Step* by Paul Pickrel. *The Yale Review* n.s. 44.4 Summer 1955 (638) 200w

J469   A review of *The Seagull on the Step* by Riley Hughes. *The Catholic World* 181.1084 July 1955 (312) 220w

J470   A review of *The Seagull on the Step* by Adrienne Foulke. *The Nation* 181.2 July 9, 1955 (28-29) 650w

J471   "Novel of French Fishing Village" by Ethel Dexter. A review of *The Seagull on the Step*. *The Springfield Republican* 77.15 July 10. 1955 (5c) 220w

J472   "Among the New Books" by Carolyn Stull. A review of *The Seagull on the Step*. *The San Francisco Sunday Examiner and Chronicle This World* 19.13 July 24, 1955 (20) 600w

J473   A review of *The Seagull on the Step*. *Book Review Digest* 51.6 August 1955

J474   A review of *The Seagull on the Step*. *The New Yorker* 31.31 September 17, 1955 (171) 160w

J475   "Good Intentions." A review of *The Seagull on the Step*. [London] *The Times* #53398 December 8, 1955 (13) 60w

J476   "Strained Relations." A review of *The Seagull on the Step*. *London Times Literary Supplement* 54.2806 December 9, 1955 (737) 90w

-1957-

J477   "Clear U.S. Aid, Novelist Wife of Disloyalty" *Chicago Tribune* 116.96 April 22, 1957 part 2 (4)

J478   "Pair Cleared in 'Risk' Case" by Herbert Foster. *The Washington Post* 80.138 April 22, 1957 (A9)

J479   A review of *Thirty Stories*. *The New Mexico Quarterly* 27.4 Winter 1957/1958 (376)

-1958-

J480   A review by Syd Bakal of the CBS Desilu Playhouse presentation of *The Crazy Hunter*. *New York Herald Tribune* (daily) 118.40935 December 30, 1958 (sec. 2 page 4)

-1959-

J481   A photograph of Kay Boyle and family. *The New York Times Book Review* 64.24 June 14, 1959 (4) J482 "Folk Tale and Fanciful Stories." A review of *The Youngest Camel Reconsidered and Rewritten. The Horn Book Magazine* 35.5 October 1959 (387) 110w

J482   "Folk Tale and Fanciful Stories." A review of *The Youngest Camel Reconsidered and Rewritten. The Horn Book Magazine* 35.5 October 1959 (387) 110w

J483   Two reviews of *The Youngest Camel Reconsidered and Rewritten;* one by Laurie Dudley 50w and one by Elizabeth Beal 80w. *Library Journal* 84.20 November 15, 1959 (3628)

-1960-

J484   "Sight and Sound." A review of *Generation Without Farewell. McCall's* 87.4 January 1960 (8) 80w

J485   "Novel About the Occupation" by Max Cosman. A review of *Generation Without Farewell. Commonweal* 71.15 January 8, 1960 (425-426) 750w

J486   A review of *Generation Without Farewell. Booklist* 56.10 January 15, 1960 (295-296)

J487   "The Light and the Dark" by Granville Hicks. A review of *Generation Without Farewell. The Saturday Review* 43.3 January 16, 1960 (59) 560w

J488   "In and Out of Books: Kay Boyle" by Lewis Nichols. *The New York Times Book Review* 65.3 January 17, 1960 (8)

J489   "There's No Armistice" by Virgilia Peterson. A review of *Generation Without Farewell. The New York Times Book Review* 65.3 January 17, 1960 (4,26) 700w

J490   "Kay Boyle's Thirteenth Novel: Occupied and Occupier" by Martha MacGregor. A review of *Generation Without Farewell. The New York Post* no volume or issue # Weekend Magazine January 17, 1960 (M12)

J491   "Lyric, Symbolic Tale of Post War Germany" by Richard Sullivan. A review of *Generation Without Farewell. The Chicago Sun Tribune* 119.3 January 17, 1960 Magazine of Books (3) 250w

J492   "Novelist's Vision of Post War Germany" by Gene Baro. A review of *Generation Without Farewell. New York Herald Tribune Book Review* 36.24 January 17, 1960 (5) 600w

J493   "Generation Without Trial" by John K. Hutchens. A review of *Generation Without Farewell. New York Herald Tribune* (daily) 119.41319 January 18, 1960 (15)

J494   "Books of the Times" by Herbert Mitgang. A review of *Generation Without Farewell. The New York Times* (daily) 109.37250 January 19, 1960 (33) 800w

J495   "Occupied Germany" by Melvin Maddocks. A review of *Generation Without Farewell. The Christian Science Monitor* 52.47 January 21, 1960 (11) 550w

J496   A review of *Generation Without Farewell* by Gouveneur Pauling. *The Reporter* 22.2 January 21, 1960 (47)

J497   "Kay Boyle's Technique in Occupied Germany" by William Hogan. A review of *Generation Without Farewell. The San Francisco Chronicle* 96.22 January 22, 1960 (23) 550w

J498   "Victors and Vanquished." A review of *Generation Without Farewell. Time Magazine* 75.4 January 25, 1960 (94, 96) 400w

J499   "One Novelist's Germany" a review of *Generation Without Farewell. Newsweek* 55.4 January 25, 1960 (92-93)

J500   "This Time the Germans Were Receiving Orders" by John Parkham. A review of *Generation Without Farewell. New York World Telegram and Sun* January 25, 1960 (21)

J501   "An Occupational Hazard" by Stephen Tonsor. A review of *Generation Without Farewell. The National Revue* 8.5 January 30, 1960 (80-86)

J502   A review of *Generation Without Farewell* by William B. Hill. *Best Sellers* 19.21 February 1, 1960 (377) 450w

J503   A review of *Generation Without Farewell* by Lelia Saunders. *Library Journal* 85.3 February 1, 1960 (674) 150w

J504   A review of *Generation Without Farewell* by F. R. *The Los Angeles Times* 79.66 February 7, 1960 Section V (6)

J505   "New Novels" by Susan Brady. A review of *Generation Without Farewell*. *The Progressive* 24.3 March 1960 (57-58)

J506   A note on *Generation Without Farewell*. *Bookmark* 19.6 March 1960 (150-151) 50w

J507   A review of *Generation Without Farewell* by Riley Hughes. *The Catholic World* 190.1140 March 1960 (380-381) 350w

J508   "Germans with Pious Compassion" by Benjamin Haimonwitz. A review of *Generation Without Farewell*. *The New Leader* 43.13 March 28, 1960 (29)

J509   A note about *Generation Without Farewell*. *English Journal* 49.4 April 1960 (276)

J510   "Kay Boyle's Fiction" by Harry T. Moore. A review of *Generation Without Farewell*. *The Kenyon Review* 22.2 Spring 1960 (323-326)

J511   A review of *Generation Without Farewell* by Belle Pomer. *The Canadian Forum* 40.473 June 1960 (66) 480w

J512   A review of *Generation Without Farewell*. *Book Review Digest* 56.4 June 1960

J513   "Novels of the Week" by Norman Schrapnel. A review of *Generation Without Farewell*. *The Manchester Guardian* July 8, 1960 (4) 160w

J514   "Big Gleeful Hood" by John Coleman. A review of *Generation Without Farewell*. *The Spectator* 205.6889 July 8, 1960 (73) 170w

J515   "In Jest and Jeopardy." A review of *Generation Without Farewell*. *The London Times Literary Supplement* 59.3045 July 8, 1960 (429) 110w

J516   A review of *Generation Without Farewell* by David Williams. *Time and Tide* 41.28 July 9, 1960 (804)

J517   "New Fiction." A review of *Generation Without Farewell*. [London] *The Times* #54823 July 14, 1960 (15)

J518   "A Summer's Dozen" by Alfred Klausler. A review of *Generation Without Farewell*. *The Christian Century* 77.35 August 31, 1960 (998) 120w

J519   "Some Recent Fiction" by William J. Stuckey. A review of *Generation Without Farewell*. *The Minnesota Review* 1.1 October 1960 (117-121)

-1962-

J520   "Voices In Varying Keys" by James H. Koch. A review of *Collected Poems*. *The New York Times Book Review* 67.36 September 9, 1962 (34) 120w

J521   A review of *Collected Poems* by Dorothy Nyren. *Library Journal* 87.17 October 1, 1962 (3457) 140w

J522   A review of *Collected Poems*. *Booklist* 59.5 November 1, 1962 (199) 80w

J523   "Two Poets and Their Muses" by David Ray. A review of *Collected Poems*. *The New Republic* 147.19 November 10, 1962 (22) 300w

-1963-

J524   "Books in Brief" by Mary E. Kelly. A review of *The Smoking Mountain*. *Library Journal* 88.4 February 15, 1963 (792)

J525   "Kay Boyle: Missionary and Scholar" by John B. Jarzavek. *Wesleyan Argies* February/March 1963

J526   A review of *Collected Poems*. *Book Review Digest* 59.1 March 1963

J527   "A Most Neglected Good Author" by Sandra Dallas. A review of *The Smoking Mountain*. *The Denver Sunday Post* March 10, 1963 Roundup (10) 450w

J528   Review of *The Smoking Mountain* by G.D. Davenport. *The National Review* 14.14 April 9, 1963 (293)

J529   "Never Stop Learning." *The New Haven Register* 151.110 April 21, 1963 The Register Magazine (3).

J530   "Love Poems" by Robert E. Knoll. A review of *Collected Poems*. *The Prairie Schooner* 37.2 Summer 1963 (176-178)

J531   "We Know What Happened, But We Don't Know Why" by Flora Lewis. A review of *The Germans: An Indictment of My People* by Gudrun Temple with an introduction by Kay Boyle. *The New York Times Book Review* 68.18 May 5, 1963 (3)

J532   "Books in Brief." A short note about *The Smoking Mountain*. *New York Herald Tribune Books Review* 39.27 May 26, 1963 (13)

J533   "Poetry Chronicle" by Richard Howard. A review of *Collected Poems*. *Poetry* 102.4 July 1963 (253-254) 500w

J534   "Kay Boyle, Champion of Understanding" by Mildred Schroeder. *The San Francisco Examiner* 219.105 October 13, 1963 Women Today Section (6)

J535   A review of *The Smoking Mountain* by Robert Atler. *Critique: Studies in Modern Fiction*. 6.3 Winter 1963\1964 (181)

-1964-

J536   A photograph of Kay Boyle, Wright Morris and Mark Harris. *The New York Times Book Review* 69.7 February 16, 1964 (6-7)

J537   "Sketch of a Poet." A note with a sketch of Kay Boyle by Helen Breyer. *The San Francisco Sunday Examiner and Chronicle* This World 27.32 April 12, 1964 (34)

J538   "Writer Kay Boyle" by Horace Schwartz. An article. *The San Francisco Examiner* 220.152 May 31, 1964 (13)

J539   "Kay Boyle: The Figure in the Carpet" by Richard C. Carpenter. *Critique: Studies in Modern Fiction* 7.2 Winter 1964\1965 (65-78)

-1966-

J540   A review of *Nothing Ever Breaks Except the Heart and Other Stories. Kirkus Review* 34.8 April 15, 1966 (448)

J541   A review of *Nothing Ever Breaks Except the Heart and Other Stories. The Saturday Review* 49.16 April 16, 1966 (34)

J542   "An Old Welcome Style: Kay Boyle's Stories" by W.G. Rogers. A review of *Nothing Ever Breaks Except the Heart and Other Stories. New York Herald Tribune* (daily) June 10, 1966

J543   A review of *Nothing Ever Breaks Except the Heart and Other Stories* by Jessie Kitching. *Publisher's Weekly* 189.24 June 13, 1966 (126) 100w

J544   "May the Good Prevail" by Thomas Lask. A review of *Nothing Ever Breaks Except the Heart and Other Stories. The New York Times* 115.39595 June 21, 1966 (41)

J545   A review of *Nothing Ever Breaks Except the Heart and Other Stories* by Glendy Culligan. *The Chicago Sun* and *Washington Post Book Week* 3.42 June 26, 1966 (12) 900w

J546   "Two Ladies—-and Elements of Style" by William Hogan. A review of *Nothing Ever Breaks Except the Heart and Other Stories. The San Francisco Chronicle* 102.181 June 30, 1966 (41)

J547   "Author Kay Boyle Spurs New Kind of Integration" by Mildred Schroeder. *The San Francisco Examiner* 224.182 July 1, 1966 (19)

J548   A review of *Nothing Ever Breaks Except the Heart and Other Stories* by Irene N. Pompea. *Best Sellers* 26.7 July 1, 1966 (130) 500w

J549   "Aristocrat of the Short Story" by Maxwell Geismer. A review of *Nothing Ever Breaks Except the Heart and Other Stories*. *The New York Times Book Review* 71.28 July 10, 1966 (4, 16) 1250w

J550   "20 Stories from a Worker in Words" by Richard Sullivan. A review of *Nothing Ever Breaks Except the Heart and Other Stories*. *The Chicago Sunday Tribune* 120.191 July 10, 1966 in the *Books Today* section. (1)

J551   "Kay Boyle to See 'For Self' in Cambodia" *The San Francisco Chronicle* 102.193 July 12, 1966 (6)

J552   "Where Have All the Children Gone?" by Theodore L. Gross. A review of *Nothing Ever Breaks Except the Heart and Other Stories*. *The Saturday Review* 49.29 July 16, 1966 (35) 800w

J553   "The Short Story: Antique or Still Relevant" by Marion Simon. A review of *Nothing Ever Breaks Except the Heart and Other Stories*. *The National Observer* 5.30 July 25, 1966 (19)

J554   "The Varied World of Kay Boyle" by M.G. A review of *Nothing Ever Breaks Except the Heart and Other Stories*. *The Christian Science Monitor* 58.205 July 28, 1966 (7) 280w

J555   A review of *Nothing Ever Breaks Except the Heart and Other Stories* by Eli M. Oboler. *Library Journal* 91.14 August 1966 (3763) 100w

J556   "5 Cambodia Trippers Bring Back Same Views." Article about Kay Boyle's visit to Cambodia. *The San Francisco Examiner* 224.223 August 11, 1966 (11)

J557   A short note about *Plagued by the Nightingale*. *Choice* 3.7 September 1966 (518)

J558   A review of *Nothing Ever Breaks Except the Heart and Other Stories*. *Book Review Digest* 62.7 September 1966

J559   An announcement for the publication of *Pinky, the Cat Who Liked to Sleep*. No review. *The Kirkus Review* 34.17 September 1, 1966 (899)

J560   "Kay Boyle's Bitter View of Johnson" An interview. *The San Francisco Chronicle* 102.258 September 15, 1966 (15)

J561   "Books for Young Adults." A review of *Nothing Ever Breaks Except the Heart and Other Stories*. *Library Journal* 91.16 September 15, 1966 (4366) 100w

J562   A review of *Nothing Ever Breaks Except the Heart and Other Stories*. *The San Francisco Examiner* September 15, 1966

J563   A review of *Nothing Ever Breaks Except the Heart and Other Stories*. *Booklist* 63.3 October 1, 1966 (156)

J564   A review of *Nothing Ever Breaks Except the Heart and Other Stories* by Bernard Dick. *The Catholic World* 204.1220 November 1966 (123)

J565   A review of *Nothing Ever Breaks Except the Heart and Other Stories*. *Booklist* 63.5 November 1, 1966 (307)

J566   "Children's Books" by Lavinia Russ. A review of *Pinky, the Cat Who Liked to Sleep*. *Publishers Weekly* 190.25 December 26, 1966 (99) 110w

J567   "A Question of Fiction" by Betty Hoyenga. A review of *Nothing Ever Breaks Except the Heart and Other Stories*. *The Prairie Schooner* 40.4 Winter 1966/1967 (370-371)

-1967-

J568   A review of *Pinky, the Cat Who Liked to Sleep* by Patricia Alice. *Library Journal* 92.2 January 15, 1967 (327) 110w

J569   A review of *Pinky, the Cat Who Liked to Sleep* by P.A. McKenzie. *The Young Reader's Review* vol. 3 February 1967 (7)

J570   A review of *Nothing Ever Breaks Except the Heart and Other Stories*. *Choice* 4.3 May 1967 (286) 280w

J571   A review of *Pinky, the Cat Who Liked to Sleep*. *The Bulletin of the Center for Children's Books* vol. 20 May 1967 (135)

J572   A note about *Pinky, the Cat Who Liked to Sleep*. *Times Literary Supplement* 66.3431 November 30, 1967 (1137)

J573   "Dramatic Heroes" by Norman Holmes Pearson. A review of *The Autobiography of Emanuel Carnevali*. *The New York Times Book Review* 72.49 December 10, 1967 (32-34) 1000w

J574   "New War Protest—-67 Arrested" An article *The San Francisco Chronicle* 103.354 December 20, 1967 (1, 15)

J575   "Draft Protesters Stay in Jail" An article *The San Francisco Examiner* year 103.153 December 20, 1967 (4)

J576   "45 Days for Joan Baez" An article *The San Francisco Chronicle* 103 355 December 21, 1967 (16)

J577   "The Tortured Poet Skipped Elegantly Out" by James Schevill. A review of *The Autobiography Emanuel Carnevali* edited and with a preface by Kay

Boyle. *The San Francisco Sunday Examiner and Chronicle This World* 31.35 December 24, 1967 (28, 31)

J578   "The Heart is Not Enough" by W. J. Stucky. A review of *Nothing Ever Breaks Except the Heart and Other Stories. Critique: Studies in Modern Fiction.* 9.2 1967 (85-88)

-1968-

J579   A review of *The Autobiography of Emanuel Carnevali* by Arthur Curley. *Library Journal* 93.3 February 1, 1968 (541) 330w

J580   A review of *Being Geniuses Together* by Glenn O. Carey. *Library Journal* 93.10 May 15, 1968 (1998) 200w

J581   A review of *The Autobiography of Emanuel Carnevali* with a foreword by Kay Boyle. *Choice.* 5.4 June 1968 (480) 280w

J582   "Those Paris Years" by Malcolm Cowley. A review of *Being Geniuses Together.* *The New York Times Book Review* 73.23 June 9, 1968 (1, 34-35) 1700w

J583   "That's How It Used To Be...in Camelot" by Mario Puzo. A review of *Being Geniuses Together. The Chicago Tribune* and *The Washington Post Book World* 2.23 June 9, 1968 (1, 3) 800w

J584   "Kay Boyle Among the Geniuses" by William Hogan. A review of *Being Geniuses Together. The San Francisco Chronicle* 104.63 June 19, 1968 (43)

J585   "Some Tampering with Molly Bloom" by William Hogan. A review of *Being Geniuses Together. The San Francisco Chronicle* 104.64 June 20, 1968 (43)

J586   "Kay Boyle: Genius at Large" by Mildred Hamilton. *The San Francisco Examiner and Herald* 1968.25 June 23, 1968 Women Today Section (4)

J587   "Again the Lost Ones" by Saul Maloff. A review of *Being Geniuses Together.* *Newsweek* 72.2 July 8, 1968 (70) 900w

J588   "The Last Time They Saw Paris" by Kathleen Cannell. A review of *Being Geniuses Together. The Christian Science Monitor* 60.192 July 11, 1968 (5) 1000w

J589   "Expatriates En Brochette" by Charles Poore. A review of *Being Geniuses Together. The New York Times* 117.40353 July 18, 1968 (31)

J590   "Kay Boyle's Ascent" by William Brandon. A review of *Being Geniuses Together. The Progressive* 32.9 September 1968 (50-51)

J591   "Notes on Current Books." A review of *Being Geniuses Together*. *The Virginia Quarterly Review* 44.4 Autumn 1968 (cix) 230w

J592   A review of *Being Geniuses Together* by William McBrien. *Commonweal* 89.5 November 1, 1968 (162, 164-166) 1600w

J593   A review of *Pinky in Persia* by Marsha J. Shapiro. *Library Journal* 93.20 November 15, 1968 (4393)

J594   "Kay Boyle Assesses San Francisco State" An interview with Bob Haesler. *The San Francisco Chronicle* 104.313 November 16, 1968 (13)

J595   "Hayakawa vs. Boyle: Meanwhile a War of Words." An article. *The San Francisco Chronicle* 104.332 December 15, 1968 (16)

J596   "S.F. State Closed for Holidays a Week Early" An article. *The San Francisco Chronicle* 104.341 December 14, 1968 (12)

-1969-

J597   A short note about *Pinky in Persia* by Rose H. Agree. *Instructor* 78.6 February 1969 (180) 50w

J598   "Spirits" by Jean Stafford. A review of *Being Geniuses Together*. *The New York Review of Books* 12.8 April 24, 1969 (26-29) 900w

-1970-

J599   A review of *Testament for My Students and Other Poems*. *Book Review Digest* 1970 annual (164)

J600   "Back from Limbo" by Saul Maloff. A review of *Year Before Last*. *The New Republic* 162.4 January 24, 1970 (30-31)

J601   A review of *Testament for My Students and Other Poems*. *Kirkus Review* 38.3 February 1, 1970 (140) 120w

J602   A review of *Testament for My Students and Other Poems* by Albert Johnson. *Publisher's Weekly* 197.5 February 2, 1970 (87) 130w

J603   "Knocking Around the Latin Quarter" by Anthony Powell. A review of *Being Geniuses Together*. *The London Daily Telegraph* April 9, 1970 (6)

J604   "First Persons" by Arthur Marshall. A review of *Being Geniuses Together*. *New Statesman* 79.2039 April 10, 1970 (512-513)

J605   A review of *Testament for My Students and Other Poems* by Patricia H. Marvin. *Library Journal* 95.8 April 15, 1970 (1486) 120w

J606   A review of *Being Geniuses Together* by John McGahern. *The Listener* 83.2143 April 23, 1970 (554-555)

J607   "Blue-eyed Boy" by Patrick Anderson. A review of *Being Geniuses Together*. *The Spectator* 224.7400 April 25, 1970 (552)

J608   "I Poems and You Poems" by Robert W. French. A review of *Testament for My Students and Other Poems*. *The Nation* 210.22 June 8, 1970 (695-698) 700w

J609   A review of *Testament for My Students and Other Poems*. *Booklist* 66.22 July 15, 1970 (1372)

J610   A review of *Testament for My Students and Other Poems* by E. Nelson. *Spirit Quarterly* 37.3 Fall 1970 (42)

J611   A review of *The Long Walk at San Francisco State and Other Essays*. *Kirkus Review* 38.19 October 1, 1970 (1126) 250w

J612   A review of *The Long Walk at San Francisco State and Other Essays* by Albert Johnson. *Publisher's Weekly* 198.16 October 19, 1970 (48) 190w

J613   "Generous Hope and Living Without Illusion" by Chad Walsh. A review of *Testament for My Students and Other Poems*. *Chicago Tribune* and *Washington Post Book World* 4.46 November 15, 1970 (6) 340w

-1971-

J614   "In a Drama of Voices" by Victor Howes. A review of *Testament for My Students and Other Poems*. *The Christian Science Monitor* 63.33 January 5, 1971 (9)

J615   "Saga of the Strike at S. F. State" by John H. Bunzel. A review of *The Long Walk at San Francisco State and Other Essays*. *The San Francisco Sunday Examiner and Chronicle* 1971.4 January 24, 1971 This World (36)

J616   A review of *The Long Walk at San Francisco State and Other Essays* by Frank C. Brown. *Best Sellers* 30.22 February 15, 1971 (492) 600w

J617   A review of *The Long Walk at San Francisco State and Other Essays* by Mark R. Yerburgh. *Library Journal* 96.6 March 15, 1971 (972) 110w

J618   A review of *The Long Walk at San Francisco State and Other Essays* by Carey McWilliams. *The Nation* 212.17 April 26, 1971 (540) 200w

J619   A review of *The Long Walk at San Francisco State and Other Essays*. *Booklist* 67.17 May 1, 1971 (713)

J620   A review of *The Long Walk at San Francisco State and Other Essays*. *Choice* 8.3 May 1971 (434) 200w

J621   A review of *The Long Walk at San Francisco State and Other Essays* by Nelson Algren. *Critic* 29.6 July/August 1971 (68-70) 1350w

J622   "Plastic Possibilities" by M.L. Rosenthal. A review of *Testament for My Students and Other Essays*. *Poetry Magazine* 119.2 November 1971 (101)

-1972-

J623   "Public and Private Poetry." A review of *Enough of Dying* by William Dickey. *The Hudson Review* 25.2 Summer 1972 (296)

J624   A review of *The Long Walk at San Francisco State and Other Essays*. *Book Review Digest* 1972 Annual (143)

J625   A review of *Enough of Dying* by Carey McWilliams. *The Nation* 214.26 June 26, 1972 (828)

J626   "Kay Boyle: The Cincinnati Years" by Richard R. Centing. *The Ohioana Quarterly* 15 Spring 1972 (11-13)

-1974-

J627   A review of *The Underground Woman*. *Kirkus Review* 42.22 November 15, 1974 (1214) 200w

J628   A review of *The Underground Woman* by Barbara Bannon. *Publisher's Weekly* 206.22 November 25, 1974 (39) 140w

-1975-

J629   "Highbrow Masculine Fantasies and Unfocused Mythology" by Larry McMurtry. A review of *The Underground Woman*. *The Washington Post* 98.32 January 6, 1975 (B4) 360w

J630   "Life with Daughter" by Peter Prescott. A review of *The Underground Woman*. *Newsweek* 85.2 January 13, 1975 (68) 450w

J631   "The New Mission of an Elegant Protester." Interview with Mildred Hamilton. *The San Francisco Sunday Examiner and Chronicle* 1975.3 January 19, 1975 Sunday Scene (7)

J632   "Woman Divided: Boyle's Fiction Contains Pertinent Facts" by Roger Ramsey. A review of *The Underground Woman. The Chicago Tribune* 128.19. January 19, 1975 Book World Section 7 (1)

J633   A review of *The Underground Woman. The New Yorker* 50.48 January 20, 1975 (97) 140w

J634   A review of *The Underground Woman* by Gail Harlow. *Library Journal* 100.3 February 1, 1975 (309-310) 190w

J635   A review of *The Underground Woman* by J.D. O'Hara. *The New York Times Book Review* 80.5 February 2, 1975 (4) 430w

J636   "Fine Print: Kay Boyle, et al." by Doris Grumbach. A review of *The Underground Woman. The New Republic* 172.6 February 8, 1975 (33)

J637   A review of *The Underground Woman* by Sister Joseph Marie Anderson. *Best Sellers* 34.22 February 15, 1975 (512) 350w

J638   "Kay Boyle: A Study in Paradox" by Blake Green. *The San Francisco Chronicle* 111.48 February 17, 1975 (12, 14) "People" section

J639   A review of *The Underground Woman. Booklist* 71.13 March 1, 1975 (668)

J640   "Prisoner of an Ancient Reality" by Robert Kirsch. A review of *The Underground Woman. The Los Angeles Times* vol.94 No Number March 6, 1975 Sec. IV (2) 400w

J641   "The Telling of the Story" by Phillip Corwin. A review of *The Underground Woman. The Nation* 220.11 March 22, 1975 (347) 1300w

J642   "Books Briefly." A review of *The Underground Woman. The Progressive* 39.4 April 1975 (45)

J643   A review of *The Underground Woman* by Fay Stender with John Kelly. *The San Francisco Review of Books* 1.1 April 1975 (1, 10, 18)

J644   "Fiction Chronicle" by Blanche H. Gelfant. A review of *The Underground Woman. The Hudson Review* 28.2 Summer 1975 (315-316) 530w

J645   A review of *The Underground Woman* by Sister J.M. Anderson. *Choice* 12.5 & 6 July/August 1975 (680) 210w

-1976-

J646   "Kay Boyle: A Profile." An interview with Charles Fracchia. *The San Francisco Review of Books* 1.12 April 1976 (7-9)

J647   "Jails Don't Daunt Protesting Grandmother" by Kathy Drew. *Lost Generation Journal* 4.1 Winter 1976 (14-15, 22-23)

J648   "Kay Boyle Dedicates Self to Human Dignity" by Kathy Drew. *Lost Generation Journal* 4.1 Winter 1976 (23)

-1977-

J649   A review of *Monday Night. The Reprint Bulletin Book Review*. 22.4 October 4, 1977 (30)

-1978-

J650   "Siftings" by Doris Grumbach. A review of *Monday Night. The Saturday Review of Literature* 5.7 January 7, 1978 (41)

J651   "A Literary Legend Who Refuses to Rest on Her Laurels" by Mickey Friedman. *The San Francisco Examiner* 104.263 September 27, 1978 (21)

J652   "A Bibliography of Works by and about Kay Boyle" by Roberta Sharp. *Bulletin of Bibliography and Magazine Notes*. 35.4 October/December 1978 (180-189, 191)

-1980-

J653   A review of *Fifty Stories* by Barbara Bannon. *Publisher's Weekly* 218.4 July 25, 1980 (147) 120w

J654   A review of *Fifty Stories. Kirkus Review* 48.16 August 15, 1980 (1119)

J655   "Fiction: Fifty Stories" by Carol Cook. A review of *Fifty Stories. The Saturday Review* 7.13 September 1980 (70) 170w

J656   A review of *Fifty Stories* by William Dudley Hooper. *Booklist* 77.2 September 15, 1980 (98)

J657   "Kay Boyle's 50" by William Hogan. A review of *Fifty Stories. The San Francisco Chronicle* 116.218 September 26, 1980 (55)

J658   "Distant Landscapes" by Earl Rovit. A review of *Fifty Stories. The Nation* 231.9 September 27, 1980 (286-287) 1000w

J659   "Moving and Maturing" by Vance Bourjaily. A review of *Fifty Stories. The New York Times Book Review* 85.39 September 28, 1980 (9, 32) 2400w

J660   A review of *Fifty Stories. The Saturday Review* 7.14 October 1980 (117)

J661   A review of *Fifty Stories* by Michael A. Haynes. *Library Journal* 105.17 October 1, 1980   (2103-2104) 140w

J662   "Kay Boyle: Writing with an Eye for Detail" by Cyra McFadden. A review of *Fifty Stories. Chicago Tribune Book World* (No volume or number) October 12, 1980 (3) 700w

J663   A review of *Fifty Stories. Publisher's Weekly* 218.16 October 17, 1980 (8-9)

J664   "Verities of the Human Heart" by Susan Wood. A review of *Fifty Stories. Washington Post Book World* 10.42 October 19, 1980 (4) 1200w

J665   "Power and Delicacy from Kay Boyle" by Beth Ruby. A review of *Fifty Stories. The Christian Science Monitor* 72.244 November 10, 1980 (B6-B7) 580w

J666   A review of *Fifty Stories. Quill and Quire* 48.12 December 1980 (36)

J667   "Kay Boyle Stories Make the Past Vital" by Edward M. White. A review of *Fifty Stories. The Los Angeles Times* (no volume or #) December 10, 1980 Sec V (27) 700w

J668   "Kay Boyle Has Led Remarkable Life" by Barbara Venton. *Siesta Key Pelican* December 18, 1980 (B4)

-1981-

J669   "Saints and Other Folk" by Peter LaSalle. A review of *Fifty Stories. America* 144.4 January 31, 1981 (84-85)

J670   "Sensitive to Life" by Richard J. Lietz. A review of *Fifty Stories. The Bloomsbury Review* 1.2 January/February 1981 (19)

J671   A review of *Fifty Stories. The Virginia Quarterly Review* 57.2 Spring 1981 (59)

J672   A review of *Plagued by the Nightingale* by Patricia Craig. *The Times Literary Supplement* 80.4072 April 17, 1981 (430)

J673   A review of *Fifty Stories. Publisher's Weekly* 220.6 August 7, 1981 (77)

J674   A review of *Fifty Stories* by Frank Gado. *Studies in Short Fiction* 18.4 Fall 1981 (459)

J675   A review of *Fifty Stories. The New York Times Book Review* 86.45 November 8, 1981 (51)

-1982-

J676   "Fiction and Failure" by Adrian Poole. A review of *Fifty Stories. The London Review of Books* 4.7 April 15 to May 5, 1982 (18) 600w

J677   "Special Notices" by William Boyd. A review of *Fifty Stories. London Magazine* 22.3 June 1982 (96-97) 700w

J678   "Security: Some Notes on The Shaping of Kay Boyle's Art" by David Koch. *Pembroke Magazine* Number 14 1982 (153-160)

J679   "Fred Zimmerman Distills a New Film from an Old Realm" a review of "Five Days One Summer" by Benedict Nightingale. Adapted from "Maiden, Maiden" *The New York Times Arts and Leisure* Section II, November 7, 1982 (1, 16)

-1985-

J680   A review of *Words That Somehow Must Be Said* by Genevieve Stuttaford. *Publisher's Weekly* 227.18 May 3,1985 (59) 140w

J681   A review of *Words That Somehow Must Be Said* by John Brosnahan. *Booklist* 81.18 May 15, 1985 1289)

J682   A review of *Words That Somehow Must Be Said. Kirkus Review* 53.10 May 15, 1985 (453-454)

J683   A review of *Words That Somehow Must Be Said* by Linda Simon. *Library Journal* 110.11 June 15, 1985 (62) 110w

J684   "Boyle's Moral Essays Chart the Centuries Contours" by Tom D'Evelyn. A review of *Words That Somehow Must Be Said. The Christian Science Monitor* 77.145 June 19, 1985 (21-22) 700w

J685   "The Writer as a Moral Force" by Emily Leider. A review of *Words That Somehow Must Be Said. The San Francisco Chronicle* 1985.27 July 7, 1985 Review Section (3)

J686   "Kay Boyle: From the Left Bank to the New Left" by Robert W. Smith. A review of *Words That Somehow Must Be Said. The Washington Post Book World* 15.28 July 14, 1985 (10)

J687   "In the City of Flesh" by David MacLean. A review of *The Devil in the Flesh* as translated by Kay Boyle. *Body Politic* August 1985 (37)

J688   "Books in Short" by Karen Fitzgerald. A review of *Words That Somehow Must Be Said*. *Ms* 14.2 August 1985 (74) 420w.

J689   A review of *Babylon* by Rene Crevel with an afterword by Kay Boyle. Reviewed by Merle Rubin. *The Los Angeles Times Book Review* 104.244 August 4, 1985 (5)

J690   "60 years of Passion and Compassion" by Hugh Ford. A review of *Words That Somehow Must Be Said*. *The New York Times Book Review* 90.34 August 25, 1985 (20) 1800w

J691   "Difficult Times" by Faith Evans. A review of *Words That Somehow Must Be Said*. *The Observer* [London]. August 25, 1985 (17)

J692   "The Surprise of the Floor" by Robert Boucheron. A review of *Babylon* by Rene Crevel translated by Kay Boyle. *The New York Native* No. 123 August 26 to September 1, 1985 (36)

J693   "The Maid Drinks Kerosene" by Clayton Eshleman. A review of *Babylon* by Rene Crevel with an afterword by Kay Boyle. *The New York Times Book Review* 90.38 September 22, 1985 (31)

J694   A review of *This Is Not a Letter and Other Poems* by Sybil Steinberg. *Publisher's Weekly* 228.13 September 27, 1985 (93) 150w

J695   "Virtues of Dissent" by Anne Chisolm. A review of *Words That Somehow Must Be Said*. *Times Literary Supplement* 84.4304 September 27, 1985 (1076) 700w

J696   A review of *Words That Somehow Must Be Said* by Susan Slocum Hinerfeld. *The Los Angeles Times Book Review* 104.300 September 29, 1985 (10)

J697   A review of *Babylon* by Rene Crevel with an afterword by Kay Boyle. Reviewed by Irving Malin. *Review of Contemporary Fiction* 5.3 Fall 1985 (198)

J698   A review of *Words That Somehow Must Be Said* by Gail Pool. *The Wilson Library Bulletin* 60.3 November 1985 (68) 400w

J699   "The Tall Banana Trees." A review of *Words That Somehow Must Be Said*. *Manas* 38.46 November 13, 1985 (3-4, 8)

J700   "Saturday Review Talks to Kay Boyle" by Kevin Murphy *The Saturday Review* 11.6 November/December 1985 (72)

J701   A review by Janice Eidus of *Words That Somehow Must Be Said*. *The Saturday Review* 11.6 November/December 1985 (72) 360w

J702   "Literary Rebel Sees the Poet as a 'Sentient Harpsichord'" by Joanna Oetter. A review of *Babylon* by Rene Crevel with an afterword by Kay Boyle. *The St. Louis Post Dispatch* December 14, 1985

J703   "Moral Witness" by Annette Kobak. A review of *Words That Somehow Must Be Said*. *Times Educational Supplement* 76.3625 December 20, 1985 (17)

J704   "Strictly San Francisco" by Robert Linkous. A review of *Words That Somehow Must Be Said*. *The San Francisco Review of Books* 10.2 and 3 Fall/Winter 1985 (5)

-1986-

J705   A review of *This Is Not a Letter and Other Poems*. *Booklist* 82.10 January 15, 1986 (727)

J706   "Kay Boyle's Promises Are for Keeping" by Ruth Bauerle. *Columbus Dispatch* 115.259 March 16, 1986 (8F)

J707   A review of *This Is Not a Letter and Other Poems* by Janet Lewis. *The Los Angeles Times Book Review* 105.131 April 13, 1986 (9)

J708   A review of *This Is Not a Letter and Other Poems*. by R. Whitman. *Choice* 23.9 May 1986 (1386)

J709   "Lifetime Anti-Fascist Writer Speaks Her Piece" by Lee Heller. *People's Daily World* June 25, 1986 (A11)

J710   A review of *Year Before Last*. *The Washington Post Book World* 16.40 October 5, 1986 (12) 120w

J711   "Kay Boyle: A Writer's Duty to Speak for the Disenfranchised" by Kay Mills. *The Los Angeles Times Opinion* 105.313 October 12, 1986 (3, 6)

J712   "Still a Rebel at 84" by Kay Mills. *The Houston Chronicle* 86.4 October 17, 1986 sec 5 (3)

J713   "At 84, Writer Kay Boyle Still Speaks for the Disinherited" *The Norfolk Virginia Pilot* October 17, 1986 (B10)

J714   "A Radical Disguised as a Lady" by Hugh Ford. *The Los Angeles Times Book Review* (No volume or number) November 9, 1986 (2)

J715   A review of *Year Before Last*. *The New York Times Book Review* 91.46 November 16, 1986 (42)

J716   A review of *My Next Bride*. *The New York Times Book Review* 91.46 November 16, 1986 (42)

J717   "Take the Old Fury in Your Empty Arms" by David Dwyer. A review of *This Is Not a Letter and Other Poems*. *The American Book Review* 8.6 November/December 1986 (22-23)

J718   "A Genius Alone" by Nancy Ramsey. *Vogue* 176.12 December 1986 (174, 176)

-1987-

J719   "Rediscovering Love" by Robert Smith. A review of *Kay Boyle: Artist and Activist* by Sandra Whipple Spanier. *The Bloomsbury Review* 7.1 January/February 1987 (7)

J720   "Heart Over Head" by Ann Morrissett Davidon. A review of *Kay Boyle: Artist and Activist* by Sandra Whipple Spanier. The Progressive 51.2 February 1987 (44-45)

J721   "Modernism and Morality" by Peggy Phelan. A review of *Words That Somehow Must Be Said*. *The Woman's Review of Books* 4.6 March 1987 (10)

-1988-

J722   "Refusals to Mourne" by Rachel Hadas. A review of *This Is Not a Letter and Other Poems*. *Parnassus: Poetry in Review* 14.2 Fall/Winter 1988 (215-232)

J723   "Kay Boyle: Writer of Conscience" by Kate Moses. *KPFA Folio* 40.2 February 1, 1988 (5)

J724   "Kay Boyle: An 86th Birthday Valentine" by Charles Amirkhanian. *KPFA Folio* 40.2 February 1, 1988 (5)

J725   A review of *Life Being the Best and Other Stories* by Penny Kaganoff. *Publisher's Weekly* 233.10 March 11, 1988 (96) 200w

J726   A review of *Life Being the Best and Other Stories*. *Kirkus Review* 56.6 March 15, 1988 (418)

J727   "Boyle's 'Astronomer's Wife' " by Robyn Gronning. *Explicator* 46.3 Spring 1988 (51-53)

J728   A review of *Life Being the Best and Other Stories* by Brad Hooper. *Booklist* 84.16 April 15, 1988 (1390)

J729   A review of *This Is Not a Letter and Other Poems* by Ann Hornaday. *The New York Times Book Review* 93.27 July 3, 1988 (12)

J730   A review of *Words That Somehow Must Be Said*. *The Washington Post Book World* 18.37 September 11, 1988 (12) 100w

J731   "Revolution, the Woman, and the Word: Kay Boyle" by Suzanne Clark. *Twentieth Century Literature* 34.3 Fall 1988 (322-333)

J732   *"My Next Bride:* Kay Boyle's Text of the Female Artist" by Deborah Denenholz Morse. *Twentieth Century Literature* 34.3 Fall 1988 (334-346)

J733   "Sexual Politics in Kay Boyle's *Death of a Man"* by Burton Hatlen. *Twentieth Century Literature* 34.3 Fall 1988 (347-362)

J734   "Kay Boyle's High Country: *His Human Majesty"* by Ian S. MacNiven. *Twentieth Century Literature* 34.3 Fall 1988 (363-374)

J735   "Tails You Lose: Kay Boyle's War Fiction" by Edward Uehling. *Twentieth Century Literature* 34.3 Fall 1988 (375-383)

J736   "Call Forth a Good Day: The Non-Fiction of Kay Boyle" by Elizabeth S. Bell. *Twentieth Century Literature* 34.3 Fall 1988 (384-391)

J737   A review of *Life Being the Best and Other Stories* by Robert Smith. *The Cleveland Plain Dealer* September 26, 1988

-1989-

J738   A review of *Death of a Man* by Penny Kaganoff. *Publisher's Weekly* 235.11 March 17, 1989 (90) 200w

J739   "Old Novel Offers Insights into Nazism" by Steve Kettmann. A review of *Death of a Man*. *The San Francisco Chronicle* 125.207 September 14, 1989 Sec E (5)

J740   "Kay Boyle: A Long and Eloquent Life." by Beth Ashley. *The Marin Independent Journal* December 3, 1989 Sec E (1, 8)

-1990-

J741   "Classic Returns" by Michael Rogers. A review of *Death of a Man*. *Library Journal* 115.2 February 1, 1990 (113) 130w

J742   "Classic Returns" by Michael Rogers. A review of *Plagued By the Nightingale*. Library Journal 115.20 November 15, 1990 (100) 60w

J743   A review of *Three Short Novels* by Sybil Steinberg. *Publisher's Weekly* 237.51 December 21, 1990 (49)

-1991-

J744   A note about *Gentlemen, I Address You Privately*. *Belles Lettres* 6.3 Spring 1991 (45)

J745   "Power Versus Love: Author Kay Boyle" by Louise Erdrich. *Lear's* 4.2 April 1991 (76-79)

J746   "Classic Returns" by Michael Rogers. A review of *Gentlemen, I Address You Privately*. *Library Journal* 116.6 April 1, 1991 (158) 70w

J747   A review of *Gentlemen, I Address You Privately*. *The Los Angeles Times Book Review* 110.146 April 28, 1991 (6) 100w

J748   A review of *Gentlemen, I Address You Privately* by Lauren Belfer. *The New York Times Book Review* 96.18 May 5, 1991 (25) 110w

J749   A short note about *Gentlemen, I Address You Privately*. *Lambda Book Report* 2.10 May/June 1991 (37)

J750   A review of *Plagued by the Nightingale*. *The Antioch Review* 49.3 Summer 1991 (475)

J751   A review of *Collected Poems* by Penny Kaganoff. *Publisher's Weekly* 238.28 June 28, 1991 (97) 200w

J752   A review of *Collected Poems* by Ellen Kaufman. *Library Journal* 116.13 August 1991 (105) 150w

J753   A short note about *Three Short Novels*. *American Literature* 63.3 September 1991 (599)

J754   A review of *Collected Poems* by Pat Monaghan. *Booklist* 88.1 September 1, 1991 (23)

J755   "Kay Boyle's Poetic Commentary" by Emily Leider. A review of *Collected Poems*. *The San Francisco Chronicle* No volume or issue number. December 22, 1991 Review section (8)

-1992-

J756   A review of *Collected Poems*. *Multicultural Review* 1 April 1991 (73) 250w+

J757   A short note about *Fifty Stories*. *Publisher's Weekly* 239.23 May 18, 1992 (65) 10w

J758   "Classic Returns" by Michael Rogers. A review of *Fifty Stories*. *Library Journal* 117.10 June 1, 1992 (188) 100w

J759   A review of *Fifty Stories*. *The New York Times Book Review* 97.35 August 30, 1992 (24)

J760   A review of *Three Short Novels*. *Belles Lettres* 7.4 Summer 1992 (28) 500w

J761   A short note about *Fifty Stories*. *Belles Lettres* 8.1 Fall 1992 (8)

J762   "A Hot Heart and Cold Eye" by Connie Willet Everett. A review of *Collected Poems*. *Ohioana* 35.3 Fall 1992 (150-153)

J763   A review of *Collected Poems* by Molly Bendall. *The Antioch Review* 50.4 Fall 1992 (780) 350w

J764   "Kay Boyle: Novelist, Anti-War Activist" by Burt Folkart. An obituary. *The Los Angeles Times* Metro section 112.26 December 29, 1992 (B8)

J765   "Kay Boyle, Writer and Poet is Dead" by Larry Hatfield. *The San Francisco Examiner* 128.172 December 29, 1992 (A15)

J766   "Kay Boyle, 90, Writer of Novels and Stories, Dies" by Eric Pace. *The New York Times* 142.49195 December 29, 1992 (A13L)

J767   "Kay Boyle: Author, Teacher, Crusader" by Maitland Zane. *The San Francisco Chronicle* 128.298 December 29, 1992 (A20)

J768   "Kay Boyle, Poet, Author, Peace Activist Dies at 90" by Richard Pearson. *The Washington Post* 116.25 December 30, 1992 (B6)

J769   "Kay Boyle." An obituary. *Facts on File* 52.2718 December 31, 1992 (1012)

-1993-

J770   Obituary by Andrew Popper. *U.S. New and World Report* 114.1 January 11, 1993 (12)

J771   "Died: Kay Boyle" obituary. *Time Magazine* 141.2 January 11, 1993 (15)

J772   "Obituary" *Current Biography* 54.2 February 1993 (57)

J773   A short note on *Fifty Stories*. *American Literature* 65.1 March 1993 (204)

J774   A review of *Collected Poems* by Charles Daughaday *Western American Literature* 28.2 Summer 1993 (166-167)

J775   "Classic Returns" by Michael Rogers. A review of *The Crazy Hunter. Library Journal* 118.13 August 1993 (170) 70w

J776   A short note about *Collected Poems. Lambda Book Report* 3.12 September/October 1993 (45)

-1994-

J777   A review of *The Crazy Hunter* by Gale Harris. *Belles Lettres* 9.3 Spring 1994 (65)

J778   "Oh, Kay: Short Story Writer" by Meg Cohen. Harper's Bazaar 127.3389 April 1994 (229)

J779   "For Kay Boyle, Nothing Succeeded Like Excess" by William Pritchard. A review of *Kay Boyle: Author of Herself* by Joan Mellen. *New York Times Book Review* May 1, 1994 (11)

J780   "Typed Until 3 A.M." by Regina Marler. A review of *Kay Boyle: Author of Herself* by Joan Mellen. *The Los Angeles Times* August 8, 1994 Book Review Section

J781   "Abortion, Identity Formation, and the Expatriate Woman Writer: H.D. and Kay Boyle in the Twenties" by Donna Hollenberg. *Twentieth Century Literature* 40.4 Winter 1994 (499-517)

K

Dissertations

K1   "The Achievements of Kay Boyle" by Byron Jackson. DA 29.899A (Florida, 1968)

K2   "Kay Boyle: From the Aesthetics of Exile to the Polemics of Return" by Frank Gado DA29.4485A

K3   "Henry Miller and Kay Boyle: The Divided Stream in American Expatriate Literature, 1930-1940)" by Elizabeth Shugart Bell DA40 (1980) 5862A

L

Audio and Video Recordings

L1   "New Sounds in American Fiction" directed by Gordon Lish. Created and produced for Cummings Publishing Company [Menlo Park, California] by New Sounds, Inc. a division of Educational Development Company. [Palo Alto, California. [1969] A set of 12 long play records which includes "Winter Night" by Kay Boyle read by Edward Binns.

L2   "The Mind of the Third Reich: William Shirer, Richard Crossman and Kay Boyle discuss Nazi Psychology" [place?]: Center for Cassette Studies, 1971 Sound recording.

L3   "Kay Boyle" produced and edited by The American Poetry Archive and The Poetry Center at San Francisco. San Francisco: American Poetry Archive, 1975 USA: Poetry Series Video Recording. Kay Boyle reads: "Poets," "A Poem for the Students of Greece," from "Testament for My Students," from "The Winter Soldiers," "A Poem for February First 1975," "A Poem for Rosemary and Timothy Leary," "The Ruined Village," (This poem later revised and renamed "The Stones of a Seventeenth Century Village") "A Message for Babette Deutsch," (This poem later revised and renamed "A Poem for Vida Hadjebi Tabrizi.) Video cassette recorded October 12, 1975.

L4   "Kay Boyle Interview with Kay Bonetti" Columbia, Missouri: American Audio Prose Library, 1985 AAPL 5012 Recorded March 1985 at Cottage Grove, Oregon.

L5   Excerpts from "The Crazy Hunter" and "A Declaration for 1955" Columbia, Missouri: American Audio Prose, 1985 Sound cassette

L6   Frontiers/Kay Boyle. Washington, D.C.: Watershed Intermedia, 1987 Series: Signature Series/Watershed Tapes C215 Reflections from *Collected Poems, Testament for My Students and Other Poems*, and *This Is Not a Letter and Other Poems*.

L7   "Kay Boyle" Los Angeles: The Foundation, 1989 Lannan Literary Series #13 The Lannan Foundation in association with Metropolitan Pictures and EZTU. Produced and directed by Lewis MacAdams and John Dorr. Kay Boyle reads "Poets," "Advice to the Old (Including Myself)," from "A Poem for Samuel Beckett," "The New Integration," "A Poem About Black Power," "A Comeallye for Robert Carlton Brown," "A Square Dance for a Square," "A Poem for Vida Hadjebi Tabrizi" and "A Poem for the Students of Greece." She is also interviewed by Shawn Wong a former Student and a novelist in his own right. Video Cassette recorded in Los Angeles on September 11, 1989.

Index

References in this index are to item numbers in this bibliography. Capital letters are used for the titles of books described in Sections A and B. Other book titles are italicized,

A

Abbott, Bernice, A35c
Abbott, H. Porter, B80
Abernathy, Milton, B109
Able, Hilde, C170, C171
Abrahams, William, B90, H109, H130
ACCENT ANTHOLOGY, B34, H48
Adams, Agnes, J310
Adams, Bronte, H144
Age of Anxiety: Modern American Stories, The, H114
Age of the Modern and Other Literary Essays, I40
Aglion, Raoul, C188
Agree, Rose S., J597
Aichinger, Ilse, C337
Albertine, Susan, B113
Albrecht, Robert C., H108
Alexander, Sidney, J460
Algren, Nelson, J621
Alice, Patricia, J568
Allen, Fred, B14
Allen, Walter, J365, J393
Allender, Nina Evans, vii, B108, B109
Altenbernd, Lynn, H90
Alter, Robert, I96, J535
American Authors and Books 1640-1940, I9
American Authors and Books 1640 to the Present Day, I43
AMERICAN CITIZEN NATURALIZED IN LEADVILLE, COLORADO, A20
American Harvest: Twenty Years of Creative Writing in the United States, H32
AMERICAN NOVELISTS OF TODAY, B39, I16
AMERICAN POETRY ARCHIVE, B86

American Poetry Since 1970: Up Late, H136
American Short Stories: 1820 to the Present, H69
American Short Story, The, I46
American Short Story: 1900-1945, The, I73
American Women Writers: A Critical Reference Guide from Colonial Times to the Present, I60
American Writing 1943, H41
AMERICANS ABROAD, B9, H8
Amirkhanian, Charles, B109, J724
Amory, Cleveland, H84
Anchor in the Sea: An Anthology of Psychological Literature, H53
Anderson, Joseph Marie Sister, J637, J645
Anderson, Patrick, J607
Anderson, William, B65
ANTHOLOGY OF MAGAZINE VERSE FOR 1923 AND YEARBOOK OF AMERICAN POETRY, B1, H1
Anthology of Stories from the Southern Review, H75
ANTHOLOGY OF THE YOUNGER POETS, B8, H7
Art of Modern Fiction, The, H58
Articles on Women Writers 1976-1984: A Bibliography, I74
ARTISTS' AND WRITERS' COOKBOOK, B46
Ashley, Beth, J740
Aswell, Edward, xi, A24, B99
Aswell, Mary Louise, H42
AT LARGE, B49
ATTACKS OF TASTE, B71
Atwater, Richard and Florence, A16a
Atwood, Margaret, A27b

AUTHORS TAKE SIDES ON
  VIETNAM, B57
AUTHORS TODAY AND YESTERDAY,
  B10
AUTOBIOGRAPHY OF EMANUEL
  CARNEVALI, THE, B60
AVALANCHE, A19
Azaltovic, John M., B30

B

BABYLON, B96, E4
Baez, Joan, J576
Bagguley, John, B57
Bailey, Brook, I110
Bakal, Syd, J480
Baker, Howard, J214
Balakian, Nona, J404, J423
Bald, Wambly, B6, H5, J33, J34
Baldwin, Faith, B30, H39
Baldwin, James, B111
Bannon, Barbara, J628, J653
Banting, John, B6, H5
Barba, Sharon, H120
Barksdale, Lena, J269
Barlone, D, C187
Barnes, Djuna, B95, C129
Baro, Gene, J492
Barr, Beryl, B46
Barrett, Margaret, J395
Barrett, Margery, J400
Barrows, Herbert, H62
Bass, Ellen, H119
Bates, H.E., J57, J273, J303
Bates, Ralph, C173
Bates, Sylvia Chatfield, H12, I1
Bauerle, Ruth, J706
Bauersfeld, Erik, B109
Baum, Vicki, A18b
Bayliss, John, H43
Bazaar, Mona, B65
Beacham, Roger, B63
Beadle, Charles, B6, H5
Beagle, Peter S. B82
Beal, Elizabeth, J483
Becker, May Lamberton, J262
Beckett, Samuel, B80, B111, C462, C466,
  G18, L7

Bedwell, Bettina, A13
*Before Columbus Foundation Fiction
  Anthology, The*, H145
BEING GENIUSES TOGETHER, A35,
  B93
Belfer, Lauren, J748
Belfrage, Cedric, B14
Bell, Elizabeth, A40, B107, I91, I104, J736,
  K3
Bell, Graham, J146
Bemelmans, Ludwig, C327
Benchley, Robert, B14,
Bendall, Molly. J763
Benet, Rosemary Carr, J268, J324
Benét, William Rose, B30, H39, I12, J127
Benet's Reader's Encyclopedia, I82
*Benet's Reader's Encyclopedia of American
  Literature, I97*
Benny, Jack, B14
Benstock, Shari, B98, I81
Beresford, J.D., J154
Berkman, Alexander, C441
Berlandino, Jane, A6
Bessie, Alvah, J48, J84
*Bessie Graham's Bookman's Manual: A Guide
  to Literature*, I10
BEST AMERICAN SHORT STORIES
  1942, B23, H33
BEST AMERICAN SHORT STORIES
  1943, B27, H36
Best American Short Stories 1952, The, H70
BEST AMERICAN SHORT STORIES
  1967, THE, B58, H103
BEST MINDS: A TRIBUTE OT ALLEN
  GINSBURG, B97
BEST MODERN SHORT STORIES, B54
*Best Modern Short Stories Selected from the
  Saturday Evening Post*, H93
Best of the Best Short Stories 1915-1950, The,
  H71
Best of the Nation, The, H72
BEST POEMS OF 1959, B44
BEST SHORT STORIES OF 1931, THE,
  B5, H4
Best Short Stories, 1940, The, H26
Bienek, Horst, C412
Billings, Harold, B63
Bishop, John Peale, H32

BLACK SUN, B81, I53
Blackmur, Richard P., J275
Blain, Virginia, I95
Blake, William, A24
Block, Maxine, I6, J330
Bloom, Harold, viii, I77
Bloomfield, Paul, J413
Bloomsbury Guide to Women's Literature, The, I101
Bogan, Louise, J241
Böll, Heinrich, C274
Bonavoglia, Angela, B106
Bonazza, Blaze O. H100
Bonnetti, Kay, B109, L4
Book of Contemporary Short Stories, A, H16
Borchert, Wolfgang, A29, B69
Boston, Ann, H139
Boucheron, Robert, J692
Bourjaily, Vance, I66, I96, J659
Bowen, Elizabeth, B99, C180
Bowles, Paul, B6, H5
Boyd, A.C., J151
Boyd, William, J677
Boyle, Howard Peterson, vii, B109
Boyle, Jesse Peyton, vii, B109
Boyle, Joan, B99, B109
Boyle, Katherine Evans, B99, B109
Boynton, Robert W. H97
Brackett, Clare L., B6, H5
Bradbury, Malcolm, I42
Bradish, Gaynor, I37
Bradlee, Frederic, H84
Brady, Susan, J505
Bragg, Linda, D5
Braithwaite, William Stanley, B1, C4, H1
Brandon, William, J590
Brandt, E.N., B22
Brault, Richard, vii, viii, B109
BREAKING THE SILENCE, A31
Brecht, Bertolt, C303
Breit, Harvey, C257
Breuer, Bessie, A23, B76, B108, C284, G1
Brewster, Dorothy, H16
Breyer, Helen, J537
Brickell, Herschel, B19, B25, B28, B35, B36, H29, H35, H38, H50, H54, H64, J85
BRIDGES OF SAN LUIS REY, THE, B48

Brink, Carol, C272
Brooke, Sir James, A1a
Brooks, Cleanth, H75
Brooks, V.E., J195
Brophy, John, J89, J192
Brosnahan, John, J681
Broughton, Irv, B104
Broun, Heywood, B14
Brown, Ethel S., J342
Brown, Frank C. J616
Brown, Robert Carlton, B6, B8, B99, B109, H5, J180, L7
Brown, Rose, B6, H5
Bruccoli, Mathew J., A4e, A7e
Brundage, Irving, B30, I70
Bryfonski, Dedria, B94
Bryher, Winifred, J251
Buchanan-Brown, J., I47
Buck, Claire, I101
Buckman, Gertrude, J332
Buell, Ellen Lewis, J260
Bullett, Gerald, J42
Bullock, Elizabeth, J354
Bullock, Florence Haxton, J405, J425
Bunzel, John H., J615
Burdett, Osbert, J124
Burke, W. J., I9, I43
Burlingame, Ann and Roger, A18, B109
Burne-Jones, Sir Philip, A1a
Burnett, David, B58, H103
Burnett, Hallie, B51, H92, H96, H99, H102, I30
Burnett, Whit, B24, B51, B68, H10, H34, H44, H47, H92, H96, H99, H111, I30
Burra, Peter, J153, J190
Burroughs, Betty, C345
Burt, Struthers, I66, I96, J346, J388
Buss, Kate, B99
Butler, Helen L., J380
Byrne, Evelyn B., B71
Byrne, John, B78

C

Cahill, Susan, H124
Calder, Alexander, B20
Calder-Marshall, Anthony, J453
Callaghan, Morley, C327

Calvacade of the American Novel, I18

*Cambridge Guide to Literature in English,
The*, I88

*Cambridge Handbook of American Literature,
The*, I78

Campbell, Finley, B61

Campbell, James, B111

Canby, Henry Seidel, J77, J161

Cannell, Kathleen, J588

Cantwell, Robert, J47, J82

Capajon: Fifty-Four Short Stories Published
1921-1933, H9

Cardoza, Nancy, C446

CARESSE CROSBY: FROM BLACK SUN
TO ROCCASINIBALDA, B105

Carey, Glenn O. J580

Carnevali, Emanuel, viii, A7, A10, B2, B60,
J579, J581

Carpenter, Don, B82

Carpenter, Humphrey, I85

Carpenter, Richard C., B99, I66, I94, I96,
J456, J457, J539

Carr, Daphne, B6, H5

Carroll, Paul, C365

Cassell's Encyclopaedia of Literature, I21

Cassell's Encyclopedia of World Literature, I47

Cassill, R. V., H127, I109

Chamberlain, John, J75

Chan, Jeffrey Paul, G10

Chang, Diana, C282

Chapin, Ruth, J431

Charters, Ann, H146, I113, I114

Chester, Laura, H120

Chin, Frank, G10, G16

Chisholm, Anne, I94, J695

CHOICES WE MADE, THE, B106

Church, Richard, J117, J157, J191, J235

Clare, Tullis, J212, J398

Clark, Axton, B6, H5

Clark, George Herbert, J338

Clark, Suzanne, I96, I100, J731

*Classics and Commercials: A Literary
Chronicle of the Forties*, I13

Cleaver, Eldridge, B65

Clements, Patricia, I95

Clough, Benjamin Crocker, H24

Coates, Robert M., J16, J62, J64

Codrescu, Andrei, H136

Cohen, Meg, J778

Cohn, Roy, xii

Cohn, Ruby, B80

Coleman, John, J514

COLLECTED POEMS, A30

COLLECTED POEMS OF KAY BOYLE,
A43

College Short Story Reader, The, H56

Colum, Mary M., J177, J233, J308

Colum, Padraic, A35a

Comfort, Alex, H43

Conarain, Nina, x, A12b, B12, H18

Concise Dictionary of American Literature,
I22

Connell, Evan S., B82

Connolly, Cyril, J118, J203

Connolly, Jean, J328

Conover, Anne, B105

Contemporary American Authors, I5

CONTEMPORARY AMERICAN
NOVELISTS, B52

Contemporary Authors, I51, I93, I102

CONTEMPORARY AUTHORS
AUTOBIOGRAPHY SERIES, B94, I70

Contemporary Literary Criticism, I48, I54,
I66, I94

Contemporary Novelists, I44

CONTEMPORARY POETS OF THE
ENGLISH LANGUAGE, B67, I37

Cook, Carol, J655

Cooper, Lettice, J294

Cooper, Louise Field, J437

Coppel, Alfred, B82

Corcoran, Marguerite Page, J433

Corry, Andrew, J174

Corwin, Phillip, I54, J641

Cosman, Max, J485

Courtney, Winfred F., I34

Cowley, Malcolm, J322, J582

Crabtree, Jean, H102

Craig, Archibald, viii, ix, A1a, C35

Craig, Patricia, J672

Crane, Hart, C31, C353

Crane, Milton, H95

CRAZY HUNTER, THE, A44

CRAZY HUNTER AND OTHER
STORIES, THE, A17

Creating the American Novel, I2

Crevel, René, x, B96, C216, E2, E4, J689, J692, J693, J697
CRITIC AS ARTIST: ESSAY ON BOOKS, 1920-1970, THE, B74, I45
CRITICAL ESSAYS ON KAY BOYLE, B115, I115
Critical Survey of Long Fiction, I71
Critical Survey of Short Fiction, I67
Crosby, Caresse, vii, ix, A2, B79, B99, B105, B109, B113, C290
Crosby, Harry, vii, ix, A2, B81, B99, B109
Crossman, Richard, L2
Culligan, Glendy, J545
Cunard, Nancy, vii, B6, B62, C140, C416, H5
Cunningham, Sarah, B83
Curley, Arthur, J579
Current American Thinking and Writing, 2nd Series, H66
Current Biography: Who's New and Why, I6
Current Biography Yearbook, I103
Current-Garcia, Eugene, H69
Cyclopedia of World Authors II, I90

D

Dahlberg, Edward, B63, B99, B109, C353, C365, C393, G18
Dahl-Wolfe, Louise, A29, J336
Daiches, David, A22d, A39a, I77, J278
Daley, Lawrence, B30
Dallas, Sandra, J527
Dark, Sydney, C3
Dashiell, Alfred, H13
Daughaday, Charles, J774
Davenport, Basil, J220
Davenport, G. D., J528
Davidson, Ann Morrissett, J720
Davidson, Cathy N., I111
Davis, Clyde Brion, B30, H39
Davis, Margo, B92
Davis, Stuart, A6
Dawson, Margaret Cheney. J5, J10, J35, J61, J79, J175
Dazai, Osamu, C282
DEATH OF A MAN, A12
DeGaulle, Charles, C202, C214
Delteil, Joseph, x, B4, E1, J16, J14

Del Vayo, J. Alvarez, G2
Denny, Reuel, J257
De Sales, Raoul de Roussy, J327
Deshaies, Arthur, C319
Deutsch, Babette, A4a, B86, J243
D'Evelyn, Tom, J684
DEVIL IN THE FLESH, E3
Dexter, Ethel, J471
Diamond, Elin, B80
DIAMOND OF YEARS, A, B45, H85
Diamonstein, Barbaralee, B73
Dick, Bernard, J564
Dickey, William, J623
Dictionary of Literary Biography, I68, I79, I91
Dictionary of Literary Biography: American Writers in Paris, 1920-1939, I62
Dictionary of Literary Biography: Yearbook 1993, I104
Dictionary of Literature in the English Language from Chaucer to 1940, I38
Diller, Angela, A4a
Directory of American Fiction Writers, I55
Directory of American Poets, I49
Directory of American Poets and Fiction Writers, A, I63
DiYanni, Robert, H137
Dobrée, Bonamy, J87
Doi, Isami, A6
Dolphin's Arc: Poems on Endangered Creatures of the Sea, The, H138
DON JUAN, B4, E1
Dorr, John, L7
Dos Passos, John, vii
Drake, William, I83
Drew, Kathy, J647, J648
du Von, Jay, B6, H5
DUCHAMP, B114
Dudley, Laurie, J483
Duncan, Isadora, ix
Duncan, Raymond, ix
Dwyer, David, I94, J717

E

Eberhardt, Richard, J248
Editor's Choice, H13
Eidus, Janice, J701

Elkins, Marilyn, B108, B115, I105, I109, I115

Elwood, Irene, J350

Encyclopedia of World Literature in the twentieth Century, I32

Engle, Paul, I94, J467

ENOUGH OF DYING, B72, H115

Erdrich, Louise, A39d, G15, G17, J745

Ernst, Max, x, B96, E2, E4

Eshleman, Clayton, J693

Etlinger, Harold, C205

Evans, Eva S., vii

Evans, Faith, J691

Everett, Connie Willet, J762

EXILED IN PARIS, B111

F

Fadiman, Clifton, H135, J76, J100, J270, J282, J323

Fariello, Griffin, B110

Farjeon, Eleanor, J271

Farrar, Janice, H91

Farrell, James T., B6, B109, H5

Farrell, John A., B6, H5

Faulkner, William, A8c, B74, C128

Feld, Rose, J343, J376

Felheim, Marvin, H67, I17

Felton, David, C407, C408

Feminine Plural: Stories by Women About Growing Up, H116

Feminist Companion to Literature in English, A, I95

Ferber, Edna, C166

Ferguson, Anne, H118

Ferguson, Linda, C455

Ferguson, Otis, J168, J225, J301

Ferlinghetti, Lawrence, I64

FICTION! INTERVIEWS WITH NORTHERN CALIFORNIA NOVELISTS, B82

Fiction 100: An Anthology of Short Stories, H121

Fictions, H132

15 Stories and Suggestions for teaching 15 Stories, H62

Fifty Best American Short Stories, 1915-1939, H21

Fifty Best American Short Stories, 1915-1965, H94

50 Great American Short Stories, H95

FIFTY STORIES, A39

Fifty Years of the American Short Story from the O. Henry Awards, 1919-1970, H109

55 Short Stories from the New Yorker, H59

First Flowering: The Best of the Harvard Advocate, H126

FIRST LOVER AND OTHER STORIES, THE, A8

First Prize Stories, 1919-1954 from the O. Henry Memorial Awards, H78

First Prize Stories, 1919-1963 from the O. Henry Memorial Awards, H89

First Prize Stories, 1919-1966 from the O. Henry Memorial Awards, H101

First Wave: Women Poets in America: 1915-1945, The, I85

Fishback, Margaret, J265

Fitch, Noel Riley, I72

Fitts, Dudley, A6, J250

Fitzgerald, Karen, J688

FitzGibbon, Constantine, B55, C334

Flandrau, Grace, J114

Flanner, Janet, xi, A9e, B79, C207

Fleischman, Wolfgang Bernard, I32

Fleischmann, Christa, B70

Fletcher, John, B80

Flint, F. Cudworth, J366

Foley, Martha, B23, B27, B58, H10, H33, H36, H70, H71, H94, H103, H123

Folkart, Burt, J764

Ford, Charles Henri, B6, B109, H5, J3

Ford, Hugh, B62, B75, B79, B101, B109, C428, I52, I84, I94, J690, J714

FOUR LIVES IN PARIS, B101, I84

Foster, Herbert, J478

Foulke, Adrienne, J470

FOUR VISIONS OF AMERICA, B85

FOURTEEN OF THEM, B30, H39

Fox, Stella, H87

Fracchia, Charles, B99, C433, J646

Franco, Jean, I42

Franckenstein, Joseph von, x, xi, B42

Fraser, George Sutherland, J122, J255

French, Robert S., I94, J608

FRENCHMAN MUST DIE, A, A21

Friedenberg, Daniel, C304
Friedman, Mickey, J651
Frost, Elizabeth Hollister, B30, H39
Fuller, Muriel, B25, B28, B35

G

Gado, Frank, I35, J674, K2
Gaines, Ernest J. B82
Gannett, Lewis, J99, J445, J463
Gara, Larry, B89
Garber, Frederick, H107
Garchik, Leah, C454
Gardiner, Wrey, B32, H40
Gardner, Leonard, B82
Geisler, Christian, C320
Geismer, Maxwell, G7, I77, I94, J549
Gelfant, Blanche H., J644
GENERATION WITHOUT FAREWELL, A29
Geniuses Together, I85
GENTLEMEN, I ADDRESS YOU PRIVATELY, A9
Gerlach, Heinrich, C292
GERMANS AN INDICTMENT OF MY PEOPLE, THE, B47
Gerstenberger, Donna, H107
Gibbs, Wolcott, B14
Gibson, Wilfrid, J189, J286, J364
Gide, Andre, C208
Gilbert, Douglas, J360
Gilbert, Sandra, H133, I76
Gillespie, A. Lincoln, Jr., B6, H5
Gillespie, David, J216
Ginsburg, Allen, B97
Gironella, Jose Maria, C269
GLAD DAY, A, a15
Glasco, Buffy, A1a, B109
Goes, Albrecht, C273
Gold, Herbert, B82, C371, H86
Goldcar, Harry, B109
Golding, William, A26c
Goodman, Paul, B53, C342, I44
Goring, Rosemary, I108
Gourmont, Remy de, C2
Graham, Gladys, J43, J65
Graham, Judith, I103
Grass, Günter, C326

Graves, Robert, ix
Great American Horse Omnibus from Homer to Hemingway, The, H60
Great American Short Stories, H129
Great Short Stories of the World, H96
Great Women Writers: The Lives and Works of 135 of the Worlds' Most Important Women Writers from Antiquity *To the Present*, I106
Great Writers of the English Language: Novelists and Prose Writers, I61
Green, Blake, B99J638
Greenbaum, Edward, B99
Greenberg, Dan, B87
Greene, Graham, J159
Gronning, Robyn, J727
Gross, Beatrice, J331
Gross, Theodore, I94, J552
Grumbach, Doris, A7f, A7g, A27c, I54, J636, J650
Grunly, Isobel, I95
Gubar, Susan, H133, I76
Guggenheim, Peggy, x
Gunton, Sharon R., I66
Gwynn, Denis, E1

H

Ha, Im Chi, C429
Hadas, Rachel, I94, J722
Hadden, Wilbur C., B10
Haesler, Bob, C377, J594
Hagglund, B. C., B6, H5
Haimonwitz, Benjamin, J508
Hall, James B. H98, H110, I31
Hallock, Joseph, J409
Halper, Albert, A6
Halpert, Stephen, B66
Hamalian, Leo, H105
Hamilton, Mildred, C424, J586, J631
Hampson, J., J333
Hanson, Harry, B11, B16, B18, H15, H23, H27, H78, H89, H101
Hardwick, Elizabeth, J399
Harlow, Gail, J634
Harper, Michaels S., C391
Harris, Gale, J777
Harris, Julia, B76

Harris, Mark, J536
Harrison, Gilbert, A., B74, I45
Hart, Elizabeth, J102, J135
Hart, James D. I11
Harte, Barbara, I36
Harter, Evelyn, J38
Hartung, Philip T., J228, J296
Harwood, H.C., J25
Hastings, Harry W., H56
Hastings, William Thompson, H24
HASTY BUNCH, A, B84
Hatcher, Harlan, I2
Hatfield, Larry, J765
Hatlen, Burton, A12c, J733
Hauser, Marianne, J321
Havighurst, Walter, J406
Hawkins, A. Desmond, J202, J217
Hawthorne, Hazel, J71
Hayakawa, S. I., xiii
Haycroft, Howard, B10, B26, I8
Haynes, Michael A. J661
Heilman, Robert B., H63
Heinemann, Katherine, B109
Heinrich, Willi, C274
Heller, Lee, J709
Hellinger, Mark, B14
Hemingway, Ernest, vii, B14
Henderson, Wyn, A5
Heppenstall, Rayner, J302
Hersey, John, B30, H39
Herzberg, Max J., I28
Hibbs, Ben, H51
Hicks, Granville, J487
Hiler, Hiler, ix, B6, H5
Hiler, pere, B6, H5
Hill, William B., J502
Hindus, Maurice, A9a
Hine, Daryl, H128
Hinerfeld, Susan Slocum, J696
Hipp, James W., I104
Hirsch, Stefan, A6
Hirsh, Katherine,F., J201
HIS HUMAN MAJESTY, A24
Hoefer, Jacqueline, I44, I86
Hoey, Reed A., J459
Hoffman, Burton C., B24
Hoffman, Frederick J., I23
Hoffman, Hester R., I10, I26, I29

Hoffman, Paul, J143
Hofheins, Roger, B82
Hogan, William, J497, J546, J584, J585, J657
Hokenson, Jan, B80
Hollenberg, Donna, J781
Holm, John Cecil, B30, H39
Holt, Patricia, C453
Hooper, Brad, I89, J728
Hooper, William Dudley, J656
Horan, John J., B30
Hornaday, Anne, I94, J729
Howard, C. Jeriel, H114
Howard, Richard, I77, I94, J533
Howe, Florence, H119
Howe, Will D., I9, I43
Howes, Victor, J614
Hoyenga, Betty, I48, J567
Hughes, Langston, C379
Hughes, Riley, J469, J507
Hunt, Sydney, B6, H5
Hurst, Fannie, B30, H39
Hussey, Maurice, I39
Hutchens, John K., J438, J493
Hutchins, John, J441
Huxley, Aldous, E3

I

ILLUSTRATION IS WORTH A THOUSAND WORDS, AN, B87
Images of Women in Literature, H118
In Transition: A Paris Anthology. Writings and Art from transition [sic] Magazine 1927-1930, H140
Inada, Lawson, Fusao, G10
Ingalls, Jeremy, J373
Interviews and Conversations with 20th Century Authors Writing in English: An Index, I69
Introduction to Literature: Stories/Poems/Plays, H90
Introduction to the Short Story, H97
Instructor's Manual for Studies in the Short Story, I41
International Authors and Writers Who's Who, The, I56
International Who's Who in Poetry, The, I59

It's a Woman's World: A Collection of Stories from Harper's Bazaar, H42

J

Jack, Peter Monroe, J290
Jackson, Alan R., B22
Jackson, Byron, K1
Jacobs, Paul, C442
Jahn, Hans, C259
JAMES STERN: SOME LETTERS FOR HIS SEVENTIETH BIRTHDAY, B78
Janta, Alexander, C212
Janvier, Ludovic, B80
Jarzavek, John B. J525
Jefferson, Dr. R.H., B61
Jennings, C. Wade, H132
John, K., J335, J368, J387, J415
Johns, Richard, B6, B66, H5
Johnson, Albert, J602, J612
Johnson, Curt, I87, I92
Johnson, Frank J., B30
Johnson, Oakley, J30
Johnson, Robert E., B70
Jolas, Eugene, vii, ix, A8, A12, B3, B6, B20, J1, H3, H5, H30, H61, J1, J384
Jones, E.B.C., J29, J40, J55, J94, J123
Jones, J., B6, H5
Jong, Erica, B85
Jordan, Alice M., J 263
Josephson, Matthew, B75
Joyce, James, vii, ix, C368, C395
Joyce, Nora, ix
Junges Amerika: Preisgekrönte stories aus den USA, H57
JUST WHAT THE DOCTOR ORDERED, B14

K

Kaganoff, Peggy, J725, J738, J751
Kamfer, Dawn, B87
Karagueuzian, Dikran, C401
Karl, Frederick R., H105
Karno, David, J377
Kaufman, Ellen, J752
KAY BOYLE: A STUDY OF THE SHORT FICTION, B107

KAY BOYLE: ARTIST AND ACTIVIST, B99, I80
KAY BOYLE: AUTHOR OF HERSELF, B109, I107
Kay Boyle: From the Aesthetics of Exile to the Polemics of Return, I35
Kay, Ernest, I56
Kazin, Alfred, J164, J223
Kazin, Elia, A14a, B76
Kee, Robert, J414
Kees, Weldon, J213
Kelly, James, I94, J464
Kelly, John, J643
Kelly, Mary E., J524
Kemmerer, John, A6
Kenna, Richard, C327
Kennedy, Leo, J369
Kenner, Hugh, B80
Kent, George, B6, H5
Kessel, Joseph, C201
Kettmann, Steve, J739
Kielty, Bernadine, J375
Kiki, ix
Kimball, Ellen, I91
King, Moxye, B61
Kingery, Robert E., J420
Kingston, Maxine Hong, G11
Kinsman, Clare D., I51
Kirkpatrick, D. L., I44, I86
Kirkus, Virginia, J280
Kirsch, Robert, J640
Kirst, Hans Helmut, C273, C292, C294
Kitching, Jessie, J543
Klausler, Alfred, J518
Klein, Leonard C., I32
Knoll, Robert, C321, I27, I66, J530
Kobak, Annette, J703
Koch, David, I62, J520, J678
Kofka, Joseph J., B30
Komroff, Manuel, B6, H5
Kraf, Elaine, G13
Kredel, Fritz, A16
Kreymborg, Alfred, B2, B6, H2
Kritcher, L. B., B22
Kronenberger, Louis, J66, J78, J179, J222
Kouwenhoven, John A., H91
Kubly, Herbert, B49, B50, G5

Kuehl, John, B56, H106, I33
Kunitz, Stanley J., B10, B26, I8
Kupinski, Walter J., B30

L

Lai, Mark, G14
Lamont, Helen Otis, B45, H85
LANDSCAPE FOR WYN HENDERSON, A5
Lang, Peter, B108
Larousse Dictionary of Writers, I108
Larsson, Raymond Ellsworth, A6
LaSalle, Peter, J669
Lask, Thomas, J544
Laughlin, James, A14c, B15, B109, H17, H134
LAURENCE VAIL, B77
Lavin, Mary, G9
Lawrence, Margaret, I3
Lawrence, T. E., A18
Lawson, David, B109
Leary, Rosemary and Timothy, C418, L3
Leavis, Q.D., J178
Lechlitner, Ruth, J246
Lee, Laurel, C440
Lee, Lawrence, J379
LEFT BANK REVISITED, THE, B75
Leider, Emily, J685, J755
Leigh, James, B82
Leiniger, Phillip, I97
Lesbian Love in Literature, H87
Lesniak, James G., I93
Lesser, M. X., H88
Lewis, C. Day, B67
Lewis, Flora, J531
Lewis, Janet, B82, J707
Lewis, Leslie L., H90
Library of Criticism: Modern American Literature, A, I25
Liddy, James, C395
Lietz, Richard J., J670
LIFE BEING THE BEST AND OTHER STORIES, A42
LIFE OF DYLAN THOMAS, THE, B55
Lim, Genny, G14
Linklater, Eric, J52

Linkous, Robert, J704
Lish, Gordon, L1
Literary Exile in the Twentieth Century, I98
Literary San Francisco: A Pictorial History from the Beginning to the Present Day, I64
LITERATURE AND LIFE IN AMERICA, B29, H37
Littell, Robert, J307, J340
Little Victories Big Defeats, H122
Litwak, Leo, B98, C380, C467
LIVING IN WORDS: INTERVIEWS FROM THE BLOOMSBURY REVIEW, B103
LIVING OF WORDS, A, B112
Livingston, Dr. James, B61
Loeb, Harold, viii, B109
Loeb, Marjorie, viii
Löhndorff, Ernest F., A18
London, Oscar, G19
LONG WALK AT SAN FRANCISCO STATE AND OTHER ESSAYS, THE, A37
Longman's Companion to twentieth Century Literature, I39
Lorenzen, Rudolph, C318
Lorimer, Sarah, B30, H39
Loveman, Amy, J73, J318
Lowenfels, Walter, B6, B99, B109, H5
Lozowick, Louis, A6
Ludwig, Richard M., H73
Luhan, Mable Dodge, B109
Lukacovic, John A., B30
Lynch, Hubert J., B30
Lynes, George Platt, J313
Lynskey, Winifred, H74

M

MacAdams, Lewis, L7
MacAffee,, Helen, J21, J59, J106, J150, J183
Macaulay, Thurston, H60
MacDonald, Dwight, C149
MacDougall, Allan, C97
MacGregor, Martha, J490
MacInnes, Helen, B30, H39

Mack, Maynard, H97
MacKenzie, Donal, B6, H5
MacLean, David, J687
MacLeish, Archibald, B8, B71, J131
MacLeod, Norman, B6, H5
MacNiven, Ian S., J734
Madden, Charles F., B61, H112
Madden, David, H142
Maddocks, Melvin, I94, J495
Magill, Frank N., I67, I71, I90, I106
Maguire, Doris D., J465
Maher, Catherine, J349
Mainiero, Lina, I60
Major Twentieth Century Writers, A Selection of Sketches from Contemporary Authors, I99
Malaquais, Jean, C197
Malin, Irving, J697
Malouf, Saul, J587, J600
MAN OUTSIDE, THE, B69
Man Without a Country, The, A14
Mann, L.S., J448
Mansfield, Katherine, C126
Marinetti, Filippo Tommaso, B6, H5
Marini, Myra, J46
MARK IN TIME PORTRAITS AND POETRY / SAN FRANCISCO, B70
Marler, Regina, J780
Marple, Allen, A21b
Marriott, Charles, J234, J385
Marshall, Arthur, J604
Martin, Fredericka, B83
Martin, Jex, Jr., J428
Martin, W. Thornton, B22
Martine, James J., I68
Marvin, Patricia H., J605
Mascone, George, C449
Mason, H.A., J109, J126
Mason, Kenneth Oliver, H24
Masters and Masterpieces of the Short Story, H83
Match, Richard, J392
Mathews, T.S., J112
Mattram, Eric, I42
Matuz, Roger, I94
Maugham, W. Somerset, H25
Maxwell, Elsa, C207
May, Hal, I93

McAlmon and the Lost Generation: A Self Portrait, I27
McAlmon, Robert, viii, ix, xiii, A35, B6, B75, B84, B93, B99, B108, B109, C81, C300, C321, C436, G20, H5
McBrien, William, J592
McCarthy, Joanne, I32, I60, I79
McCarthy, Joseph, xi
McCarthy, Mary, J113
McClennen, Joshua, H83
McClintock, Marshall, H81
McClure, Michael, D5
McCullers, Carson, A18b, A20, A30
McFadden, Cyra, J662
McGahern, John, J606
McHargue, Georgess, H122
McKenzie, P.A., J569
McMillan,, Dougald, B80
McMinnies, Mary, C287
McMurtry, Larry, J629
McNamee, Gregory, B103
McWilliams, Carey, J618, J625
Meeker, Arthur, Jr., C170
Mehring, Walter, C204
Mellen, Joan, xiv, B109, I107
Mencken, H. L., B74
Mendelson, Phyllis Carmel. I54
Menken, Rue, B6, H5
Meredith, George, A1a
Mesher, David R., C464, I94
METAMORPHOSIZING THE NOVEL, B108, I105
Meynell, Viola, J23
Microcosm: An Anthology of the Short Story, H107
Miles, Dudley, B29, H37
Miller, Henry, B85
Miller, John, H141
Millett, Fred B. H65, I5, I14
Mills, Kay, J711, J712
Millspaugh, Clarence, J274
Milner, Florence, J172
Mirikitani, Janice, C450
Mirrielees, Edith, J391
Mishima, Yukio, C282
MR. KNIFE, MISS FORK, E2
Mitford, Jessica, C371
Mitgang, Herbert, J494

Modern Short Stories, H67
Modern Short Stories: A Critical Anthology, H63
Modern Short Stories: The Fiction of Experience, H88
MODERN SHORT STORY IN THE MAKING, THE, B51, H92
Monaghan, Pat, J754
MONDAY NIGHT, A14
Monroe, N. E., J359
Monsarrat, Nicholas, C276
Montgomery, John D., C287
Moon, Bucklin, H46
Moore, Anne Caroll, J258
Moore, Harry T., A4e, A7e, A34A, B52, I40, I54, I77, J292, J442, J510
Moore, Marianne, viii, A4, C476
Moore, Nicholas, H45
Moore, Reginald, B21
Moran, Helen, J56, J92, J149
Morehead, Ethel, viii, ix
Morgan, Bill, B97
Morris, Ira, A37
Morris, John N., H88
Morris, Wright, J536
Morse, Deborah Denenholz, I94, J732
Mortimer, Penelope, C423
Moses, Kate, J723
Moult, Thomas, J197, J208
Muir, Edwin, J86, J120, J147, J167, J211, J238, J291, J372
Mumford, Lewis, B1, H2
Murphy, Kevin, J700
Murphy, Rosalie, B67, I37
MY NEXT BRIDE, A10
Myers, Robin, I38

Neider, Charles, J341
Nelson, E., J610
Nemerov, Howard, B109, C297, C448, D6
Neue Amerika: Zwansig Erzähler der Gegenwart, H19
New Anthology of Modern Poetry: Revised Edition, A, H49
New Directions in Prose and Poetry, H17
NEW DIRECTIONS IN PROSE AND POETRY 1937, B13, H20
NEW DIRECTIONS IN PROSE AND POETRY 1939, B15, H22
New Directions in Prose and Poetry, H134
New Guide to Modern World Literature, The, I75
New Road: 1944 New Directions in European Art and Letters, H43
Newhouse, Edward, C164
Newman, Franklin B., H67, I17
Newton, Huey P., A37, C374, C392
Nichols, Lewis, J488
Nightingale, Benedict, J679
Nin, Anaïs, H120
Nine Short Stories, H73
1939, A23
No More Masks: An Anthology of Poems by Women, H119
Normansen, Henry, B30
Norton Anthology of Literature by Women, The, H133, I76
Norton Anthology of Short Fiction, The, H127
NOTHING EVER BREAKS EXCEPT THE HEART, A32
Novels and Novelists, I65
Nyren, Dorothy, I25, J521

N

Nabokov, Vladimir, C170
NANCY CANARD: BRAVE POET, INDOMITABL REBEL, 1896-1965, B62
Nash, Ogden, B14
NATIONAL BOOK AWARDS, THE, B88
Neagoé, Peter, B6, B9, B17, H5, H8, I4
Neall, A.W., B22
Nee, Edwin T., B30

O

Obligado, Lilian, A33, A34
Oboler, Eli, M. J555
O'Brien, Edward J., B5, C95, H4, H21, H26
O'Brien, Kate, J206, J297, J363
O'Conner, Rt. Hon. T.P., A1a
Odic, Jean, C218
Oetter, Joanna, J702
O'Hara, J. D., I54, J635

O. HENRY MEMORIAL AWARD PRIZE
  STORIES OF 1932, B7, H6
O. HENRY MEMORIAL AWARD PRIZE
  STORIES OF 1935, B11, H15
O. HENRY MEMORIAL AWARD PRIZE
  STORIES OF 1939, B16, H23
O. HENRY MEMORIAL AWARD PRIZE
  STORIES OF 1940, B18, H27
O. HENRY MEMORIAL AWARD PRIZE
  STORIES OF 1941. B19, H29
O. HENRY MEMORIAL AWARD PRIZE
  STORIES OF 1942, B25, H35
O. HENRY MEMORIAL AWARD PRIZE
  STORIES OF 1943, B28, H38
O. HENRY MEMORIAL AWARD PRIZE
  STORIES OF 1946. B35, H50
Ogden, Donald, B14
O'Keeffe, Georgia, B102
Olendorf, Donna, I102
100 YEARS OF THE AMERICAN
  FEMALE FROM HARPER'S BAZAAR,
  B59, H104
OPEN SECRETS: NINETY-FOUR
  WOMEN IN TOUCH WITH OUR
  TIME, B73
Ourin, Victor, C414
Ousby, Ian, I88
Owens, Olga, J283
*Oxford Companion to American Literature,
  The*, I11
*Oxford Companion to Women's Writing in the
  United States, The*, I111

P

Painter, George D., J417
Paley, Grace, A41
Palmer, Doug, B99
Palmer, Gladys, viii
Paris, Rosemary, I96, J402
Parisi, Joseph, H128
Parker, Peter, I112
Parkham, John, J500
Parsons, Geoffrey, J163
Pass, Sylvia, J142
Paul, Alice, vii
Paul, Elliot, C174
Pauling, Gouveneur, J496

Paulson, Dennis, B99
Pavey, L.A., J186, J188
Pearson, Norman Holmes, J573
Pearson, Richard, J768
Pence, Raymond Woodbury, H14
Penguin Companion to World Literature, The,
  I42
Penzler, Otto M., B71
Perkins, Barbara, I97
Perkins, George, I97
Perry, Marvin B. Jr., H73
Peters, Nancy J., I64
Peterson, Virgilia, I94, J439, J462, J489
Phelan, Peggy, J721
Philippe, Charles-Louis, x, E3f, E4
Picabia, Francis, C35
Pick, Robert, J381
Pickering, James H., H121
Pickrel, Paul, J468
PINKY IN PERSIA, A34
PINKY THE CAT WHO LIKED TO
  SLEEP, A33
Pipes, Richard, C394
*PL Book of Modern American Short Stories,
  The*, H45
PLAGUED BY THE NIGHTINGALE,
  A4
Plommer, William, J107, J116
Pocket Book of O. Henry Prize Stories, The,
  H54
*Poetry Anthology 1912-1977: Sixty-five Years
  of America's Most Distinguished Magazine,
  The*, H128
Pollitzer, Anna, B102
Pomer, Belle, J511
Pompea, Irene N., J548
Pool, Gail, J698
Poole, Adrian, J676
Pooley, Robert C., B29, H37
Poor, Henry Varnum. A23
Poore, Charles, J298, J589
Popper, Andrew, J770
Porter, David, A29, B69
Porter, Katherine Anne, A9e, A17, B109,
  I45, I66, I77, I96, J14
Potriack, Walton, H69
Pound, Ezra, vii, B6, B109, C469, H18
Powell, Anthony, J452, J603

Pozner, Vladimir, C175, C186
Prahken, Sarah L., I50
Pratt, Theodor, B6
Prescott, Peter S., I54, J630
PRIMER FOR COMBAT, A18
Primer for White Folks, H46
Pritchard, William, J779
Private Reader: Selected Articles and Reviews, The, I7
PRIZE STORIES OF 1950 THE O. HENRY AWARDS, B36, H64
PRIZE STORIES 1981 THE O. HENRY AWARDS, B90, H130
PUBLISHED IN PARIS, B79, I52
Putnam, Samuel, B6, H5
Puzo, Mario, J583

Q

Quartermain, Peter, I79
Quenell, Peter, J90, J187
Quinn, Kerker, B34, H48

R

Radiguet, Raymond, x, E3, J32
Rahv, Phillip, J293
Raine, Kathleen J., J242
Ramsey, Nancy, J718
Ramsey, Roger, J632
Randolph, John, B83
Rawicz, Piotr, C338
Ray, David, I94, J523
Ray, Man, ix, A9e
Reader's Advisor, The, I29
Reader's Advisor: A Guide to the Best in Literature, The, I34
Reader's Advisor: A Layman's Guide to Literature, I50
Reader's Encyclopedia, The, I12
Reader;s Encyclopedia of American Literature, The, I28
Reader's Guide and Bookman's Manual, The, I26
Reader's Guide to the Twentieth Century Novel, A, I112
READIES FOR BOB BROWN'S MACHINE, B6, H5

Reading Fiction: An Anthology of Short Stories, H137
Reading Fiction: A Method of Analysis with Selections for Study, H65, I14
Reading Modern Fiction: Thirty Stories with Study Aids, H74
Realm of Fiction, 61Short Stories, H98
Realm of Fiction, 65Short Stories, H110
RED SCARE: MEMORIES OF THE AMRICAN INQUISITION, B110
Rediscoveries: Informal Essays in Which Well-Known Novelists Rediscover Neglected Works by One of Their *Favorite Authors,* H112
Redmon, Ben Ray, J32
Reed, Henry, J371, J394
Reed, Ishmael, H145
Reeve, F. D., G21
Reference Guide to American Literature, I86
Reference Guide to Short Fiction, I109
Reid, Alec, B80
RELATIONS AND COMPLICATIONS, A1a
Remarkable Lives of 100 Women Writers and Journalists, The, I110
REMNANTS OF POWER, THE, B64
Resources for Teaching the Story and Its Writer: An Introduction to Short Fiction, I113
RETURN TO PAGANY, A, B66
Rexroth, Kenneth, B66
Reynolds, Mary, C207
Rheidol, Richard, J91
Rice, Virginia, B109
Richards, Robert Fulton, I22
Richards, William T., B30
Richardson, John, J435
Richardson, Maurice L., J200
Richler, Mordecai, H143
Richter, Hans Werner, C273
Ridge, Lola, viii, B99, B109
Riding, Laura, ix
Riess, Curt, B31
Riley, Carolyn, I36, I48, I54
Rinehart, Mary Roberts, B30, H39
Rising Tides: 20ᵗʰ Century American Women Poets, H120
Ritchie, Elisavietta, H138

Riveloup, Andre, C202
Rizzi, Anthony John, B30, C192
Roberts, C.E. Bechhoffer, J88, J115, J193
Roberts, Dorothy James, C283
Rodman, Selden, H49, J245
Rogers, Michael, J741, J742, J746, J758, J775
Rogers St. Johns, Adela, B30, H39
Rogers, W.G., J542
Rood, Karen Lane, I62
Root, Waverly, J41, J104
Rose, Stuart, B22
Rosenblum, Joseph, I90
Rosenfeld, Paul, B2, H2
Rosenstein, Louis, B30
Rosenthal, Bob, B97
Rosenthal, M. L., I48, J622
Ross, Arthur, I46
Ross, Harold, xi
Ross, Woodburn O., H77, I20
Rothman, Nathan L., I66, J133, J421
Roussy, Raoul de, A18b
Rovit, Earl, I66, I96, J658
Roy, Emil, H100
Rubin, Merle, J689
Ruby, Beth, J665
Rukeyser, Muriel, C456, D3, J252
Russ, Lavinia, J566
Ryan, Bryan, I99

S

Sachs, Barbara Turner, B46
Sagan, Carl, B100
Sage, Robert, B3, H3
Sahl, Hans, C323
Saint-Exupéry, Antoine de, A9a
Salome, Andreas, C330
Salzman, Jack, I78
SAMUEL BECKETT: A COLLECTION OF CRITICISM, B80
San Francisco Stories: Great Writers on the City, H141
Sanchez, Sonia, A36
Sanchez, Thomas, B85
Sandys, Frederick, A1a
Sanford, Charles, E1
Saroyan, William, B14

SATURDAY EVENING POST STORIES OF 1941, B22, H31
Saturday Evening Post Stories, 1942-1945, The, H51
SATURDAY EVENING POST STORIES 1950, B38, H68
SATURDAY EVENING POST STORIES 1952, B40, H76
SATURDAY EVENING POST STORIES 1953, B41, H79
SATURDAY EVENING POST STORIES 1954, B43, H82
Saunders, Lelia, J503
Scheville, James, C376, C382, J577
Schilling, Wilfrid, C302
Schine, G. David, xii
School of Femininity, The, I3
Schorer, Mark, C371
Schrapnel, Norman, J513
Schriftsgiesser, Karl, J63
Schroeder, Mildred, J534, J547
Schwartz, Delmore, J253
Schwartz, Horace, J538
Schwartz, Narda Lacey, I74
Scoggin, Margaret C., J361
Scott, Evelyn, A11, B99, B109
Scott, Virgil, H113, I41
SEAGULL ON THE STEP, THE, A26
Seaver, Russell W., J136
SECOND AMERICAN CARAVAN, THE, B2, H2
SEEDS OF LIBERATION, B53
SELECTED WRITING, B21
Sentimental Modernism : Women Writers and the Revolution of the Word, I100
Sewell, Elizabeth, B61
Seymour, Sir Albert, A1a
Shackleton, Edith, J156
Shakespeare, William, B14
Shape of Fiction: British and American Short Stories, The, H105
Shapiro, David, G6
Shapiro, Marsha, J., J593
Sharp, Roberta, J652
Shattuck, Charles, B34, H48
Sheidley, William E., I113
Sherman, S. E., J317
Shinkman, Elizabeth Benn, B91

Shirer, William, A 25d, C306, C385, L2

SHORT STORIES, A2

Short Stories: A Collection of Types of the Short Story, H24

Short Stories from the New Yorker, H28

Short Stories in Context, H77, I20

Short Stories of Today, H14

Short Story Criticism, I96

Short Story Hits, 1932: An Interpretive Anthology, H11

The Short Story in America, 1900-1950, I19

Short Story Writers and Their Work: A Guide to the Best, I89

Sidjakov, Nicolas, B46

Simon, Linda, J683

Simon, Marion, J553

Sinclair, Upton, C170

Sladky, Paul, I109

Slawson, John, A31

Smart, William, H125

Smith, Henry, J182

Smith, Martin Seymour, I57, I65, I75

Smith, Robert W., I94, J686, J719, J737

Smoley, Richard M., H126

Smock, Frederick, B112

SMOKE AND OTHER EARLY STORIES, B95

SMOKING MOUNTAIN: STORIES OF POST WAR GERMANY, THE, A25

SO LITTLE DISILLUSION, B91

Sokolsky, George E., B14

Solano, Solita, C207

Solbert, Ronnie, A28

Sometimes Magic: A Collection of Outstanding Stories for the Teenage Girl, H102

Sommers, Martin, B22

Sorenson, Villy, C281

Soskin, William, J226, J284

Spanier, Sandra Whipple, xiv, A42, B99, B109, I80, I96, J719, J720

Spearhead: 10 Years' Experimental Writing in America, H55

Spector, Herman, B6, H5

Spencer, Claire, A7b

Spender, Stephen, B69

Spinner, Stephanie, H116

Stafford, Ann, H117

Stafford, Jean, J598

Stallman, Robert Wooster, H58

STATEMENT, A, A6

Steel, Kurt, B30, H39

Stegner, Wallace, B82, J306

Stein, Gertrude, vii, A1a, B6, H5

Steinberg, S. H., I21

Steinberg, Sybil, J694, J743

Steinhoff, William R. H67, I17

Stender, Fay, J643

Stephenson, David L., H86

Stern, James, B78, B109

Stern Lloyd, B6, H5

Stevenson, Adlai, B64

Stevik, Philip, I73

Stewart, R. W., J266

Stieglitz, Alfred, B109

Still, James, C164

Stories of Modern America, H86

Story and Its Writer: An Introduction to Short Fiction, The, H146

Story and Its Writer: An Introduction to the Short Story, The, I114

Story Anthology 1931-1933, A, H10

Story Jubilee. H99, I30

Story Pocket Book, The, H44

Stout, Wesley Winans, B22, H31

Strachey, Richard, I96, J53

Strong, L.A.G., J22, J44, J236

Stucky, William J., I96, J519, J578

Studies in Fiction, H100

Studies in the Short Story, H113

Study Aids for Teachers of Modern Short Stories, I17

Stull, Carolyn, J424, J440, J472

Stull, Christopher, J289

Stuttaford, Genevieve, J680

Suggestions for Teaching Fifteen Stories, I15

Sullivan, Nancy, H131

Sullivan, Richard, J461, J491, J550

SUNDOWN BEACH, B76

Swados, Felice, C166

Swallow, Alan, B32, H41, H53

Swinnerton, Frank, J295

SWORN STATEMENT OF KAY BOYLE FRANKENSTEIN, B42

Sykes, Gerald, I77, J8

Sylvia Beach and the Lost Generation: A History of Literary Paris in the Twenties and Thirties, I72

T

Tabrizi, Vida Hadjebi, C437, L3, L7
Takahashi, Yasunari, B80
Taken at the Flood, H52
Talbot, Daniel, H80
TALKS WITH AUTHORS, B61
Tambimuttu, B21
Tate, Allen, H32
Tate, Trudi, H144
Teacher's Manuel for the Realm of Fiction: 61 Stories, I31
Teller of Tales: 100 Short Stories from the United States, England, France, Russia and Germany, H25
Temple, Gudrun, B47, J531
Terrell, Donna M., C 434
Terry, Ellen, A1a
TESTAMENT FOR MY STUDENTS AND OTHER POEMS, A36
That Kind of Woman, H144
Theis, Louise, B109
THEY WERE THERE: THE STORY OF WORLD WAR II AND HOW IT CAME ABOUT BY AMERICA'S FOREMOST CORRESPONDENTS, B31
Thielen, Benedict, J194
THIRTEEN STORIES, B32, H40
THIRTY STORIES, A22
THIS IS MY BEST 1942, B24, H34
THIS IS MY BEST 1970, B68
This Is My Best in the Third Quarter of the Century, H111
THIS IS NOT A LETTER AND OTHER POEMS, A41
THIS MEADOW OF TIME: A PROVENCE JOURNAL, B112
Thomas, Dylan, A14c, J239
Thompson, Ralph, J219, J229, J422
365 DAYS, B12, H18
THREE SHORT NOVELS, A27
Through the Looking Glass, A8
Thruelsen, Richard, B22

Time to Be Young: Great Stories of the Growing Years, H47
Tomkins, Calvin, B114
Tonsor, Stephen, J500
Tooker, Dan, B82
Towne, Charles Hansen, J12
Toynbee, Phillip, J334
Tracz, Francis, H114
Trahey, Jane, B59, H104
TRANSITION STORIES, B3, H3
Transition Workshop, H61
Trask, Willard, J254
Treasury of American Short Stories, The, H131
Treasury of Mountaineering Stories, A, H80
TRIAL OF HUEY NEWTON, THE, B65
Trilling, Diana, J353
Trimmer, Joseph F., B88, H132
Troyar, Howard, J434
Trueblood, Kathryn, H145
Tucker, Meredith, I98
Twenties: American Writing in the Postwar Decade, The, I23
Twentieth Century American Literature, I77
TWENTIETH CENTURY AUTHORS, B26, I8
Twentieth Century Short Stories, H12, I1
Two Hundred Contemporary Authors, I36
200 Years of Great American Short Stories, H123

U

Uehling, Edward, I94, I96, J735
UNDERGROUND WOMAN, THE, A38
Uzzell, Thomas H., H11

V

Vail, Laurence, x, xi, A2, A3, A10, A12b, B6, B12, B77, B99, B109, C67, C81, H5, H18
Valensi, Frances, J139
Van Doren, Mark, J141, J169
Van Gelder, Robert, B33, C161, J101, J158
Van Gundy, Justine, B72, H115
Van Vechten, Carl, B17

Vanity Fair: A Calvacade of the 1920s and 1930s, H84
Venton, Barbara, J668
Vercors, C198
Verna, Stan A., I69
VERTICAL, B20, H30
VETERANS OF THE ABRAHAM LINCOLN BRIGADE, B83
Vinson, James, B67, I37
Vittorini, Elio, G3
VOICES OF SURVIVAL IN THE NUCLEAR AGE, B100
Votteler, Thomas, I96

W

Wagenknecht, Edward, I18
Wagner-Martin, Linda, I111
Walbridge, Earl, J128
Walker, Adelaide and Charles, A9
Walker, Mildred, J444
Wallace, A. Dayle, H77, I20
Wallace, Doreen, J, 204
Walsh, Chad, I94, J613
Walsh, Ernest, vii, viii, ix, A1a, A9
Walton, Edith, J103, J134
Walton, Richard J., B64
Ward, A. C., I39
Warfel, Harry R., B39, I16
Warren, Robert Penn, H75
Watkins, Ann, B99, B109, H52
Watson, Noelle, I109
Wave Me Goodbye: Stories of the Second World War, H139
Weber, Max, A6
WE MODERNS, B17, I4
WEDDING DAY AND OTHER STORIES, A3
Weeks, Edward, J411
Weiss, Anne, I43
Weiss, Irving, I43
Wells, Oliver, B8, H7
Welty, Eudora, C166
West, Anthony, J288
West, Jessamyn, B82
West, Ray B., Jr., C380, H58, I19, J339
Westcott, Glenway, viii, B101
Whearty, Raymond, C340

When Women Look at Men: An Anthology, H91
WHILE THERE IS A SOUL IN PRISON, B80
WHISTLEING ZONE, THE, B50
White, Edward M., J667
WHITE HORSE OF VIENNA AND OTHER STORIES, THE, A11
White, Peter, J432
White, Stewart Edward, B14
Whitman, Alden, B94
Whitman, R., J708
Who's Who in Twentieth Century Literature, I57
Who's Who in U.S. Writers, Editors and Poets: A Bibliographical Directory 1986-1987, I87
Who's Who in Writers, Editors and Poets, I92
Who's Who of American Women: A Biographical Dictionary of Notable Living American Women Writers, I24
Wicker, Tom, C426
Wickes, George, C383
Widdermer, Margaret, B30, H39
Wiechert, Ernst, C292
Wilder, Thornton, B48
Wilkins, Sophie, B47
Williams, Blanche Colton, B7, H6
Williams, David, J516
Williams, William Carlos, viii. A9e, A30, B6, B109, C25, C53, H6, J2, I96, J1
Williams-Ellis, Annabel, J272
Wilner, Herbert, C380
Wilson, Angus, J454
Wilson, Edmund, I66, I77, J347
Wilson, T.C., J83
Wilson, Ted, J58
Wolff, Geoffrey, B81, I53
WOMAN ON PAPER, A, B102
Women and Fiction; Short Stories by and about Women, H124
Women and Literature: An Annotated Bibliography of Women Writers, I58
Women and Men, Men and Women: An Anthology of Short Stories, H125
WOMEN OF THE LEFT BANK PARIS, 1900-1940, B98, I81
Women on the Wall, H81

Women Poets in English: An Anthology, The, H117

WOMEN WRITERS OF THE WEST COAST, B92

Wong, Shawn, A43, C399, G12, H145, L7

Wood, Susan, J664

Woolf, Cecil, B57

Worden, Helen, B30, H39

WORDS AND MUSIC: COMMENT BY FAMOUS AUTHORS ABOUT THE WORLD'S GREATEST ARTISTS, B37

WORDS THAT MUST SOMEHOW BE SAID, A40

World of Fiction, The, H142

World of Short Fiction, The, H108

World of the Short Story: A Twentieth Century Collection, The, H135

Wright, Charles, C411, G4, G8

Wright, Richard, B111

WRITE AND REWRITE: A STUDY OF THE CREATIVE PROCESS, B56, H106, I33

WRITERS AND WRITING, B33

WRITER'S MIND: INTERVIEW WITH AMERICAN AUTHORS, THE, B104

Writers on World War II, H143

Wylie, I.A.R., C166

Y

Yalom, Marilyn, B92

YEAR BEFORE LAST, A7

YELLOW DUSK, A13

Yerburgh, Mark R., J617

Young, K.T., A6, B6, H5

YOUNGEST CAMEL, THE, A16

YOUNGEST CAMEL RECONSIDERED AND REWRITTEN, THE, A28

Yung, Judy, G14

Z

Zabel, Morton Dauwen, J276

Zane, Maitland, J767

Zeifman, Hersh, B80

Zimmerman, Fred, J679